SHARING JESUS EFFECTIVELY in the BUDDHIST WORLD

SHARING JESUS EFFECTIVELY in the BUDDHIST WORLD

David Lim,

Steve Spaulding,

& Paul De Neui, eds.

Sharing Jesus Effectively in the Buddhist World

Cover design: Amanda Valloza

Book design: Sharon Edwards

Published by William Carey Library, an imprint of William Carey Publishin
10 W. Dry Creek Cir | Littleton, CO 80120 | www.missionbooks.org

William Carey Publishing is a ministry of Frontier Ventures
1605 E. Elizabeth St. | Pasadena, CA 91104 | www.frontierventures.org

Printed in the United States of America
22 21 20 19 18 6 5 4 3 2 BP

ISBN 0-87808-509-2

Printed in the United States of America

Contents

Introduction vii

David Lim, Steve Spaulding, & Paul De Neui

1. Christian Opportunities in the Changing Demographic Context of Global Buddhism 1

Todd M. Johnson & Bobby Jangsun Ryu

2. Christian Mission in the Context of Buddhist Mission 49

Terry Muck

3. Difficulties and Devices in Depicting the Deity of Christ to the Theravada Buddhist Mind 65

M. S. Vasanthakumar

4. Gentle Strength and *Upāya*: Christian and Buddhist Ministry Models 109

Russell H. Bowers, Jr.

5. Meekness: A New Approach to Christian Witness to the Thai People 147

Nantachai Mejudhon

6. Where Are Your Temples? Do Christianity and Buddhism Share a Temple Ethos? 187
Steve Spaulding

7. Islands in the Sky: Tibetan Buddhism and the Gospel 243
Marku Tsering

8. Structural and Ministry Philosophy Issues in Church Planting among Buddhist Peoples 263
Alan R. Johnson

9. People Movements in Thailand 283
Alex Smith

10. A People Movement among the Pwo Karen in Northern Thailand 327
Jim Morris

11. Incarnational Approaches to the Japanese People using House Church Strategies 353
Mitsuo Fukuda

References 363

Introduction

Welcome to our book in the first three-volume "Sharing Jesus in the Buddhist World" series. These works are written by a group of Evangelical mission "reflective practitioners," who are committed to develop more biblical and more effective ways to win the Buddhist peoples of the world to the saving grace and transforming power of our Lord Jesus Christ.

The chapters in this volume were first presented as papers at a Missiological Forum held at the start of the sixth assembly of SEANET in January 2004 in Chiang Mai, Thailand. Some chapters have been revised by the authors in response to the feedback gained at the Forum. The editors have played minor roles in the final editing of these articles and the literary styles of the authors have been retained. We take pride in including them as qualitative works worthy of serious consideration by the intelligent Christian public, especially those concerned about evangelizing people of other faiths.

This book consists of three types of articles. The opening chapter is a "situationer" of where the Buddhist people groups are, and the next six describe some of the best models of mission approaches to reaching Buddhists. The last four chapters depict some past and present attempts at effective "people movements" or "church planting movements" in Thailand and Japan.

Chapter 1, "The Changing Demographic Context of Global Buddhism," contains the most recent update on the statistics about the Buddhist world as we enter the 21st century. We thank its two authors for compiling and analyzing the data for the global church. Todd M. Johnson is the Director of the Center for the Study of Global Christianity (CSGC) at Gordon-Conwell Theological Seminary. He is co-author of the *World Christian Encyclopedia, 2nd ed.* (Oxford University Press, 2001) and *World Christian Trends: AD 30–AD 2000* (William Carey Library, 2001). Bobby Jangsun Ryu, a Master of Divinity student at Gordon-Conwell, has helped at its CSGC.

Chapter 2 serves as the introductory article to Chapters 3-7. In "Christian Mission in the Context of Buddhist Mission," Terry Muck describes and analyzes the five major mission approaches that have been used to reach Buddhists. (The next five chapters are samples of each of these five types of missions.) Professor of Mission and World Religion at Asbury Theological Seminary, Muck wrote his Ph.D. dissertation on Sri Lankan Buddhism for Northwestern University in Evanston, Ill. He edited the journal *Buddhist-Christian Studies* for nine years and has been editing another journal, *Missiology,* for the past two years.

Terry Muck's first type, "concept comparisons," is exemplified in Michal Solomon Vasanthakumar's chapter on "The Deity of Jesus Christ for Theravadan Buddhists in Sri Lanka." Vasanthakumar, who holds a Master of Theology from the British Open University, has taught in Lanka Bible College and is currently on a study sabbatical in London. He has also authored more than 20 Bible study books in the Tamil language.

The next chapter by Russell H. Bowers, Jr., "Gentle Strength and *Upaya*: Christian and Buddhist Ministry Models," is a sample of finding similarities and differences (in this case, a major difference) in some particular "cultural forms." Bowers has a Ph.D. in Systematic Theology from Dallas Theological Seminary.

Chapter 5, "Meekness: A New Approach to Christian Witness to Thai People" by Nantachai Mejudhon, demonstrates a third approach to evangelizing Buddhists—through "scientific witness," using a concrete way to relate to people and address a practical need in the culture. Mejudhon has a D.Miss. from Asbury Theological Seminary and has been leading the culturally-sensitive Muangthai Church in Bangkok and directing the Cross-Cultural Communication Training Center there with his wife.

The next chapter focuses on Terry Muck's fourth category of comparing the "ritual practices" of religions. In "Where are Your Temples? Do Christianity and Buddhism Share a Temple Ethos?" Steve Spaulding evaluates the origins and present practices of constructing buildings for worship in the two faith systems. Born and raised in Japan, Spaulding has a M.A. in Missiology from Fuller Theological Seminary and has been the Associate for Southeast Asia of DAWN Ministries.

The final chapter of this section, "Islands in the Sky: Tibetan Buddhism and the Gospel" by Marku Tsering (pseudonym), shows the fifth type of mission approach: that of highlighting the "folk religious functions." In this instance, using "root-cause worldview analysis," the author dissects the Buddhist Tibetan shamanistic occult-magical view of reality.

The last four chapters contain stories on how effective multiplication of converts and churches has occurred among some Buddhist peoples in Thailand and Japan. In Chapter 8, Alan R. Johnson introduces the "Structural and Ministry Philosophical Issues in Church Planting among Buddhist Peoples," focusing on the values and goals for developing dynamic churches based on his experiences as an Assemblies of God missionary in Thailand. Johnson has been the program director of the Institute of Buddhist Studies at the Asia Pacific Center for the Advancement of Leadership and Mission in Baguio City, Philippines.

We are pleased that Alex Smith could contribute a fourth chapter to our three-volume series, this time using his previous historical studies to write about "People Movements in Thailand." Smith was an Overseas Missionary Fellowship (OMF) missionary in Thailand for 27 years and in recent years, has been a mission mobilizer for OMF in the US. He has a D.Miss. from Fuller Theological Seminary.

In Chapter 10, "A People Movement among the Pwo Karen in Northern Thailand," we have Jim Morris' analytical narration of his own experiences. Morris has sought to evangelize the Pwo Karen people group since 1957, having finished his undergraduate studies from Prairie Bible Institute.

Last but not least is the chapter on "Incarnational Approaches Using House Church Strategies in Japan" by Mitsuo Fukuda. This short but thought-provoking essay describes how the author is leading a new mission paradigm to reach the seemingly hard-to-reach Shinto Buddhists of Japan. Fukuda, who has a D.Miss. from Fuller Theological Seminary, has been heading the Rethinking Authentic Christianity Network from Osaka, Japan.

With this book, we conclude our first set of the "Sharing Jesus in the Buddhist World" series. Special thanks are due to Paul De Neui (Ph.D., Intercultural Studies, Fuller Theological Seminary) for helping in the last stages of editing this book. We look forward to editorial help from him and Kang San Tan (D.Miss., Trinity International University) in the next set of "Reaching Buddhists for Christ" series.

We invite our readers to access the previous volumes, *Sharing Jesus in the Buddhist World* and *Sharing Jesus Holistically with the Buddhist World*, both edited by David Lim and Steve Spaulding. All of these works provide concrete models of contextualized witness to adherents of various Buddhist faiths, which number one billion in the world today. All three books are rich resources for those committed to effective evangelization and transformation of "nations" in our generation.

May God continue to help us facilitate this type of sharing of the "best theologies" and "best practices" in reaching Buddhist peoples for Christ in their varied contexts, and may we be found faithful and more effective in fulfilling the Great Commission among them, so that the end may come (cf. Matt. 24:14; 2 Pet. 3:9). Maranatha!

David Lim, Steve Spaulding, & Paul De Neui

Quezon City, Philippines

August 2005

1

Christian Opportunities in the Changing Demographic Context of Global Buddhism

Todd M. Johnson & Bobby Jangsun Ryu

Introduction

Images of the Buddha, ancient and new, are ubiquitous around the globe. The diversity and continuity of the images are astonishing—ranging from the Buddha's gaunt appearance in India to his portly image in the Far East. Hundreds of millions of Buddhists turn to these varying images as objects of religious devotion and affiliation. Thus, in today's world, one encounters "Buddhisms", as well as "Buddhism." This is consistent with the first meaning of *sāsana* which can be rendered as the religion or tradition of a particular nation.[1] In this localized sense, Buddhism represents the practice and ritual of an ethnic, linguistic, or cultural community. At the same time, local Buddhists will be aware that they belong to a wider religious community. It is this second meaning of *sāsana* that gives Buddhism its transcendental and universalizing vision. All local Buddhist communities (*sāsana*) are part of a larger global community of Buddhists (*sāsana*).[2]

Our task here is to consider from a demographic perspective the local-global reality of Buddhism and its relation to the mission of the Christian church. In this regard, data from the World Christian Database[3] have been sorted and arranged into the tables below with particular emphases on the present affiliation, influence, responsiveness, and diversities of Buddhist peoples. It is the authors' intention that a better grasp of the current state of global Buddhism will enable Christians to continue engaging in higher levels of contextualized discourse and evangelism strategies in the Buddhist world.

Before turning our attention to the demographic data, it will be helpful to understand the present and future states of global Buddhism against its historical backdrop. The transnational arc of Buddhism from localized *sāsana* to its place today as a truly global religion will be briefly traced in the next section.

From Localized to Global *Sāsana*

Transnational Expansion of Buddhism

The expansion of Buddhism from India into major cultural basins occurred within one hundred years of the death of its founder, Siddharta Gautama.[4] Largely because of the consolidation of Buddhism in northern India by Mauryan King Asoka, Buddhists would eventually be found in Sri Lanka, Myanmar, Central Asia, Southeast Asia, and China—contexualizing their precepts and practices into the distinct cultural and linguistic traditions of each culture. Consequently, when Buddhism came into contact with the Western world, it already represented a vast mosaic of local diversities. By the 20th century, Buddhism was a major global faith, even though its core communities were still located mainly in Asia.

Movement of Buddhist Peoples

In modern times, emigration (and consequently, immigration) has fueled Buddhist growth beyond Asia. The first wave was the global movement of the Chinese in the mid-nineteenth century. More recent waves of Southeast Asians (Vietnamese, Cambodians, Thai, and others) have resettled outside of Asia and represent one of the fastest growing populations in the USA.

Buddhist Practice in Pluralistic Societies

Appropriating the non-theistic aspects of Buddhism as compatible with secular worldviews, key Enlightenment figures in Europe championed the spread and development of Buddhism by focusing largely on Theravada Buddhism while ignoring the deistic and supernatural aspects of the Mahayana tradition. In the late nineteenth century, Theosophists in America reinvigorated Buddhism in both its rationalistic and new age forms. As these two forms emerged as powerful forces in the Western world the vision to purify Buddhism traveled back to South and Southeast Asia, where reformers like Dharmapala sought to strengthen Buddhism in its homelands by appealing to its nationalistic character. Today, in its New Age form, Buddhism is found everywhere in the Western world.[5]

Globalization as Means for Global Buddhism

In recent decades, globalization provided the means by which Buddhism has become truly global. The following observations represent some of the ways in which Buddhism and globalization might continue to interact in a positive way:

- Meditation is a central feature of Buddhism and has become a dominant trait in the eyes of most Western converts.

- Meditation, taught now through the media and, lately, over the Internet, could become one of the most global of all characteristics.
- Meditation can facilitate the search for meaning in a postmodern world.
- Asian immigrants in the West see their Buddhism as a way of reasserting their identity in a foreign land.
- The increased visible presence of the Dalai Lama has made Buddhism widely-known and respected.
- Buddhism is critical of Western greed and has this appeal as an alternate lifestyle in the Western world.

The Demography of Global Buddhism Today

The discussion above has briefly summarized the trajectories by which Buddhism has developed and expanded as a global *sāsana* along manifold strands and structures of localized *sāsanas*. Bearing this in mind, the ensuing section examines the present demographic picture of Buddhism as a global religion in terms of the current affiliation, groupings, influence, responsiveness, and diversities of Buddhist peoples.

Understanding Buddhist Affiliation

The starting point for our analysis is the question: Who is a Buddhist? Fundamentally, it is a person who identifies himself or herself as a Buddhist. Self-identification is foundational to religious affiliation and emerges as a quantitative indicator mainly in censuses and polls. However, this demographic inquiry masks the fact that many people who would not call themselves "Buddhists" nonetheless practice Buddhism in some significant way. This is especially true of the Chinese, for example, who are often called "popular" religionists. Their two ways of identifying Buddhists are explored next in the concepts: "Core Buddhism" and "Wider Buddhism."

Core Buddhism and Wider Buddhism

Table 1 "Core Buddhism and Wider Buddhism by UN Continents, 1900-2050" outlines the demographic situation of Buddhism over a time span of 150 years. The main features of this table show adherents to Buddhism in its different forms. The first feature is the Core Buddhist component, which can be viewed in terms of the major schools of Buddhist thought such as Mahayana and Theravada. In demographic terms this group in the year 2000 represented more than 360 million people or about 6% of the world's population.[6]

However, it is well known that popular religion in China draws on the "Three Teachings," one of which is Buddhism.[7] This understanding of Chinese popular religion raises the suggestion that the religious group known as "Chinese folk-religionists"[8] could be considered "Buddhists." Such enumeration may better reflect the broader influence and inclusion of Buddhism among the Chinese. Additionally, in practice, even the nonreligious in China are seriously impacted by Buddhism in both worldview and key rituals. The concept of wider Buddhism, then, would include all Buddhists of Core Buddhism plus all Chinese folk-religionists and Chinese nonreligious. This produces an astonishing 1.28 billion adherents in 2000, making Buddhism the third largest religion in the world with slightly less adherents than Islam.

Equally significant, however, is the expected decline of Buddhism as a percentage of the world's population. This is largely due to the low birth rates found in core countries such as Japan or China. Well into the twenty-first century, Christians and Muslims are expected to have more children than either Hindus or Buddhists. By 2050 it is possible that Core Buddhists will represent only 5.25% of the world's population (down from 7.85% in 1900) and Wider Buddhists only 15.6% (down from 31.3% in 1900).[9] This expected decline, however, will be attributed primarily to low birth rates in Asia; by contrast, in Europe, North America and Oceania, the respective percentages of Buddhists will rise through immigration.

Buddhist Countries

Table 2 "Top 20 Buddhist countries by Buddhist population in 2000" enumerates the world's largest Buddhist countries. Not surprisingly, China is the only country with more than 100 million Buddhists. If the definition is expanded to include Chinese-folk religionists and the nonreligious in China on the premise of Wider Buddhism explained above, then this number would approach 1 billion. The USA ranks number 12 on this list showing the impact of both immigration (from Asia) and some conversions of non-Asians. These forces of immigration and conversion will likely continue to fuel the rise of Buddhists in the USA. Table 1 projects the number of core Buddhists in North America in 2050 at 8.6 million, which, if transposed to Table 2, would make the USA/Canada the eighth largest Buddhist country in the world!

Table 3 "Top 20 Buddhist countries by percentage Buddhist in 2000" highlights those countries with the highest percentage of Buddhists. Not surprisingly, most of the top 10 are found in Southeast Asia. Australia, now over 2% Buddhist, again illustrates the impact of immigration of Asians. United Arab Emirates, number 20 on the list, highlights another trend—the guest worker phenomenon in Western Asia.

Buddhist Peoples

The next two tables focus on the impact of Buddhism on the world's peoples. Table 4 "Top 20 Buddhist peoples by number of Buddhists in 2000" sorts peoples by the number of Buddhists in any people, whether heavily Buddhist or not. All of these are found in Asia in the heartlands of Buddhism. Table 5 "Top 20 Buddhist peoples (over 5% Buddhist) by population in 2000" sorts the number of individuals in the largest peoples over 5% Buddhist. This highlights the fact that the largest "Buddhist" people group is the Han Chinese speaking standard Mandarin. Note that several other Han Chinese peoples appear on the list.

Responsive Buddhist Peoples

Table 6 "Top 20 most responsive Buddhist peoples in 2000" and Table 7 "Top 20 most responsive Buddhist megapeoples in 2000" explore the concept of "evangelism responsiveness" in relation to Buddhist peoples. Evangelism responsiveness is a measure of the number of baptisms per million hours of Christian evangelism. The higher the number, the greater the evidence of responsiveness to the Christian gospel. Note that only one people over 500,000 and six over 100,000 make it on to this list.

In Table 6 one sees the promise for Christian mission in Bhutan, which ranks number 15 in Table 2 on the list of Top 20 Buddhist countries by Buddhist population in 2000 (1.6 million) and ranks number 3 in Table 3 on the list of Top 20 Buddhist countries by percentage Buddhist in 2000 (77.44%). We see evidence of response to the gospel in Bhutan even though there has been very little Christian outreach.

Responsiveness of Buddhist Peoples

Table 7 asks, "What are the most responsive Buddhist peoples over 1,000,000 in population?" This list is spread evenly over the Buddhist world. Interestingly, three immigrant communities are among the top 10 responsive peoples: the Han Chinese and Northern Khmer (Cambodian), both in Thailand, and the Vietnamese in the USA. As mentioned previously, this reflects two increasing realities concerning the globalization of Buddhism. First, the impact of transnational migration on Buddhist growth in receptor countries means that countries long viewed as traditional Buddhist strongholds, such as Thailand, cannot be characterized as monolithic expressions of Buddhism, but rather, as complex layers of diverse Buddhist traditions and transitory people groups. Second, the Christian church must rethink the traditional lines of cross-cultural missions and develop strategic methods to target (and differentiate between) specific people groups in core Buddhist countries. Note that the highest value on this list is 2.8 times smaller than that in Table 6.

Film and Scriptures among Buddhist Peoples

Table 8 "Top 20 Buddhist peoples with no Jesus film in their language in 2000" examines the status of the Jesus Film among Buddhist peoples in the year 2000. Table 9 "Top 20 Buddhist peoples with no scriptures in their language in 2000" asks the same question with scriptures. Some of these peoples are surprisingly large, considering the extensive reach of the film and the current ambitious translation programs underway. These peoples are all minorities among the larger peoples of Asia. These two tables raise the larger (and often sensitive) issue of resource allocation in missions work today. For the sake of illustration, note that Table 8 shows that the Central Bhutanese (Bhotia) and Eastern Bhutanese (Sharchop), both of which have a population exceeding 100,000, are listed among the top 10 most responsive Buddhist peoples in 2000 (Table 6), ranking sixth and seventh, respectively. These two groups also rank second and fourth, respectively, in Table 9 (Top 20 Buddhist peoples with no scripture in their language in 2000).

The juxtaposition of these two demographic realities underscores the importance of improving the allocation of mission resources and strategies. By viewing certain quantitative indicators of need (Tables 8 and 9) in light of the responsiveness index (Table 6), the following question, at the very least, should be considered: Are sufficient resources and efforts being allocated to provide the responsive Central Bhutanese (Bhotia) and Eastern Bhutanese (Sharchop) with translated scriptures? This degree of critical thinking and strategizing has, until now, often been overshadowed by the status quo, the lack of demographic awareness and tools, and/or the sometimes counterproductive influence of donor aspirations. Better grasp of demographic indicators should equip missions thinkers and workers to prioritize and allocate their limited resources in a sea of unreached peoples and needs.

Christian Peoples and Buddhism

Table 10 "Top 20 majority Christian peoples with more than 0.5% Buddhists in 2000" asks "What are the largest majority Christian peoples (over 50% Christian) that have more than 0.5% Buddhists." The purpose of this table is to help Christians to understand where dialogue with Buddhists might take place within Christian contexts. Surprisingly, the top five countries are South Africa, USA, Brazil, the Philippines, and Myanmar! Note as well that twelve of the twenty top people groups come from the "Big Three" of the Pacific Rim: China, Japan and South Korea. These countries will continue to grow economically in the ensuing decades and will likely strengthen their ties with the West, meaning more points of contact with Western Christianity, e.g., students learning English in church-based ESL programs. Christianity is expected to continue to grow in China and South Korea as well. Thus another significant trend will likely involve Christians from these countries interacting with Christians from the rest of the world (including Africa and Latin America). One also sees second-generation Chinese, Japanese and Koreans Christians from overseas returning to their homelands as professionals. What do these trends imply for future prospects of Buddhist-Christian contact?

Table 11 "Top 20 peoples with more than 500,000 Christians and 500,000 Buddhists in 2000" approaches the same question from the standpoint of size. This table illustrates where both Christians and Buddhists respectively exceed 500,000 in a single people. Not surprisingly the Han Chinese and Japanese are on the top of the list. Number 3, however, is the Maratha of India and number 5 is the Hindi speakers in Northern India. India, normally thought of as a

Hindu country, could be a major player in Christian-Buddhist interaction.[10]

The Many Varieties of Buddhism

Finally, Table 12 "274 varieties of Buddhism with number of adherents in 2000" sets out 274 varieties of Buddhism.[11] This list is intended to show some of the significant variations within Buddhism. Note that the varieties are not mutually-exclusive and therefore should not be totaled. The major implication of this table for Christian mission is the need for Christians to study and understand these 274 varieties of Buddhism. Without fluency in these varieties, Christians will not be inclined to truly contextualize the gospel among Buddhists.

Conclusion

Taking a demographic view of the Buddhist world draws attention to its status as one of the world's truly global religions, and, from a Christian point-of-view, the need for a much more deliberate and contextualized Christian engagement of Buddhists. Although the primary thrust of this paper is demographic in nature, it is well worth noting that the data presented herein must be seen neither in abstraction nor isolation, but rather, with an aim toward sharper contextualized thinking and more effective missional enterprise. The proffered data, at the very least, raises the inference that the Buddhists of the world have yet to see the face of Jesus through their own cultural lenses.[12] The irony for the existing Christian world is that without these Buddhist "faces" of Jesus, Christians are missing crucial perspectives on Jesus. The successful mission of preaching the gospel among Buddhists will have the unexpected benefit of enlarging the Christian understanding of the Savior of all humanity.

List of Tables

Source: *World Christian Database*

Table 1: Core Buddhism and Wider Buddhism by UN Continents, 1900-2050.

Table 2: Top 20 Buddhist countries by Buddhist population in 2000.

Table 3: Top 20 Buddhist countries by percentage Buddhist in 2000.

Table 4: Top 20 Buddhist peoples by number of Buddhists in 2000.

Table 5: Top 20 Buddhist peoples (over 5% Buddhist) by population in 2000.

Table 6: Top 20 most responsive Buddhist peoples in 2000.

Table 7**:** Top 20 most responsive Buddhist megapeoples in 2000.

Table 8: Top 20 Buddhist peoples with no Jesus film in their language in 2000.

Table 9: Top 20 Buddhist peoples with no scriptures in their language in 2000.

Table 10: Top 20 majority Christian peoples with more than 0.5% Buddhists in 2000.

Table 11: Top 20 peoples with more than 500,000 Christians and 500,000 Buddhists in 2000.

Source: *World Christian Trends*

Table 12: 274 varieties of Buddhism with number of adherents in 2000.

Table 1. Core Buddhism and Wider Buddhism

UN Continent	Major Religion	Pop 1900	%
Africa	Buddhists	3,400	0.00
	Chinese folk-religionists	1,900	0.00
Asia	Buddhists	126,619,501	13.24
	Chinese folk-religionists	379,914,740	39.73
	Chinese nonreligious	30,000	0.00
Europe	Buddhists	401,000	0.10
	Chinese folk-religionists	0	0.00
Latin America	Buddhists	5,930	0.01
	Chinese folk-religionists	1,600	0.00
Northern America	Buddhists	40,410	0.00
	Chinese folk-religionists	75,120	0.00
Oceania	Buddhists	6,530	0.10
	Chinese folk-religionists	12,678	0.20
Core Buddhism (Buddhists only)		127,076,771	7.85
Wider Buddhism (Buddhists and all Chinese)		507,112,809	31.31

by UN continents, 1900-2050.

Pop 2000	%	Pop 2025	%	Pop 2050	%
139,382	0.02	284,950	0.02	507,600	0.03
32,685	0.00	57,690	0.00	111,950	0.01
358,302,853	9.76	440,444,380	9.22	474,993,680	8.75
389,455,266	10.61	454,732,000	9.52	483,252,880	8.90
524,252,518	14.28	564,186,300	11.81	480,000,000	8.84
1,528,874	0.21	2,197,920	0.32	2,859,040	0.47
261,511	0.04	357,600	0.05	443,200	0.07
657,864	0.13	1,081,660	0.16	1,650,330	0.20
193,243	0.04	277,920	0.04	377,150	0.05
2,862,135	0.01	5,420,020	0.01	8,600,020	0.02
665,392	0.00	965,000	0.00	990,000	0.00
472,498	1.55	874,450	2.18	1,206,770	2.56
123,108	0.40	234,550	0.59	302,130	0.64
363,963,606	6.01	450,303,380	5.67	489,817,440	5.25
1,278,947,329	21.12	1,471,114,440	18.54	1,455,294,750	15.61

Table 2. Top 20 Buddhist countries by Buddhist population in 2000.

Country	Pop 2000	Buddhists	Buddhist%
China	1,260,036,000	107,393,511	8.52%
Japan	127,096,314	70,153,662	55.20%
Thailand	62,805,574	52,036,050	82.85%
Viet Nam	78,136,913	38,364,974	49.10%
Myanmar	47,748,939	34,992,083	73.28%
Sri Lanka	18,923,749	12,944,908	68.41%
Cambodia	13,104,030	11,266,161	85.97%
South Korea	46,740,141	7,158,330	15.32%
India	1,008,937,356	6,987,396	0.69%
Taiwan	22,401,000	4,677,128	20.88%
Laos	5,278,563	2,577,202	48.82%
USA	283,230,243	2,500,500	0.88%
Nepal	23,042,704	2,007,834	8.71%
Indonesia	212,092,024	1,913,389	0.90%
Bhutan	2,085,136	1,614,658	77.44%
Malaysia	22,218,485	1,505,860	6.78%
Bangladesh	137,439,261	747,516	0.54%
Singapore	4,018,114	581,684	14.48%
Russia	145,491,166	577,185	0.40%
Mongolia	2,533,299	570,092	22.50%
Total of these 20 countries	**3,523,359,011**	**360,570,123**	**10.23%**

Table 3. Top 20 Buddhist countries by percentage Buddhist in 2000.

Country	Pop 2000	Buddhists	Buddhist%
Cambodia	13,104,030	11,266,161	85.97%
Thailand	62,805,574	52,036,050	82.85%
Bhutan	2,085,136	1,614,658	77.44%
Myanmar	47,748,939	34,992,083	73.28%
Sri Lanka	18,923,749	12,944,908	68.41%
Japan	127,096,314	70,153,662	55.20%
Viet Nam	78,136,913	38,364,974	49.10%
Laos	5,278,563	2,577,202	48.82%
Mongolia	2,533,299	570,092	22.50%
Taiwan	22,401,000	4,677,128	20.88%
South Korea	46,740,141	7,158,330	15.32%
Singapore	4,018,114	581,684	14.48%
Christmas Island	3,424	419	12.24%
Nepal	23,042,704	2,007,834	8.71%
China	1,260,036,000	107,393,511	8.52%
Brunei	328,305	24,795	7.55%
Malaysia	22,218,485	1,505,860	6.78%
Northern Mariana Is	72,786	3,825	5.26%
Australia	19,131,420	404,608	2.11%
United Arab Emirates	2,605,958	51,846	1.99%
Total of these 20 countries	**1,758,310,854**	**348,329,630**	**19.81%**

Table 4. Top 20 Buddhist peoples by

Country	People Name	Autoglossonym
Japan	Japanese	hyozyun-go
China	Han Chinese (Mandarin)	guo-yu
Viet Nam	Vietnamese (Kinh)	viêt general
Myanmar	Burmese (Myen, Bhama)	bama central
Thailand	Central Thai (Siamese)	thai central
Thailand	Northeastern Tai (Isan)	isan
Sri Lanka	Sinhalese (Singhalese)	sinhala general
Cambodia	Central Khmer (Cambodian)	khmae central
China	Han Chinese (Cantonese)	yue central
China	Han Chinese (Wu)	Shanghainese
South Korea	South Korean	onmun south
Thailand	Northern Tai (Yuan, Phyap)	lanna
China	Central Tibetan (Hsifan)	utsang
India	Maratha (Maharathi)	Wider Marathi
Taiwan	Taiwanese (Hoklo)	quan-zhang-taiwan
Thailand	Han Chinese	thai central
China	Han Chinese (Jinyu)	jinyu
Thailand	Southern Tai (Pak Thai)	pak-thai
China	Han Chinese (Hakka)	hakka
Myanmar	Burmese Shan (Thai Yai)	shan
Total of these 20 peoples		

number of Buddhists in 2000.

Pop 2000	Buddhists	Buddhist%
121,643,336	66,551,069	54.71%
767,663,451	53,736,442	7.00%
65,988,069	35,765,533	54.20%
26,631,608	25,845,976	97.05%
20,182,571	19,294,538	95.60%
16,643,477	16,310,607	98.00%
12,762,555	12,021,051	94.19%
11,447,572	10,816,811	94.49%
51,708,097	10,341,619	20.00%
94,580,444	6,715,212	7.10%
45,355,231	6,576,508	14.50%
6,657,391	6,464,327	97.10%
5,105,288	5,003,182	98.00%
74,459,577	4,616,494	6.20%
15,926,968	4,411,770	27.70%
5,175,179	4,140,143	80.00%
47,256,138	3,307,930	7.00%
4,936,518	3,258,102	66.00%
31,526,857	3,152,686	10.00%
3,103,681	3,085,059	99.40%
1,428,754,008	**301,415,058**	**21.10%**

Table 5. Top 20 Buddhist peoples (over 5%

Country	People Name	Autoglossonym
China	Han Chinese (Mandarin)	guo-yu
Japan	Japanese	hyozyun-go
China	Han Chinese (Wu)	Shanghainese
India	Maratha (Maharathi)	Wider Marathi
Viet Nam	Vietnamese (Kinh)	viêt general
China	Han Chinese (Cantonese)	yue central
China	Han Chinese (Jinyu)	jinyu
South Korea	South Korean	onmun south
China	Han Chinese (Hakka)	hakka
Myanmar	Burmese (Myen, Bhama)	bama central
China	Han Chinese (Min Nan)	Taiwanese
Thailand	Central Thai (Siamese)	thai central
China	Han Chinese (Jin)	Wider Jin
Thailand	Northeastern Tai (Isan)	isan
Taiwan	Taiwanese (Hoklo)	quan-zhang-taiwan
China	Northern Zhuang (Chwang)	wu-ming
Sri Lanka	Sinhalese (Singhalese)	sinhala general
Nepal	Nepalese (Eastern Pahari)	nepali
Cambodia	Central Khmer (Cambodian)	khmae central
China	Manchu (Man)	manchu
Total of these 20 peoples		

Buddhist) by population in 2000.

Pop 2000	Buddhists	Buddhist%
767,663,451	53,736,442	7.00%
121,643,336	66,551,069	54.71%
94,580,444	6,715,212	7.10%
74,459,577	4,616,494	6.20%
65,988,069	35,765,533	54.20%
51,708,097	10,341,619	20.00%
47,256,138	3,307,930	7.00%
45,355,231	6,576,508	14.50%
31,526,857	3,152,686	10.00%
26,631,608	25,845,976	97.05%
25,830,738	2,324,766	9.00%
20,182,571	19,294,538	95.60%
20,160,576	1,411,240	7.00%
16,643,477	16,310,607	98.00%
15,926,968	4,411,770	27.70%
12,770,213	2,426,340	19.00%
12,762,555	12,021,051	94.19%
12,108,598	968,688	8.00%
11,447,572	10,816,811	94.49%
10,915,818	1,089,399	9.98%
1,485,561,894	**287,684,679**	**19.37%**

Table 6. Top 20 most responsive

Country	People Name	Autoglossonym
Bhutan	Khen	khen-kha
Bhutan	Dzalakha	Wider Sharchagpa
Bhutan	Gurtu	kurtopa-kha
China	Jyarung (Rgyarong)	North Jarong
China	Zhongzhai (Western Jiarung)	jiarong west
Bhutan	Central Bhutanese (Bhotia)	Kebumtamp
Bhutan	Eastern Bhutanese (Sharchop)	sharchagpa-kha
India	Monba (Memba, Menpa)	Monba
Bhutan	Sangla	tsangla
China	Namuyi	namuyi
China	Tu (Monguor, Tu-jen)	hu-zhu
China	Guiqiong	guiqiong
Myanmar	Rumai Palaung	rumai
China	Zhaba	zhaba
China	Northern Pumi	p'umi north
China	Queyu	queyu
Bhutan	Chali	tshalingpa
Bhutan	Chocangacakha	chocangacakha
India	Lalung	lalung
China	Southern Pumi	p'umi south
Total of these 20 peoples		

Buddhist peoples in 2000.

Pop 2000	Buddhists	Buddhist%	Evangelism Responsiveness
46,916	46,869	99.90%	2,803
17,515	17,497	99.90%	2,292
11,677	11,665	99.90%	2,084
161,285	161,237	99.97%	2,029
53,300	53,284	99.97%	1,570
615,171	614,556	99.90%	1,481
399,512	399,312	99.95%	1,465
47,925	47,364	98.83%	1,457
161,598	161,582	99.99%	1,401
6,174	6,051	98.00%	1,263
212,946	212,882	99.97%	1,241
7,308	7,162	98.00%	1,220
201,902	191,807	95.00%	1,219
8,064	8,024	99.50%	1,208
44,101	44,013	99.80%	1,205
7,308	7,162	98.00%	1,179
7,924	7,916	99.90%	1,166
23,354	23,331	99.90%	1,092
23,609	23,519	99.62%	1,089
25,201	25,151	99.80%	1,081
2,082,790	**2,070,383**	**99.40%**	**1,477**

Table 7. Top 20 most responsive

Country	People Name	Autoglossonym
China	Khamba (Khams Bhotia)	kham
Myanmar	Yangbye (Yangye)	yangbye
Myanmar	Arakanese (Maghi, Mogh)	arakan
China	Central Tibetan (Hsifan)	utsang
China	Yunnanese Shan (Dai)	shan
Cambodia	Central Khmer (Cambodian)	khmae central
Thailand	Han Chinese (Min Nan)	Taiwanese
Thailand	Northern Khmer (Cambodian)	khmeer north
USA	Vietnamese	viêt general
Thailand	Northeastern Tai (Isan)	isan
Thailand	Southern Tai (Pak Thai)	pak-thai
Myanmar	Burmese Shan (Thai Yai)	shan
Myanmar	Burmese (Myen, Bhama)	bama central
Thailand	Northern Tai (Yuan, Phyap)	lanna
Thailand	Central Thai (Siamese)	thai central
Laos	Lao (Laotian Tai, Lao-Lu)	lao
Japan	Eta	hyozyun-go
Japan	Japanese	hyozyun-go
Viet Nam	Vietnamese (Kinh)	viêt general
Sri Lanka	Sinhalese (Singhalese)	sinhala general
Total of these 20 peoples		

Buddhist megapeoples in 2000.

Pop 2000	Buddhists	Buddhist%	Evangelism Responsiveness
1,703,695	1,702,843	99.95%	999
1,073,138	965,824	90.00%	785
2,005,455	1,604,364	80.00%	667
5,105,288	5,003,182	98.00%	580
1,139,325	911,460	80.00%	558
11,447,572	10,816,811	94.49%	428
1,318,917	527,567	40.00%	400
1,117,588	1,069,532	95.70%	356
1,189,567	618,575	52.00%	341
16,643,477	16,310,607	98.00%	320
4,936,518	3,258,102	66.00%	305
3,103,681	3,085,059	99.40%	269
26,631,608	25,845,976	97.05%	256
6,657,391	6,464,327	97.10%	200
20,182,571	19,294,538	95.60%	193
2,542,976	2,000,559	78.67%	182
2,541,926	1,779,348	70.00%	148
121,643,336	66,551,069	54.71%	142
65,988,069	35,765,533	54.20%	105
12,762,555	12,021,051	94.19%	64
314,909,832	**219,736,470**	**69.78%**	**365**

Table 8. Top 20 Buddhist peoples with no

Country	People Name	Autoglossonym
Japan	Central Ryukyuan	luchu
Sri Lanka	Rodiya	rodiya
Bhutan	Central Bhutanese (Bhotia)	Kebumtamp
China	Bai (Baizi, Whites)	bai
Bhutan	Eastern Bhutanese (Sharchop)	sharchagpa-kha
China	Ongbe (Be)	lingao
Myanmar	Silver Palaung (Bonglong)	pale
China	Tu (Monguor, Tu-jen)	hu-zhu
Nepal	Limbu	tajeng-pan
Myanmar	Rumai Palaung	rumai
Myanmar	Golden Palaung (Shwe)	shwe
Bhutan	Sangla	tsangla
China	Jyarung (Rgyarong)	North Jarong
Thailand	Phuthai (Puthai)	Phu
Myanmar	Mro Chin	mrung
Japan	Kunigami	kunigami
Laos	So (Kah So, So Makon)	kah-so
China	Bulang (Pula, Samtao)	Bulang
Viet Nam	White Tai (Thai Trang)	tai-kao
Japan	Northern Amami-Oshima	amami north
Total of these 20 peoples		

Jesus film in their language in 2000.

Pop 2000	Buddhists	Buddhist%
984,285	944,914	96.00%
946,187	891,214	94.19%
615,171	614,556	99.90%
1,772,619	540,649	30.50%
399,512	399,312	99.95%
654,211	327,106	50.00%
257,539	257,024	99.80%
212,946	212,882	99.97%
299,555	209,689	70.00%
201,902	191,807	95.00%
200,073	180,066	90.00%
161,598	161,582	99.99%
161,285	161,237	99.97%
170,379	153,341	90.00%
137,765	130,877	95.00%
124,046	120,573	97.20%
114,595	103,136	90.00%
91,479	88,735	97.00%
252,539	88,389	35.00%
76,042	73,000	96.00%
7,833,728	**5,850,085**	**74.68%**

Table 9. Top 20 Buddhist peoples with no

Country	People Name	Autoglossonym
Sri Lanka	Rodiya	rodiya
Bhutan	Central Bhutanese (Bhotia)	Kebumtamp
China	Bai (Baizi, Whites)	bai
Bhutan	Eastern Bhutanese (Sharchop)	sharchagpa-kha
China	Ongbe (Be)	lingao
Myanmar	Silver Palaung (Bonglong)	pale
China	Tu (Monguor, Tu-jen)	hu-zhu
Nepal	Limbu	tajeng-pan
Myanmar	Rumai Palaung	rumai
Myanmar	Golden Palaung (Shwe)	shwe
China	Jyarung (Rgyarong)	North Jarong
China	Bulang (Pula, Samtao)	Bulang
China	Molao	mu-lam
Japan	Southern Ryukyuan (Miyako)	miyako
China	Southern Chiang (Qiang)	taoping
China	Zhongzhai (Western Jiarung)	jiarong west
India	Monba (Memba, Menpa)	Monba
Bhutan	Khen	khen-kha
Japan	Yayeyama	yaeyama
China	Northern Pumi	p'umi north
Total of these 20 peoples		

scriptures in their language in 2000.

Pop 2000	Buddhists	Buddhist%
946,187	891,214	94.19%
615,171	614,556	99.90%
1,772,619	540,649	30.50%
399,512	399,312	99.95%
654,211	327,106	50.00%
257,539	257,024	99.80%
212,946	212,882	99.97%
299,555	209,689	70.00%
201,902	191,807	95.00%
200,073	180,066	90.00%
161,285	161,237	99.97%
91,479	88,735	97.00%
177,035	71,699	40.50%
67,653	65,826	97.30%
82,532	57,772	70.00%
53,300	53,284	99.97%
47,925	47,364	98.83%
46,916	46,869	99.90%
47,636	46,683	98.00%
44,101	44,013	99.80%
6,379,577	**4,507,786**	**70.66%**

Table 10. Top 20 majority Christian peoples with

Country	People Name	Autoglossonym
South Africa	Xhosa	i-si-xhosa
USA	Korean	p'yojun-o
Brazil	Japanese	hyozyun-go
Philippines	Han Chinese (Min Nan)	Taiwanese
Myanmar	Kachin (Chingpo, Singpo)	jing-pho
USA	Hawaiian Creole	hawaiian-creole
China	Chingpo (Kachin, Jinghpaw)	jing-pho
Peru	Japanese	hyozyun-go
Canada	Korean	p'yojun-o
China	Vietnamese (Gin, Jhing)	viêt general
Thailand	Eurasian	English
Myanmar	Eurasian (Anglo-Burmese)	English
New Zealand	Han Chinese (Cantonese)	yue central
Australia	Korean	p'yojun-o
Madagascar	Han Chinese	guo-yu
Brazil	Korean	p'yojun-o
Jamaica	Han Chinese (Hakka)	hakka
Argentina	Korean	p'yojun-o
Trinidad & Tobago	Han Chinese (Hakka)	hakka
Mauritius	Sino-Mauritian (Hakka)	hakka
India	Kachin (Singpho)	jing-pho
Total of these 20 peoples		

more than 0.5% Buddhists in 2000.

Pop 2000	Christian%	Buddhists	Buddhist%
6,582,998	88.40%	32,915	0.50%
2,041,240	70.00%	204,124	10.00%
1,363,250	63.50%	272,650	20.00%
812,312	89.90%	41,428	5.10%
703,108	60.00%	70,311	10.00%
283,230	90.00%	14,162	5.00%
132,556	55.00%	13,256	10.00%
122,150	50.80%	18,323	15.00%
92,270	61.00%	18,454	20.00%
50,401	75.00%	7,560	15.00%
50,244	55.00%	19,846	39.50%
47,749	95.00%	2,387	5.00%
41,558	51.00%	11,054	26.60%
40,293	55.00%	4,029	10.00%
39,926	70.00%	3,993	10.00%
38,018	55.00%	13,306	35.00%
31,428	84.70%	314	1.00%
27,770	80.00%	4,166	15.00%
20,891	65.00%	2,089	10.00%
20,637	55.00%	1,651	8.00%
20,179	70.00%	1,009	5.00%
12,562,208		**757,027**	**6.03%**

Table 11. Top 20 peoples with more than 500,000

Country	People Name	Autoglossonym
China	Han Chinese (Mandarin)	guo-yu
Japan	Japanese	hyozyun-go
China	Han Chinese (Wu)	Shanghainese
India	Maratha (Maharathi)	Wider Marathi
Viet Nam	Vietnamese (Kinh)	viêt general
India	Hindi (High Hindi)	hindi formal
Indonesia	Javanese (Orang Jawa)	jawa general
China	Han Chinese (Cantonese)	yue central
China	Han Chinese (Jinyu)	jinyu
South Korea	South Korean	onmun south
China	Han Chinese (Min Nan)	Taiwanese
Thailand	Central Thai (Siamese)	thai central
China	Han Chinese (Jin)	Wider Jin
Taiwan	Taiwanese (Hoklo)	quan-zhang-taiwan
Sri Lanka	Sinhalese (Singhalese)	sinhala general
China	Han Chinese (Min Pei)	min-bei
Indonesia	Han Chinese (Peranakan)	paranakan
China	Han Chinese (Cantonese):HK	yue central
Total of these 20 peoples		

Christians and 500,000 Buddhists in 2000.

Pop 2000	Christians	Christian%	Buddhists	Buddhist%
767,663,451	58,803,020	7.66%	53,736,442	7.00%
121,643,336	4,002,066	3.29%	66,551,069	54.71%
94,580,444	12,200,877	12.90%	6,715,212	7.10%
74,459,577	3,722,979	5.00%	4,616,494	6.20%
65,988,069	5,279,046	8.00%	35,765,533	54.20%
62,554,116	1,251,082	2.00%	500,433	0.80%
53,075,690	7,138,680	13.45%	1,061,514	2.00%
51,708,097	1,758,075	3.40%	10,341,619	20.00%
47,256,138	3,307,930	7.00%	3,307,930	7.00%
45,355,231	18,813,350	41.48%	6,576,508	14.50%
25,830,738	2,841,381	11.00%	2,324,766	9.00%
20,182,571	504,564	2.50%	19,294,538	95.60%
20,160,576	1,008,029	5.00%	1,411,240	7.00%
15,926,968	716,714	4.50%	4,411,770	27.70%
12,762,555	588,354	4.61%	12,021,051	94.19%
12,610,692	1,261,069	10.00%	630,535	5.00%
5,620,439	2,472,993	44.00%	843,066	15.00%
4,680,152	561,618	12.00%	842,427	18.00%
1,502,058,840	**126,231,827**	**8.40%**	**230,952,147**	**15.38%**

Table 12. 274 Varieties of Buddhism with

#	Variety of Buddhism	Adherents	Main country	Begun
1	Buddhists	363,963,606	Japan	
2	Sino-American Buddhist Association	800,000	USA	1968
3	Folk-Buddhists	10,000,000	Japan	
4	Kasogatan	30,000	Indonesia	c1500
5	Lamaists	21,490,000	China	640
6	Kagyudpas	9,000,000	China	c1030
7	Drukpa Kagyudpa	50,000	China	c1170
8	Drigung Kagyudpa	4,000	China	c1180
9	Karmapas	6,000,000	China	c1150
10	Taklung Kagyudpa	50,000	China	c1190
11	Nyingmapas	7,000,000	China	c790
12	Rimaypas	600,000	China	c1860
13	Sakyapas	5,000,000	China	1073
14	Dolma	1,000	China	
15	Tsharpa	500,000	China	c1540
16	Phuntsok	1,000	China	c1960
17	Ngorba	500,000	China	1429
18	Njushi-ryu	100,000	China	
19	Mongolian Buddhism	600,000	Mongolia	
20	Mahayanists	202,232,757	Japan	
21	Chinese Buddhists	90,000,000	China	60
22	Falun Gong	30,000,000	China	
23	Hua-yen	3,000,000	China	690
24	Indian Buddhists	7,249,384	India	1956
25	Korean Buddhists	7,100,000	South Korea	372
26	Chogye Chong	7,001,000	South Korea	372
27	Chongwhajong	712,000	South Korea	1969
28	Chontaijong	1,182,000	South Korea	594
29	Bulgyohwoi	563,000	South Korea	1975
30	Kwanumjong	618,000	South Korea	1940
31	Mitajong	1,026,000	South Korea	1943
32	Taego Chong	3,133,000	South Korea	1356
33	Won Buddhism	600,000	South Korea	1916
34	Popsong	1,000,000	South Korea	
35	Japanese Buddhists	71,000,000	Japan	
36	Nichiren Shu	2,100,000	Japan	c1260
37	Nichiren Honshu	34,760	Japan	
38	Nichiren Komonshu	26,556	Japan	
39	Nichirenshu Saijokyo	7,018	Japan	
40	Nichiren Hokkeshu	14,020	Japan	

number of adherents in 2000.

Note

Buddha-dharma. Followers of the Buddha in several hundred schools and sects.
SABA. Chinese Buddhist polity. Strict standards.
Popularized religion mixing Buddhist elements with local deities or cults.
Javanese local variety of Buddhism; with Mahayana, Theravada, forms amalgam Buddhayana.
Tibet. Worldwide diaspora. Mantra 'Om mani padmi hum'. 1959, 6,000 monasteries destroyed.
Followers of the Oral Teaching Lineages. One of 4 main Lamaist orders/sects. In Europe, USA.
Dragon Kagyudpa. Tibet, and Bhutan state religion.
Third largest of surving Kagyudpa Lamaism. Many monasteries in Ladakh.
Karma Kagyudpas, largest surviving Tibetan Lamaist Kagyudpa schools. Black Hats.
Smallest of 4 surviving Kagyudpa schools of Tibetan Buddhism.
Red Hat lamas. Followers of the Ancient Teachings. Tibet's oldest Buddhist order; unreformed.
Eclectic Movement. Nonsectarian, spiritual/cultural renaissance, unify the many Lamaist sects.
Grey Earth School. One of 4 major sects of Tibet Lamaism. Logicians, debaters, philosophers.
Subgroup within Sakyapa Lamaism.
One of 2 rival branches of Sakyapa tradition of Tibetan Buddhism.
Subgroup of Tibetan Buddhist Sakyapa school.
Branch of Sakyapa tradition of Tibetan Buddhism. Monasteries across Tibet.
Tibetan. Variety of Lamaism.
Viciously suppressed by Stalinists from 1917 to 1990. Now revived.
Greater Vehicle of Salvation. Family of lineages. Main cultures: Tibeto-Mongol, Sino-Japanese.
Violently suppressed in AD 452, 574, and 845.
A Buddhist motivation-based sect. 1999 clashes with Communist regime.
Kegon (Flower Adornment), a major school of Chinese Buddhism. F=Fa-tsang.
Reformed Buddhism reintroduced by B.R.Ambedkar for Dalits (Untouchables).
Mahayana Buddhism.
Daihan-Bulgyo-Chongyejong strict Korean Son (Zen) Buddhism (Chongye), unified 1935.
Daihan-Bulgyo-Chongwhajong (Korean Buddhist Sect of Chongwha; Mahayana).
Daihan-Bulgyo-Chontaijong (Korean Buddhist Sect of Chontai; Mahayana).
SGI Hankuk-Bulgyohwoi/Korean Buddhist Council. Emphasis upon world peace.
Daihan-Bulgyo-Kwanumjong (Korean Buddhist Sect of Sattva).
Daihan-Bulgyo-Mitajong (Korean Buddhist Sect of Sattva).
Hankuk-Bulgyo-Taigojong (Korean Buddhist Sect of Taigo). Liberal, rivaling traditionalists.
Won Bulgyo (Round Circle). Modernized Zen/Taoism/Confucianism/Chondogyo/Christianity.
Korean version of Mahayana Buddhism. Zen elements. 1935, unified as Chogye Chong.
Mainly Mahayana, but many varieties. Total Buddhist sects in Japan: 180.
'Sun Lotus'. The original movement begun by monk Nichiren (1222-1282). HQ Ota-ku, Tokyo.
HQ Sakyo-ku, Kyoto-shi.
HQ Okayama-ken.
HQ Okayama-ken.
HQ Fukushima-shi.

Table 12. 274 Varieties of Buddhism with

#	Variety of Buddhism	Adherents	Main country	Begun
41	Nichirenshugi Butsuryuko	2,048	Japan	
42	Nichirenshu Fujufuseha	16,697	Japan	c1610
43	Nara Buddhists	2,262,202	Japan	c550
44	Daijokyo	409,975	Japan	
45	Honke Myoshu Renmei	1,354	Japan	
46	Honmon Hokkeshu	251,250	Japan	
47	Daiekai Kyodan	29,895	Japan	
48	Honpa Nichirenshu	45,650	Japan	
49	Honmon Kyooshu	6,732	Japan	
50	Hokkeshu Jinmonryu	145,680	Japan	
51	Fujifuse	20,000	Japan	c1600
52	Hokke Nichirenshu	25,500	Japan	
53	Hokke Shinshu	3,098	Japan	
54	Honmon Butsuryushu	447,186	Japan	1857
55	Hokkeshu Honmonryu	368,570	Japan	
56	Hokkeshu Shinmonryu	64,610	Japan	
57	Hosshikai Kyodan	141,752	Japan	
58	Honke Nichirenshu	2,500	Japan	
59	Bussho Gonenkai Kyodan	912,807	Japan	
60	Myochikai Kyodan	670,102	Japan	
61	Nipponzan Myohoji	200,000	Japan	1917
62	Myodokai Kyodan	155,098	Japan	
63	Zaike Nichirenshu Jofukai	24,582	Japan	
64	Nihonzan Myohoji Daisanga	24,326	Japan	
65	Saijo Inarikyo	232,352	Japan	
66	Seigikai Kyodan	36,432	Japan	
67	Shobokai	12,571	Japan	
68	Shishinkai	70,162	Japan	
69	Kokuchukai	28,731	Japan	
70	Shobo Hokkeshu	18,659	Japan	
71	Nakayama Myoshu	565,650	Japan	
72	Pure Land Buddhists	21,000,000	China	c380
73	Gugan Shinshu	1,489	Japan	
74	Bukkyo Shinshu	5,500	Japan	
75	Buddhist Churches of America	120,000	USA	1899
76	Chinzei	7,000	Japan	
77	Japanese Pure Land Buddhists	20,941,500	Japan	c1180
78	Shinshu Jokojiha	25,062	Japan	
79	Jishu	87,410	Japan	
80	Shinshu Kita Honganjiha	9,153	Japan	

number of adherents in 2000 (*contd.*).

Note

HQ Aichi-ken.
HQ Okayama-ken.
Nara sects were first forms of Buddhism in Japan. Now 7 distinct Nara sects.
HQ Nagoya-shi.
HQ Kanagawa-ken.
HQ Kamigyo-ku, Kyoto-shi.
HQ Osaka-fu.
HQ Osaka-fu.
HQ Chogu-shi, Tokyo.
HQ Toshima-ku, Tokyo.
A Nichiren branch of secret believers until 1874 state recognition. HQ Okayama.
HQ Osaka-shi.
HQ Shinagawa-ku, Tokyo.
HQ Kamigyo-ku. No priesthood. Lay-run.
HQ Toshima-ku, Tokyo.
HQ Kamigyo-ku, Kyoto-shi.
HQ Iwate-ken.
One of numerous Nichiren adaptations.
HQ Minato-ku, Tokyo.
HQ Shibuya-ku, Tokyo.
Wondrous Law of the Lotus Sutra. Global fame for 'peace pagodas'. 1,500 ascetics.
HQ Osaka-shi.
HQ Shinjuku-ku, Tokyo.
HQ Shibuya-ku, Tokyo.
HQ Okayama-ken.
HQ Chiba-ken.
HQ Shinagawa-ku, Tokyo.
HQ Kita-ku, Tokyo.
HQ Edogawa-ku, Tokyo.
HQ Kita-ku, Kyoto-shi.
HQ Chiba-ken.
Ching-Tu. Begun China (F=Hui-yuan), then Japan (Jodo Shy). Now almost all in Japan.
HQ Fukui-shi.
HQ Kumamoto-ken.
Jodoshinshu. Japanese Americans.
A school of Jodo (Pure Land) Buddhism.
F=Honen. Several rival sects. God=Amitabha/Amida, a god presiding over Western Paradise.
HQ Niigata-ken.
HQ Kanagawa-ken.
HQ Otaru-shi, Hokkaido.

Table 12. 274 Varieties of Buddhism with

#	Variety of Buddhism	Adherents	Main country	Begun
81	Shinshu Koshoha	145,680	Japan	
82	Seizan Jodoshu	131,100	Japan	
83	Shinshu Izumojiha	11,980	Japan	
84	Kurotani Jodoshu	406,955	Japan	
85	Jodoshu Seizan Zenrinjiha	156,730	Japan	
86	Jodo Shu	5,778,316	Japan	c1180
87	Jodoshu Shaseiha	4,150	Japan	
88	Makoto no Jodo Shinshu Jokojiha	168,868	Japan	
89	White Lotus School	10,000	China	402
90	Shinshu Yamamotoha	4,000	Japan	
91	Yuzu Nenbutsu Shu	101,144	Japan	
92	Jodoshu Seizan Fukakusaha	81,300	Japan	
93	Ji Buddhism	100,000	Japan	1270
94	Shinshu Takadaha	261,875	Japan	
95	Shinshu Shojojiha	21,490	Japan	
96	Shinshu Sanmontoha	19,000	Japan	
97	Shinshu Choseiha	1,073	Japan	
98	Montoshu Ichimiha	2,700	Japan	
99	True Pure Land Buddhists	14,000,000	Japan	c1270
100	Jodo Shinshu Dobo Kyodan	1,216	Japan	
101	Jodo Shinshu Honganjiha	6,662,362	Japan	1220
102	Jodo Shinshu Otaniha	6,715,135	Japan	1220
103	Fudoshu	1,706,858	Japan	
104	Hossoshu	600,000	Japan	661
105	Kegon	705,000	Japan	736
106	Shingon Risshu	443,800	Japan	c1250
107	Risshu	23,300	Japan	754
108	Myohoshu	4,920	Japan	
109	Ritsu	500,000	Japan	
110	Kegon Shu	70,486	Japan	740
111	Shotoku Shu	12,838	Japan	1950
112	Shingon Buddhists	11,000,000	Japan	810
113	Issaishu	156,270	Japan	
114	Guze Kannon Shu	11,700	Japan	
115	Ishizuchisan Shingonshu	94,550	Japan	
116	Hasshukengaku Shinshukyo	15,880	Japan	
117	Chizan-ha	1,101,000	Japan	
118	Buzan-ha	1,372,000	Japan	
119	Fudokyo	3,800	Japan	
120	Shingonshu Reiunjiha	6,700	Japan	

number of adherents in 2000 (*contd.*).

Note

HQ Shimogyo-ku, Kyoto-shi.
HQ Kyoto-fu.
HQ Fukui-ken.
HQ Kyoto-shi.
HQ Kyoto-shi.
Original parent Pure Land Buddhism. F=Honen.
HQ Higashiyama-ku, Kyoto-shi.
HQ Fukuoka-shi.
School of Celestial Platform/Pure Land: Pai-lien Tsung, Tien-Tai (in Japan, Tendai). F=Hui-yuan.
HQ Fukui-ken.
HQ Osaka-shi.
HQ Kyoto-shi.
Ji='Time', a sect of Pure Land Buddhism. F=Ippen. Wandering preachers.
Largest Pure Land sect in Japan, with 600 temples. HQ Mie-ken.
HQ Fukui-ken.
HQ Fukui-shi.
HQ Yokohama-shi.
HQ Kitami-shi, Hokkaido.
Jodo Shinshu. Also termed Shin Buddhism. Many monks. c1650, splits in 2 sects.
HQ Ishikawa-ken.
F=Shinran. Major subgroup in True Pure Land. Nishi (Western). 10,000 temples (HQ Kyoto).
True Pure Land Sect. Eastern Temple. 16,890 clergy, 9,980 temples. HQ Shimogyo-ku, Kyoto.
HQ Okayama-ken.
One of 6 Nara sects of Japanese Buddhism. 40 temples. 1945, 57,042 adherents. HQ Nara-shi.
Mutual identity of phenomena and great Buddha Dainichi (AD 749). HQ Nara-shi. 1945: 50,915.
A subgroup of Risshu; 90 temples. HQ Nara-shi. F=Eizon.
One of 6 Nara sects of Japanese Buddhism. Strict monasticism. HQ Nara-shi. F=Ganjin/Ching.
HQ Nara-ken.
Emphasis on Buddhist monastic precepts.
Nara sect. Name in Chinese: Hua Yen. 60 temples, 900 clergy. HQ Nara-shi.
A modern form of Japanese Mahayana. 1950, ex Hossoshu. HQ Nara-ken.
True Word. F=Kukai. Tantric Buddhism; 45 sects. God=Great Sun Buddha. HQ Kyoto.
HQ Yamaguchi-ken.
HQ Wakayama-shi.
HQ Ehime-ken.
HQ Kumamoto-shi.
One of the 2 main branches of Shingon Buddhism.
Larger of 2 main branches of Shingon Buddhism (Shingonshu).
HQ Nakoya-shi.
HQ Bunkyo-ku.

Table 12. 274 Varieties of Buddhism with

#	Variety of Buddhism	Adherents	Main country	Begun
121	Shingonshu Shugenha	62,242	Japan	
122	Shingonshu Ishitetsuha	8,000	Japan	
123	Shingonshu Hokakujiha	15,030	Japan	
124	Shingonshu Gochi Kyodan	10,000	Japan	
125	Shingonshu Senyujiha	39,196	Japan	
126	Shingonshu Murojiha	27,520	Japan	
127	Shingonshu Inunakiha	21,421	Japan	
128	Meisan Shingonshu	12,800	Japan	
129	Komyo Shingonshu	102,181	Japan	
130	Shinnyoen	190,631	Japan	1935
131	Shingonshu Kyushu Kyodan	9,820	Japan	
132	Shingonshu Kongoinha	42,180	Japan	
133	Kannon Shu	490,000	Japan	
134	Tenshu	20,000	Japan	
135	Shingonshu Kokubunjiha	81,560	Japan	
136	Koyasan Shingonshu	4,876,300	Japan	815
137	Shingonshu Kojinha	5,100	Japan	
138	Shingonshu Omuroha	141,768	Japan	
139	Shingon Sanboshu	156,340	Japan	
140	Shigisan Shingonshu	496,415	Japan	c1000
141	Nakayama Shingo Shoshu	456,902	Japan	1921
142	Shin Bukkyo Kukaishu	30,000	Japan	
143	Shin Shingonshu	4,150	Japan	
144	Shin-nyo En	2,100,000	Japan	
145	Shingi Shingonshu	212,970	Japan	
146	Shingonshu Kazan'inha	6,100	Japan	
147	Manji Kyodan	275,900	Japan	
148	Shingonshu Sumaderaha	49,640	Japan	
149	Shingon Birushana Shu	4,942	Japan	
150	Shingon Kyodan	4,400	Japan	
151	Shingonshu Yamashinaha	53,712	Japan	
152	Shingon Misshu	21,980	Japan	
153	Shingonshu Daigoha	353,693	Japan	
154	Ryosenji Shingonshu	16,097	Japan	
155	Shingonshu Tojiha	56,470	Japan	
156	Shingonshu Daikakujiha	37,990	Japan	
157	Shingi-Shingonshu Yudonosanpa	20,000	Japan	
158	Shingonshu Chizanha	1,205,187	Japan	1585
159	Shingonshu Buzanha	879,341	Japan	1580
160	Shingon Shu	282,740	Japan	

number of adherents in 2000 (*contd.*).

Note

HQ Kogawa-ken.
HQ Ehime-ken.
HQ Nara-ken.
HQ Aichi-ken.
HQ Kyoto-shi.
HQ Nara-ken.
HQ Osaka-fu.
HQ Wakayama-shi.
HQ Wakayama-ken.
HQ Tachikawa-shi, Tokyo.
HQ Fukuoka-shi.
HQ Hyogo-ken.
HQ Osaka-shi.
One of many Shingon sects with differentiated practices.
HQ Osaka-shi.
HQ Wakayama-ken. Oldest sect of Tantric Buddhism in Japan.
HQ Hyogo-ken.
HQ Kyoto-shi.
HQ Huogo-ken.
HQ Nara-ken.
HQ Saga-ken.
HQ Hyogo-ken.
HQ Higashi Osaka-shi.
'Garden of the Truth of Buddha'. Lay movement with 500 workers. Focuses on Nirvana Sutra.
HQ Taito-ku, Tokyo.
HQ Hyogo-ken.
HQ Fukuoka-ken.
HQ Kobe-shi.
HQ Higashi Osaka-shi.
HQ Tochigi-ken.
HQ Kyoto-shi.
HQ Toyama-ken.
HQ Kyoto-shi.
HQ Nara-shi.
HQ Kyoto-shi.
HQ Kyoto-shi.
HQ Yamagata-ken.
Based on 'New Interpretation of Shingon' with Pure Land elements.
HQ Bunkyo-ku, Tokyo.
A broader form of modified Shingon.

Table 12. 274 Varieties of Buddhism with

#	Variety of Buddhism	Adherents	Main country	Begun
161	Shingon Shotenshu	4,374	Japan	
162	Shingonshu Dainichiha	15,000	Japan	
163	Tendai Buddhists	5,000,000	Japan	c550
164	Enjoshu	16,274	Japan	
165	Ishizuchishu	10,000	Japan	
166	Kodo Kyodan	391,399	Japan	1948
167	Shinshu Bukkojiha	137,844	Japan	
168	Kongoshu	142,486	Japan	
169	Tendai Jimonshu	400,310	Japan	c850
170	Jodo Shinshu Kenkoinha	15,000	Japan	
171	Kokawa Kannon Shu	18,616	Japan	
172	Kurama Kokyo	7,440	Japan	
173	Taiwashu	104,725	Japan	
174	Washu	2,015,550	Japan	1949
175	Owari Koyasan	72,090	Japan	
176	Shugenshu	91,008	Japan	
177	Shugendo	104,149	Japan	c1050
178	Nenpo Shinkyo	511,438	Japan	1925
179	Kinpusan Shugen Honshu	254,764	Japan	1945
180	Kenjoshu	4,893	Japan	
181	Seizanshu	4,000	Japan	
182	Tendai Shinseishu	74,680	Japan	
183	Myokenshu	227,223	Japan	
184	Yogacara	10,000	India	c350
185	Zen Buddhists	13,000,000	Japan	1191
186	Ichibata Yakushi Kyodan	110,184	Japan	
187	Isson Kyodan	1,580	Japan	
188	Chan Buddhism	1,000,000	China	c500
189	Rinzaishu Kokutaijiha	2,265	Japan	1327
190	Rinzaishu Koshojiha	3,116	Japan	
191	Rinzaishu Myoshinjiha	1,628,000	Japan	1337
192	Rinzaishu Nanzenjiha	91,157	Japan	1291
193	Rinzaishu Tenryujiha	82,580	Japan	1339
194	Obaku Shu	244,584	Japan	1650
195	Rinzaishu Shokokujiha	53,750	Japan	1382
196	Rinzaishu Tofukujiha	5,000	Japan	1239
197	Tsao-tung	800,000	China	1108
198	Nyoraikyo	33,371	Japan	
199	Ningen Zen Kyodan	5,170	Japan	
200	Senshin Kyodan	36,553	Japan	

number of adherents in 2000 (*contd.*).

Note

HQ Hyogo-ken.
HQ Tochigi-ken.
Tendaishu. Introduced from China. Rationalist monastic order, ascetic, meditative. 20 sects.
Sect of Tendai Buddhism. HQ Kyoto-shi.
Sect of Tendai Buddhism. HQ Ehime-ken.
Sect of Tendai Buddhism. HQ Yokohama-shi. F=Okano Shodo and wife Kimiko.
HQ Kyoto-shi.
Sect of Tendai Buddhism. HQ Ehime-ken.
Schism ex Tendai by F=Enchin. HQ Shiga-ken. Esoteric. Many schisms and sects.
Sect of Tendai Buddhism. HQ Kyoto-shi.
Sect of Tendai Buddhism. HQ Wakayama-ken.
Sect of Tendai Buddhism. HQ Kyoto-shi.
Sect of Tendai Buddhism. HQ Iwate-ken.
Largest of the 20 sects of Tendai Buddhism. HQ Osaka-shi.
Sect of Tendai Buddhism. HQ Aichi-ken.
Sect of Tendai. HQ Kamagawa-ken.
Way to control central power. Lay, hostile to clergy. 180 temples.
Sect of Tendai Buddhism. HQ Osaka-shi.
Sect of Tendai Buddhism. HQ Nara-ken. Mountain worship, magical rituals.
Sect of Tendai Buddhism. HQ Hiroshima-ken.
Sect of Tendai Buddhism. HQ Kyoto-shi.
HQ Shiga-ken.
Sect of Tendai Buddhism. HQ Osaka-fu.
Yoga-practice. Vijnanavada. Philosophical school 'Mind Only' of Mahayana Buddhism.
Brought to Japan from China. Now 22,000 temples in Japan.
HQ Shimane-ken.
HQ Ishikawa-ken.
Form of Zen meditation rooted in Indian Buddhism and developed in China and Japan.
HQ Toyama-ken.
HQ Kamigyo-ku, Kyoto-shi.
Largest Rinzai sect in Japan. 3,000 temples. Declining. HQ Kyoto. Members in USA, Mexico.
HQ Kyoto-shi.
HQ Ukyo-ku, Kyoto-shi.
One of 3 schools of Zen in Japan. F=Ingen. 460 temples. HQ Kyoto-fu.
HQ Kyoto-shi.
HQ Kyoto-shi.
Chan (Zen) school of Buddhism in China. Soto (Japanese). The 5 Ranks/Ways.
HQ Nagoya-shi.
HQ Chiba-ken.
HQ Mie-gun, Mie-ken.

Table 12. 274 Varieties of Buddhism with

#	Variety of Buddhism	Adherents	Main country	Begun
201	Sanbo Kyodan	2,737	Japan	
202	Soto Shu	6,841,720	Japan	c1240
203	Rinzaishu Kenninjiha	24,000	Japan	1202
204	Rinzaishu Eigenjiha	13,630	Japan	1361
205	Rinzaishu Buttsujiha	98,502	Japan	1395
206	Rinzaishu Kenchojiha	89,380	Japan	1253
207	Rinzaishu Kogakujiha	30,100	Japan	1380
208	Rinzaishu Daitokujiha	14,731	Japan	1324
209	Rinzaishu Hokojiha	588,900	Japan	1384
210	Rinzai Zen Buddhists	3,000,000	Japan	1191
211	Rinzaishu Enkakujiha	178,000	Japan	1282
212	nonreligious Buddhists	54,408,000	Japan	c1950
213	Chinese Buddhist Association	60,000,000	China	1954
214	Indonesian Buddhayana Council	1,930,000	Indonesia	1954
215	Buddhist Society of India	6,000,000	India	1951
216	Buddhist Federation of Australia	241,000	Australia	c1970
217	All Indonesia Fed of Buddhist Orgs	2,000,000	Indonesia	1978
218	All Ceylon Buddhist Congress	12,500,000	Sri Lanka	1918
219	Buddhist Association of Thailand	52,382,000	Thailand	1934
220	All Japan Federation of Buddhist Sects	81,300,000	Japan	
221	Buddhist Society of Great Britain and I	3,000	Britain	1907
222	Federation of Buddhists of Thailand	52,000,000	Thailand	1975
223	Sri Lankan Dharmadhuta Society	2,000,000	Sri Lanka	1952
224	Unified Vietnamese Buddhist Church	39,000,000	Vietnam	1963
225	Lao United Buddhists Association	2,650,000	Laos	1977
226	Western Buddhist Order	500,000	Britain	1967
227	Majelis Upasaka Pandita Agama BI	500,000	Indonesia	c1975
228	Gelugpas	100,000	China	c1450
229	Mulavamsa	12,000	Sri Lanka	c1900
230	Dwara Nikaya	3,000	Myanmar	c1850
231	Hngettwin Nikaya	1,000	Myanmar	c1850
232	Dhammarakkhitavamsa	5,000	Sri Lanka	c1900
233	Dhammayut Nikaya	1,500,000	Thailand	c1870
234	Shwegyin Nikaya	50,000	Myanmar	c1850
235	Siyam Nikaya	12,000	Sri Lanka	1753
236	Thuddama Nikaya	450,000	Myanmar	1780
237	Mahanikaya	200,000	Thailand	c1700
238	Saddhammavamsa	6,000	Sri Lanka	
239	Ramanna Nikaya	2,000	Sri Lanka	1865
240	Thomayat	2,300	Cambodia	

number of adherents in 2000 (*contd.*).

Note
HQ Kanagawa-ken.
Zen Buddhism with temples, priests, rites. China origin. F=Dogen. Popular Buddhist teaching.
F=Myoan-Eisai (1141-1218)
HQ Shiga-ken.
HQ Kyoto-shi.
HQ Kanagawa-ken.
HQ Yamanashi-ken.
HQ Kita-ku, Kyoto-shi.
HQ Shizuoka-ken.
Japanese Zen. F=Lin Chi (Chinese). Overall aim to reproduce Enlightenment experience.
HQ Kanagawa-ken.
Persons with Buddhism as family religion but professing no personal religion.
Government-control after virtually destroyed in Cultural Revolution, 1966-1979.
Majelis Buddhayana Indonesia (MBI). Java.
Neo-Buddhism of BR Ambedkar; mass conversion of Dalits, 1956. Marathi.
Huge Nan Tien Temple is part of a Taiwan-based 110 monastery network.
Acronym WALUBI. Represents all Buddhist sects to government.
Theravadins. Leadership of YMBA.
75 provincial associations (14 Chinese).
Nihon Bukkyo Kai. 60 sects, 60 other organizations.
I=Ireland. All traditions taught.
FBT. Begun by Mahanikaya monks.
Begun from World Fellowship of Buddhists for Theravada missions worldwide.
United Buddhist Association, uniting Theravadins and Mahayanists.
LUBA. 7,000 monks, 10,000 novices, in 2,800 monasteries.
Friends of the Western Buddhist Order (WBO). Quasi-monastic. F=Venerable Sangharakshita.
MUABI. Council of Buddhist Lay Spiritual Advisors of Indonesia. Married, no monastic rules.
Virtuous Ones. Yellow Hat Lamaist monastic order (Dalai Lama's sect); emphasis scholarship.
Prominent monastic grouping within Amarapura Nikaya.
Small Burmese Theravada monastic fraternity. Rationalist.
Smallest monastic fraternity in Burma; around Mandalay.
Prominent monastic grouping within Amarapura Nikaya.
Thammayut. Theravada monastic community with 1,500 monasteries.
Smaller school: 50,000 monks. Strict, puritanical.
Oldest fraternity of Theravada monks in Ceylon. Strict hierarchy.
80% of monastic fraternity in Burma. 250,000 ordained monks.
Largest Theravada fraternity in Thailand: 95% of 28,000 monasteries, with 200,000 monks.
Monastic grouping within Amarapura Nikaya.
One of 3 main divisions of Theravada monks.
Order of the Law. Close to Thai Thammayut. Destroyed 1975, restored 1991. 104 monasteries.

Table 12. 274 Varieties of Buddhism with

#	Variety of Buddhism	Adherents	Main country	Begun
241	Anagarika	30,000	India	BC 800
242	Hoguk Sungdan	20,000	South Korea	c1950
243	Order of Buddhist Contemplatives	2,000	USA	1970
244	Fukudenkai	2,451	Japan	
245	Gedatsuko	234,131	Japan	
246	Bauddha Dharmankur Sabha	500,000	India	1892
247	Buddhist Sunday Schools Movement	3,000,000	Thailand	1958
248	Vietnamese Buddhists	39,533,000	Vietnam	c50
249	Theravadins	136,259,000	Sri Lanka	BC c250
250	Burmese Theravadins	32,000,000	Myanmar	
251	Cambodian Buddhism	9,500,000	Cambodia	AD 400
252	Laotian Theravada Buddhism	2,500,000	Laos	
253	Neo-Buddhism	6,000,000	India	1951
254	English Sangha Trust	150,000	Britain	
255	Dhammadana Association	3,000	Thailand	c1940
256	German Dhammaduta Society	84,000	Germany	1957
257	Getambe Group	1,000	Sri Lanka	1980
258	Amarapura Nikaya	50,000	Myanmar	c1850
259	Maha Bodhi Society	10,000,000	Sri Lanka	1900
260	Lanka Vipassana Bhavana Samitiya	1,000	Sri Lanka	1952
261	Siyane Vipassana Bhavana Samitiya	3,000	Sri Lanka	1955
262	Santi Asok	30,000	Thailand	1975
263	Sarvodaya Sramadana	2,400,000	Sri Lanka	1958
264	Thammakaai Religious Foundation	1,000,000	Thailand	1970
265	Vinaya Vardhana Society	5,000	Sri Lanka	1932
266	Vajrayana Buddhism	1,000,000	China	400
267	Buddhist Publication Society	300,000	Sri Lanka	1958
268	Sadahnm Mithuru Samuluwa	1,000,000	Sri Lanka	1962
269	Internat Network of Engaged Buddhists	1,500,000	Thailand	1989
270	Bharatiya Buddha Mahasabha	400,000	India	
271	Chittagong Buddhist Association	30,000	Myanmar	1887
272	World Buddhist Sangha Council	5,000,000	Sri Lanka	1966
273	World Fellowship of Buddhists	359,000,000	Thailand	1950
274	Buddhayana	1,930,000	Indonesia	1954

number of adherents in 2000 (*contd.*).

Note

Organized Buddhist homeless ascetics who do not enter the sangha.
Monks Militia for National Defence (Chogye order).
OBC. Order in Soto Zen. Abbeys in UK, USA, Canada.
HQ Okayama-shi.
HQ Shimogyo-ku, Kyoto-shi.
Begun in Calcutta, reviving West Bengal Buddhism.
Many schools around Bangkok.
Theravadin and Mahayanist from early stage.
Theravada, 'Way of the Elders'. Also termed Hinayana (Lesser Vehicle of Salvation).
Theravada heavily influenced by animism, nats, Hinduism.
2 orders in 1970: Mahanikay (3,230 monasteries: 62,700 monks), Thomayat (139: 2,300).
State religion until 1975.
Conversion of 4 million Outcastes: Buddhism of social protest (B. R. Ambedkar, Maharashtra).
Supporting Britain-based monks.
Modernizing urban grouping attacking superstition.
German wing of Buddhist world mission.
Lay meditation society. F=P. Sorada.
One of 3 main Theravada divisions, in Amarapura, Burma. 1,000 monasteries, 3,000 monks.
MBS. Great Enlightenment Society. Worldwide missions.
Lanka Insight Meditation Society. Lay meditation.
Modern Sri Lankan lay meditation society.
This-worldly TV moral reformists in urban 'dhamma families'. Use of Buddha images rejected.
Buddhist model of social development, reaching 20% of Ceylon's villages. F=A. T. Ariyaratna.
Media, prosperity, flaunting of wealth. Lay asceticism. Conservative.
Association for the Protection of Buddhist Discipline. Anticlerical.
Thunderbolt Vehicle. Esoteric Buddhism, based on Tibetan-language Vajrayana tradition.
BPS. HQ Kandy. Mission to the West.
Saddhamma Friends Society (SFS). Reformed Theravada.
INEB. Social activist stance.
Indian council for guiding Buddhist affairs.
Buddhist welfare organization representing Buddhists in Burma.
WBSC. HQ Colombo. To assist Theravada bhikkhu mendicant missions around world.
F=Malalasekera (Ceylon). Centralized. HQ Bangkok. 1969 Ninth General Conference.
Syncretistic amalgam of Mahayana, Theravada, with Kasogatan (local Javanese Buddhism).

Notes

[1] This concept is summarized in Gananath Obeyesekere's superb treatment of global Buddhism in *Global Religions*, ed. Mark Juergensmeyer (New York: Oxford University Press, 2003), 63-77.

[2] This represents a close parallel with Walls' concept of Christianity utilizing both an "indigenizing" principle (contextualizing in local culture) and "pilgrim" principle (all Christians unified because none are fully at home in any culture). See A. Walls, *The Missionary Movement in Christian History: Studies in the Transmission of Faith* (Maryknoll: Orbis, 1996).

[3] Now available online at www.worldchristiandatabase.org.

[4] Nonetheless Buddhists still view India as their homeland where Siddharta Gautama first preached. Today there are thousands of significant places of pilgrimage in India visited every year by Buddhists and others from around the world.

[5] For a summary of the spread of Buddhism in the Western world, see Martin Baumman, "Global Buddhism: Developmental Periods, Regional Histories, and a New Analytical Perspective," *Journal of Global Buddhism* 2 (2001), 1ff. www.globalbuddhism.org.

[6] See Table 1-1 in Part 1 "World Summary" in *World Christian Encyclopedia, 2nd ed.* D. B. Barrett, G. T. Kurian, and T. M. Johnson, (New York: Oxford University Press, 2001, 2 vols.), 4.

[7] The other two are Confucianism and Daoism.

[8] Also known as popular religionists or universists who are 'followers of a unique complex of many elements: universism (yin/yang cosmology with dualities earth/heaven, evil/good, darkness/light, originating as far back as BC 3000), ancestor cult, Confucian ethics, divination, festivals, folk religion, goddess worship, household gods, local deities, mediums, metaphysics, monasteries, Neo-Confucianism, popular religion, sacrifices, shamans, spirit-writing, Taoist and Buddhist elements.' D. Barrett and T. Johnson, "Annual Statistical Table on Global Mission: 2004" in *International Bulletin of Missionary Research*, Vol. 28, No.1, January 2004, 24-25.

[9] However, in Singapore, Nepal and a few other countries, as evidenced in recent census figures, a Buddhism renaissance is taking place. If this spreads to China, then the projected figures for 2025 and 2050 may be

much higher and Buddhists might grow as a percentage of the world's population.

[10] In their book, *Christianity and Buddhism: A Multi-Cultural History of their Dialogue*, Whalen Lai and Michael von Bruck provide insightful observations on the future of Buddhist-Christian dialogue in India. Based upon a thorough discussion of the historical contacts between Buddhism and Christianity in India, they observe the following points: (i) Buddhist-Christian dialogue is fruitful and builds trust; (ii) dialogue that is academic in nature (e.g., subtle theological differences) is unlike the encounter situations taking place at the street level in villages, monasteries, and communities; (iii) doctrine of *upaya* (transmitted means) is helpful to further dialogue; (iv) Indian Christians, more so than their Buddhist counterparts, are more ready to problematize their own tradition (and doctrinal views), but both fear loss of identity as result of dialogue, and as such, stress symbolic exchange (not absolute, conversion-like dialogue) and share the understanding that interreligious dialogue is a process of common search for truth. Whalen Lai and Michael von Bruck, *Christianity and Buddhism: A Multi-Cultural History of their Dialogue* (Maryknoll: Orbis, 2001), 38.

[11] For the full context see Part 17 "Religiometrics" in D. B. Barrett and T. M. Johnson, *World Christian Trends, AD 30–AD 2200* (Pasadena: William Carey Library, 2001).

[12] Of course, this appraisal is nothing new. In fact, the perception of Christianity as "foreign" has persisted for decades in Asia. "The failure of the church to break through the social solidarity of Buddhist communities," observed the Lausanne working committee in its Occasional Paper on Buddhism published in 1980, was one of three identified causes for the "lack of permanent self-perpetuating Christian communities among Buddhist peoples." Whalen Lai and Michael von Bruck recently reiterated that Christians need to engage in meaningful "existential encounter and experience" with Buddhists as opposed to speculative reason. Ibid., 102-103.

2

Christian Mission in the Context of Buddhist Mission

Terry Muck

This chapter elucidates five of the most common approaches in Christian mission, particularly in the context of Buddhist mission to win adherents from people of other faiths, namely: concept comparisons, cultural forms, scientific witness, ritual practices, and folk religion functions. It also shows the strengths and weaknesses of each.

Concept Comparisons

Easily the most common form of missiological approaches to Buddhism, the comparison of concepts, has been widely and capably articulated. Perhaps the single greatest reason why it is so popular is that it follows the course of Christian doctrine: the way doctrine is conceptualized, the way it is taught, and the way it is used to evangelize. Historically, at least since the contact of the early church with Greek philosophical forms, doctrine has been the heart of the expressions of Christian faith. The steps taken to do this kind of missiological interaction seem obvious. They seem like simplicity itself:

1. Analyze a philosophy or religion into its doctrines/teachings.
2. Compare/contrast doctrines using both content and function.
3. Compare/contrast overall systems using measures of coherence and effectiveness.
4. Present an argument as to why the Christian doctrine is better: more effective, more logical, more revelatory, more characteristic of God's nature.

Of course, the reason they seem so obvious and simple are probably the same reasons why this method is so widely used. It is used because those of us in Western cultures are conditioned and trained to think this way. It is at the heart of Western rationality, Greek philosophy, including Aristotelian logic.

I have in front of me, temporarily thumb-tacked to my office wall, a huge chart entitled "Beliefs of the World's Great Religions." Across the top are the column headings: indigenous, Hinduism, Jainism, Sikhism, Confucianism, Taoism, Judaism, Christianity, and Islam. Down the left margin are the headings of the rows: God, Spirit, Creation, Fall, Redemption, and Ethics. It is obvious that these are Christian theology inspired headings. Yet, even if they were translated into something a bit more generic—Transcendent, Spirit Realms, Cosmology, Lack, Solution, Morality—it still would represent a Christian theology simply because it privileges doctrine as the essence of religion and the way to compare different religions.

A good example of this method of mission work is a book written by long time Methodist missionary to India, J.T. Seamands. *Tell it Well: Communicating the Gospel Across Cultures* uses the concept comparison method brilliantly. To effectively communicate the gospel, Seamands says, one must understand the needs and background of the listener. The author explains the background and major tenets of Buddhism, including: The Life of Buddha, Four Noble Truths, and Nirvana. Then the author lists the places where each of these doctrines positively correlate with similar Christian doctrines (compare) and where they negatively correlate with Christian doctrines of the same function (contrast). An overall comparison of the two religions, Buddhism and Christianity, emerges. Finally, a model is offered which illustrates very practically how to communicate the gospel to a Buddhist in a way that he or she may understand. Many other books use this method as well. It is the most common way to teach a course on how to argue that the Christian way is better.

Interestingly, Buddhists have also used this way for the superiority of Buddhism. One instance of this is cited by Whalen Lai in an article in volume 18 of the *History of Religions*, "Limits and Failure of *Ko-I* (Concept Matching) Buddhism" (1978). Lai's article tells the essence of a story revealed by a set of six letters written by two Buddhist monks and a Confucian scholar. At question in the letters is whether or not concepts integral to Buddhism can be translated adequately into Chinese Confucian thought forms. It is apparent that this conversation is part of an ongoing Chinese attempt by neo-Taoist intellectuals in the fourth century to match Buddhist and Taoist concepts, a process that came to be claimed *ko-I fo-chiao* (concept matching). The overall effect of the letters is to point up the limitations of this kind of concept matching. For some Buddhist teachings there are no comparable Chinese Confucian forms (for example, the idea of *asamkarta dharmas* or uncompounded realities). But the letters also give the impression that for most of the ideas of Buddhism, there are comparable Chinese Confucian equivalents. And because there are, it is possible to argue their relative strengths and weaknesses, particularly in the overall systems of thought.

The strengths of this type of argumentation are evident, especially for those of us who are immersed in Western systems of thought. First, it makes the teachings of a foreign religious tradition understandable. By putting the teachings in the forms we recognize we can grasp what it is the Buddha, or Confucius or Lao-Tzu taught. Second, because it puts them in comparable form, it makes them easier to evaluate. We can find out more quickly the limitations of each.

The weaknesses, however, are also evident. First, the temptation is to immerse these thoughts in ways that will make them easily defeatable. Concept-matching is not that easy to do. It is something that we must honestly acknowledge. As Lai says, "The practice of finding comparable ideas in Taoism to ease the transitions into Buddhism had the advantage of making an alien faith palatable, but it is also risked reducing the Buddha *dharma* to the teaching of Lao-Tzu" (1979:238). Second, not all concepts have equivalent structures or forms in other religions and other cultures. Sometimes a new idea comes along, and needs to be presented as such. To settle for an almost equivalent is the same as stating the idea in a false way.

Cultural Forms

Adoniram Judson (1788-1850), American Baptist missionary to Burma, developed the second approach to Burmese Theravada Buddhists that can be best called a cultural forms approach. He adapted a cultural building, a *zayat*, for what amounted to a Christian coffee house.

Judson discovered in his early ministry in Burma that Burmese were reluctant to come to Christian churches for two reasons: one, because of the social stigma of going to a Westernized religious building; and two, because the mission compound from which he worked was too remote to the working people of Rangoon. He decided to erect a *zayat*, an indigenous open aired gazebo devoted to discussion. At first money was a problem. Then he raised enough ($200) and decided to build one on Pagoda Road, the main thoroughfare in Rangoon that connected the city to Shwe Dagon pagoda, an important Buddhist shrine. Thousands of religious Buddhist walked down the road every day and the numbers increased to tens of thousands on the four monthly worship days (full, half, and quarter moon days) and religious holidays.

Many *zayats* lined Pagoda Road. Some were large, some quite small, just four pillars and a roof, like a bus stop. They were really shelters where travelers could rest, men gather to talk or listen, and Buddhist lay teachers could teach. Buddhist priests only used them to teach on special occasions.

Judson's *zayat* was small, thirty feet by twenty feet. It had a porch where Judson planned to sit and engage people in conversation. The enclosed portion was one room made of painted boards with a large glass-less window in each wall where the men could study and public worship could be held. Like all buildings in Burma, it stood on posts about four feet above the ground. It wasn't as nice as most of the many Buddhist *zayats* along Pagoda Road, but it was nice and it was like the other *zayats*.

It worked to attract Burmese curious about the foreign religion. It worked well enough that it produced the first Burmese Buddhist convert Maung Nau. And that worked well enough to bring about several waves of persecution. First, from the local government which levied a series of very expensive taxes on the new *zayat*. Then from Buddhist priests who began to teach against the new religion in no uncertain terms. And finally from the emperor himself in a series of laws that limited the Christian witness.

But the *zayat* worked to the extent that it attracted people. Once Judson and his wife Nancy also made the format of the service like that which one would find in a Buddhist temple—sitting on mats on the floor, the teacher on a low stool at the front, men on one side women on the other—they almost always had a small group of ten to twenty people for their discussions. These were more people than they would have attracted to a typical Western church.

One hundred and fifty years later it is interesting to see a Buddhist organization, the Soka Gakkai, discover a similar lesson of indigeneity in America. Soka Gakkai is a Japanese Buddhist lay association that has grown out of the teachings of thirteenth century

Buddhist teacher, Nichiren. Nichiren taught that the essence of Buddhism is captured in the Lotus Sutra, particularly the invocation that opens the teaching. "Nam-myoho-renge-kyo" (homage to the Lotus Sutra) and the three cardinal values: benefit, beauty, and goodness. Nichiren's followers were strongly evangelistic. Conversions in Japan were numerous and by 1958 the membership was 750,000 families. Under the third president, Ikeda Daisaku, Soka Gakkai continued to grow in the Buddhist climate of Japan (10 million by the mid-1980s) but much more slowly elsewhere. Ikeda decided to indigenize the teachings in something dear to Western, and academic meetings of world peace advocates. In 2000, Soka Gakkai founded Soka University, a four-year liberal arts college in Orange County, Calif.

By adopting both the civil institutions and the basic tenets of American civil religion, Ikeda has made a "foreign" religion palatable to American tastes. It represents a textbook case of American civil religion being used to promote ideas. Contextualization writ large. As one observer of the movement put it, "For members of Soka Gakkai, salvation implies social, political, and cultural responsibility. The phrase "obutsu myogo" ("the union of king and Buddha") used by the society may legitimize its involvement in the secular sphere, its work for world peace, human welfare, and enlarged cultural and educational opportunities, and its goal of reforming all human activities by introducing Buddhism into the sphere of everyday life as the basis for the creation of values" (Wilson 407).

The strengths of this cultural equivalence approach are obvious. In particularly difficult countries, that is, countries where because of religious competition it is difficult for Christianity to even get a hearing, adapting the teaching to a cultural form may be the only way to get a toehold. Without such an effort, the religion continues to sound strange, foreign, and suspicious. With it, the medium tension needed to get a hearing for a new idea is created. If it isn't new, people won't be intrigued enough to consider it. If it is too new, they will be frightened away. Medium tension between the new teaching and the prevailing culture is the ticket. Further, it creates a situation where it is not necessary to create a new culture in order to gain a place for gospel teaching. The existing culture works just fine.

The weaknesses of this approach are in the ever-present danger of doing so much adapting of the teaching that the essence of the teaching is lost. Not everything is culturally adaptable. Not everything can be couched in the indigenous culture's terms. Some things about the existing culture must be spoken against. Critical contextualization is an art that takes work—and prayer—to accomplish.

1. Identify a common cultural form or issue that communicates confidence, trust and importance.
2. Show how that form or issue is or can become integral to the new language.
3. Work toward instituting that form or solving the issue.

Scientific Witness

Some believe that all witness should come from concrete actions alone, actions that contribute to human flourishing. A very simple "three steps" characterize this approach to mission to Buddhist:

1. Discern the physical need: food, clothing, shelter, medicine, education.
2. Address the need.
3. Let the satisfaction of the need be the witness to the faith.

Some believe that this is all that witness should be and believe it because they don't believe any other action respects the freedom of individual human beings to choose their own religion path. We should, they believe, simply take care of physical needs so that the people administered to can freely choose their way, choose with full stomachs, warm bodies, and clear minds.

For others, scientific witness is the only witness possible for reasons outside of their control. One such place is Nepal. In Nepal it is illegal to witness openly to one's faith in Jesus Christ. It is illegal to convert from one religion to another or to entice person to convert from one religion to another. Thus, the only witness allowed is to do good deeds for another person.

One group of Christians in the Nepalese context decided that their witness should be health care for the class of people who not only collected the trash of Katmandu for a living but lived in the midst of the dump where the trash was discarded and collected. A small city of people lived in huts carved out of mountains of trash; streets crisscrossed the immense trash heap that grew larger day by day. As one might imagine, the potential for disease plagued the inhabitants of Trash City. They did not make enough money for proper health under the best of conditions, and they certainly could not afford the specialized care their special living circumstances created.

A group of Christian doctors and health care workers set up small clinics at several key spots in the trash heap and provide low cost or no cost health care to all who come and ask for it. They do not verbally witness to their faith in Jesus Christ, but they do not hide the fact that they are Christians either. Symbols of their Christian faith decorate the walls of their waiting areas and treatment rooms. Bibles lay on their office desks and waiting room coffee tables. They are always ready to give the reasons for why they are doing what they are doing—because they believe that contributing to human flourishing in this way honors God—if they are ever asked. But if they are not asked they believe their witness still shines brightly.

Others in Nepal do similar witness by providing family health care services in small villages throughout the countryside. People travel great distances to learn about family planning and infant care. Small diseases are treated on the spot. Regular classes in sanitation prevent their return. The four keys to clean water and good health are repeated like a mantra. And the people know they are Christians by their love.

A group of Buddhists also engage in scientific witness. They call themselves engaged Buddhists. Engaged Buddhists believe that their religious beliefs have the potential to contribute to the welfare of all sentient beings. Engaged Buddhists can be found operating in two prominent world theaters.

The first is rural village life in Asia. Engaged Buddhists believe that the values of small village life in Asian villages that traditionally have been dominated by Buddhism have been changed due to colonization and industrialization. By departing from subsistence and agricultural forms of vocation, and changing instead to increasingly global marketing economics, they have also changed value systems. Usually this change is unconscious. Usually it is disastrous to their way of life. The old religion seems irrelevant to life. No satisfactory new religion takes its place. In the absence of any transcendent values to maintain their social structures, the purely economic values of buying and selling, the values of the marketplace, have to suffice. They are insufficient for humane living. Drugs, prostitution, and crime become rampant.

The second is Western secularized societies. In these societies the evils of war and environmental degradation run rampant. Engaged Buddhists preach the values of dhamma to teach listeners of selfless living, the lessons of impermanence, and the lessons of equanimity.

The strengths of scientific witness are obvious. People are helped in immediate and life changing ways. The change is measurable and self-evident. The good, at first glance anyway, seems so transparent as to be uncontestable. The Bible is filled with admonishments to us to walk humbly, do good for the poor, and fear God. Woes are pronounced in abundance to those who neglect their duty to the less privileged of society, particularly the poor, the widowed, and the orphaned. Scientific witness gives us an immediate way to live out our faith in the context of a world in need.

The weaknesses of scientific witness only become evident over time. Over time, one learns the lessons of the chimera of simple effects of good deeds. One cannot always be sure that by helping one group of people in this sector of society one is not doing harm in another sector of society. Further, the help provided by scientific witness helps in this life only, and when measured against eternity or timelessness it is temporary at best. By viewing suffering and life as the ultimate evils and the ultimate goods, other values are lost; e.g., the value of learning gained through suffering, the temporaries of life which at their best end all too quickly, and the loss of focus on what happens at death.

Ritual Practices

One of the most overlooked methodologies that is being used most fruitfully today with Buddhists is the use of Buddhist rituals themselves to introduce the gospel. Or to transform cultures in which Buddhism dominates into gospel-sensitive cultures.

A. H. Mathias Zahniser, professor emeritus of mission and world religions at Asbury Theological Seminary, advocates the use of critically contextualized rituals in introducing Buddhists to the gospel. Ritual, Zahniser believes, is one of the most overlooked resources in the missionary's arsenal. It is overlooked because many Christians have forgotten ritual's value in their own spirituality, and thus can hardly be expected to see it as a valuable missiological ally.

Zahniser explores the use of religious ritual in article in *Missiology* (January 1991). The title of the article is "Ritual Process and Christian Discipling: Contextualizing a Buddhist Rite of Passage." Zahniser asks the question of whether a Theravada Buddhist ritual used as a rite of passage of a Burmese young boy into the Buddhist monastic order can be a model for either discipling new Christians or introducing young Christian children into the responsibilities of adult Christian life. In other works, particularly his book, *Symbol and Ceremony: Making Disciples Across Cultures* (1997), Zahniser also explores the possibilities of using the Jewish Sabbath and the Muslim concept of pilgrimage to teach important, cognate Christian truths.

In order to explain the method, Zahniser uses Glasnapp and Victor Turner's extensive work on the three moments of ritual experience: (1) the leaving of all the social constraints of life as it has been lived to engage in the ritual proper, (2) the entering into a liminal state of no constraints and new possibilities, and (3) the reentry into life with a new role, and what Zahniser calls a bonding to religious meaning that has occurred because of the possibilities created by liminality. Zahniser then walks us through the three-days of ceremony that usher a Burmese Buddhist young man into the monkhood, showing us how all three stages are evident, and then suggesting that a similar process could be used in order to introduce Christian young people to new roles or adult roles.

This method of mission can be helpfully broken down into four steps:

1. Identify a meaningful ritual that appears to have cross religious applications.
2. Analyze the ritual into its constituent parts, clearly listing what actually happens in each and then attempt to identify the more abstract purposes of each of the constituent parts.
3. Identify a cognate ritual or need in Christianity.
4. Transpose the form of the ritual practice to its new religious setting.

Buddhists have also used other religions' rituals in doing its work of spreading the dhamma to all sentient beings. One of the clearest examples of this is the existence of a literary work called the "Questions of King Milinda (Milindapanho)." The work itself uses a literary device of rhetorical questions and answers in order to communicated some of the essentials of Theravada Buddhist teaching. The questioner is a Greek king called Milinda in the text, but often identified with a Greek king Menander who pushed Greece's military interests into central Asia in the third century, B.C. The answerer of the questions is a Buddhist monk called Nagasena.

The form of the work is what represents the Buddhist borrowing of a ritual practice. The form is rhetorical questioning and answering of a kind common to early Greek philosophy and religion, a form that became extremely common in early Christian theological works after the hellenization of early Hebrew thinking. The practice of a questioning, intelligent seeker asking probing metaphysical questions of a reflective religious teacher is quite foreign to Eastern religion in general and Buddhism in particular. The Buddha, in fact, expressly decried the use of such disputations in a sermon where he simply refused to answer such questions brought to him by an inquirer. The Buddha's position was that religious teaching was soteriological in nature, not philosophical; and therefore the religious seeker was wasting his or her time (not to say the Buddha's) by asking such questions. It should be obvious that the time could more profitably be spent working out one's spiritual practice.

The Buddha illustrates his point with the famous example of the burning building. When a person is trapped in a burning house, he said, is that person's response to ask Why the building is on fire? or Who set the fire? or How the building was burning down? No, the Buddha said, the person's response is to get out of the house. Similarly, religion is not a matter of asking Why? Or Who? Or How? Rather the problem is to work out one's own salvation.

The strengths of the ritual practices approach is that it develops an acceptable level of continuity with a person's existing religion—assuming the transposition of ritual is done with full doctrinal integrity. The weakness of the position is that such is not always the case. As Zahniser puts it, "Cross-cultural discipling requires learning from non-Christian as well as Christian religious traditions. It involves adapting local symbols and rituals to the Spirit's task of enabling believers to realize that the ultimate God wishes to relate to them intimately and to be a relevant partner with them in dealing with their most vital life issues together in community. Without incorporation of symbols and ceremonies familiar to them, their new faith runs the risk of irrelevance. With the use of these features from their pre-Christian religious environment their faith runs the risk of distortion" (1997:160).

Folk Religion Functions

Last but not least, the lowest common denominator approach to Buddhism means treating all Buddhism as folk religionists. Instead of confronting the ideas and institutions of Buddhism directly, simply treat each Buddhist as one would treat an animist or a generic, everyday religious person. Emphasize the parts of Christianity that focus on everyday needs regarding family, friends, and job, and leave the metaphysical debates for much later.

The person most associated with this approach is Paul Hiebert, who in an article in *Missiology* (1982) developed the idea of the "excluded middle." The excluded middle is that part of religion that is located halfway between high religion and scientific religion, and is often referred to as folk religion.

High religion is formal religion. It includes doctrine and statements of faith, and answers the ultimate questions of life, such as: Who am I? What am I doing here? and Where am I going after this life? Answers to these questions come from revelations provided by God or the gods. High religion is what we normally think of when we think of Christianity, Islam, Hinduism, and Buddhism.

In contrast, science is that part of religion that is reason-based. Science provides religion with answers to questions that have to do with empirical matters, those facets of religion that deal with biology, psychology and sociology. Questions about individual religious behavior and the value of religion to society are subjects that specialists in these areas of religious study excel in answering.

Folk religion is religion that falls between high religion and scientific religion. In participates in both, acknowledging the reality of transcendent wisdom, but also respecting the contributions of science. Folk religion addresses four questions, however, that tend to be ignored by high religion and science: What is the meaning of my current life and impending death? How can I deal access the power of the good spirits and avoid the power of the bad? How can I attain the good life? And How can I deal with everyday disorder and sin? It is in answering these everyday questions of life management that folk religionists deal.

Historically, Christian missionaries have their greatest successes when dealing with people whose religions focus on those questions. Historically, Christian missionaries have had the least success in dealing with people with firmly established high religions, such as Hinduism, Buddhism, and Islam. Recent scholarship by anthropologists and historians of religion have made it clear that even people who adhere to a high religion also mix with those high religious beliefs a good deal of folk religious practice. Since Christians have had more success at the folk religion level than the high religion level, why not just focus on the folk religious level.

The methodologies of this approach then tend to deal with the Christian answers to everyday problems of living, especially those at the intersection of worldly success and transcendent power. Can Christianity provide me with a safe job, a healthy family, a good life? Can Christianity protect me from evil spirits? Can Christianity insure me a death that leads to life, a better life of some sort? When it comes to competing metaphysical worldviews, this approach says Why bother?

It is very interesting that Buddhism *dharmadhatus* consistently used a similar approach in their forays into China and Japan. In each place, Buddhism found well-established high religions. In China the metaphysical outlook of Taoism and the social religion of Confucianism were so well established that competition was futile. Early Buddhists focused on the contributions that Buddhism could make to the folk religion level, the level of everyday rites of passage: birth, adulthood, marriage, death. These areas were treated minimally if at all in the high religious systems of Taoism and Confucianism, although at certain periods Taoism also attempted to extend its cultural influence by providing folk religious services. Buddhism won its way by providing folk religious services instead of competing high religion explanations.

In Japan, early Buddhists encountered a country that had developed an elaborate and firmly entrenched national mythos as represented by the religion of Shinto. This mythos included both a cosmology and a system of social obligation. Instead of attempting to compete with that mythos, the Buddhists simply addressed the everyday religious gaps not served by Shinto and served instead by a plethora of folk religious practices. It was at this level and the level of practical religious meditation that the *dharmadhatus* won their way in Japan.

The strength of the lowest common denominator approach is its emphasis on what has been a strength of Christian missions since the beginning. Success with indigenous and animist religions has never been a problem for Christian missionaries. It is a stroke of genius to recognize that it is at this level that Christianity is most effective and that the findings of the social scientists regarding the ubiquity of folk religion mean all people are amenable to the treasures of Christianity in addressing everyday problems. A further strength of this approach is that it is much more sensitive to local cultures than the older mission methodologies that stressed Christianity's high religion aspects.

The weaknesses of the lowest common denominator approach is that as the other world religions, particularly Hinduism, Buddhism, and Islam compete with Christianity for world market share, they too are appealing on the folk religious level in ways that are almost as successful as Christianity. Those religious marketing technologies and skills will improve. In this kind of religious competition it seems that what is going to happen is that Christians will be forced, sooner or later, to compete directly with the high religious aspects of those other religions. This may be a few years away yet, but it seems to be the future trend with which Christian missionaries will have to deal.

1. Discern the folk religion need: meaning, spiritual power, spiritual need.
2. Explain how Christianity addresses the need.
3. Work to address the need.

3

Difficulties and Devices in Depicting the Deity of Christ to the Theravada Buddhist Mind

M. S. Vasanthakumar

Christian mission since its inception has presented Jesus Christ as the God of the universe, and proclaimed salvation to human beings through His atonement. Even though some of the contemporary Christian theologies discard and even deny this fundamental biblical truth, Evangelical Christianity still presents Jesus Christ as God and defends his deity in all possible ways. In theistic societies Jesus Christ could appear as the God or one of the gods according to their belief systems. Therefore, evangelists could easily find ways to present Jesus Christ as God in such societies. But, in societies where the world-view does not have a place for theistic conceptions, it is extremely difficult to proclaim the Christian message to the people. Especially, in Theravada Buddhist societies, it is not an easy task to convince the people about the absolute deity of Jesus Christ and his unique role in offering salvation to mankind. All our defenses concerning Jesus Christ will appear to the Buddhists as futile and they think of Jesus Christ similar to that of Buddha prior to his enlightenment or like one of the Hindu gods. This essay is an analysis of the difficulties involved in proclaiming Jesus Christ as God in Buddhist societies, especially in Sri Lanka, and some attempts to find ways to overcome these obstacles.

The Buddhist Perception of Jesus Christ

The Buddhist perception of Jesus Christ is in contradistinction with that of the biblical teaching concerning him. The fundamental tenets of Buddhism differ to a great extent from Christianity, especially in the doctrines that are related to the metaphysical realms and realities. Buddhism denies some of the vital Christian conceptions such as God, human soul and eternal life. To the Buddhist mind these were not only incomprehensible illusions but non-existing entities or imaginary absurdities. In fact, the Buddhist perception of Jesus Christ is conditioned by these Buddhist rationalities. Consequently, in the Buddhist mind Jesus Christ occupies the lowest position. There are various theological suppositions and historical realities behind this Buddhist view of Jesus Christ. Analyzing these factors will help us to understand the difficulties that are involved in presenting Jesus Christ as God and Savior to the Buddhists.

Theological Factors

Theologically, Buddhism and Christianity differ to a great extent. While Buddhist tenets are based on human comprehensions, Christian doctrines are derived from the supernatural revelation of God. According to Buddhism human beings are capable of attaining *nibbana* by their own efforts, but Christianity sees all people as sinners who cannot do anything for their salvation, apart from the gracious atonement of Jesus Christ. Even the ultimate objectives of both religions do not reach the same destination. In Buddhism people are strived to get rid of the endless cycles of birth and death. Christianity, on the other hand offers eternal life to believers. Christian mission needs to comprehend this theological chasm between Buddhism and Christianity, because the difficulties in communicating the Christian message to the Buddhists emerge from the different orientations of these religions. In view of the different presuppositions, the deity of Jesus Christ becomes incomprehensible and unconvincing to the Buddhists for the following reasons.

Unacceptable Theism: Buddhism basically denies the existence of an absolute, eternal, and omnipotent God. According to the tenets of Buddhism, everything (including the gods but excluding the state of *nibbana*) is subject to impermanence (*anicca*), selflessness/soullessness or non-substantiality (*anatta*) and unsatisfactoriness (*dukkha*).[1] In Buddhism these were the hallmarks of existence which point to the fact that all existence in its absolute entirety is but a flux-in-process (*anicca*), having nothing permanent or enduring in the process of change (*anatta*), and hence inherently incapable of producing any lasting satisfaction (*dukkah*). Therefore, Buddhism cannot think of God to whom it can refer as Creator, Lord, Savior, etc, who can be described as eternal, omniscient, omnipotent, etc. Consequently the Buddhists are unable to accept Christian theism, especially the deity of Jesus Christ.

In Buddhist literature the Brahma and other gods do not have the meaning and function they have in Hindu or Brahmanic religion. Brahma has been stripped off all of his divine attributes and reduced to a mere heavenly being subject to change and impermanence. Enlightened individuals, by virtue of their enlightenment, have gone beyond the gods and therefore above gods (Marasinghe 1974:84). The Buddha and the enlightened-ones having attained *nibbana* are superior to the gods and the ultimate objective of the gods is to arrive at this higher state. In the Buddhist texts, it is the gods who admire and respect the Buddha and the enlightened-ones and seek the association of the Buddha and the enlightened-ones whether for clarification of a doubt that has arisen in their minds or for a friendly call as they find solace in their company. Similarly it was not the Buddha who came to the Brahma but the Brahma who came to the Buddha requesting advice or instruction and the Brahma never became advisor to the Buddha (84–85). Hence the superiority of the Buddha is well recognized by the Brahmanic gods in the Buddhist literature (39).

Throughout the Pali *Nikayas*, the Buddha is always referred to as the teacher not only of men, but of the gods as well… When we come from Brahmanism to Buddhism, the position of the gods is in fact, reversed. Instead of the men seeking gods, it is the gods who seek the enlightened men for spiritual guidance (Marasinghe 1974:86). According to Buddhist cosmology, the gods are as much a part of the world of *samsara* as are the human beings or any other type of living beings. They too are therefore, subject to the same conditions of change and impermanence and the heavens are not spheres of eternal bliss. Consequently, the gods in Buddhism are not objects of prayer or of sacrifice (43). Brahmanic theistic notions were rejected by the Buddha as "unsatisfactory solution[s] for men's needs… [and] a misconception of reality which is morally harmful and not at all conducive to Liberation" (Wijebandara 1993:113). Hence the Buddha rejected all such notions as false concepts and "foolish and blind talk" (116). Therefore, according to the Buddhist perspective of Jesus Christ too is devoid of his divine attributes. Since theistic faiths are deemed as "unsatisfactory religions" (Dharmasiri 1998:xi) by the Buddhists, Christianity has fallen into an unwelcome state in Sri Lanka. The Buddhists find it extremely difficult to accept the deity of Jesus Christ.

Unscientific Religion: The Buddhists criticize Christianity as an unscientific and primitive faith in contrast to Buddhism, which according to them is scientific, logical, relevant, and meaningful to the modern context. They contend that "over four hundred years, Christianity has waged war on science and lost every engagement. Today science lies at the heart of our culture and has become an irresistible force, while Christianity has been pushed into a corner" (Du Pre 1984:146). Since Christianity is based on the supernatural revelation of God, and science is considered as a purely human enterprise of discovery, Buddhists conclude that Christianity and Jesus Christ are totally opposed to science (Kirthisinghe 2004:2).

In fact, Buddhists condemn all religions that are based on supernatural beings and faith as "erroneous," remarking that the scientific progress in the West "was made not because of faith and belief in the supernatural, but largely by rejecting it or being indifferent to it" (Kirthisinghe 2004:2). They say that "more progress could have been made and with less agony if religion had not interfered with scientific interpretation of reality" (3). According to the Buddhists, scientific discoveries have disproved the fundamental beliefs of Christianity. For them, "the Bible ignores the rest of the universe, and sees the earth as the centre, controlled by God....Christian theology is unable to accommodate certain scientific discoveries, notably evolution" (Peiris nd:14). They are content that the cosmology of Copernicus and Galileo is contrary to the geocentric depiction of the biblical universe. Darwinian biology is often invoked to criticize the biblical account of the creation and the fall of humanity. And modern psychology is brought forward to deny the concept of an eternal soul within the constitution of human beings. Above all, it is argued that science has denied the necessity of God. Hence, the Buddhists conclude that, "not only did science controvert the specific dogmas of the Western religion [i.e., Christianity], but it... [has] undermined the foundations as well as the fundamental concepts implicit in a religious outlook on things" (Jayatilleke 1996:14).

While criticizing Christianity as unscientific, Buddhists claim that the Buddha was a "scientist" (Jayatilleke 1996:4) and "the founder of scientific psychology" (Du Pre 1984:147). According to them "Buddhism is a science" (92) and the Buddhist system is a "scientific endeavour" (Spencer 1990:17). They go to the extent of saying that Buddhism "is not a religion, or a philosophy, but a science" (95). They claim that "every new discovery in the domain of science helps us to appreciate the sublime teachings of the Buddha" (Guruge 1965:439). It is their contention that "the scientific revolution does not have the same adverse effect on Buddhism as it had on other religious traditions" (Jayatilleke 1996:10). The Buddhists justify their claim by pointing out that the methodology used by the Buddha to discover the reality of the human predicament and to diagnose its causes and finally to describe a remedy for it are scientific procedures (Kirthisinghe 2004:4). The Buddhists insist that what the Buddha had discovered in a scientific way was in harmony with modern scientific knowledge, (Spencer 1990:18) while Christianity seems "utterly foolish" when confronted with science. Consequently Jesus Christ appears to the Buddhists as an unscientific, primitive person with an irrelevant message to the modern world (Guruge 1965:439–475).

Under Buddhist Monks: Another reason for the lower attitude of many Buddhists toward Christianity and Jesus Christ is the myth of Jesus' supposed visit to India and his supposed study under the Buddhist monks. Since the Gospels do not give an account of Jesus' life prior to his public ministry from the age of twelve, some have imagined and invented fanciful stories that had brought Jesus Christ to India. This novel concept was invented for the first time by a Russian journalist called Nicolai Notovich in 1894 and many have believed it to be a true account and built their hypothesis on it.[2] From time to time in Sri Lanka, popular newspapers have carried articles defending such a myth. In recent times Holger Kersten's writings on this subject have been popularized in Sri Lanka. Kersten has not only argued for an Indian visit of Jesus Christ but he has also emphasized the supposed Christian borrowings of Buddhism in the gospel narratives (Kersten 1994). Consequently, the majority of the Buddhists do not see the need to know the teachings of Jesus, for they think that such an endeavor will not benefit them since they claim to have the original teachings of the Buddha without any distortion by the Jewish background of Jesus and later additions of the Christian church.

H. Kersten, as well as the Buddhists who are influenced by him, argue that Jesus had come to India in search of truth. Kersten bases his thesis on the account of Notovich (Kersten 1994:7–20). Notovich claimed to have found a Tibetan scroll, which depicted Jesus as wandering in India and Tibet prior to his work in Palestine (2004:218). According to the supposed scroll, Jesus had left

Palestine at the age of thirteen with the object of perfecting himself in the divine word and of studying the laws of the great Buddhas. He supposed to have spent six years with the Brahmins at Juggeraut, Rajagriha, Benares, and other Indian sacred cities. Brahmanic priests are supposed to have "taught him to read and understand the Vedas, to cure by aid of prayer, to teach, to explain the holy scriptures to the people, and to drive out evil spirits from the bodies of men, restoring unto them their sanity" (219). During that time Jesus is said to have preached to the "low caste" people of India and the "higher castes" had sought to kill him (221–2). He is then purported to have left Juggernaut, gone to Gautamides, the birthplace of the Buddha, and begun to study Buddhism and after six years become a Buddhist preacher. He is then thought to have left Nepal and the Himalayan Mountains, descended into the valley of Rajputana, and gone towards the west, preaching to diverse peoples the supreme perfection of man (222–3).[3]

Hence, many Buddhists argue that Jesus' teachings, particularly their ethical norms, were pure Buddhism. A. Dharmapala insisted that the Sermon on the Mount was borrowed from Buddhism (Guruge 1965:696). Kersten argues, that "the Buddhist thought is found in Jesus' teachings" (1994:99–102) and states that the Sermon on the Mount is a "condensed version of Buddhism" (Gruber and Kersten 1995:vii). Kersten draws several parallels between Buddhism and the New Testament, not only in the teachings of the Buddha and Christ but also in their lives (79–167). It was his contention that the Q source in the synoptic tradition as well as the Gospel of Thomas[4] are the oldest materials containing the original teachings of Jesus and that they are highly influenced by Buddhism. Further, they are "more authentic than the canonical Gospels and saturated with Buddhist ideas" (112). Basing his argument on J. Kloppenborg's analysis of the Q source,[5] Kersten goes on to assert that the materials found in Q1 are taken from the Buddhist *Dhammapada*[6] and *Undanavarga*[7] (123). He concludes, that "the original Jesus taught Buddhist ideas, lived the life of a Buddhist wandering monk, and instructed his disciples in following the

Buddhist path" (142–3). Therefore, several contemporary Sri Lankan Buddhists have concluded that Christianity is a distorted and inferior counterfeit of their own religion. They agree with Kersten that "the orientation towards Buddhism reveals discontent with the Christian tradition and makes apparent a feeling that the Buddhist religion is more authentic" (viii). Hence, Jesus Christ appears inferior to the Buddha to the Buddhist mind.

Historical Factors

Theologically, the theistic position of Christianity, its seemingly unscientific outlook, and the myth of Jesus' supposed study under the Buddhist monks create difficulties in presenting Jesus Christ as God and Savior to the Buddhist mind. These theological difficulties had become worse due to some historical realities, especially the events of the European colonial expansion. As in other colonized countries, in Sri Lanka the Christian mission was coincided with western colonial rule.[8] The Portuguese (1505-1658), followed by the Dutch (1658-1796), held the coastal areas of Sri Lanka under their subjugation. Then the British, who expelled the Dutch from the country in 1796, conquered the central Kandyan kingdom in 1815 and became the sole rulers of the whole country until 1948 when Sri Lanka became an independent state. It was under these colonial regimes Christianity was spread in Sri Lanka.[9] Hence the events that coincided with the Christianization of Sri Lanka had conditioned the Buddhist response to Christ. Colonial rule distorted and marred the image of Jesus Christ and his teachings in the minds of the Buddhists.

Unfriendly Figure: In contrast to the peaceful arrival of Buddhism to Sri Lanka,[10] Christianity came to the island as a dreadful conquering Western force when the Portuguese arrived in the country in 1505 (Tennent 1998:1–3). It has been often pointed out that the conversions made by the Portuguese were "the product of the bludgeon" (Williams 1951:83) for Christianity was "forced upon the people by means of inquisition" (Percival 1975:8). Hence contemporary Sri Lankans allege that Christianity was introduced to the country by the "power of the sword" (Malalasekera 1995:263). Such accusations have become a subject of controversy in modern times for the opinions on this matter among scholars differ to some extent.[11] Nevertheless, whether the Portuguese had used force or not in making converts, contemporary Buddhist opinion is that Christianity was forced on Sri Lankans. The use of force may not always have taken the form of threatening the people at the point of a sword; in many instances it was bringing pressure on the people that eventually led or forced them to become Christians.[12] Yet it cannot be denied that "in cases where inducements were ineffective, the use of terror and severe reprisals followed" (Phadnis 1976:44).

Christianity was the privileged religion of the subsequent colonial governments. During Dutch rule various laws were passed which brought pressure on non-Christians to accept baptism (Malalasekera 1995:264). Even though religious freedom was allowed under the British,[13] the government favored Christianity. Therefore, contemporary Sri Lankans are of the opinion that not only the Portuguese but also the subsequent Western colonial regimes used force in attempting to Christianize the natives. The Report of the Buddhist Committee of Inquiry[14] says that the Portuguese "occupied the maritime provinces and remained here for 150 years, oppressing and harassing the people of this country in a manner hitherto unknown" and depicts them as "the ruthless Catholic invader from Portugal."[15] Regarding the Dutch the report says that they were "treacherous and aggressive people who were in some respects as cruel as the Portuguese."[16] All Christian enterprises, including the British period, are described as the "menace of missionary activity" (Tambiah 1992:54). Hence Christianity is viewed as a religion that sanctions and encourages the use of force to convert people and as a religion of cruelty and violence. It was natural, therefore, for the Sri Lankans to conclude that "there must be something defective or unreal in a religion which required coercion and persecution to enforce its adoption" (Tennent 1998:70).[17]

Contemporary Buddhists see Christianity as a Western religious sect that came to Sri Lanka mainly to destroy their religion. During the Portuguese rule, several Buddhist and Hindu temples were demolished in the Maritime Provinces of Sri Lanka, statues of the Buddha and of the deities were destroyed, and many monks were killed.[18] The Sri Lankan Chronicle *Culavamsa* depicts the Portuguese as cruel enemies of Buddhism" (Geiger 1998:231–2).[19] Contemporary Buddhists consider them as "cruel, inhuman, rapacious, bigoted and savage persecutors of Buddhism in their endeavour to impose their faith… on the people of Sri Lanka" (Perera 1998:60). Hindu temples in the kingdom of Jaffna also suffered a similar fate.[20] In fact the destructions of the temples were considered by the Portuguese historians as one of the greatest achievements of the missionaries, and according to the Portuguese historians "numerous" idols were destroyed. "The memory of Portuguese persecution, maladministration, corruption and greed lingers in Sri Lanka Ceylon to the present day" (de Silva 1941:4).

While the Dutch and the British did not follow the Portuguese in demolishing Buddhist and Hindu temples, the activities of the missionaries of that period were aimed at the overthrow of Buddhism and Hinduism in Sri Lanka. The missionaries would have continued the "temple destroying mission" if the government had agreed to their requests. Dutch clergymen constantly urged the Dutch East Indian Company to suppress all non-Christian worship and destroy their temples and statues. But the Company was unwilling to follow the missionaries as it did not want to take any action that might be detrimental to its commerce. Nevertheless, the Dutch "looked upon Buddhism as a form of paganism, something that the Protestant Christians could not allow to exist or to prosper" (Karunaratna 1988:145). British missionaries similarly hoped for the day when temples and idols would be completely wiped out in Sri Lanka. The Methodist missionary B. Clough expressed his dream thus: "And O! What a sight that will be when the Temples of the Heathen are forsaken, Their (idols? Goods?) demolished and when the name of Christ shall echo thro the… Eastern World."[21]

The main objective of the education system of the colonial period seems to have been the eradication of native religions and the establishment of Christianity as the country's sole religion. During the Dutch period, "education was crucial to the new policy of conversion for the children had to be indoctrinated with the faith at an early age" (Arasaratnam 1997:221). It was mainly on the schools that the Dutch built their hopes for establishing the Reformed religion on this island.[22] The British had similar objectives in education.[23] In fact, "the Christian missionaries saw education primarily as a means of conversion" (de Silva 1987:195). Quoting a letter written by Governor Brownrigg, W. Rahula says, "this should reveal to the reader how the British Government tried to destroy Buddhism and Buddhist culture in Ceylon and to spread Christianity and western culture in its place" (1974:89). Hence, Buddhists often accuse Western colonial powers of destroying Buddhism and forcing Christianity on the natives.[24] The persecutions of Buddhism under colonial rule have created a negative disposition towards Christianity, and for contemporary Buddhists, Jesus Christ is not a friendly figure but a formidable foe of their religion.

Unspiritual Ideology: Further, the Buddhists do not consider Christianity as a spiritual religion but as an unspiritual ideology. This was due to the fact that in the past Christianity had functioned as a commercial instrument of the Western colonial powers. In fact, the major concern of the colonial rulers had been commerce and not religion. "The primary objective of the Portuguese Crown in the east was the control of East-West commerce" (de Silva 1987:126). The Portuguese spread their religion with the hope that the citizens of the conquered country would be faithful to the king of Portugal and would not become a hindrance to their commercial enterprise. For, religious conversion was considered as "a link that would bind the new subjects to their colonial masters" (Don Peter 18). The Portuguese search was for "Christians and Spices" and these dual goals "epitomised the religious and economic motives, which brought the Portuguese to the East at the end of the fifteenth century" (Boxer 185–224).

The subsequent Dutch rule also had the same emphasis on commerce. The Dutch rule in Sri Lanka consisted of the administration in the hands of the Dutch East India Company,[25] and the "primary aim of the Dutch in the first few decades of the seventeenth century was the securing of a monopoly of the spice trade" (de Silva 1987:134). The Dutch Reformed Church in Sri Lanka was dominated by "the East Indian Company with its prevailingly commercial and political interests" (Greenway 17). Hence the church "did not enjoy the status of an independent mission" (de Silva 1981:196), but "it was a department of government, and all its operations were subject to the scrutiny of the Governor and his council" (Greenway 165). Such control of the Company over the affairs of the church created a negative impression upon the Buddhists concerning Christianity. The Buddhists, therefore, think that Christianity was nothing other than an arm of the commercial enterprise of the colonial rulers.

The Dutch rule in Sri Lanka came to an end in 1796 and the British East India Company replaced the Dutch Company in the east. The island was transferred from the British East India Company to the British Crown by the Treaty of Amiens in 1802.[26] Even though this brought religious tolerance and freedom to the country, the British continued to give prominence to commerce by introducing the plantation industry—beginning with coffee, and then tea, rubber, and coconut. The growth of the plantation sector contributed to the increasing control of the economy by the colonial rulers (de Silva 1987:181). Even the missionaries of that era were of the opinion that commerce and industry were a proper sphere for English Protestantism (Hardy 1858:191–195). They "propagated the view that capitalism was a divinely sanctioned economic system destined to uplift the heathen" (Jayawardena 2001:252). All three colonial regimes focused much attention on commerce in order to increase their materiel wealth. Therefore, contemporary Buddhists, by comparing them with King Asoka who sent his son and daughter to Sri Lanka to spread Buddhism without expecting anything from Sri Lankans,[27] conclude that the Indian emperor is spiritually higher than the European colonists and that Buddhism is superior to Christianity in the sense that the former is devoid of selfish gain and the later is full of corruption, exploitation, and injustice. Consequently, Jesus Christ has been perceived as an imperialist, who "supports the whole process of colonisation and domination" (Wessels 1990:75).[28]

Undermining Debates: The prevailing lower view of Christianity and Jesus Christ in contemporary Sri Lanka is mainly due to the victory of the Buddhists in the historic controversies with Christians in the latter part of the 19th century. These controversies, which undermined Christianity to a lowest level in the minds of the Buddhists, consisted of many confrontations between the Buddhists and Christians in five major memorable public debates, in which both religious spokesmen challenged each other in face-to-face confrontations in order to defend and assert the superiority and authenticity of their respective religions.[29] These debates, and the controversies surrounding them, did nothing to further the objectives of the missionaries who initiated them. Instead, they became counterproductive, inspiring a revival in Buddhism and hardheartedness towards Christianity. Further, the debates and the activities of the Christians of that century remain embedded in the collective memory of modern Sri Lankan Buddhists as examples of Christian arrogance and its callous castigation of Buddhism. It is not an exaggeration to say that what the Crusades have ultimately done to the modern Islamic response to Christianity has also been done to Sri Lankan Buddhists by the missionary castigation of Buddhism, and especially by these historic debates.

Sri Lankan Buddhists, past and present, regard the nineteenth century religious debates as highly significant events in their 2,500 years of religious history (de Silva 1981:9). The final and decisive debate held at Panadura in August 1873 has became "a landmark in Buddhist-Christian relationship in the island" (Karunaratna 1988:125), for "this debate marked the culmination of the process of inter-religious encounter that went back to the very arrival of Christianity in the island" (Thilekaratne 229). Sri Lankan Buddhists consider this controversy to be "the fortunate event that saved Buddhism from being destroyed by the foreign missionaries backed by the then government" (Gunaratne and L. De Silva 17). Hence, for them, "it was an epoch-making event" (Malalasekera 1995:301) and "a cornerstone of the modern society in which we live today" (Kariyawasam VIII) and proudly point out that, in that controversy, the Buddhists had refuted the missionaries and defended Buddhism.[30] In fact, for them it has "closed down a dark period in Sri Lankan Buddhism and ushered in a new bright era" (Perera 1988:81).

The Buddhist disdain for Christianity, which the nineteenth century controversies did so much to shape, was not confined to that century only. There is a continuing contention between Buddhists and Christians in Sri Lanka. The controversies, especially the Panadura debate, have been popularized to such an extent that the Buddhists question the value of Christianity as a religion worthy of following. In the subsequent century, the account of the Panadura controversy has been published several times[31] is taught in schools, and serves as a frequent point in ongoing religious discussions. In August 1973, the centenary of the Panadura debate was celebrated "with great devotion and enthusiasm in several parts of the island" (Gunaratne and L. de Silva 17). The centenary of the death of Gunananda (1823-1890), the victorious Buddhist hero of the controversies, was also "celebrated with pomp and pageantry... [obtaining] the blessings of the highest authority of the country" (Somaratna 50). "The present Buddhist leaders look up to this era [i.e., the 19th century] with awe and respect. In fact some of those leaders [of the 19th century] who treated Christians with contempt have been treated in school textbooks as national heroes. This has had a serious impact on the minds of the younger generation that are taught to look upon the Christians as traitors" (Ekanayake 16). The contemporary Buddhists are proud to point out that "the crumbling bastions of Christian dogmatic theology were reduced to a heap of smoking rubble....The Panadura controversy, which was intended to bring discredit to the Buddhists, sounded instead the death-knell of

Christian influence in Sri Lanka, so that never again did Catholic or Protestant dogmatism venture to cross swords with Buddhist wisdom" (Sangharakshita 18).

The majority of the Buddhist in Sri Lanka consider Christianity as a dead religion of the past and Buddhism as the living religion of today. According to them "Christianity, or what remains of it, is fast dying...The Christian religion is dissolving before our eyes" (Wijayawardhana 1993:502). For them, the 19th century controversies settled the religious issues concerning Buddhism and Christianity once and for all. In such a context, the Buddhists generally do not see any reason to renounce their highly valued religion and embrace a seemingly insignificant and inferior religion called Christianity. Contemporary Buddhist feelings and attitudes toward Christianity are aptly expressed in the report of the Buddhist committee of inquiry. Though this report is fifty years old now, its depiction of the Buddhist attitude towards Christianity remains largely valid. The report says:

> For twenty three centuries Lanka has been nourished with the quintessence of human thought, the sublime teaching of the *Sambuddha*, the Supremely Enlightened One, and now the people of this Buddhist Lanka are being asked to give it up for crude teachings of the unenlightened teachers, for exploded beliefs, outworn theories and played-out philosophies. The Buddhists do not want to exchange gold for lead, or bread for filth; they want to hold fast to their compassionate, refined, and reasonable view of life, and their noble culture, which is founded, on the *Dhamma* (III-V).

It should not be forgotten that the initial efforts of the missionaries to propagate Christianity did not encounter opposition.[32] "The Buddhist priesthood… continued to resort to the missionaries and invited their attendance at the temples, to furnish answers to their interrogatories as to the proofs and principles of Christianity" (Tennent 1998:312).[33] In fact, the missionaries had enjoyed warm welcome and generous hospitality even from the

Buddhist monks (Hardy 1860:312–3).[34] This enabled the missionaries to gather large audience for their preaching (Hardy 1864:209).[35] Nevertheless, the missionaries were accustomed to criticize Buddhism and Buddhist ceremonies in derogatory manner (Malalgoda 1976:223).[36] The missionaries condemned Buddhism as "false, absurd, blasphemous, dangerous… [and a] gigantic system of error" (Small 1964:74). According to them Buddhist worship and temple ceremonies were all "horrifying and appalling, abominable and wicked" (Hardy 1860:321). "superstitious, idolatrous and devil worshipping" (Selkirk vi). They asserted that "Buddhism makes a fool of man by promising to guide him to safety, while it leads him to the very verge of the fatal precipice" (Hardy 1993:210)[37] which is "accompanied by the worship of demons and the propitiation of malignant infernal spirits" (Hardy 1841:11–12). Hence they tried "to pull down this stronghold of Satan" (Gogerly 1831) and "expose the so-called "errors of Buddhism."[38] It is their contention that "to be a Christian a man must regard Buddha as a false teacher, and his claim to supremacy as a sin against Almighty God" (Hardy 1841:216). For them, the Buddhists converts are in fact, "converted from the error of their own way (Hardy 1841:227). The missionaries studied Buddhism, but their main objective in such endeavours was to expose its "defects and errors" (Hardy 1841:XI), "their absurdity and sinfulness" (Harvard 1823:234) eventually "disestablish Buddhism" (Hallisey 39). Due to such continued provocative preaching, the Buddhists began to reject the missionaries and eventually opposed their activities. In fact, they "withdrew their tolerance and … turned against Christianity" (Malalgoda 1976:212).

Initially the Buddhists, of course, sent petitions to the government (Malalgoda 1976:588),[39] believing that the "British in general would see that a wrong had been done to them" (Malalgoda 1976:587). But, the government apparently only intervened in some instances, and requested the missionaries not to upset the Buddhists. Nothing was done to prevent the anti-Buddhist activities of the missionaries. The missionaries altogether ignored the occasional advice and admonition of the Governors, believing that a Christian government should not hinder the progress of the missionary work.[40] Concluding that the sending of petitions to the colonial government would not prevent provocative missionary activities, the Buddhists began to respond to missionary tracts by writing replies to them.[41] Subsequently both parties castigated each other's publications, and defended their religions vigorously, until they came forward to have public debates.[42] In 1848, the Christians published D. J. Gogerly's *Kristiyani Prajnapti* (Institutes of the Christian Religion), which "suspended all the previous polemical writings issued by the missionary presses and sounded the effective beginnings of the Buddhist Christian controversy" (Malalgoda 1976:217), for "it touched off the first serious opposition to Christianity on the part of Buddhism" (Small 1964:159) and brought the two parties together in face-to-face confrontations.[43] On the one hand this book had brought several Buddhists to Christianity (Pannananda 685), but on the other hand these conversions also functioned as an eye opener to the Buddhist monks, and consequently they "organised themselves into a strong opposition to react against these publications" (Kariyawasam 190).[44]

Although the title of Gogerly's publication suggests that it was rather for the instruction of Christians than an attack on Buddhism, the book contains an exposition of Buddhism based on the author's research on the Pali canon. Apart from his expositions of Christian doctrines, Gogerly had made a comparison of Buddhist and Christian doctrines in relation to essential theological issues. The aim of this comparison was to refute the Buddhist doctrines and to establish the truth of the Christian. Gogerly thought that when the Buddhists really understand their religion, they "would realise what nonsense they were and so Buddhism would lose its hold on the country" (Small 1964:157). Hence, the missionaries rejoiced, "here we have all the arguments needed to disprove certain positions that are declared to have been laid down by Buddha" (Hardy 1864:293). Christian missionaries repeatedly challenged the Buddhists to disprove, if they could, the main thesis of Gogerly's work. In addition to the book, several small tracts based on it were circulated widely challenging the Buddhists to disprove Gogerly's thesis. The missionaries made frequent quotations from this book in their sermons.

In *Kristiyani Prajnapti* Gogerly had pointed out the inconsistencies between the canonical teachings and the contemporary Buddhist practices and beliefs. In contradistinction to the canonical teachings, the Buddhists of that time venerated and even worshipped the Buddha (Selkirk 378–9)[45] and believed in the transmigration of souls. In addition to this, on the basis of the scientific discovery concerning the shape of the globe, Gogerly had also criticized the Buddhist cosmology. However, the main controversy around *Kristiyani Prajnapti* was directed against the chapter in which Gogerly had attempted to prove, from the canonical texts,[46] that Buddha was not omniscient (Gogerly 1885:2). The Buddhist monks responded by denying the genuineness of the passage cited by Gogerly by questioning his competence in Pali, and denying that the entreaty of Sahmaptai had occurred thrice on which Gogerly had based his arguments.[47] The Buddhists raised this issue until their canon was revised in 1867.[48] Further, the Buddhists pointed out that the Buddha's omniscience is a soteriologically relevant awareness, i.e. the Buddha became aware of specific things in the range of knowables successively in contrast with the biblical notion of an all-knowing capability from the beginning (Nikaya 167–71). The Christians, without comprehending this phenomenal aspect of Buddha's knowledge, criticized him from their Christian point of view.[49]

Since Christians had ridiculed the Buddha for not being omniscient, the Buddhists began to criticize Jehovah in similar manner. They pointed out that the biblical verses used to defend the omniscience of Jehovah are contradicted by the passages in which he is depicted as a repenting God (Abhayasundara 65–66). Further, they remarked that in the exodus event Jehovah was unable to distinguish the houses of the Israelites without an outward and visible sign which indicates that he is not omniscient (Abhayasundara 66).[50] Since God performed miracles one after the other on the basis that if people did not listen and obey after one miracle that another would be performed in the exodus event, the Buddhists argued, this demonstrated that Jehovah was not omniscient for he did not know the response of the people until the miracle was performed (Abhayasundara 67). Thus, contrary to the expectations of the missionaries, they encountered unexpected criticisms against the omniscience of Jehovah, finding it difficult even to defend their own concepts and disprove the Buddhists' arguments. Consequently, the Buddhists, instead of doubting the omniscience of the Buddha, denied and even denounced the claims made by Christians about the knowledge of Jehovah. This episode is a reminder that challenging a concept or a doctrine of other religions just to disprove and condemn it often brings similar criticisms and even unanswerable arguments against one's own faith.

Likewise, since the missionaries condemned Buddhism as demonism, they were provoked to criticize Christianity in similar terms. Hence they said that the blood sacrifices of the Bible demonstrate that the Christian God is bloodthirsty evil spirit, seething with anger, greed and delusion. According to them it is gods who receive offerings of incense, flowers, garlands, and light while devils receive fish, flesh, bones, fried meat, and burned meat and offerings of blood. Since the Old Testament is full of blood sacrifices, the Buddhists concluded that Jehovah is not God, but only a devil (Young and Somaratna 1996:136).[51] In addition to the Old Testament sacrifices, the Buddhists referred to the act of Zipporah when God sought to kill Moses (Ex. 4:24), stating that it was similar to that of the devil dancers of Sri Lanka who appease the wrath of the devils by offering blood sacrifices (Abhayasundara 1993:68). According to the Buddhists, God's injunction to circumcise Moses' son, "betray his fondness for human blood in common with evil spirits having similar tastes" (84). They have even cited the sacrifice of Jephthah's daughter to substantiate this criticism (91). Further, they remarked that it was to kill more people that Jehovah had hardened the heart of the Pharaoh. Citing Judges 1:19, the Buddhists said, since it is only devils who are scared of iron objects, Jehovah, who was afraid of iron chariots, was nothing else than a devil (69)[52] Hence it is counterproductive, for Christians attributed Buddhism and the Buddha to the devil, but Buddhists instead of renouncing their religion and embracing Christianity, depicted Jesus Christ and Christianity as demonism.[53]

The missionaries were of course optimistic about the outcome of the controversies.[54] They "believed that the Buddhist system of belief was so absurd that in an open contest between the two faiths Christianity would prove its superiority and would prevail" (Small 1964:76). Thus they asserted, that "the cross must triumph… the time will come when the *wihara* will be deserted, the *dagoba* unhonoured, and the *banna* unread" (Hardy 1993:162–3). The missionaries dreamt that such a Christianized society would be established in Sri Lanka subsequent to the controversies (Hardy 1993:VIII-IX). Nevertheless the Buddhists were able to answer the missionary criticisms, and the hopes of the missionaries diminished because, the Buddhists claimed that they had defeated Christianity and established the truth that Buddhism is authentic and superior to Christianity. Therefore, these nineteenth century controversies indicate to the majority of the contemporary Buddhists that a serious consideration of Christianity and its teaching adds nothing to their spirituality. To them, the controversies have long since settled the issue of religious truth. According to them today's conversions to Christianity "are not conversions through conviction but through enticement with the offer of food shelter and clothing to the poverty-stricken" (Abeyasekera 103). For the Buddhists, questions of religious truth had already been settled by the nineteenth century controversies. The only ground left open for conversion, therefore, must by implication, is material advantage (Abeyasekera 103).

Christian Presentation of Jesus Christ

As the theological and historical survey above has pointed out, it is difficult to present Christ as Savior and God to the Buddhists. The Buddhist perception of Jesus does not have a place for His divinity. According to them, Jesus is scientifically primitive and religiously inferior to the Buddha. Further the colonial rule and the controversies had reduced the statues of Jesus Christ to the lowest position. He has become a western crusader who came to Sri Lank to destroy Buddhism and Sinhalese culture. Some Buddhists even went to the extent of depicting Jesus Christ as a devil or evil spirit. Nevertheless Christians had continued to present Jesus Christ as the savior and God to the Buddhists even to the present day. Some follow the footsteps of the missionaries of the colonial era, but others have pointed out the need to modify—to contextualize this Christian message to the Buddhists. Many still believe that Christians should start their message with God when communicating with the Buddhists. But such a message will not make much sense to the Buddhist mind, which does not believe in the existence of a supreme God.[55] As I have pointed out in my last year paper, Christian missiology among the Buddhists should begin with anthropology and not with theology.[56] Like the Buddha, we must analyze the human predicament first and lead them to God who can deliver them from their pathetic state.

Terminological Approach

Since traditional Christian missiology is irrelevant to the Buddhist context, some have proposed different approaches to present Jesus Christ and his message to the Buddhists. One such methodology that is developed in Sri Lanka is terminological approach which expresses the Christian message in Buddhist terms.[57] It is true that some of the typical terminologies are far removed from the context of Buddhism and they are incomprehensible to the Buddhists. The missionaries of the colonial era expressed Christianity in western terms, which did not convince the Buddhist mind at large. Therefore, instead of using western Christian terms it has been suggested that employing Buddhist terms would communicate the Christian message well and convince the Buddhists about the Christian gospel.[58] In this approach, sometimes just using a term from Buddhism may suffice to communicate the

Christian message. But in most instances we need to explain the Christian concept in detail in order to avoid possible and potential misunderstandings.

In adopting the terminological approach, however, Christians need to be extremely cautious and wise, for a major disadvantage in employing non-Christian terms in Christian messages is their susceptibility to being misunderstood. Since non-Christians are familiar with these terms they will understand them according to their own contexts and meanings. They may not get the intended meaning of the Christians. For instance, it may seem helpful to use the term "rebirth" instead of "regeneration" when conversing with a Buddhist. Christians may assume that the term rebirth will convey the ideas that are intended by the Christian concept of regeneration. But the Buddhists will not comprehend the Christian concept of regeneration from the term "rebirth" without a detailed explanation. The Buddhist mind will naturally ponder about the endless cycles of births and deaths whenever they hear the term "rebirth."[59] Hence, in order to avoid unnecessary misunderstandings, it is necessary for Christians to avoid familiar terms.[60]

In the 19th century Buddhist-Christian controversies, one of the criticisms leveled against the Christian missionaries was on such grounds. In the Panadura debate, the Buddhists accused the Christians for deceiving non-Christians by adopting their religious terms and concepts. They pointed out, that in Calcutta, Christ was called son of *Iswara* with the view to enlisting the sympathies of the Hindus who held the god *Iswara* in great reverence. Similarly, in Sri Lanka, Jehovah went by the name of "*dewiyanwahanse*" as this term existed amongst the Sinhalese to denote the gods in whom they believed. Even when Christians explained that "this was not with the view of deceiving the people, but the language could not offer any other better word," the Buddhists continued to insist that "the intention of the Christians was to deceive the Hindus" (Abhayasundara 63, 73-74).[61] It is true that divine names cannot be rendered in other languages without using the common terminologies that connote divinity in those dialects. Nevertheless, employing the names or titles of other deities for Jesus is not a proper methodology for the Christian mission, for it will be seen as another cunning device of the Christians to win adherence deceitfully. It will also give a wrong impression to the non-Christians about the personality of Jesus Christ, for they will attribute all the qualities and characteristics of their gods to him. Therefore, it is better to use the names already in use (i.e., Jesus Christ and Jehovah) instead of adopting Buddhist names just for the sake of contextualization.

Theological Approach

In this approach, a theological concept from Buddhism is used to present the Christian message to the Buddhists. Many use the Buddhist concept of *pattidana* (merit transference) to explain the gospel to Buddhists. Even though this Buddhist concept was developed within the Mahayana tradition, it is practised in Theravada societies in South East Asia as well" (Schumann 1973:92). Early Mahayana Buddhists came to believe in a process of merit transference, through which practitioners, especially a Buddha or a Bodhisattava, could apply merit to persons less advanced on the path (Lefebure 1993:24). Even though such a concept does not exist among the Sri Lankan Buddhists, they are accustomed to transfer their merits to their dead relatives. Hence it is pointed out that within the framework of this practice of merit transference, we can explain the concept of imputation of Christ's righteousness to the believers, and our sins to Jesus Christ (Weerasingha 1989:72–76).

Likewise, the concept of God can be explained to the Buddhist by using their doctrine of *anatta*.[62] In Buddhist philosophy *anatta* means there is nothing called self/soul or any unchanging abiding substance in human beings (Rahula 1959:52). Although Buddhism denies the existence of God, as Lynn de Silva has pointed out, the concept of *anatta* necessitates such a belief. While denying the self (this is the crux of *anatta*), Buddhism teaches that man must depend on himself for his deliverance. For de Silva, this is "one of the deepest dilemmas in Buddhism."[63] So he asks, "What is the self that denies the self and at the same time asserts that it alone can save the self?" *Nibbana*, deliverance from the ongoing endless cycles of births and deaths, the ultimate goal to which Buddhist morality is directed, is expected in Buddhism purely by self effort. Buddhism asserts that people have the power to achieve this goal. Therefore de Silva says, "To deny the self and to affirm self-sufficiency is a contradiction."[64] According to him it is the Bible, which takes the doctrine of *anatta* seriously and points out the inability of human beings to save themselves. Thus he remarks, "it can be shown that the Bible takes what is implied in the doctrine of *anatta* more seriously than Buddhism does, for the biblical teaching is that man is nothing by himself and can do nothing by himself about his salvation. The doctrine of *anatta* therefore points to the truth that man cannot save himself by his own efforts and is in need of saving grace." De Silva positively affirms, "it is in relation to the unconditioned (God) that the full depth and significance of *anatta* can be understood" (L. de Silva 1979:58). In other words, in view of *anatta* God becomes indispensable. Thus by emphasizing *anatta* de Silva makes an attempt to convince Buddhists of the necessity of divine help in attaining the ultimate goal (L. de Silva 1967).

Practical Approach

Terminological as well as theological approaches to communicate the Christian message to the Buddhists are too sophisticated and philosophical in nature. Hence these approaches may not convince the ordinary people. Therefore, another practical approach is necessary in order to convince the Buddhist laity about the tenets of Christianity. In Sri Lanka there exists a contradiction between philosophical Buddhism and practical Buddhism. While philosophical Buddhism rejects the theistic notions of religion, practical Buddhism in Sri Lanka has absorbed almost all the deities of Hinduism.[65] Therefore, contemporary Buddhist assertion of non-theistic character of their religion is intended mainly to emphasize the unacceptability of Christian theism. The Buddhists in Sri Lanka worship not only the Buddha, but also other Hindu deities in their pantheon, making offerings to the statues and pictures of the Buddha and other Hindu deities and recite Pali verses.

> Sinhalese Buddhists state that their religion was founded by the Buddha, who was a human being and is now dead. Cognitively this position is held by every Buddhists from the most learned monk to the most ignorant layman. Yet they usually behave as if the Buddha appears to them as a powerful and omnibenevolent god, a supreme being who is still in some way present and aware. For instance, if assailed by dangerous demons a pious Buddhist will recite the qualities of the Buddha and thus keep any malevolent forces at bay.... Moreover, Buddhists have dealings with the Buddha in which they behave as if he were at least numinously present; in particular, offerings are made before the statues.[66]

In Sri Lanka every Buddhist monastery[67] has a temple with at least one statue of the Buddha, and most homes have a small shrine or at least a picture of the Buddha with tiny altar before it. In front of these representations of the Buddha people conduct themselves as if in the presence of an important person or God. The Buddhist's explanation for such conduct is that of respect for the memory of Buddha, but "the demeanour of the average worshipper is reminiscent of theistic devotion rather than of philosophic contemplation."[68]

> At least one ceremony is so obviously motivated by fear that it cannot be rationalised in terms of respect and affection for the memory of an omni benevolent Buddha, whether dead or alive. This is the ceremony of consecrating a statue. Only when a statue has been consecrated can it be an object of worship, and this fact is sufficient to show that a Buddha statue is more than a mere reminder of the Buddha (Gombrich 1966:24).

In fact the very act of consecration indicates that the statue of the Buddha is being brought to life. The ceremony consists of only a single performance of painting the eyes or carving the pupils. Once this ceremony is over the statue is considered nothing else than divine. "Before the Eyes are made, it is not accounted a God, but a lump of ordinary Metal, and thrown about the shop with no more regard than anything else…The eyes being formed, it is thenceforward a God" (Knox 1681:130).

The consecration ceremony of a statue of the Buddha and its subsequent veneration clearly indicate that the Buddhists worship the statue contrary to their rational explanation. In the meantime they worship the gods of spirit religion and Hinduism contrary to the teachings of the Buddha. Hence when A. Dharmapala, began to reform Buddhism in the nineteenth century, his primary objective was "to separate canonical teachings from popular religious practices" (Amunugama 1985:720). The Buddhists in Sri Lanka generally avoid asking worldly blessing from Buddha; rather they go to the gods and other cultic rituals for such blessings. Dharmapala pointed out the inconsistency of Buddhist doctrines and of such religious observations of the people. Hence it was his firm conviction that "no intelligent Buddhists… would ever care to invoke a god who is only a step higher in the evolutionary scale of progress than man" (Guruge 1965:638). Many of the rituals, which did not have a direct scriptural rationale, were dismissed as "excrescence survivals of Hindu practices, which were antithetical, or at least irrelevant, to Buddhism" (Amunugama 1985:720).

Despite the reforms of Dharmapala, the Buddhists still have their gods and engage in ritualistic ceremonies. In fact contemporary Sri Lankan Buddhism is a "composite of canonical Buddhism, deity worship and magical animism… It is a blend of cultic and occultic practices within a derived concept from orthodox canonical Buddhism" (Weerasingha 1989:45). Astrology, occultism and worship of territorial spirits and gods are common features of Sri Lankan Buddhism (Gombrich and Obeyesekere 1988). Prior to the arrival of Buddhism in the third century BC, the religious belief of Sri Lanka was basically animistic and people's religious convictions were conditioned by their fear of gods and demons (Paranavitana

1929:302–327). Even though by the first century BC Buddhism had spread into every part of the country (Mendis 1998:10), the earlier animistic religion "flourished side by side among the masses and has persisted down to modern times" (Paranavitana 1929:305). Its early developments in Sri Lankan Buddhism "absorbed various cults, rituals, and ceremonies that had been practised in the country… This popular aspect of Buddhism in Sri Lanka developed into a system capable of serving the varied religious needs of society (Ilangasinha 1992:183).

Since the gods are higher than human beings, they are sought for various practical problems and needs. It is not an exaggeration or an error to say that Buddhists in Sri Lanka need gods for their day today practical life. They cannot live with philosophical explanations alone. Hence, they worship the gods while trying to obtain *nibbana* through Buddha's eight-fold path. But rituals and ceremonies are the predominant features of contemporary Sri Lankan Buddhism. This clearly indicates their need for a god or a supernatural being who could help them in their numerous problems and difficulties that have engulfed their lives. It is at this point that Christians need to point out the power and divinity of Jesus Christ to the Buddhists. But the major obstacle in this endeavor is the Buddhist's view of Jesus Christ. As it had been pointed out in the first part of this paper, theologically and historically Jesus Christ has been reduced to a lowest level in the minds of the Buddhists. Hence it is the paramount duty of Christians to raise the status of Jesus Christ in the minds of the Buddhists. Hence the following practices are suggested.

Apology for the wrongs done to Buddhism in the past: As pointed out earlier, missionaries of the colonial era were accustomed to condemn all religious systems other than their own and attributing them to Satan or falsehood. Much damage had been done to Buddhism in Sri Lanka under the colonial rule. Christians need to understand that the Buddhists have not forgotten their colonial past which most Christians are accustomed to disregard or ignore. Contemporary Sri Lankan Buddhism has its roots in the nineteenth-century revival which drew much of its strength from Buddhist reaction to the anti-Buddhist activities of the Christians. As far as the Buddhists are concerned the colonial heritage of contemporary Christian mission is unfitting to the religious ethos of the country. Therefore it is necessary for Christians whose theology emphasizes repentance, to repent of their colonial attitude and express the true spirit of Christ in all their activities.

Acknowledging the sins of a nation or a community is nothing new to the Christian Bible. The Old Testament contains many instances in which the leaders acknowledged and repented of the sins of their forefathers or contemporaries. Since Christian treatment of Buddhism in Sri Lanka was wrong, an appeal was made in 1969 to the Christians to recognize the dark side of their history and make a public act of repentance.[69] Considering the nineteenth century missionary activities, it was pointed out in 1997 that "repentance for this sad history was the only way forward"[70] for the Christians in Sri Lanka. It is sad that this important advice has been totally ignored by many Christians who continue to follow their colonial forefathers in aggressive or polemical evangelism. The nineteenth century controversies are a reminder to contemporary Christians that argumentative and aggressive forms of evangelism are unfitting to the message of Christ, a message saturated with undeserved love to humanity.

Appreciation for the wisdom of the Buddhist precepts: The missionaries of the colonial era are accustomed to criticize and condemn Buddhism and its practices. Unfortunately such derogatory activities still prevail among certain sections of evangelical and mainline churches in Sri Lanka.[71] They often argue that there is nothing wrong or inappropriate in condemning Buddhism and other non-Christian religions citing incidents from the Bible.[72] However, it should be observed that such condemnation in the Bible was not aimed at converting the people of other faiths. It was mainly addressed to the Jews (in OT) and Christians (in NT) to discourage them from turning to other gods. Therefore biblical condemnation of idolatry ought not to be used as a precedent or an excuse for criticizing non-Christian religions in order to convert adherents of these faiths.

According to the Bible all religions are nothing other than human responses to divine revelation even when they do not conform to the Judeo-Christian standards.[73] They are "a mixture of human response and divine revelation" (Wright 1997:109). As the Bible declares, and human experience demonstrates, people are religious because of the intuitive awareness they have regarding the divine (Ecc. 3:11). This innate knowledge is due to the divine image within the constitution of human beings,[74] and the divine self-disclosure in human conscience.[75] Human religions do have diabolical and immoral aspects, but they are due to the sin, ignorance and fallibility that are inherent in human nature. Nevertheless, people with all their errors and evils seek God in response to divine revelation, and it is the responsibility of Christians to recognize this religious instinct without condemning it and attributing everything in other religions to Satan. In this respect, the greatest apostle of Christianity, Paul set an excellent example in Athens. Although that city was full of idols, and idolatry was condemned by God, and whilst Paul was greatly distressed by the religious practices of the people (Acts 17:16), instead of condemning them, he commended their religious observances (Acts 17:22). Paul was not endorsing or sanctioning idolatry, but neither was he approaching the non-Christians with a polemical mentality similar to that of the missionaries of the colonial era and many contemporary evangelical minded Christians in Sri Lanka. In Paul's approach, "we have a respectful recognition of religious endeavours" (Larkin 1995:255), for it was "a cultured compliment to the distinguished audience" (Dunn 1996:234). Such a positive attitude and broadmindedness are vital when encountering the people of other faiths.[76]

Christians need to recognize that the moral code that the Buddha expounded was similar to the ethical codes of the Bible. Furthermore, the theology of the missionaries was systematized by utilizing Greek philosophy, which is a human ideology similar to

Buddhist doctrines. It is clearly unreasonable to attribute Eastern philosophy to Satan and Western philosophy to God. In fact there are many good things in Buddhism which Christians can and should appreciate. We need to look for the good and positive aspects in other religions and appreciate them without totally discarding them. There are certain things in Buddhism which could enrich our Christian walk. Christians need to develop an attitude of appreciation of non-Christian religious wisdom and ways without attributing everything to the devil.

Articulation of a Wide-Missiology to the Buddhist populace: Finally, in contrast to the "Narrow-Missiology" of the colonial missionaries we need to develop a "Wide-Missiology" which instead of having an exclusive biblical theology formulates Christian Missiology in the light of Buddhist doctrines and in relation to Buddhist realities. However, this does not mean to deny the unique revelation of the Bible or dilute the gospel message. On the contrary it is systematizing Christian missiology in view of Buddhist doctrines and ethos. Wide-Missiology includes dialogue with Buddhists instead of having only a one-way direct preaching. However, it does not totally discard the direct preaching method. It proposes a non-confrontational preaching method; avoiding arrogant, and defamatory criticism of Buddhism. Hence it includes proclaiming the Christian gospel without criticizing or condemning Buddhism and engaging in religious dialogues with the Buddhists.

In dialogue with the Buddhists in Sri Lanka, Lynn de Silva has contributed much.[77] As already pointed out his emphasis on the Buddhist concept of *anatta* to point out the necessity of God to Buddhist is an excellent way to reach the non-theistic minds of the Buddhists. He took the Buddha's discovery of the three marks of human predicament, *anicca*, *anatta*, and *dukkha* as the fundamental characteristics of all existence and the proper starting point of Christian theology in a Buddhist context. Since traditional Christian theology's theistic starting point may sound incomprehensible to the non-theistic Buddhist mind, de Silva's attempt to begin his theology where the Buddha had begun is commendable and should became the norm for Christian missiology in a Buddhist context. However, even though de Silva's missiological construction has valuable insights, his thesis has some weaknesses too, for he ends up by giving Buddhist meanings to Christian concepts and harmonizes both religious concepts in a syncretistic way,[78] instead of communicating the Christian message to the Buddhists.[79]

In contemporary Sri Lanka Aloysius Peiris also contributed much to Buddhist-Christian dialogue.[80] Concluding that existing Asian Christologies "are all out of place in Asia"[81] Peiris insists that Asian Christian theology as well as the Church must be baptised in the "Jordan of Asian Religions" and crucified in the "Calvary of Asian poverty."[82] By this dictum Peiris has made an appeal to Christians to give up their colonial identity and submit their theologies to the judgement of other non-Christian soteriologies and socialism.[83] In recent times, however, rejecting syncretism and synthesis as violations of the unique identity of each religion, he has ventured to develop a mutual relationship between Buddhists and Christians to learn from and edify each other. Depicting this process as "symbiosis," Peiris remarks that in such an engagement people of one religion expose themselves to another religion and in the process learn more about what is significant and unique in their own tradition through the judgments and witness of the other.[84] Evangelical Christians may reject such a proposal, but Christians can and should learn about their own faith and enrich their spirituality by such encounters with Buddhists and vice versa. Nevertheless, it should not be forgotten that Christianity is not just a learning process. The intrinsic nature of Christianity is its fundamental obligation to express its unique message to the non-Christian as well.

In any dialogical approach, the tendency is to discover and affirm the commonness of the different faiths with the hope of bringing a mutual understanding and harmony between the diverse religious communities that are divided by religion. Such a process is vital and necessary for the mutual engagement of discovering the depths and the true nature of religions, but the endeavor should also challenge the people involved to evaluate their own religious concepts objectively and if necessary, make changes to become better. In any inter-faith dialogue, learning as well as teaching should occur in a reciprocal way. Such a process must begin on a common ground and proceed to discover the differences and if necessary borrow from the other side to complement one's own religious pursuit. I have pointed out in a previous paper that the message of the book of Ecclesiastes and the Four Noble Truths[85] of the Buddha should become an important topic in any Buddhist-Christian dialogical encounter. For both the Buddha and the author of Ecclesiastes take a common and important subject to investigate and discover the root causes of the human predicament and propose solutions in their own cultural and religious contexts. With this subject, both Buddhists and Christians could engage in a common search to find out how both religions seek to solve the human predicament and follow whichever path they see appropriate.

Notes

[1] For an exposition of this Buddhist doctrine see S. Tong, *The Real Facts of Life: Practical Reflections on the Three Marks of Existence*. Kandy: Buddhist Publication Society, 2000.

[2] For instance see Levi Downing, *The Aquarian Gospel of Jesus the Christ*, CA: Devorss & Co, 1981; Elizabeth Clare, *The Lost Years of Jesus*, Livingston, MT: Summit University Press, 1984 and Janet Bock, *The Jesus Mystery*. Los Angeles: Aura Books, 1984.

[3] For a critical evaluation of this novel theory see R. Rhodes, *The Counterfeit Christ of the New Age Movement* (Grand Rapids: Baker, 1991), 13-113; D. Groothuis, *Revealing the New Age Jesus* (Leicester: IVP, 1990), 147-173.

[4] This apocryphal text was discovered by Egyptian peasants in a grave at Nag Hammadi near Luxor, together with 48 other tracts from a library of Gnostic texts in Coptic (the Middle Egyptian language) in 1946. Until then the existence of this lost text is known only from the early Christian writings.

[5] J. Kloppenborg has divided the Q material into three sections. Q1 contains the oldest material, which comprises the wisdom sayings of Jesus. Q2 has the later additions of the prophetic and apocalyptic texts and Q3 is also a later addition, which comprises the temptation story and number of linking sections (Ibid., 113).

[6] *Dhammapada* is a part of the *Tipitaka.* It has 423 verses arranged in twenty six chapters, and is included in the *sutta-pitaka*, the discourses of the Buddha.

[7] *Undanavarga* is an extended collection based on the Dhammapada. Originally it was R. C. Amore who suggested that the Q source had partly originated in Buddhism. He concluded, "part of the Q source was heavily influenced by the Dhamapada and by the biography of the Buddha" (*Two Masters, One Message*, 181).

[8] Although there is evidence for the presence of small groups of Christians in the island prior to the colonial regime, no serious attempt seems to have been made to convert the Buddhists to Christianity until the country has been conquered by the western powers in the sixteen century. (Cf. "The Antiquity of St. Thomas church, Gintupitiya" *Ceylon Churchman*, Nov/Dec, 1990; G. P. V. Somaratna, "Christianity in Sri-Lanka in the Anuradhapura Period" *Dharma Deepika* 2 (December 1996), 22-24; Senarat Paranavitana, *Story of Sigiriya,* Colombo: Lake House Investments Ltd., 1972, 44-46, 94, 120; M. Quere "Christianity in Sri-Lanka before the Coming of the Portuguese" *The Aquinas Journal* 4 (December 1987), 127-145.

[9] The Portuguese rule introduced Roman Catholicism to the country. Cf. S. Gannaprakasar, *A History of The Catholic Church in Ceylon: Period of beginnings 1505–1602* (Colombo: Literature Committee of the Catholic Union of Ceylon, 1924); M. Quere, *Christianity in Sri-Lanka Under the Portuguese Padroado*, (Colombo: Catholic Press, 1995). The Dutch introduced their reformed faith. Cf. R. S. Greenway, *The Dutch Reformed Church in Ceylon,* unpublished MTh Dissertation (Grand Rapids: Calvin Seminary, 1963). During the British period many missionary organizations began their work in Sri Lanka. Cf. J. E. Tennent, *Christianity in Ceylon* (London; 1850); C. N. V. Fernando, *A*

Study of the History of Christianity in Ceylon in the British Period from 1786–1903, with Special Reference to the Protestant missions, unpublished B.Litt. dissertation (Oxford University, 1942).

[10] Buddhism comes to the island about the middle of the 3rd century BC (W. Rahula, *History of Buddhism in Ceylon*, 48). The Sri Lankan Chronicle *Mahavamsa* narrates the arrival of Mahinda, son of King Asoka who brought Buddhism to the country and the acceptance of Buddhism by the natives (W. Geigher, tr. *The Mahavamsa*, 88-115). By the 1st century BC, Buddhism had spread into every part of the island (G. C. Mendis, *The Early History of Ceylon*, 10).

[11] That the Portuguese, "compelled the natives to accept Christianity" is totally denied by some Christian scholars. Cf. D. Peter, *Education in Sri-Lanka under the Portuguese*, 64-67; S. G. Perera, *A Note on Portuguese Missionary Methods in the East*, 77. Christians quote J. E. Tennent's statement, "I have discovered nothing in the proceedings of the Portuguese in Ceylon to justify the imputation of violence and constraint," to substantiate their argument (D. Peter, *Education in Sri-Lanka under the Portuguese*, 65). Although Tennent said this in 1850 (*Christianity in Ceylon*, 66), he also pointed out that "the records of their government have entirely disappeared; they were taken to Goa on the conquest of the island by the Dutch, whence they were removed to Lisbon, and afterwards transferred to Brazil" (ibid., 7-8). Hence he remarked, "in their absence there is little or no historical evidence of the system of proselytism pursued by their clergy, or the amount of the success, beyond the imperfect notices of the Dutch historians, and the still existing traditions of the Sinhalese themselves" (ibid., 8). Christians generally fail to take note of this information provided by J. E. Tennent. Further, nine years later when Tennent had access to the Portuguese records he had remarked, "there is no page in the story of European colonisation more gloomy and repulsive than that, which recounts the proceedings of the Portuguese in Ceylon" (*Ceylon: An Account of the Island Physical, Historical, and Topographical*, 547). Referring to Faria V Souza's *Asia Portuguese* (Lisbon: 1666-75), Tennent remarked, "they appeared in the Indian Seas in the threefold character of merchants, missionaries, and pirates. Their ostensible motto was 'amity, commerce, and religion.' Their expeditions consisted of soldiers as well as adventurers, and included friars and a chaplain-major. Their instructions were, "to begin by preaching, but, that failing, to proceed to the decision of the sword" (*Ceylon: An Account of the Island*, 547-548). After analysing the Portuguese missionary methodologies C. R. Boxer made

the following observation: "Many other instances could be given to exemplify the fact that the Portuguese sometimes used force, or the threat of force, to forward their conversion policy in the East… When all due reservations and allowances have been made, the fact remains that many of the Portuguese in the East regarded themselves as forming the spearhead of militant Roman Catholic Christianity, and as such they took literally the Biblical injunction (Luke XIV, 23) to compel them to come in" ("A note on Portuguese Missionary Methods in the East," 88, 90).

[12] D. Peter, *Education in Sri-Lanka Under the Portuguese*, 67. C. R. Boxer, *Christians and Spices: Portuguese Missionary Methods in Ceylon*, 348.

[13] In 1799, three years after British occupation of the Costal areas of Sri Lanka, the British Governor issued an historic edict defining the British policy of toleration towards Christians and non-Christians alike. Cf. G. C. Mendis, ed., *The Colebrooke-Cameron Papers Volume II*, 161.

[14] This committee was set up to inquire into state of Buddhism in Sri-Lanka by the All Ceylon Buddhist Congress in 1954. The committee held its sittings throughout the island for a whole year and surveyed the attitudes and aspirations of the Buddhists. As S. J. Tambiah has correctly observed, this report reflects "the views of some of the islands foremost Buddhist scholars and educators, both clerical and lay" (*Buddhism Betrayed? Religion, Politics, and Violence in Sri-Lanka*, 31).

[15] The Report of the Buddhist Committee of Inquiry, VIII.

[16] The report admits the fact that they "did not persecute the Buddhist; all their venom was directed against the Roman Catholics," X.

[17] This comment of J. E. Tennent concerning the Dutch period is equally applicable to the entire colonial period.

[18] "In Kotte city itself, a group of *bhikkhus* led by *bhikkhu* Buddhavamsa roused the people who attacked the king's bodyguard with sticks and stones. The riot was quelled only after Portuguese reinforcements arrived from Colombo and, in retaliation, thirty *bhikkhus* were seized and put to death."

[19] W. Geiger, tr. *Culavamsa*, 231-232. For a similar criticism in the 19th century see A. Guruga, ed. *Return to Righteousness*, 482.

[20] S. Mudaliyar, "Relics of the Portuguese Rule in Jaffna" *Ceylon Antiquary and Literary Register* V, 12. Cf. Boxer, *Christians and Spices*, 351.

[21] B. Clough, *Missionary Letter* 27 September 1814, quoted in Y. Gooneratne, *English Literature in Ceylon 1815-1878*, 90. Similarly, another Methodist missionary R. Newstead wrote in 1818, that the Temples of Heathenism will be forsaken and alone – the grass shall grow in their courts and the Owls lodge in their Mausoleums – The idols shall be dishonoured and thrown down and they who worshipped them shall tread upon them and the whole gloomy machinery of the worship of demons shall gradually sink into decay and eternal oblivion while the glorious living temple of the Lord of Hosts shall rapidly tho' silently arise (quoted in Gooneratne, 90).

[22] R. L. Brohier, *The Dutch Period of the Church in Ceylon*, 109.

[23] For instance, A. Dharmapala has stated that "the missionaries said very frankly, we come to teach you not English but Christianity" A. Guruge, ed. *Return to Righteousness*, 684.

[24] For instance A. Dharmapala said the Christian thinks himself to be the chosen of God, and the example of the Hebrews who destroyed the tribes of Canaan is copied by the invader when he is dealing with the native races of conquered countries (Guruge, *Return to Righteousness*, 405).

[25] The Dutch East India Company was founded in 1602 and obtained the State General of United Netherlands for the monopoly of trade in the East Indian seas. The management of the company was vested in a committee of seventeen directors. The Company though started as a commercial enterprise, in course of time became a political power in the East and conquered several countries there.

[26] From 1798-1802 British possessions in Sri Lanka were ruled by a governor appointed by the Crown but working under the Governor-General of India and the directors of the east India Company. This system of 'dual control' proved unsatisfactory and in 1802 the Maritime Provinces were made a British Crown Colony controlled directly from London. The East India Company, however, retained a monopoly of the cinnamon trade for a further twenty years (Chandra R. de Silva, *Sri Lanka: A History*, 165).

[27] It has been pointed out that Asoka's Rock Edict II contains a reference to Sri Lanka as one country influenced by the emperor and helped by him in the sphere of medical work. Even though some think that Tambapamni in Asoka's inscription refers to the valley of the Tamaraiparani river in South India, others has pointed out that it refers to Sri Lanka since one of Sri Lanka's ancient names is Tapprobane

(Tamraparni) resembles with this name (W. Rahula, *Buddhism in Sri Lanka*, 10-13; R. K. Mookerjee, *Asoka*, 132).

[28] A. Wessels, *Images of Jesus*, 75. Commenting on the way the Bible came to Asia, R. Sugirtharajah says, that "it came as an ideological manifesto of the imperialist" (*The Bible and its Asian Readers*, 55).

[29] These debates were "verbal confrontations in which the tenets of Buddhism and Christianity were critically examined with the view to demonstrating to the audience gathered for the occasion the superiority of Christianity" (K. M. de Silva, *A History of Sri Lanka*, 340). They were held in the following locations: at Baddegama (twelve miles from Galle) in 8 February 1864, at Waragoda (near Kelaniya) in August 1865, at Udanwita in 1 February 1866, at Gampola in 6, 9 and 10 January 1871, and at Panadura in 26 and 28 August 1873. For an analysis of these debates, see R. F. Young & G. P. V. Somaratna, *Vain Debates: The Buddhist Christian Controversies of Nineteenth-Century Ceylon.* (Vienna: Institute of Indology University of Vienna, 1996). How these debates emerged and inspired a counterproductive revival in Buddhism and continues to condition the minds of Buddhists against Christianity see my *The Legacy of the Controversies: The Continuing Impact on Interfaith Encounters in Sri Lanka of Nineteenth-Century Controversies between Buddhists and Christians*. Unpublished MPhil Dissertation, England: The Open University, 2001).

[30] The Buddhists point out that, the controversy ended with victory for the Buddhists. The Buddhist orator (Gunananda Thera) not only replied effectively to the fallacies of the Christian speakers, but also enlightened them on the principles and tenets of the Buddhist doctrine. When the Christians retired from the debate defeated, the Buddhists were overjoyed. Festivities were held in every temple to mark their triumph and the effigy of Gunananda Thera was carried in procession in every village. The triumph of the Buddhists over their Christian adversaries at Panadura controversy flushed into their veins vigour and enthusiasm to work for the recovery of their glory (H. R. Perera, *Buddhism in Sri Lanka*, 78-79).

[31] It has been published in 1947, 1955, 1990 and 1994.

[32] In fact, tolerance of other faiths was a well established Buddhist tradition in Sri Lanka (K. M. de Silva, *A History of Sri Lanka*, 128; W. Rahula, *What the Buddha Taught*, 5). Even the Portuguese as well as Dutch historians had praised the Buddhists for their religious tolerance (F. Queyroz, *The Temporal and Spiritual Conquest of Ceylon*, 700; K. W.

Goonewardena, *Dutch Policy Towards Buddhism in Sri Lanka*, 319). Among the British authors, we have a seventeenth century witness to this fact (cf. R. Knox, *An Historical Relation of the Island of Ceylon in the East Indies*, 83, 102). For a nineteenth century witness, see R. Percival, *An Account of the Island of Ceylon*, 210). Even the Christian missionaries had testified to the spirit of tolerance among the Buddhist. Cf. D. J. Gogerly, *An Introductory Sketch of Buddhism*, 4; R. S. Hardy, *Eastern Monachism*, 412; B. Clough, *Missionary Letter*, 25 January 1814, SOAS Library Archives, London).

[33] J. E. Tennent, *Christianity in Ceylon*, 312. Missionaries' writings testify this fact. See *Methodist Magazine* XXXIX (1816), 398 and *CMS Proceedings for Asia 1821-1823.* Cited in E. J. Harris, *Crisis and Competition*, 14.

[34] For instance, a Methodist missionary R.S. Hardy wrote about his experience as: In travelling through unfrequented parts of the interior… I usually took up my abode at the *pansal* [Buddhist temple], and seldom was I refused a night's lodging or a temporary shelter during the heat of the day. The priests would bring out the alms-bowl, when they saw that I was hungry… or they would bring tobacco or some other luxury, to express their satisfaction at my visit (*Eastern Monachism*, 312-313).

[35] R. S. Hardy, *Jubilee Memorials of the Wesleyan Mission*, 209; *Methodist Magazine* XXXIX (1816), 154; *Ibid.* XXXIX (1816), 190; Ibid., XL (1817), 197; B. Clough, *Missionary Letter*, 3 November 1815, SOAS Library Archive, London.

[36] K. Malalgoda, *Buddhism in Sinhalese Society*, 223; J. Selkirk, *Recollection of Ceylon*, 441-450.

[37] R. S. Hardy, *The Legends and Theories of the Buddhists, Compared with History and Science*, 210.

[38] *Tract Society Annual Report* (London: Baptist Missionary Society, 1833), 35-36.

[39] K. Malalgoda says that "these petitions reveal the tolerance of the *Sanga* in the early years and their belief that an appeal to reason and harmony would have a positive result" (*Buddhism in Sinhalese Society*, 588).

[40] *Tract Society Report*, 35-36. For a detailed account of these petitions and the responses to them see my *The Legacy of the Controversies*, 41-45.

[41] Buddhist writings were of course limited to some extent until they acquired their own printing press in 1862.

[42] For details of this aspect of Buddhist Christian controversies see Young and Somaratna, 51-111; M. S. Vasanthakumar, *The Legacy of the Controversies*, 45-47.

[146] *Kristiyani Prajnapti* was considered a "much dreaded book" by the Buddhists and as Hardy had observed in 1864, "there is now scarcely a single publication issued from the Buddhist press in which there is not some notice of it" (*Jubilee Memorials*, p. 292). After its first publication in 1848, *Kristiyani Prajnapti* was reissued in 1849 and 1853. In 1857 it was issued again at the rate of 2000 copies for each edition. In 1862, Gogerly added to it a long introduction of seventy eight pages. In 1861 another 7000 copies were printed.

[44] T. Kariyawasam, *Religious Activities and the Development of New Poetical Tradition*, 190. T. Kariyawasam goes to the extent of saying that "the revival of the Buddhist interest in their own religion can be entirely and directly assigned to the reaction shown to the compositions of the Rev. D. J. Gogerly" (ibid., 188). In fact, "nearly every religious movement in the different parts of the island owes its origin to the reading of Gogerly's Christian Institutes" (R. S. Hardy, *Missionary Letter*, 30 May 1865).

[45] Cf. J. Selkirk, *Recollections of Ceylon*, 378-379.

[46] Gogerly has cited a passage in the Mahawaga of the Vinaya Pitaka 1.5-1.6.8.

[47] Since Gogerely's Buddhist Scriptures were his own copy from the manuscripts that he found in the temple libraries in the Matara area, the accuracy of his citations naturally depended on the reliability of his manuscripts. Even though only fragments are extant Young and Somaratna remark that "in comparing the citations in the *Prajnapti* with the editions of the Pali Text Society we have discovered only minor discrepancies in a few instances" (Young & Somaratna, 82).

[48] The Majjhima Nikaya (1.168-69), the Samyutta Nikaya (1.137-38), and the Buddhavamsa-atthakatha (11-12) all mention only one entreaty. The Vinaya texts (Mahavagga and Mahapadanna) on the other hand mention three entreaties. Three entreaties are also found in the Mahavastu and the Lalitavistara.

[49] According to Gorgerly, the Pali *sabbannu* and its Sinhalese cognate *sarvajna* mean "he who knows all things." But he had "imposed on the Pali canon a philosophical model of omniscience more congenial to the Judeo-Christian tradition than to Buddhism" (Young & Somaratna, 85).

[50] Ibid., 66. It is their contention that "because the Christian's God required an outward and visible sign to distinguish objects, [and] he did not possess the power of knowing everything" (ibid., 83).

[51] Young and Somaratna, *Vain Debates*, 136. There were similar stories about Jehovah written by the Buddhists. Young and Somaratna mention such a palm leaf manuscript, in which Jehovah is compared to the terrifying Alavaka, whose story is told in the commentary to the *Sutta Nipata*. This was a *yakkha* (demon) who could only be appeased by the sacrifice of human victims until he was converted by the Buddha (ibid., 138).

[52] They pointed out, "It was usual amongst the natives of this country to have a small piece of iron when food was carried from one place to another, and when decoctions were prepared it was customary to tie a string with a piece of iron hanging from it round the pot in which is the medicine. This was done to keep away devils and sundry evil spirits; and that was the meaning of the God of the Hebrews fearing iron chariots (ibid., 69).

[53] For the entire account of Panadura debate see P. Abhayasundara, ed., *Controversy at Panadura*, Colombo.

[54] This is characteristic of the nineteenth century Christian missionaries. As D. King has remarked, the missionaries were "overestimated their success, and in relation to the prospects of the missionary cause, allowed themselves to indulge in hopes which facts have not justified" (*The State and Progress of Jamaica*, 130).

[55] J. R. Davis, points out the difficulties involved in using the famous gospel text John 3:16 to the Thai Buddhists. In the phrase *God so love the world* the word "God" could refer to several things to the Thai Buddhist but not the Christian God. Further, since all desires, good or bad, is bad according to Buddhism and they presupposes relationships and attachments, God loving the world will appear to the Buddhists, like a god or a person prior to the enlightenment. Finally, believing, or trusting is also totally contrast to the Buddhist way of salvation (J. R. Davis, *Poles Apart: Contextualizing the Gospel*, 10-11).

[56] Cf. M. S. Vasanthakumar, "A Christian Supplement to the Buddhist Search: An Exploration of the Book of Ecclesiastes in the Light of Buddha's Four Noble Truths," *Sharing Jesus Holistically in the Buddhist World,* William Carey Library, 2005.

[57] Cf. D. T. Niles, *Eternal Life Now: A Presentation of the Christian Faith to the Buddhists*. Colombo: Ceylon Printers, 1946; T. Weerasingha, *The Cross and the Bo Tree: Communicating the Gospel to the Buddhists*. Taichung: Asia Theological Association, 1989; L. de Silva, *Emergent Theology in the Context of Buddhism*. Colombo: Ecumenical Institute, 1979.

[58] Even some of the missionaries of the colonial era recognised this important truth in communicating the Christian message to the non-Christians. For instance Ricci (1552-1610), an early missionary to China, recognised the need to meet Chinese culture at the religious and philosophical level (Dyrness 1990:125). Likewise, immediately upon their arrival in India William Carey and his colleagues saw that they must understand not only the language but also "the thought world of those to whom the gospel is preached (Neill 1964:264).

[59] Biblical narratives illustrate this well (cf. John 3:4; 4:11). Such examples could be multiplied and so extra caution and additional explanations are necessary when employing non-Christian terms and concepts in Christian message. For Jesus himself explained the terms he had employed in his conversation with Nicodemus and Samaritan woman in great detail (cf. John 3:5-8; 4:13).

[60] An excellent example of this is the way the Tamil Bible translators rendered the Greek *ergon* in their translation. They "purposely avoided the word *karma* to translate the Greek *ergon* (deed), lest the original context of the word *karma* be brought to the memory of the reader" (D. Francis, *The Relevance of Hindu Ethos for Christian Presence*, p. 10). So the term *Kriya* was preferred to *Karma*. Such kind of caution is necessary to avoid possible and potential misunderstandings.

[61] P. Abhayasundara, ed., *Controversy at Panadura*, 63, 73-74.

[62] Buddhists consider this to be the cardinal doctrine of their religion. Hence they say this is "the bedrock of Buddhism… All other teachings of Buddha are intimately connected with it" (G. P. Malalasekera, *The Buddha and His Teachings*, 34). Thus, "with this doctrine… stands or falls the entire Buddhist structure" (Nyanatiloka Mahathrea, *Buddhist Dictionary*, 3).

[63] L. de Silva, "Good News of Salvation to the Buddhists," 450.

[64] Ibid., 451.

[65] Cf. G. Obeyesekere, "The Buddhist Pantheon in Ceylon and Its Extensions." *Anthropological Studies in Theravada Buddhism.* M. Nash, ed. (New Heaven: Yale University of Southeast Asia Studies, 1966), 1-26; R. Gombrich & G. Obeyesekere, *Buddhism Transformed: Religious Change in Sri Lanka* (Delhi: Motilal Banarsidass Publishers, 1990), 65-199; R. Gombrich, *Theravada Buddhism: A Social History from Ancient Benares to Modern Colombo* (London: Routledge, 1996), 146.

[66] R. Gombrich, "The Consecration of a Buddhist Image," 23. The usual offerings to a Buddha image, which may be made at any time, are flowers, lights and incense.

[67] A Monastery is not merely where monks live but the complex of buildings associated with such living quarters. This complex includes a temple containing Buddha images and other religious art.

[68] R. Gombrich, "The Consecration of a Buddhist Image," 23.

[69] This appeal was made by T. Balasuriya in *Daily News* 11 May 1969, Quoted in E. J. Harris, "Building Friendship between Buddhists and Christians: An Exploration," 37.

[70] Ibid., 38.

[71] Cf. E. J. Harris, "Of Conversion and Evangelism: Reflection from Sri Lanka," 4, 8.

[72] The author has encountered such attitudes in personal conversations with evangelical Christians in Sri Lanka. These standpoints can be witnessed in contemporary evangelical gospel presentations.

[73] According to Romans 1 idolatry and immorality are the natural consequences of the total or partial rejection of the divine revelation.

[74] The Bible explicitly states that human beings are created in the image of God (Gen. 1:26-27). Though the Fall has affected the divine image to a considerable extent (Gen. 3), it is not totally destroyed by human sin but distorted because of it. Even after the fall human beings are depicted as possessors of the divine image (Gen. 9:6, Jas. 3:9).

[75] According to Psalm 19:1, Romans 1:18-20 God has revealed himself both in creation and in human conscience. Paul says that the non-Jewish communities had divine laws inscribed in their hearts (Rom. 2:14-15). The similarities between the ethical precepts of Moses and Hamurabi were also due to this phenomenon.

[76] In Acts 17:22 the Greek word translated as 'religious' (*deisidaimonesterous*) could be used either in good or bad sense. The KJV rendering 'Ye are too superstitious' implies criticism. Hence "it is an unlikely way to start an evangelistic speech" (A. Fernando, *Acts: The NIV Application Commentary*, p. 475). F. F. Bruce, however, citing an ancient writer Lucian, says, it cannot be a complimentary expression, for "it was forbidden to use complimentary exordia in addressing the Areopagus court, with the hope of securing its goodwill" (F. F. Bruce, *The Books of Acts: The New International Commentary*, 355). Nevertheless, we cannot be certain on how far Paul was abiding by this prohibition and the NIV rendering is more positive. Moreover, the Athenians' reputation for religious piety is well attested (W.J. Larkin, *Acts: The IVP New Testament Commentaries*, 255). Hence Paul was expressing commendation in his address, as K. Grayston has pointed out, "to provide a way into his address that would engage the attention of the audience" (Quoted in I. H. Marshall, *Acts: Tyndale New Testament Commentaries*, 285).

[77] L. de Silva, a Methodist minister of Sri Lanka, was actively involved in promoting Christian-Buddhist dialogue for three decades until his death in 1981. He served as the director of the Ecumenical Institute in Colombo. It was de Silva who introduced Buddhist studies as well as Buddhist-Christian dialogue as a central concern of the institute.

[78] For instance, he equates the Buddhist concept of rebirth with Christian hope of resurrection. And his theory of progressive sanctification almost teaches universalism.

[79] For a critical examination of de Silva's missiology se my *Christian Mission and its Christological Messages: An Examination and Evaluation of Selected Asian Attempts to Communicate the Christian Faith in Buddhist and Hindu Contexts*, Unpublished MA Dissertation, England: All Nations Christian College, 1997.

[80] A. Peiris, the editor of the Dialogue since the death of L. de Silva, has contributed much to the liberation theology and Buddhist-Christian relationship. In 1974, he founded Tulana Research Centre to foster Buddhist-Christian understanding.

[81] Cf. A. Peiris, "Does Christ Have a Place in Asia? A Panoramic View" in *Any Room for Christ in Asia?"* Leonard Boff & Virgil Elizondo ed., London/Maryknoll: SCM Press/Orbis, 1993.

[82] A. Peiris' theology is found in *Asian Theology of Liberation*. Maryknoll: Orbis, 1988, *Love Meets Wisdom: A Christian Experience of Buddhism*. Maryknoll: Orbis, 1988, and *Fire and Water: Basic Issues in Asian Buddhism and Christianity*. Maryknoll: Orbis, 1996.

[83] An evangelical critique of A. Peiris' theology is made in V. Ramachandara, *The Recovery of Mission: Beyond the Pluralist Paradigm* (Carlisle: Paternoster, 1996), 38-70.

[84] A. Peiris, "Inculturation in Asia: A Theological Reflection on an Experience" in *Concilium*, (November-December 1994).

[85] The Four Noble Truths are the fundamentals of Buddhism. This comes from the initial sermon of the Buddha after his enlightenment known as *Dhamma-cakka-pavattana-sutta* (setting in motion the wheel of truth) and recorded in the *Samyutta-nikaya* LVI.

4

Gentle Strength and *Upāya*: Christian and Buddhist Ministry Models

Russell H. Bowers, Jr.

Introduction

Every religion seeks to spread itself. Christianity and Buddhism are no exceptions. Convinced adherents naturally try to share the gospel or *dharma* with the uninitiated. But how do they go about doing that? Are their philosophies of ministry similar? Just as the messages of the two faiths display superficial similarities perched atop deep philosophical differences so may the methods (Bowers 1995:140-144). And, just as learning the *what* of Buddhism can help Christians understand themselves as well as Buddhists, so may reflecting on the *how*. Many Christians would no doubt benefit from contemplating the *how*, since the contradictory practices of different churches (and the meager results of some) suggest inattention to the question.

So then, how should Christians seek to minister to their Buddhist neighbors? Some reply that the biblical Christian is like a strongman with bulging muscles and icy stare. He is not intimidated by, nor does he cede the smallest territory to, those outside his faith.

The minister as strongman

For example, the Cambodian church continues to mushroom numerically since its legalization in 1990. New converts from Buddhist-animism often wonder how they should now relate to family members and neighbors who continue to practice a faith so different from Christianity. Some pastors, fearing that they will be criticized by fellow pastors as compromisers if they maintain cordial relations with Buddhists, urge their congregations to sever all ties with the past, withdraw to Christian enclaves, and openly ridicule the *sangha* and the *dharma*. The Christian, they say, is strong and uncompromising in matters of faith.

Others are not so sure. How can we attract converts if our attitude repels them? In a society that values respect, how can disrespect encourage acceptance? Isolation in believing ghettos only reinforces the notion that Christianity is a foreign faith. Rejection and ridicule only harden people to defend their heritage and dignity. Maybe the strongman is not such a good image after all. Perhaps Paul's description of himself as "a nursemaid caring for her little children"(1 Th. 2:7) is more appropriate.

Actually, both images are useful, though neither tells the whole story. Each conveys *some* truth about how faithful Christians

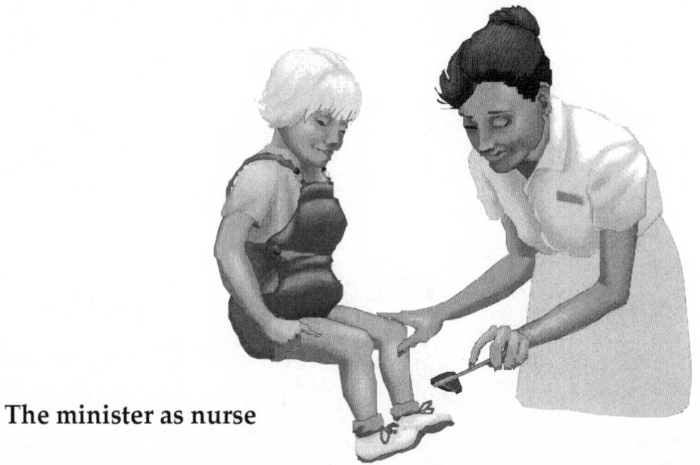

The minister as nurse

behave, but each picture needs to be modified by the other. The Christian minister must be *both* strong *and* gentle.

To sharpen our focus on this biblical approach that tempers strength with gentleness, we may ask how it compares with the Buddhist ideal of *upāya*. The Sanskrit word *upāya* describes a Buddha's or *bodhisattva's* skillful use of various means—stories, parables, similes, or actions—to explain the *dharma* to the unenlightened. *Upāya* is the "father of buddhas and bodhisattvas."[1] It implies an impetus to teach, perceptivity into the hearer's spiritual acumen, and wisdom in choosing the best method to awaken and inform her mind. Those raised in the West, for example, assume a worldview quite different from the Buddhist one, so they will need time and effort to grasp the core of the *dharma*. Hence the *bodhisattva* will start with the pupil where she is, and gradually, skillfully lead her to understanding. The twin concepts of the *bodhisattva* and *upāya* have accelerated Mahayana's missionary success.

Adapting the message to the hearer in this way may seem to parallel the biblical ideal of gentleness. But, although parallels do exist and lessons may be learned from Buddhist *upāya*, significant differences warn us not to equate this approach with biblical Gentle Strength and embrace it *carte blanche*.

A Christian Ministry Model: Gentle Strength

This chapter will discuss Gentle Strength (i.e., Strong for the Truth, Gentle with People) as the biblical model for ministry to non-Christians. It will then introduce the Buddhist ideal of *upāya*, and finally suggest why the former excels the latter.

Strong for the Truth

Christianity is not a weak faith. The Bible calls for strength on the part of its followers in at least three ways: discernment, decisiveness, and deeds. To put it differently, believers are to be strong in mind, strong in will, and strong in action.

Discernment: The Bible rules out both the blending of incompatible belief systems into a tertium quid on the one hand, and the assertion that (since no system is inherently true or false) any one will do on the other. Rather, the Christian must be strong in mind to distinguish truth from error. Both syncretism and philosophical pluralism entail an intellectual laxity (to say nothing of a volitional weakness) resulting in a bland acceptance of (almost) everything. But mutually-exclusive propositions cannot simultaneously be true. Critical strength of mind is required to discern truth from error, or better from best; and strength of will to opt unequivocally for what one discovers to be truth, even when popular opinion demands otherwise.

Biblical passages that urge such discernment are numerous. Here are a few. 1 Thessalonians 5:19-21 outlines the wise response when encountering new teaching ("prophecies"). First, do not ignore it (i.e., put out the Spirit's fire by treating it with contempt). But second, do not uncritically swallow it; *test* what is said. Third, hold onto whatever you find in it to be good, and shun whatever is wrong (evil).

One audience that profitably followed this method was the Berean Jews (Ac. 17:10-15). When Paul and Silas introduced the news about Jesus, the Bereans did not ignore it. But neither did they mindlessly accept it. Rather, they received the message with great eagerness and proceeded to test it scripturally. As a consequence many believed.

Doctrinal discernment extends not only to one's initial decision to choose between Christianity and another faith, but later to distinguish between fraudulent and genuine forms of Christianity. The apostle John warned his readers not to "believe every spirit, but [to] test the spirits to see whether they are from God, because many false prophets have gone out into the world" (1 Jn. 4:1). There is every danger that Christians might be "led astray from [their] sincere and pure devotion to Christ" and follow "a Jesus other than the Jesus [the apostles] preached" (2 Cor. 11:3-4), or desert "the one who called you by the grace of Christ and [turn] to a different gospel—which is really no gospel at all" (Gal. 1:6-7). Christians must stop thinking like children and think like adults (1 Cor. 14:20).

Discernment is not a once-for-all *satori*-like experience, but a continual and ever more finely-tuned exercise throughout individual and corporate Christian life. That is why Paul prayed that the Philippians' love "abound more and more in knowledge and depth of insight, so that [they] may be able to discern what is best..." (Phil. 1:9). Here discernment has moved beyond deciding between the truth claims of Christianity versus a non-Christian religion, and between a bogus and a genuine Christianity, to deciding out of a field of "good" options what is "best." The point for this paper is that Christianity throughout calls for strength of mind to discern truth and excellence from error and mediocrity. It does not pretend all ways are equal.

Decisiveness: Once the truth is discerned, God does not want Christians to be half-hearted for it. He wants us to neither sit on both sides of the fence, nor to have both feet firmly planted in midair. The Bible throughout calls for a strong, decisive, unambiguous commitment. Mature Christianity is not for the faint of heart.

Some verses suggest that God would rather people be strong in their commitment—even if it is to an errant belief system—than wishy-washy. Joshua wanted Israel to choose their god, even if that meant another than Yahweh (Josh. 24:14-15). Elijah urged an indecisive Israel to go ahead and serve Baal if he truly were god, but by all means to stop wavering between two opinions (1 Ki. 18:21). Jesus wished the Laodiceans were either hot or cold (Rev. 3:15). If the resurrection is not true we should "eat and drink, for tomorrow we die" (1 Cor. 15:30). Significance in the kingdom is reserved for those who decisively deny themselves, "hate" their natural relatives, take up their cross, and follow (Lk. 9:23-27; 14:26-27). It does not follow those indecisive souls who put their hand to the plow and then look back (Lk. 9:62). Being a Christian means being a Christian, not being a Christian and worshiping the spirits at the same time.

Deeds: Having exercised critical strength of mind to discern the truth and decisive strength of will to side with it, the Christian is urged to demonstrate active strength of engagement. She is to live for the truth.

This is true, first, for all of life in general. But in particular the Bible requires the Christian community to stand against error. Being strong for the truth entails being strong against wrong. When Judaizers sought to compel circumcision and observance of the Law, Paul and Barnabas entered into "sharp dispute and debate with them" (Acts 15:2). Apparently, errant ideas aroused in the apostles an urgency to oppose them. This is because false teaching is not an innocuous difference of opinion on ethereal matters. Rather it can both destroy the faith of individuals and ruin whole households (1 Tim. 2:18; Tit. 1:11). Only by watching his doctrine closely can the Lord's servant save both himself and his hearers (1 Tim. 4:16). Consequently early church leaders did not smilingly welcome wrong doctrine and practice but vigorously opposed them, even if doing so meant publicly opposing the chief of the apostles (Gal. 2:11). The glorified Lord commended Ephesus for exposing false apostles. By contrast he rebuked Pergamum for having people who held to the teaching of Balaam and the Nicolaitans, and Thyatira for tolerating "that woman Jezebel" who called herself a prophetess (Rev. 2:2-20). Swerving from true doctrine can lead to loss of reward, and welcoming those who teach it entails sharing in their wicked work (2 Jn. 7-11). Early church leaders felt compelled to urge their followers to "contend for the faith that was once for all entrusted to the saints" (Jude 3).

Underlying Assumptions: At least three assumptions underlie this desideratum: 1) there is such a thing as truth in religion, 2) truth matters, and 3) truth can be known (even if not perfectly or exhaustively).

That there is such a thing as truth in religious matters is contested in pluralist and postmodern societies. Defending the affirmative lies outside the scope of this article. I will simply assume that, just as there are objective, non-negotiable answers to such questions as, "Does two plus two equal four?" and "In what year did George Washington die?", there are similar answers to such questions as, "Did Jesus of Nazareth physically rise from the dead?" and "Does throwing rice in the wat feed and pacify the ghosts of my ancestors?"

If there is such a thing as truth and, as a consequence, such a thing as error, then it seems natural to conclude that truth matters. Just as a bridge that is built on the belief that two plus two equals three may face collapse, so a life that is built on wrong (even if sincere) religious or metaphysical beliefs may be headed for disaster. Hosea lamented that God's people were destroyed for lack of knowledge; and Jesus said it was the truth that would set people free (Hos. 4:6; Jn. 8:32).

But the existence and importance of religious or metaphysical truth would hardly matter if that truth were abstruse. The Bible does affirm that God's thoughts vastly surpass human thoughts (Isa.

55:8-9; 1 Cor. 1:25). Nevertheless, he has made the essence of his plan so plain (Deut 30:11-14 [cited in Rom 10:5-13]; 2 Tim 3:15; cf. Mic 6:6-8) that a child serves as the model for entrance into the kingdom (Mt. 18:2-3). God in his grace has so revealed himself in nature, conscience, history, scripture, and Christ, that people may know him truly, even if imperfectly and not exhaustively. Sufficient and true religious truth is accessible to the masses.

To summarize: There are such things as truth and error in religious teachings. The biblical Christian needs to be strong in mind to discern the truth, strong in will to commit himself exclusively to it, and strong in action to promote the truth and expose error. The strongman does in fact represent one aspect of Christian leadership and ministry.

Gentle with People

But does the strongman tell the whole story? In particular, *how* should strength be displayed? The Christian minister is clearly to be strong vis-à-vis the truth. But what is her demeanor toward *people*?

The General Pattern: The general pattern is gentleness. Both by prescription and example, the New Testament urges gentleness as the manner in which to commend truth and expose error. The scriptures do not promote a proud, prickly approach to proclamation.

2 Timothy 2:23-26. Paul's second epistle to Timothy is probably his last surviving letter. In it the apostle instructs his protégé how to carry on the ministry after he himself is gone. The letter introduces the pattern of tempering strength for the truth with gentleness toward people.

The idea of strength emerges early when Paul says that God did not give us a spirit of timidity. Therefore Timothy should not be ashamed to speak about the Lord, but willing to join Paul in suffering for the gospel (1:7-8). He must keep the pattern of sound teaching, and guard the good deposit that was entrusted to him

(1:13-14). Strong in God's grace, Timothy is repeatedly to pass on that deposit (2:1-2, 14a), taking care to handle accurately the word of truth (2:15). Occupied thus with good teaching, he should shun foolish arguments (2:14a, 16, 23).

But *how* should Timothy pursue this ministry of strength for the truth?

> [T]he Lord's servant must not quarrel; instead, he must be kind to everyone, able to teach, not resentful. Those who oppose him he must gently instruct, in the hope that God will grant them repentance leading them to a knowledge of the truth, and that they will come to their senses and escape from the trap of the devil, who has taken them captive to do his will (2:24-26).

Μαξομαι means first to fight physically, and second to fight verbally: *quarrel, wrangle, and dispute*. It implies a serious conflict—intensive and bitter. Such combativeness the servant of the Lord must renounce. Rather, he or she must be ηπιον. The word means *gentle*, and is used to describe the way a mother cares for her little children (1 Th. 2:7). She is not harsh but patient, even when they require firm instruction or correction. Here is where the image of the nurse calming her young patient, rather than the strongman wielding his barbell, is appropriate. Further, the Christian minister must be ανεχικακοφ, *not resentful*—that is, *able to endure difficulties without becoming angry or upset*. Rejecting resentment, the strong servant of the scriptures *gently* instructs his opponents. The word behind *gently* is πραυτηφ, *gentleness of attitude and behavior in contrast with harshness in one's dealings with others*.

Chapter 4 offers a reprise of this pattern of Strong for the Truth, Gentle with People. In view of the wickedness of the last days and the persecution that awaits the godly (2 Tim. 3), as well as the proclivity of people to prefer smooth talk to sound teaching (4:3-4), the Christian leader is to preach the word (i.e., be strong for the truth) (4:2). He must capitulate neither to evil nor to the spirit of the age. But again we ask, *how* is he to preach the word? "With great patience and careful instruction." The word behind *patience* is not υπομονη *perseverance*, but μακροθυμια *longsuffering*, the prolonged restraint of θυμοφ (*passion, anger, rage*). Μακροθυμια is "a state of emotional calm in the face of provocation or misfortune and without complaint or irritation" (Louw and Nida 2001:167). Timothy and his successors are urged not to fly off the handle against antagonists, but to suffer long their calumny or ridicule; not to rant, scold, or wax sarcastic, but to reply with *careful instruction*. Uncompromising commitment to the truth neither requires nor implies reckless behavior toward opponents. Strong for the truth but gentle with people.

1 Peter 3:15-16. Peter parallels Paul's prescription. "Strong for the truth" is communicated in Peter's opening directives that his readers should 1) in their hearts set apart Christ as lord, and 2) always be prepared to explain and defend their hope. Strength for the truth is displayed first in unwavering decisiveness to follow Christ, and second in clarity of mind and boldness of character to render an απολογια for their faith. Critics will often ask for a λογοφ, a *logical discourse* or *reason*, for the hope that we have; Christians should be prepared and strong to give an απολογια, a speech in defense of themselves.

"Gentle with people" follows in the apostle's instructions regarding *how* this strong, reasoned defense is to be made: "with gentleness and respect…." For "gentleness" Peter employs the same πραυτηφ that Paul did in 1 Thessalonians 2. The word is used eleven times in the NT: 1 Cor. 4:21; 2 Cor. 10:1; Gal. 5:23; 6:1; Eph. 4:2; Col. 3:12; 2 Tim. 2:25; Tit. 3:2; Jas. 1:21; 3:13; 1 Pet. 3:16. The word translated "respect" is φοβοφ. *Phobos* stands behind the English word "phobia" and all its compounds, and in classical times could be used for the panic that prompts flight. It could also denote profound awe for deity. Because of who God is, people approach him with fear and respect. That is the kind of attitude we should have toward other people, even those who question our Christian faith. We should neither be flippant, sarcastic, haughty, nor disinterested. Paul suggests the same when he teaches that we should "show true humility toward all men" (Tit. 3:2), and James when he warns against cursing men (Js. 3:9-12).

Reasons to Deal Gently: But why be gentle? Why not be strong in our dealings with people, just as we are strong in our commitment to the truth? The Bible suggests several reasons:

We also have weaknesses. In describing Old Testament worship, Hebrews says that the high priest "is able to deal gently with those who are ignorant and are going astray, since he himself is subject to weakness" (Heb. 5:2). Recalling our own sinfulness is good medicine against the malady of hubris. Paul echoes this sentiment when, in the context of urging peaceable ness, consideration, humility, and rejection of slander, he muses that "[a]t one time we too were foolish, disobedient, deceived and enslaved by all kinds of passions and pleasures. We lived in malice and envy, being hated and hating one another" (Tit. 3:3). Both our present weaknesses and past follies should incline us toward humility and the gentle treatment of those who are themselves going astray.

Others may be right. Some Christians believe that they have all the truth and only the truth, whereas others hold exclusively to error. Neither is true. Abraham is one of the most revered Old Testament figures. He was the founder of the Jewish nation and is "the father of all who believe" (Rom. 4:11-12, 16-17). His faith made him the friend of God (Js. 2:23). Yet these did not make him always right.

On one occasion Abraham moved to Gerar. The patriarch lied about his wife, and Sarah ended up in Abimelech's harem. To rectify this situation, God did not speak to Abraham but, of all people, to a Philistine king (Gen. 20:1; 21:22, 34)! Through his lack of faith and reliance on unethical stratagems, Abraham had rendered himself incapable of hearing God's voice on resolving the present crisis. God instead warned Abimelech, who immediately restored Sarah, and tacitly rebuked Abraham in the process. Abraham, the believer, the covenant partner, the friend of God and father of all who believe, only heard God's voice on this occasion through the mouth of a pagan, Philistine king. He had acted deviously because he falsely assumed, as Christians sometimes do today, that there was "no fear of God in this place" (Gen. 20:11).

This instance is not unique. Josiah was a godly Judean king, who "did what was right in the eyes of Yahweh and walked in the ways of his father David, not turning aside to the right or to the left" (2 Chr. 34:1). He presided over a Passover celebration unlike any that had been celebrated since the days of the Judges (2 Ki. 23:22-23; 2 Chr. 35:1-19). His zeal led to the assessment that "[n]either before nor after Josiah was there a king like him who turned to Yahweh as he did—with all his heart and with all his soul and with all his strength, in accordance with all the Law of Moses" (2 Ki. 23:25).

By contrast, the Pharaohs of Egypt are not generally portrayed as paragons of spirituality. Yet when Neco marched out to fight Babylon, he warned Josiah with these words not to oppose him: "God has told me to hurry; so stop opposing God, who is with me, or he will destroy you." Tragically, the text records that Josiah "would not listen to what Neco had said *at God's command* but went to fight him on the plain of Megiddo." He was shot by archers and died (2 Chr. 35: 20-24). The godly king had refused to listen to God's voice coming from an unexpected source.

Jesus observed that "the people of this world are more shrewd in dealing with their own kind than are the people of the light" (Jude 8-10). Proverbs counsels listening to ants (Prov. 6:6-11). Even donkeys and stones may on occasion have things to say (Num. 22:28; Lk. 19:40). Only if we have more faith and a closer walk with God than did Abraham, and more zeal for Yahweh than did Josiah, can we afford to ignore those outside our community of faith. Though the believing community may be the usual channel of divine communication, it may not be the only.

Abusive speech is the tool of false teachers. Although some people confuse the loudness of a speaker's voice with the logic of her words, the two are unrelated. Slander and abusive speech are the tools of false teachers, who employ them to mask the weakness of their arguments and persuade the simple-minded. It is "godless men" and "dreamers" who "slander [even] celestial beings" and "speak abusively against whatever they do not understand." They stand in sharp contrast with the archangel Michael, who dared not bring a slanderous accusation against even so obvious an enemy as Satan (Jude 8-10).

Peaceful words coupled with godly living is the wise pattern. On the contrary, the wise teacher controls his tongue, not using it to "curse men, who have been made in God's likeness." He demonstrates his wisdom "by his good life, by deeds done in the humility that comes from wisdom." Heavenly wisdom is neither envious nor ambitious; but pure, peace-loving, and considerate (Js. 3:9-18).

Jesus dealt gently. This is the way Jesus ministered. In seeking to characterize Jesus' ministry Matthew cited Isaiah:

> Here is my servant whom I have chosen, the one I love, in whom I delight; I will put my Spirit on him, and he will proclaim justice to the nations. He will not quarrel or cry out; no one will hear his voice in the streets. A bruised reed he will not break, and a smoldering wick he will not snuff out, till he leads justice to victory. In his name the nations will put their hope (Mt. 12:18-21, cf Is. 42:1-4).

Verse 19 was not intended to suggest utter silence, for the previous verse speaks of his proclaiming justice. Rather, the picture is one "of gentleness and humility (11:29), of quiet withdrawal … and a presentation of his messiahship that is neither arrogant nor brash" (Carson nd). When Peter wants to epitomize Jesus' ministry, he talks about "how God anointed Jesus of Nazareth with the Holy Spirit and power, and how he went around doing good and healing" (Ac. 10:38). Jesus was not characteristically confrontational.

When to Break the Pattern: There were, however, occasions when Jesus did speak harshly. In Matthew 23 he pronounced seven woes against the teachers of the law and Pharisees, whom he named hypocrites, sons of hell, blind guides and fools, whitewashed tombs, snakes, and a brood of vipers. This is not exactly the Dale Carnegie approach. In addition to Jesus, one can think of Elijah with the prophets of Baal (1 Ki. 18:27), Paul with Elymas (Ac. 13:9-11), and Isaiah with idol worshippers (Isa. 44:9-20). Why this dramatic departure from the designated design?

One key seems to be that the recipients of harsh critique are those who should have known better. The lawyers and Pharisees had long studied God's law; their godlessness was the result not of lack of opportunity but of willful misreading. Elymas was a Jew who also should have had access to the truth, but who instead turned to false prophecy and sorcery. Paul's treatment of him differed strikingly from the lack of personal invective against the pagans in Acts 14:11-18. The Israelites whom Elijah confronted should have known Yahweh. The idolaters Isaiah satirized had failed to engage in the most basic kind of thinking (see esp. Isa. 44:19-20). The culpability of these thus exposes them to rebuke rather than entreaty.

Second, the objects of censure were often not simply self-deluded, but were leading others astray. The lawyers and Pharisees were not just blind, but blind *guides*. Elymas was deterring Sergius Paulus from the truth. Paul personally opposed Peter in the presence of others (implying a possible loss of face for Peter) because "other Jews joined him in his hypocrisy" and "even Barnabas was led astray" (Gal. 2:11-13). He later urged Titus to sharply rebuke legalists "because they are ruining whole households" (Tit. 1:10-13).

We may conclude that the general pattern for ministry—certainly the initial approach—is that of gentleness. This is what the prescriptive passages teach and many historical pericopes illustrate. There are, however, occasions when people so culpably and actively embrace error that *they* must be opposed as strongly as the doctrines they espouse.

Three Mechanics of Gentleness

The preferred procedure, however, and the one that should be followed first, is to distinguish between a false teaching and the person who happens to hold it. The former is the problem; the latter is not.

Separate the Person from the Problem: In their seminal work on negotiation, Fisher, Ury, and Patton devote a chapter to separating the person from the problem. They remind us that negotiators are people first, and that every negotiator has two kinds of interests—substantive and relational. The chapter considers the issues of perception, emotion, communication, and prevention, and concludes by asserting, "Separating the people from the problem is not something you can do once and forget about; you have to keep working at it. The basic approach is to deal with the people as human beings and with the problem on its own merits" (1991:39).

McGrath picks up this attitude toward negotiating business differences and adapts it to Christian apologetics. He suggests the following:

> Suppose you are talking to a lifelong atheist about his ideas. The superficial agenda may be about whether or not God exists. But beneath the surface, there may be a conflict going on within this person, unnoticed. Thoughts like this might be flashing through his mind: "I've been an atheist for twenty-five years now. That's a long time. And everyone knows that I'm an atheist. If I change my mind now, people will laugh at me. I'll lose face. My personal reputation is tied up with my atheistic views. I'm locked into this situation. Somehow, my atheism and my personal identity have become mixed up with each other. If I change my mind on this one, I'll somehow be condemning my whole past." The apologist can very easily reinforce such prejudices through a tactless and insensitive approach to the matter (McGrath 1993:88).

To reduce the likelihood of exacerbating the problem, McGrath suggests first separating the people from the problem, and then making it easy for them to change their minds.

Scripture tacitly commends this approach. Returning to 2 Timothy 2:24-26, we note that Paul urges gentle treatment of the erring *person* in the hope that he will abandon his wrong *ideas*. The enemy in this case is the devil who has ensnared those who oppose apostolic doctrine. Gentle instruction and God's intervention may open the eyes of the blinded to see and accept the truth. Second Corinthians 4:1-6 takes much the same tack. Paul talks about how the god of this age has blinded the minds of unbelievers. He is therefore the problem, as well as the doctrine he espouses. The proper response is to set forth the truth plainly and commend oneself to every man's conscience, preaching Jesus as Lord and themselves as servants. Both the above phrases fit the template of being strong for the truth yet gentle on people.

Gentleness may seem to be merely an attitude, a demeanor that is hard to quantify or prescribe. While it is these, there are procedures that can be used to assure a gentle, user-friendly approach. Separating the person from the problem is one. Listening before speaking, and using familiar terms are two more. Taken together they promote a sense that the speaker is not so self-satisfied that he spouts his speech with a careless, "Take it or leave it."

Listen Before Speaking: "He who answers before listening—that is his folly and his shame" (Prov. 18:13). There is wisdom in hearing and understanding another before talking with her, especially if the speaker wishes to discuss worldview or religion. Failure to do so may lead to incomprehension at best and needless offense at worst.

Paul practiced this approach by not just looking, but looking *carefully* at the Athenians' shrines before addressing the Areopagus (Acts 17:23). This occasion reflected his overall strategy of becoming all things to all people so as to win as many as possible.

His goal was not to detachedly dump a load of words on an audience, but to win as many converts as possible (1 Cor. 9:19-22).

There are what may be called "[s]tandard techniques of good listening." These are

> to pay close attention to what is said, to ask the other party to spell out carefully and clearly exactly what they mean, and to request that ideas be repeated if there is any ambiguity or uncertainty. Make it your task while listening not to phrase a response, but to understand them as they see themselves. Take in their perceptions, their needs, and their constraints (Fisher, Ury and Patton 1991:34).

Such active, detailed listening does not imply agreement with what is being said.

> Understanding is not agreeing. One can at the same time understand perfectly and disagree completely with what the other side is saying. But unless you can convince them that you do grasp how they see it, you may be unable to explain your viewpoint to them. Once you have made their case for them, then come back with the problems you find in their proposal (:35).

We may, in fact, disagree vehemently with another and yet do well to listen and understand.

> The reason [entering into another's worldview] is important is that we want to get at the facts. What Hitler thought and felt and did were facts. The inner facts about Hitler help to explain a lot of the outer ones, and we need to know the inner Hitler as well as we can, if we wish to understand the terrible history of those times. Likewise if we wish to explore the nature of Buddhism we need to get at the meanings which are held by the Buddhist texts and Buddhist people. *Our* views are not facts about *them*, but facts about us. Later, when we have found what Buddhist Buddhism is we can shape our own (Smart 1987:4).

Present Christ in Familiar Terms: Those who place high value on their content but little on their audience often couch their message in forms familiar to themselves, regardless of whether they communicate. Who cares if I have made what I have to say attractive, comprehensible, or relevant to my listeners? I have made my grand speech. What I said was clear enough to me. If they want to get it, they will simply have to work harder.

Perhaps this overstates the case. But the effective communicator—the gentle communicator—will master her audience as well as her subject. She will then tailor the latter to fit the former. Gentleness with people entails understanding them and easing their work of listening.

Recently I attended a meeting for rural Asian pastors, many illiterate, some from restrictive political contexts. These were people hungry for encouragement and instruction. The seminar, organized by a wealthy, well-known Western evangelistic organization, was convened in our capital city. No doubt the organization's intentions were noble. But when the keynote speaker orated through translation about their live satellite simulcasts to a litany of alliterated national names, he left his audience in a fog, and hungry still. By contrast, he was followed by a local leader who talked for three or four minutes: "Brothers, some of us know how to use the toilets, and others do not. Those who do must not laugh at those of us who do not, but rather help them learn. And here in the city, it is impolite to spit on the walls or floor of the hotel. I know some of you do that in your villages, but here is not a good testimony to do so. If you have to spit, use your bathroom or go outside, but do not spit on the walls or floor of the hotel." The latter knew his audience. His address, though lacking the erudition and polish of the first, accomplished much more.

God has worked not only to communicate with humanity, but to make his communication plain. This is a major purpose of the incarnation. No one has ever "seen" God in his essence and glory—with either the physical eye or the eye of the mind. The best we can hope for is that he put us in a cleft in the rock and cover us with his hand until he has passed by. Then he can remove his hand so we can "see" his back, but never his face (Jn. 1:18; Ex. 33:22-23). Because God in his nature and character excels us—living "in unapproachable light"—no one has seen or can see him (1 Tim. 6:16). The incarnation was God's method of communicating himself in a form humanity could grasp. "God, the One and Only, who is at the Father's side, has made him known" (Jn.1:18).

Jesus spoke in familiar terms—talking about wells and water with the woman of Sychar; seeds, weeds, and crops with his agricultural audiences. Paul dressed his identical message in different clothing when speaking to Jews and Greeks, making it easy for each group to hear (Compare Acts 13:14–43 with Acts 17:16–34). Gentleness with people entails fitting our message to our hearers.

Dealing With Opponents

Ministering in such a way that we are strong for the truth but gentle with its adversaries is likely to raise opposition. Non-Christians will most likely object to our being strong for the truth; whereas fellow Christians may suspect that a gentle approach constitutes compromise. How should we handle these objections?

Non-Christian Opponents: Most religions are exclusivistic. Even those like Baha'i that urge the value of all religions reject the exclusive claims of any particular one, insisting that their all-embracive approach alone is valid. The exclusive claims of Christ will inevitably clash with adherents of other faiths and ideologies.

When this happens we may recall that it is not necessary to be combative when opposing error, even though we don't believe that error. Daniel 3 records neither sarcasm nor vitriol when Hananiah, Mishael, and Azariah rejected Nebuchadnezzar's decree to worship his golden image. They simply stated their commitment to Yahweh, and consequent refusal to bow to any other god. Three chapters later, Darius outlawed prayer except to himself. Daniel made no public scene in response, but simply continued his own faithful practice. When Festus raised his voice and accused Paul of insanity, the apostle did not reply in kind. He merely answered that what he was saying was "true and reasonable," respectfully addressing him as "most excellent Festus" (Acts 13:14-43 cf. Acts 17:16-34). More strikingly, when the cured Namaan apologized in advance for bowing down (in body, not in heart) with the king in the temple of Rimmon, the uncompromising Elisha told him, "Go in peace"(2 Ki. 5:15-19). All of these disagreed without being disagreeable.

Christian Opponents: By contrast, Christians are more likely to object to a gentleness that seems to get evangelists too close to their unbelieving audiences, sniffing compromise somewhere. His foes repeatedly accused Jesus of befriending tax collectors and sinners, forgetting that it is the sick who need a physician (e.g., Mt. 9:10-13), and failing to grasp the depth of God's love for the lost and the lengths he goes to retrieve them (Lk. 15:1-2). Jewish Christians criticized Peter for eating with the uncircumcised. The apostle had to detail for them the certainty of God's summons to visit Cornelius and the latter's subsequent conversion (Acts 11:1-18). In view of these precedents, it is not surprising that some Christians today criticize others for getting too close to outsiders they are trying to reach.

When this happens, each side should extend the benefit of the doubt to the other, recalling that in this disputable matter as in others, Christians may in good faith adopt different positions. Unless compromise or sin is clearly and biblically at stake, Christians should restrain from despising or condemning others whose practice is different. Each will one day give an account of himself, not of others (Rom. 14:1-15:4).

A Buddhist Ministry Model: Skill-in-Means

Gentleness without strength robs us of a sure message that addresses either our pains in this life or our prospects for the next. Strength without gentleness builds walls around rather than doorways into the hearts of our hearers. The effective, biblical minister will embody both—the strength of discernment, decisiveness, and deeds when the issue is truth; the gentleness of separating, listening, and adapting when the issue is presenting that truth to people.

Specifically, those who serve in Christ's name must distinguish between being strong in the Christian faith and being arrogant in the way they present it. They need to act differently toward mistaken ideas and the people who believe them. We must uncompromisingly hold to our faith while respecting those who embrace another. It is crucial to learn humility and the ability to listen even when we are convinced that we hold to the truth. Such an attitude suggests that Christians should engage with non-Christians whenever possible rather than withdrawing in isolation from them.

In Christian theology, even though God's thoughts far outdistance our own, the essence of his plan is plain enough to be understood by children. The clarity and ubiquity of God's self-revelation renders those who reject it culpable (Rom 1:18–23) This doctrine of the perspicuity of the scriptures contrasts with the Buddha's warning about the opacity of the *dharma*.

The Need for Skill-in-Means: The Inaccessibility of the Dharma

The Lotus Sutra is an early Mahāyāna text in which a divinized, eternal Buddha invites all other beings to join him in full enlightenment. The problem delaying this process is that his teaching is so hard to grasp.

> The wisdom of the Buddhas is infinitely profound and immeasurable. The door to this wisdom is difficult to

> understand and difficult to enter.... If pratyekabuddhas, acute in understanding, without outflows, in their last incarnation, should fill the worlds in the ten directions, as numerous as bamboos in a grove, though they should join together with one mind for a million or for countless kalpas, hoping to conceive of the Buddha's true wisdom, they could not understand the smallest part of it (Lotus Sutra Chapter 2).

Difficult as this teaching is, the Buddha himself has attained it: "I also announce to you, Shariputra, that this profound subtle and wonderful Law without outflows, incomprehensible, I have now attained in full. Only I understand its characteristics, and the Buddhas of the ten directions do likewise" (Lotus Sutra Chapter 2). Fortunately, this otherwise incomprehensible dharma may be elucidated by the Buddha through *upāya*, his skillful use of means.

> I announce this to the assembly of voice-hearers and to those who seek the vehicle of the pratyekabuddha; I have enabled people to escape the bonds of suffering and to attain nirvana. The Buddha, through the power of expedient means, has shown them the teachings of the three vehicles prying living beings loose from this or that attachment and allowing them to attain release (Lotus Sutra Chapter 2).

Only through parable, similes, and other skillful means may ordinary people learn the dharma and escape suffering: "This Law is not something that can be understood through pondering or analysis. Only those who are Buddhas can understand it.... The Buddhas ... wish to open the door of Buddha wisdom to all living beings, to allow them to attain purity." How do they open the door of Buddha wisdom? Through their skillful use of various means:

> [I]n order to bring peace and comfort to living beings I employ various different doctrines to disseminate the Buddha way. Through the power of my wisdom I know the nature and desires of living beings and through expedient means I preach these doctrines, causing all living beings to attain joy and gladness.... [T]he Buddhas of the past used countless numbers of expedient means, various causes and conditions, and words of simile and parable in order to

> expound the doctrines for the sake of living beings (Lotus Sutra Chapter 2).

Such expedient means do not always entail truth. They may, at times, deceive.

> In the Buddha lands of the ten directions there is only the Law of the one vehicle, there are not two, there are not three, *except when the Buddha preaches so as an expedient means*, merely employing provisional names and terms in order to conduct and guide living beings.... [P]eople of small wisdom delight in a small Law, unable to believe that they themselves could becomes [sic] Buddhas. Therefore we employ expedient means, making distinctions and preaching various goals. But though we preach the three vehicles, we do it merely in order to teach the bodhisattvas (Lotus Sutra Chapter 2).

Upāya is central to the Buddhist philosophy of ministry.

> The problem the historical Buddha faced was how to communicate his experience, and this was resolved with the nascence of *upāya*.... Fully realizing the inadequacies of human language, which is based on a conceptualized view of reality, he knew that the degree a single individual would profit from his preaching was highly dependent on diverse factors such as the existent spiritual level, past experience, present environment, psychological needs, and so on. He also was aware that it was possible for a layman to benefit as much as a learned monk if the teachings were presented in a manner comprehensible to the layman; thus different varieties and the intellectual modes of approaches were necessary. All these forms of communication constituted *upāya* (Matsunaga 1974:53).

Thus, "The concept of *upāya* is inseparable from the notion of Buddha, since it is his means of communication with the unenlightened" (Matsunaga 1974:54). Further, since enlightenment grows out of a radical non-dualism that does not distinguish between oneself and others, communicating the *dharma* to others follows naturally. The ignorant may see preaching as an evidence of compassion, whereas in fact "The bodhisattva is no more motivated by pity or kindness than is the hand when it disentangles the foot from a snarl of vines" (:69). He knows that in the act of helping others he is helping himself. Consequently, "*upāya* becomes not a mere 'device' or secondary teaching, but rather represents the most crucial concept of Mahāyāna philosophy" (:72).

The Elasticity of Skill-in-Means: A New Definition of "Not Lying"

What is important in the Buddha's teaching is not whether its content is *true*, but whether following it leads its hearers to release from ignorant clinging into dispassionate nirvana. The *dharma* is only a raft designed to conduct its passenger to the far shore. Once that shore is reached, the raft may be discarded. And it does not matter if the raft leaked or was built of rotten logs.

For example, the Buddha compared his teaching to a man who promised to give toys to his unsuspecting children in order to lure them from a burning house. Though he neither had nor gave what he promised, the father did a noble thing by speaking as he did. So too with the Buddha.

> Shariputra, suppose that in a certain town in a certain country there was a very rich man. He was far along in years and his wealth was beyond measure. He had many fields, houses and menservants. His own house was big and rambling, but it had only one gate. A great many people—a hundred, two hundred, perhaps as many as five hundred—lived in the house. The halls and rooms were old and decaying, the walls crumbling, the pillars rotten at their base, and the beams and rafters crooked and aslant.
>
> At that time a fire suddenly broke out on all sides, spreading through the rooms of the house. The sons of the rich man, ten, twenty perhaps thirty, were inside the house. When the rich man saw the huge flames leaping up on every side, he was greatly alarmed and fearful and thought to himself, 'I can escape to safety through the flaming gate, but my sons

are inside the burning house enjoying themselves and playing games, unaware, unknowing, without alarm or fear. The fire is closing in on them, suffering and pain threaten them, yet their minds have no sense of loathing or peril and they do not think of trying to escape!'

Shariputra, this rich man thought to himself, 'I have strength in my body and arms. I can wrap them in a robe or place them on a bench and carry them out of the house. And then again he thought, this house has only one gate, and moreover it is narrow and small.

'My sons are very young, they have no understanding, and they love their games, being so engrossed in them that they are likely to be burned in the fire. I must explain to them why I am fearful and alarmed. The house is already in flames and I must get them out quickly and not let them be burned up in the fire!'

Having thought in this way, he followed his plan and called to all his sons, saying, 'You must come out at once!' But though the father was moved by pity and gave good words of instruction, the sons were absorbed in their games and unwilling to heed them. They had no alarm, no fright, and in the end no mind to leave the house. Moreover, they did not understand what the fire was, what the house was, what the danger was. They merely raced about this way and that in play and looked at their father without heeding him.

At that time the rich man had this thought: 'The house is already in flames from this huge fire. If I and my sons do not get out at once, we are certain to be burned. I must now invent some expedient means that will make it possible for the children to escape harm.'

The father understood his sons and knew what various toys and curious objects each child customarily liked and what would delight them. And so he said to them, 'The kind of playthings you like are rare and hard to find. If you do not take them when you can, you will surely regret it later. For example, things like these goat-carts, deer-carts and ox-carts. They are outside the gate now where you can play with them. So you must come out of this burning house at once. Then whatever ones you want, I will give them all to you!'

At that time, when the sons heard their father telling them about these rare playthings, because such things were just what they had wanted, each felt emboldened in heart and, pushing and shoving one another, they all came wildly dashing out of the burning house.

At that time the rich man, seeing that his sons had gotten out safely and all were seated on the open ground at the crossroads and were no longer in danger, was greatly relieved and his mind danced for joy. At that time each of the sons said to his father, 'The playthings you promised us earlier, the goat-carts and deer-carts and ox-carts—please give them to us now!'

Shariputra, at that time the rich man gave to each of his sons a large carriage of uniform size and quality. The carriages were tall and spacious and adorned with numerous jewels. A railing ran all around them and bells hung from all four sides. A canopy was stretched over the top, which was also decorated with an assortment of precious jewels. Ropes of jewels twined around, a fringe of flowers hung down, and layers of cushions were spread inside, on which were placed vermilion pillows. Each carriage was drawn by a white ox, pure and clean in hide, handsome in form and of great strength, capable of pulling the carriage smoothly and properly at a pace fast as the wind. In addition, there were many grooms and servants to attend and guard the carriage.

What was the reason for this? This rich man's wealth was limitless and he had many kinds of storehouses that were all filled and overflowing. And he thought to himself, 'There is no end to my possessions. It would not be right if I were to give my sons small carriages of inferior make. These little boys are all my sons and I love them without partiality. I have countless numbers of large carriages adorned with seven kinds of gems. I should be fair-minded and give one to each of my sons. I should not show any discrimination. Why? Because even if I distributed these possessions of mine to every person in the whole country I would still not exhaust them, much less could I do so by giving them to my sons!'

At that time each of the sons mounted his large carriage, gaining something he had never had before, something he had originally never expected. Shariputra, what do you think of this? When this rich man impartially handed out to his sons these big carriages adorned with rare jewels, was he guilty of falsehood or not?

Shariputra said, "No, World-Honored One. This rich man simply made it possible for his sons to escape the peril of fire and preserve their lives. He did not commit a falsehood. Why do I say this? Because if they were able to preserve their lives, then they had already obtained a plaything of sorts. And how much more so when, through an expedient means, they are rescued from that burning house! World-Honored One, even if the rich man had not given them the tiniest carriage, he would still not be guilty of falsehood. Why? Because this rich man had earlier made up his mind that he would employ an expedient means to cause his sons to escape. Using a device of this kind was no act of falsehood. How much less so, then, when the rich man knew that his wealth was limitless and he intended to enrich and benefit his sons by giving each of them a large carriage."

The Buddha said to Shariputra, "Very good, very good. It is just as you have said. And Shariputra, the Thus Come One is like this. That is, he is a father to all the world. His fears, cares and anxieties, ignorance and misunderstanding, have long come to an end, leaving no residue. He has fully succeeded in acquiring measureless insight, power and freedom from fear and gaining great supernatural powers and the power of wisdom. He is endowed with expedient means and the paramita of wisdom, his great pity and great compassion are constant and unflagging; at all times he seeks what is good and will bring benefit to all.

He is born into the threefold world, a burning house, rotten and old. In order to save living beings from the fires of birth, old age, sickness and death, care suffering, stupidity, misunderstanding, and the three poisons; to teach and convert them and enable them to attain anuttara-samyak-sambodhi.

He sees living beings seared and consumed by birth, old age, sickness and death, care and suffering, sees them undergo many kinds of pain because of their greed and attachment and striving they undergo numerous pains in their present existence, and later they undergo the pain of being reborn in hell or as beasts or hungry spirits. Even if they are reborn in the heavenly realm or the realm of human beings, they undergo the pain of poverty and want, the pain of parting from loved ones, the pain of encountering those they detest—all these many different kinds of pain.

Yet living beings drowned in the midst of all this, delight and amuse themselves, unaware, unknowing, without alarm or fear. They feel no sense of loathing and make no attempt to escape. In this burning house which is the threefold world, they race about to east and west, and though they encounter great pain, they are not distressed by it.

Shariputra, when the Buddha sees this, then he thinks to himself, I am the father of living beings and I should rescue them from their sufferings and give them the joy of the measureless and boundless Buddha wisdom so that they may find their enjoyment in that.

Shariputra, the Thus Come One also has this thought: if I should merely employ supernatural powers and the power of wisdom; if I should set aside expedient means and for the sake of living beings should praise the Thus Come One's insight, power and freedom from fear, then living beings would not be able to gain salvation. Why? Because these living beings have not yet escaped from birth, old age, sickness, death, care and suffering, but are consumed by flames in the burning house that is the threefold world. How could they be able to understand the Buddha's wisdom?

Shariputra, that rich man, though he had strength in his body and arms, did not use it. He merely employed a carefully contrived expedient means and thus was able to rescue his sons from the peril of the burning house, and afterward gave each of them a large carriage adorned with rare jewels. And the Thus Come One does the same. Though he possesses power and freedom from fear, he does not use these. He merely employs wisdom and expedient means to rescue living beings from the burning house of the threefold world, expounding to them the three vehicles, the vehicle of the voice-hearer, that of pratyekabuddha, and that of the Buddha.

He says to them, 'You must not be content to stay in this burning house of the threefold world! Do not be greedy for its coarse and shoddy forms, sounds, scents, tastes and sensations! If you become attached to them and learn to love them, you will be burned up! You must come out of this threefold world at once so that you can acquire the three vehicles, the vehicles of the voice-hearer, the pratyekabuddha and the Buddha. I promise you now that you will get them, and that promise will never prove false. You have only to apply yourselves with diligent effort!'

The Thus Come One employs this expedient means to lure living beings into action. And then he says to them, 'You should understand that these doctrines of the three vehicles are all praised by the sages. They are free, without entanglements, leaving nothing further to depend upon or seek. Mount these three vehicles, gain roots that are without outflows, gain powers, awareness, the way, meditation, emancipation, samadhis, and then enjoy yourselves. You will gain the delight of immeasurable peace and safety.'

Shariputra, if there are living beings who are inwardly wise in nature, and who attend the Buddha, the World-Honored One, hear the Law, believe and accept it, and put forth diligent effort, desiring to escape quickly from the threefold world and seeking to attain nirvana, they shall be called [those who ride] the vehicle of the voice hearer. They are like those sons who left the burning house in the hope of acquiring goat-carts.

If there are living beings who attend the Buddha, the World-Honored One, hear the Law, believe and accept it, and put forth diligent effort, seeking wisdom that comes of itself, taking solitary delight in goodness and tranquility, and profoundly understanding the causes and conditions of all phenomena, they shall be called [those who ride] the vehicle of the pratyekabuddha. They are like the sons who left the burning house in the hope of acquiring deer-carts.

If there are living beings who attend the Buddha, the World-Honored One, hear the Law, believe and accept it, and put forth diligent effort, seeking comprehensive wisdom, the insight of the Thus Come One, powers and freedom from fear, who pity and comfort countless living beings, bring benefit to heavenly and human beings, and save them all, they shall be called [those who ride] the Great Vehicle. Because the bodhisattvas seek this vehicle, they are called mahasattvas. They are like the sons who left the burning house in the hope of acquiring ox-carts.

Shariputra, that rich man, seeing that his sons had all gotten out of the burning house safely and were no longer threatened, recalled that his wealth was immeasurable and presented each of his sons with a large carriage. And the Thus Come One does likewise. He is the father of all living beings. When he sees that countless thousands of millions of living beings, through the gateway of the Buddha's teaching, can escape the pains of the threefold world, the fearful and perilous road, and gain the delights of nirvana, the Thus Come One at that time has this thought: I possess measureless, boundless wisdom, power, fearlessness, the storehouse of the Law of the Buddhas. These living beings are all my sons. I will give the Great Vehicle to all of them equally so that there will not be those who gain extinction by themselves, but that all may do so through the extinction of the Thus Come One.

To all the living beings who have escaped from the threefold world he then gives the delightful gifts of the meditation, emancipation, and so forth, of the Buddhas. All these are uniform in characteristics, uniform in type, praised by the sages, capable of producing pure, wonderful, supreme delight.

> Shariputra, that rich man first used three types of carriages to entice his sons, but later he gave them just the large carriage adorned with jewels, the safest, most comfortable kind of all. Despite this, that rich man was not guilty of falsehood. The Thus Come One does the same, and he is without falsehood. First he preaches the three vehicles to attract and guide living beings, but later he employs just the Great Vehicle to save them. Why? The Thus Come One possesses measureless wisdom, power, freedom from fear, the storehouse of the Law. He is capable of giving to all living beings the Law of the Great Vehicle. But not all of them are capable of receiving it.
>
> Shariputra, for this reason you should understand that the Buddhas employ the power of expedient means. And because they do so, they make distinctions in the one Buddha vehicle and preach it as three.[2]

Another example is when the Buddha said that although in fact he would not enter extinction, he spoke as though he would. If people thought he were going to remain in the world indefinitely, shallow persons would become lax, pursue worldly attachments, and fail to respect him properly and strenuously pursue their own enlightenment. "Therefore the Thus Come One, though in truth he does not enter extinction, speaks of passing into extinction." The shortness of his time here on earth would, he thought, encourage diligent pursuit of the Buddha path. Speaking deceitfully this way is not lying: "Good men, the Buddhas and Thus Come Ones all preach a Law such as this. They act in order to save all living beings, so what they do is true and not false." He then illustrates with the story of a physician who lies to save his children from poison, and acts nobly in doing so (Lotus Sutra chapter 16).

> Suppose, for example, that there is a skilled physician who is wise and understanding and knows how to compound medicines to effectively cure all kinds of diseases. He has many sons, perhaps ten, twenty, or even a hundred. He goes off to some other land far away to see about a certain affair. After he has gone, the children drink some kind of poison

that makes them distraught with pain and they fall writhing to the ground.

"At that time the father returns to his home and finds that his children have drunk poison. Some are completely out of their minds, while others are not. Seeing their father from far off, all are overjoyed and kneel down and entreat him, saying: 'How fine that you have returned safely. We were stupid and by mistake drank some poison. We beg you to cure us and let us live out our lives!'

"The father, seeing his children suffering like this, follows various prescriptions. Gathering fine medicinal herbs that meet all the requirements of color, fragrance and flavor, he grinds, sifts and mixes them together. Giving a dose of these to his children, he tells them, 'This is a highly effective medicine, meeting all the requirements of color, fragrance and flavor. Take it and you will quickly be relieved of your sufferings and will be free of all illness.'

"Those children who have not lost their senses can see that this is good medicine, outstanding in both color and fragrance, so they take it immediately and are completely cured of their sickness. Those who are out of their minds are equally delighted to see their father return and beg him to cure their sickness, but when they are given the medicine, they refuse to take it. Why? Because the poison has penetrated deeply and their minds no longer function as before. So although the medicine is of excellent color and fragrance, they do not perceive it as good.

"The father thinks to himself: My poor children! Because of the poison in them, their minds are completely befuddled. Although they are happy to see me and ask me to cure them, they refuse to take this excellent medicine. I must now resort to some expedient means to induce them to take the medicine. So he says to them: 'You should know that I am now old and worn out, and the time of my death has come. I will leave this good medicine here. You should take it and not worry that it will not cure you.' Having given these instructions, he then goes off to another land where he sends a messenger home to announce, 'Your father is dead.'

> "At that time the children, hearing that their father has deserted them and died, are filled with great grief and consternation and think to themselves: If our father were alive he would have pity on us and see that we are protected. But now he has abandoned us and died in some other country far away. We are shelter-less orphans with no one to rely on!
>
> "Constantly harboring such feelings of grief, they at last come to their senses and realize that the medicine is in fact excellent in color and fragrance and flavor, and so they take it and are healed of all the effects of the poison. The father, hearing that his children are all cured, immediately returns home and appears to them all once more.
>
> "Good men, what is your opinion? Can anyone say that this skilled physician is guilty of lying?"
>
> "No, World-Honored One."
>
> The Buddha said, "It is the same with me. It has been immeasurable, boundless hundreds, thousands, ten thousands, millions of nayuta and asamkhya kalpas since I attained Buddhahood. But for the sake of living beings I employ the power of expedient means and say that I am about to pass into extinction. In view of the circumstances, however, no one can say that I have been guilty of lies or falsehoods" (Lotus Sutra Chapter 6).

Perhaps not everyone would agree with this last statement of the Buddha. The Japanese translation of *upāya* is *hōben*. For many Japanese, *hōben* has come to connote "lies," even though that is not what the word means (Holte 2003).

This use of falsehood as *upāya* is not just a theoretical concept of the past, but a practical usage of the present:

> The Tibetan Rituals of Death, much like the parable of the burning house, illustrate the significance and *the potential positive nature of mistruth within upaya.*. While allegedly aiding the dying, the institution of these rituals appears to have been for the benefit of the living....

> They are given an opportunity to demonstrate their great compassion, both in action and thought…
>
> Why then are the rituals professed to be meant for the dying? For the same reason that the father misleads his children to save them from the burning house. Through skillful means, *it is possible to manipulate people for their own good* [emphasis added] ("Death Rituals" 2003).

Upāya may employ not only teachings that are admittedly not true, but also practices generally considered immoral. As *upāya* does not insist on truth in its ideas, perhaps neither does it require decency in its actions. For example, a central tenet of Buddhism is nondualism—belief in the profound essential oneness of all that is. If nondualism is true, then *nirvāna* is *samsāra* and *samsāra nirvāna*, and "the worldly passions are precisely enlightenment" (Stone 1995:20). No essential difference distinguishes the Buddha from the grossly unenlightened. While the antinomian licentiousness that sometimes results from this concept doubtless runs counter to its intent,[3] it must be noted that tantric Buddhism consciously seeks enlightenment through sensual indulgence and ritual intercourse. If practitioners claim they find release from ignorant clinging (Buddhism's ultimate desideratum) through such practices, who can judge them wrong? If the end justifies the means and the end is reached, who can denounce the means as improper? Rather, ritual sex becomes a way in which women can impart enlightenment to men.

What Tantric Buddhism shares with the more traditional schools is: (1) the goal of the abandonment or transcendence of the self, and (2) the belief in the illusory nature of the physical world. It differs in how to respond to these tenets. First, in Tantric Buddhism the favored method to transcend the self is "the ecstasy of ritual sexual intercourse and orgasm." Second, all we need to do to be liberated from the physical world is to realize its illusory nature. Once we do it makes no difference how we act, and we remain undefiled by it (Members 2003).

A very different use of the female as *upāya* for the male is the depiction of her decomposing corpse to teach impermanence. Meditation on the foulness of corpses is known as *asubabhavana* (Chin 1998:282). Images of that which is most desirable graphically succumbing to nine stages of decay forces the observer to acknowledge human frailty and death, and so discourages lust and attachment. The stages are: death, bloating, blood oozing, putridness, being consumed, blueness, white bones linked, scattered bones, and tomb (Chin 1998:280–281). "Since the female body was a source of desire for men, meditations on the decaying corpse became a form of aversion therapy for monks" (Chin 1998:294). This use of the female body as *upāya* is quite the opposite of that in tantric Buddhism. Here the tool is abhorrence and aversion; there desire and indulgence.

These opposing uses of women to teach the *dharma* illustrate a conundrum that haunts nondualism. Does it lead to pessimism vis-à-vis this world and to asceticism, or to licentious indulgence (Lewis 1943:8)? The Buddha sought to avoid these extremes through his Middle Way. But the strictness of some of the precepts (shunning a luxurious bed, refusal of silver and gold) and the austerity of some Theravadan *arhats* suggest an initial inclination toward the former, whereas tantric excesses travel far into the latter. Clearly the "skillful means" by which one reaches enlightenment are not only varied but mutually contradictory.

To sum up, *upāya* parallels the Christian concept of gentleness, in that out of compassion for the untutored it labors to present its message in ways they will understand. It differs from the Christian ministry model in that it consciously employs untruth to do so.

Comparing Gentle Strength and Upāya: The Issues of Truth, Goodness, and Beauty

Truth: This question of truth is the most obvious difference between the Christian and Buddhist ministry models. Christianity insists that its doctrines and history are true. The Bible uses parables and stories as well, but presents these as such without pretending they are factual.

For example, Peter assures his readers that "We did not follow cleverly invented stories when we told you about the power and coming of our Lord Jesus Christ" (2 Pet. 1:16). The truthfulness of the transfiguration of which he speaks should encourage his readers to heed the prophetic scriptures and shun the heresies and debaucheries of the false teachers who exploit their hearers with "stories they have made up" (2:3). The Buddha, as we have seen, encouraged the use of cleverly invented stories, and did not consider presenting them as factual to be lying.

The reason that truth is important is that Christians may be called to lay down their lives for their faith. Why should they do that for a fable? As Paul said, if the doctrine of resurrection is not true, then rather than endangering ourselves every hour and dying every day Christians should eat and drink, for tomorrow we die (1 Cor. 15:30-32). The God of the scriptures is described as incapable of lying (Tit. 1:2; Heb. 6:18); those who speak in his name shun the practice as well (Cf. Jn. 21:24; Rom. 9:1; 2 Cor. 11:31; 1 Tim. 2:7).

Goodness: Christianity insists that good and evil, God and Satan, right and wrong, are *not* non-dual. "God is light; in him there is no darkness at all." Hence Christians must not "do evil that good may result" (Rom. 3:8). Evil must be avoided both as an end and as a means. Sadly, the church has not always practiced this ideal, or even embraced it. Rejection of evil in all its forms remains, however, the biblical pattern for the church.

However, with its philosophical commitment to non-dualism and no transcendent standard of right and wrong, Buddhism has produced sects that openly advocate immorality. Its tantric practices parallel those of the Nicolaitan Gnostics, which Christian must shun as mentioned in Rev. 2:6 & 15-16 (Members 2003). For the Tantric Buddhists, "As a way of proving that one is enlightened, all sorts of forbidden acts should be engaged in: fornication, thieving, eating dung, and so forth." Similarly, one can "use the physical world and one's perceptions of it as a means towards enlightenment. All activities, including sex, can be used as a meditative technique" (Tantrism 2003).

Such doctrines and practices more legitimately fall within Buddhism than do libertarian movements such as the Nicolaitans, the Brethren of the Free Spirit, or the 17th-century Ranters within Christendom. The Bible clearly denounces such evils, whereas if good and evil are non-dual it is hard to see how to deny them legitimacy. Thus while it is not *necessarily* or even *primarily* immoral, Buddhism seems to be *potentially* so.

Beauty: The prolonged and detailed contemplation of decaying corpses doubtless teaches lessons, but it does so ambiguously and pessimistically. Precisely what message is the observer to deduce from the oozing blood and carrion birds picking the skeleton? Certainly physical life ends, and decay is unpleasant, but what exactly do we learn beyond that? What positive, practical instruction is thereby conveyed to guide the thinking and conduct of the living? Whatever teaching the pictures may convey is ambiguous in that it is subject to varying applications. It is pessimistic as well. Buddhists often object to people characterizing their thought as pessimistic, but this practice possibly suggests one reason for doing so.

It is true that the Old and New Testaments also depict negative didactic images. Among the most vivid are those of Lamentations, which the graphically describe the effects of famine in Jerusalem, besieged and captured because of her sin. Israel's history and sufferings are not fortuitously inserted in the scriptures, but were placed there "as examples to keep us from setting our hearts on evil things as they did" (1 Cor. 10:6). But while these images are instructive and prevent Christianity from descending into Pollyannaism, they are not the primary foci of Christian contemplation. The primary focus is rather overwhelmingly positive. Paul states the general principle in Philippians 4:8, "Finally, brothers, whatever is true, whatever is noble, whatever is right, whatever is pure, whatever is lovely, whatever is admirable—if anything is excellent or praiseworthy—think about such things." Specifically, the Christian is transformed by renewing his mind (Rom. 12:2), and by contemplating Christ. Thus the Christian faith proposes a positive object of contemplation with specific, detailed lessons to be learned. Christian contemplation is not primarily revulsion *from* an ugly something, with no clear objective of where to go, but rather attraction *toward* an object (the person of Christ) with specific lessons to be learned. The "evil" toward which believers should be "infants" may include natural or aesthetic as well as moral (1 Cor. 14:20).

Conclusion

It would be unfair to compare the *ideals* of one religion with the *practices* of another. We must not argue, for example, "Look at the lofty ethic of Christianity, and see how it excels the poor practices of some Buddhists." No, ideals can only be compared with ideals, and practice with practice. The truth is, of course, that Christianity has had in the past and continues to harbor in the present many harmful, wicked proponents and practices, from the Crusades to the Inquisition to complicity in the Holocaust to Jim Jones. The purpose of this paper has been to compare neither the ideals of Christianity with the practices of Buddhism, nor the practices of the two faiths. Rather, this has been a preliminary attempt to compare the professed *ideals* of Christianity and Buddhism regarding philosophy of ministry as expressed in central documents of these faiths and in the writings of recognized leaders.

First, a case was made that the New Testament model of ministry for the church is one of *Gentle Strength*. That is, the church considers truth to be a primary value in all it teaches and does, and seeks to propagate it without compromise. The church attempts to be *strong for the truth*. But the manner in which this truth is both held and propagated is tempered by *gentleness toward people*. Especially in the area of "disputable matters" there may be more than acceptable view (Rom. 4). At times we may be wrong. Others may grasp certain ideas more clearly. Teaching must be adapted to the capacities, interests, and sensitivities of the hearer. But in our *gentleness* we never are to compromise established *content*. The faith, after all, has been "once for all entrusted to the saints."

By contrast, *upāya* represents a key Buddhist ministry concept. Not just in its practices, then, but in its professed *principles*, Buddhism proposes that even non-truthful means to move listeners toward its proposed end of enlightenment and non-attachment are legitimate. Unless trantric Buddhism can somehow be demonstrated to be aberrant and hence outside of true Buddhism, its proposals must be included in assessing what the faith teaches. Should we choose to disregard tantrism, however, even so central a Buddhist document as the Lotus Sutra clearly advocates the use of non-truth as a ministry method. By contrast, the Inquisition or Jim Jones can be shown from its scriptures to be illegitimate deviations from Christianity, and hence out of line with what it actually teaches. The professed Christian ideal is thus not tarnished by these lamentable practices in its name.

Buddhism, then, seems to promote non-rationality, falsehood in its *upāya*, immorality in its tantrism, and ugliness in its contemplation of corpses. *Upāya* is *gentle* in that it evaluates the capacities of the listener and adapts its presentation so that it can be understood and received. But it lacks the *strength* of the Christian commitment to truth. This contrasts with the strong rational character of Christianity, its insistence on truth and holiness, and its predisposition toward beauty. These contrasts, I suggest, make the Christian model of ministry preferable to the Buddhist one in their *methods* as well as their *content*.

Notes

[1] The phrase was used by José Cabezon. See Lai and von Brück 2001:225. He calls *prajna* (wisdom) the mother.

[2] "The Lotus Sutra," chap. 3. Punctuation and spelling have been slightly altered. The three vehicles referred to are: (1) The *sravaka*, a hearer or disciple. A disciple may be a monk or a nun, a layman or a laywoman. Bent on his or her liberation, a *sravaka* follows and practices the teaching of the Buddha and finally attains nirvana. He also serves others, but his capacity to do so is limited. (2) The *pratyekabuddha* (individual buddha), a person who realizes nirvana alone by himself at a time when there is no *samyaksambuddha* in the world. He also renders service to others, but in a limited way. He is not capable of revealing the truth to others as a *samyaksambuddha* does. (3) The *bodhisattva*, a monk or layman who is in a position to attain nirvana as a *sravaka* or as a *pratyekabuddha*, but out of great compassion *(maha karuna)* for the world, renounces it and goes on suffering in *samsara* for the sake of others, perfects himself during an incalculable period of time, and finally realizes nirvana and becomes a *samyaksambuddha*, a fully enlightened buddha. He discovers the truth and declares it to the world. His capacity for service to others is unlimited. (Adapted from Rahula 2003).

[3] See, e.g., Küng 1986:417–19. Compare a similar misunderstanding of the Christian concept of grace in Paul's letter to the Romans. The apostle had argued that people cannot achieve righteousness before God through religious observance, but rather must receive it as a gift of his grace through Jesus Christ (3:20, 24, 28). An objector responds: "What shall we say, then? Shall we go on sinning so that grace may increase? Shall we sin because we are not under law but under grace?" (6:1, 15) Paul's response indicates that those who proposed these responses had yet to grasp the meaning of both sin and grace.

5

Meekness: A New Approach to Christian Witness to the Thai People

Nantachai Mejudhon

Introduction

All textbooks on the history of Christian mission in Thailand mention low percentages of Christian conversion. The Roman Catholic priests came to Thailand in 1511 (Jeng 1983:90). They planted only six churches during their 300 years of mission work (Wells 1958:5). The first attempt to propagate Protestantism in Siam seems to have been in the early part of the nineteenth century (Latourette 1944:243). The first missionary of Protestantism came to Siam in 1828 (Kim 1974:39). The first Thai convert appeared in 1859, nineteen years after the American Presbyterian church entered in 1840 and remained faithful (Kane 1978:97). Even after 165 years of aggressive evangelism, professing Christians still numbered only 0.6 percent in 1980 (Barrett 1982:664).

This study investigates the cultural and religious behavior pattern of "meekness" and suggests using this pattern as the new approach to Christian witness for missionaries and Thai Christians. I will determine if there is something culturally inappropriate with past and present approaches to Christian witness that missionaries and Thai Christians have used for perhaps the last century related to ignoring or undervaluing this cultural and religious pattern.

Thai people are characteristically kind and gentle. Missionaries are welcomed wholeheartedly and can preach anywhere. There has been no persecution of missionaries in Thailand. The government donates much money to Christian organizations in Thailand. The constitution provides freedom for all religions. Missionaries can preach in public places, but the number of foreign missionaries is strictly controlled. At present, there are approximately 1,000 missionaries and 128 Christian organizations in Thailand. All seem to experience the same reception—friendliness and good will, but an almost unalterable repugnance to the idea of conversion (Neill 1990:293). The growth in all churches is very slow.

Missionaries' attitudes toward Buddhism, the predominant religion in Thailand, have often been negative, and some consider Buddhism evil. In the nineteenth century, Siam was the only country in Asia which succeeded in fully maintaining its political independence from aggressive Western powers (Latourette 1944:240). Historically, Thailand also has successfully maintained its spiritual independence in spite of aggressive, Western missionary strategies by simply using the cultural and religious behavior pattern of meekness as a shield to escape spiritual colonization.

In the same manner, I believe that the Christian church in Thailand is viewed as having violated the cultural and religious values of reciprocity and harmony by its use of aggressive methods and is now deprived of the opportunity to initiate dialogue about the gospel.

Theoretical Framework

This study develops an alternative method of evangelism appropriate for use in Thailand by combining the theoretical frameworks and models of intercultural communication of Carley H. Dodd (1995:6), the elenctic witness in cross-cultural study of religion of J. H. Bavinck (1960:247-272), and the model of vulnerability of elenctic witness offered by Mathias Zahniser (1994:71-78).

Success in intercultural communication depends on three factors: culture, personality, and the interpersonal relationships between the receiver and the sender (Dodd 1995:6). Effective intercultural communication begins with recognition that a focus on task alone is insufficient. Communication relationships must be planted, watered and cultivated along with our task orientation for successful intercultural communication experiences (Dodd 1995:15).

Dodd provides a comparison of a number of cultural values between North Americans and Asians. He also suggests a guide for communicators to improve their communication skills. Dodd's suggestions help people to come closer to each other and listen to each other seriously.

Dodd suggests that the sender of the message should assume the burden of communication (Dodd 1995:15). Communication with a person from a different culture poses proportionately more ambiguities and uncertainties. Some form of predictability is needed to combat the uncertainty. Dodd suggests that the first phase of reducing uncertainty involves precontact impression formation. Communicators reduce uncertainty on a simple and efficient level during this first phase (Dodd 1995:21).

In this study, a comparison between American and Thai values will indicate problems of intercultural communication. The character of the Thai nine-value clusters, recently researched by

Suntaree Komin, a Thai scholar (1991:132-218), reveals various facets of Thai meekness. We will see how application of the character of the Thai nine-value clusters can help missionaries in their strategies of witnessing to the Thai.

Bavinck's main feature of an elenctic approach to evangelism (1960:247-272) rests upon the faithfulness of Jesus Christ. The elenctic approach to evangelism accepts the responsibility for mediating and acknowledging conviction in one's self and in the community of faith. To be really able to convict anyone else of sin, a person must know himself and the hidden corners of his heart very well. The Holy Spirit first convicts us, and then through us he convicts the world. Anyone who in humility lets the Holy Sprit convince him of his sins may be the means by which the Holy Spirit discloses to others the hidden sources of the their willingness to really take God seriously.

Zahniser goes further in developing the meekness approach by introducing the role of vulnerability in elenctics (the witness that is concerned with the convincing and convicting work of the Holy Spirit) (1994:71-78). The idea is to open our minds, our lives, and ourselves so we can learn more from the Thai. By doing so, both their lives and ours will reach a point of unity where we can begin to understand, love, and help each other. Zahniser provides three crucial dimensions of Christian witness among non-Christians (especially Muslims): the importance of intimate dialogue, the work of God's Spirit in prevenient grace, and the role of vulnerability in being convincing. Taken together, these dimensions, Zahniser suggests, compose an approach or model for evangelism which he calls, "close encounters of the vulnerable kind" (Zahniser 1994:72).

Dr. Suntaree Komin, a Fulbright scholar and a Thai, suggested that the psychology of the Thai people has nine value clusters: ego orientation; grateful relationship orientation; smooth interpersonal relationship orientation; flexibility and adjustment orientation; religio-psychical orientation; education and competence orientation;

interdependence orientation; fun-pleasure orientation; and achievement-task orientation.

Paul Fieg is a scholar who worked in Thailand as an American Peace Corps volunteer in Thailand for many years. Fieg divided Thai cultural values into eight conceptual domains: time, work and play, youth vs. age, equality vs. hierarchy and rank, materialism vs. spirituality, change vs. tradition, confrontation vs. indirection (avoidance), and dependence vs. independence.

I will examine the differences between American values and Thai values for each domain. The resulting comparison will produce a number of elements to meekness which in turn will serve as a summary of characteristic elements found in a meekness approach to witnessing for pursuing answers to the study.

Understanding Thai Value Systems and Behavioral Patterns

Dodd suggested that communication with a person from a different culture poses proportionately more ambiguities and uncertainties. Understanding Thai value systems and behavioral patterns helps missionaries and Thai Christians to manage ambiguities and uncertainties in intercultural communication. This, in turn, draws the Thai to missionaries, to Thai Christians and to Christ.

Dr. Suntaree Komin researched for ten years to find Thai values and behavioral patterns. The findings of Thai instrumental values reveal the culturally learned patterns of social interaction, whereby Thai people learn to survive and function effectively in their society.

Missionaries and Thai Christians who apply any approaches which the Thai perceive as aggressive will automatically break the relationship, and effective intercultural outcomes will not occur. The Thai social system is reflected in the following nine value clusters on a continuum of psychological importance, from high to low, as enumerated below.

Value Clusters According to Their Relative Significant Position in the Thai Cognitive System

It should be borne in mind that the higher the number in the order, the closer to the self and the more likely to be activated to guide actions (Komin 1991:133). Under each value cluster, a description of behavioral patterns is provided. The elements of these descriptions and interpretations are recognizable to the Thai.

1. Ego Orientation: The Thai are first and foremost ego oriented, characterized by the highest ego value of being independent, being one's self (*Pen tua Khong tua eng*), and having high self-esteem (Komin 1991:133). Thai people have big egos, a deep sense of independence, pride, and dignity. They cannot tolerate any violation of the "ego" self whether that be Buddhism, the king, the nation, or parents (Komin 1991:134). Despite their cool and calm front, they can be easily provoked to strong emotional reactions if the "self", or anybody close to the "self," like one's father of mother, is insulted. Basically, it boils down to the question of "face" and "dignity."

Since Thai culture values "ego" and "face," straightforward, negative performance feedback, strong criticism, and face-to-face confrontation techniques and challenges should be avoided (Komin 1991:135). "Face-saving" is a key criterion in handling all person-related decisions, particularly negative ones. Compromise is often used as an effective means to save face and to keep the "surface harmony" even at the expense of some task.

Christians should not compare religions verbally (LCWE 1980:6). They should have a sympathetic understanding of the Buddhists (1980:10). Christians must show their sensitivity to the cultural concepts of those to whom they go and their credibility among the people they are reaching (1980:10).

2. Grateful Relationship Orientation: Reciprocity of kindness, particularly the practice of being grateful, is a highly valued characteristic in Thai society (Komin 1991:139). The Thai have been socialized to value this grateful (*Katanyu*) quality in a person. A person should be grateful to persons who render *Bunkhun* (goodness, helps, favors) to him or her (Komin 1991:140). *Bunkhun* must be returned, often on a continuous basis and in a variety of ways, because Bunkhun should not and cannot be measured quantitatively in material terms (Komin 1991:139-143).

This reveals why a missionary who taught science and English to a Thai King for only eighteen months, received numerous gifts and rights such as a place to teach Christianity in a Buddhist temple, lands, and the Edict of Religious Toleration in return. At the same time, this fact also reveals why missionaries who served as medical doctors and helped many Thai people from sickness and death could not convince them of the love of Christ. Because the Thai have a strong ego, when missionaries contributed great *Bunkhun* to the Thai while looking down on Buddhism and idol worship, the ego was disturbed. They saw the grateful relationship turning into a power-dominated relationship. The relationship became a "transactional interaction" where there was no deep psychological bond. The ego was kept intact and independent, and the duration of the relationship had no meaning (Komin 1991:139-143).

Christians should maintain good relationships (Komin 1991:200). This could be done by developing friendly relationships with families in communities over a period of time (LCWE 1980:13) without any strings attached (LCWE 1980:12).

3. Smooth Interpersonal Relationship Orientation: Unlike American's top values which tend to focus on self-actualization, ambition, and achievement, the Thai also place high value on a group of "other-directed" social interaction values, designed to project a picture of smooth , kind, pleasant, no-conflict interpersonal interactions, in short, the surface harmony observed by many (Komin 1991:143).

This orientation is characterized by the preference for a non-assertive, polite, and humble type of personality (expressed through appearance, manners, and interpersonal approach), as well as the preference for relaxed, and pleasant interaction which accounts for the smiling and friendly aspects of the Thai people that fascinates most foreign visitors (1991:143).

This group of "other-directed" social interaction values are called "social smoothing" values (1991:143). The persons demonstrating these are caring and considerate; kind and helpful; responsive to situations and opportunities; self-controlled, tolerant, and restrained; polite and humble; calm and cautious; contented; and socially-related.

Komin continues to say that the findings of this group of values are significant for three reasons: First, five out of about eight interpersonal related values emerged on the Thai value list but not on the American value list. They are: caring and considerate, responsive to situations and opportunities, calm and cautious, contented, and socially-related (Komin 1991:144). Second, some of the "social smoothing" values have consistently secured the Thai significantly high rankings in the Thai value system. Third, this finding means these values are deeply internalized and functional in the everyday life of the Thai. By knowing these five values, missionaries and Thai Christians are able to learn how to manage the interaction stage in intercultural communication because the Thai are intuitive at observing and practicing these subtle social rules (Komin 1991:144).

4. Flexibility and Adjustment Orientation: Evidently, besides ego and smooth interpersonal relationships, the Thai are flexible and situation-oriented (Komin 1991:161). Komin provides data which indicates that while most Thai favor sincere interactions, they also value the flexible (*Alum aluy*) characteristics in persons (Komin 1991:164).

In general for the Thai, there is nothing as serious as being rigid or unchangeable (Komin 1991:164). Because of this value, it is not surprising to find a "decision-shifting" behavior pattern quite common for the Thai, such as denying or postponing decisions to accept Christ, baptism, or appointments even though they said "yes" weeks prior. They might even switch their principles.

The Thai view the missionaries and what they do in various situations as more important in their conversion to Christianity than dogma or doctrines. If the doctrines can radiate through missionaries' lives, it helps the Thai come to Christ. This also helps missionaries in developing the meekness approach to the Thai.

5. Religio-Psychical Orientation: Theravada Buddhism as the main religion of the country is professed by 95 percent of the total population. Undoubtedly it has directly and indirectly exerted strong influence on people's everyday lives. Most of them have little deep knowledge about it. In general, the Thai do not make conscious efforts to reach *nirvana*, nor do they fully and succinctly believe in reincarnation. They generally have serious doubts about the truth and validity of those other-worldly doctrines or notions such as rebirth, *nirvana*, and to a lesser extent, *Karma* (Komin 1991:171). They are not taken very seriously. The Thai hold more of a "this worldly" orientation.

This finding helps missionaries and Thai Christians develop what we call "a meekness approach to witnessing." Theological arguments and apologetic approaches may fit those who hold high religion. But Komin (1991) suggested that the Thai do not make conscious effort to reach *Nirvana* or to hold high religion, nor do they fully and succinctly believe in reincarnation (1991:176). Presently, missionaries and Thai Christians try to persuade the lost to come to Christ so they will go to heaven, however, Buddhists are not interested in going to heaven or reaching *Nirvana* (Komin

1991:171). The future is not as important to them as is the present. They have numerous felt needs, and they apply the affective approach of folk religions in Thailand to feed their psychological hunger in a modernistic world. A rational or apologetic approach may not work well with the majority of the Thai people, but an intuitive, feeling, or affective approach, seeing Christ as the "Man for others" and the one who can deliver them from all fears, may be considered as a new way of meekness in Christian witnessing (Koyama 1968:16). For the Thai, religion is felt emotionally, not rationalized cognitively (Komin 1991:171-186).

6. Education and Competence Orientation: With regard to the value of education, the findings of the study revealed that educational values and competence hold a medium level of importance (Komin 1991:186). Knowledge for its own sake did not receive a high value in the cognition of the Thai in general. Education has been perceived more as a means of climbing up the social ladder, in terms of higher prestige and higher salary, than as an end in itself (Komin 1991:186).

This finding can help missionaries adjust their focus. The Thai people are not interested in the content of missionaries' teaching. If being Christian enabled them to get benefits and helped in finding jobs, knowing English, and opening up chances for a better life, they might consider being Christians.

7. Interdependence Orientation: In many cultures, cooperation is fundamental (Dodd 1995:122). Some Asian cultures emphasize group cohesion and loyalty (1995:122). This value orientation reflects more of the spirit of community collaboration, and in a sense, the values of co-existence and interdependence (Komin 1991:190). The value of helping one another motivates cooperative behavior in the community and reinforces a sense of neighborhood. When a family is ill, suffers a death, or celebrates a wedding, neighbors will come and help that family in times of need or crisis. They bind their relationship through reciprocal services such as assistance and exchanges of food (Komin 1991:190).

8. Fun and Pleasure Orientation: Thailand has been known as the "land of the smile," a stereotyped image accompanied by the myth of the Thai being easy-going, enjoying everyday pleasures with happy carelessness, not letting troubles touch them easily, viewing life as something to be enjoyed not endured, and not doing anything that is not *sanuke* (to have fun, to enjoy oneself, and have a good time) (Komin 1991:191). They are easily bored or *bua*, not because of having nothing to do like the Westerners but because of the repetitive activities they do that are not *sanuke* (fun, enjoyable).

Does this smiling, friendly interaction with joyful behavior give a true indication that fun and pleasure are valued as ends in themselves, or are they a necessary means to function effectively in Thai society? Research findings suggest that this fun-pleasure value functions as an imperative mechanism, as a means to support and maintain the more important interpersonal interaction value.

9. Achievement-Task Orientation: This is characterized by the achievement need emphasizing the internal drive toward achievement through hard work. Believing that hard work alone will propel one along the road to success, the Western work ethic has emphasized personal achievement, what one has done or achieved through one's best ability and hard work (Komin 1991:197). Because of this Thai value, missionaries and Thai Christians who are work-oriented and perceive Christian missions as something they have to strive to do by their own efforts, and who evaluate their success by the number of saved souls, may be disappointed and discouraged constantly in their Christian witness to the Thai.

Komin's research data shows the achievement value of being ambitious and hardworking to attain one's goals has been consistently ranked as least important. All Thais, without exception, ranked the hardworking achievement value much lower than the group of social relationship values. A closer look reveals that 64.9

percent of the Bangkok Thai and 55.2 percent of the rural Thai perceive maintenance of good relationships as more important than work (Komin 1991:200). A good relationship, not tasks, wins all.

Missionaries and Thai Christians who deal aggressively with Buddhist friends when it comes to religion usually must endure shaky relationships. Generally, the longer they are Christians, the fewer Thai Buddhist friends and relatives they have. This seems to be a fact in many Thai churches in Thailand. Although missionaries and Thai Christians had no intention of being aggressive, nevertheless when this orientation was demonstrated through Christian witness, it was judged aggressive by Thais because of their value of meekness in developing relationship with others.

In conclusion, task-achievement value for the Thai is usually inhibited by social relationship values. While submissiveness and good relations, with or without work, have always paid off, tasks, especially those seen as threats or without submissive reactions to superiors, do not lead to success in life in the Thai cultural context. Achievement in the Western sense would not fit in a culture which values strong social relations.

A number of missionaries have the idea that Christians have to count souls and report to a church or organization as a way of evaluating their success. They may be work-oriented. When they meet together, they will end up asking how many members each group has. The question such as, "How many members do you have in your church?" was rarely asked in New Testament accounts. Good relationships with friends and relatives do not come into their conversations. Heroes are those who aggressively win souls for Christ. This may be a reason why mission work in Thailand fails. A new approach of applying meekness to the Christian witness in Thailand will be easier for Thai Christians than American missionaries. If they accept their failure and are willing to adjust, I believe they will see success in their Christian witness.

Understanding the Differences between Cultural Values of the Thai and Americans

This section is concerned with the contrast of eight cultural domains in which the distinctiveness of cultural values of the Thai and Americans can be understood. The contrast will help readers understand the reasons why missionaries and Thai Christians who follow missionaries' methods and strategies need to change their way of witnessing. The result of my study in this section will also be used to design a meek approach in Christian witness to the Thai.

The Concept of Time

To Americans time is money (Dodd 1995:122). But in Thailand, particularly in rural areas, time is not generally equated with earning a living. Most farmers do not think of themselves as having lost money if they are forced to waste time. In fact, the Thai do not appear to have a strong notion of wasting time at all. Living close to nature's cycles and wishing to avoid the anxieties of preparing for the future or lamenting the past causes the Thai villagers to live mostly in the present time, enjoying all the passing moments.

By knowing this orientation, allowing sufficient time for developing an intimate relationship, diffusion of the gospel and evangelizing whole families rather than evangelism of individuals, affirms this cultural value (LCWE 1980:11; Nida 1990:179). This value suggests that whole families and groups of families should be won to Christ if viable churches are to be planted and are to make an adequate impact on the community, and individual converts should be used to win their families (LCWE 1980:7). Delaying of a water baptismal service for a new convert in order to win the whole family is affirmed by the suggestion of this cultural value.

The Concept of Work and Play

Many cultures separate work and play. In these cases, work demands diligence, concentration, even tedium. Since play is considered frivolous, combining work and play is unreasonable. Work and play do not mix. That view dominates some North American thought. In contrast, other cultures blend work and play. For the North American to insist on the divorce of work from frivolity and to judge others negatively is to invite estrangement (Dodd 1995:121).

From the Thai standpoint, if something is not *sanuke*, it is scarcely worth doing. Unlike the compartmentalized approach of Americans, Thais have the expectation that all of their activities will contain *sanuke*. Work, study, and even religious service must have at least an element of *sanuke* if they are to retain the Thai's interest (Ayal 1963:47-48). In fact, one reason why there are so few Thai converts to Christianity is undoubtedly due to the failure of the missionaries to make Christianity appear more *sanuke* (1963:58).

The story of Christ is *sanuke* by nature, because God loves us and decided to be a man named Jesus. Thais' minds and hearts should be touched by the gospel. Thai people do not like anything serious. Making the gospel alive is the key to evangelism. Verbal and non-verbal communication should be used in sharing the gospel. Indigenous media is the best for evangelization (LCWE 1980:8). Missionaries who love *sanuke* can be used greatly in Thailand. Storytelling should also be used as much as possible

Christians should not dump the information explicitly (Dodd 1995:99). They should communicate the person of Christ, not Christianity as religion (LCWE 1980:6). Christians should build personal relationships with them and seek to serve them humbly and lovingly (LCWE 1980:10).

The Concept of Youth versus Age

The respect North Americans have for their elderly is indeed pale compared with the high value placed upon the elderly in other cultures (Dodd 1995:117). Value of parental authority also varies culturally. North Americans typically stress individuality and making one's own decisions by the mid-teens (Dodd 1995:117). Accompanying this emphasis seems to be a disregard for parental authority and diminished communication with parents (1995:117).

Thai people show respect for the elderly and ancestral generation. Culturally speaking, a younger person should begin by *wais* (a gesture of respect which consists of placing one's hands together at the breast and bowing) to an older person (Fieg 1989:58). Thai law does not allow men or women to sue their parents in court (Supap 1994:62). To honor one's parents throughout life is considered one of the highest virtues. The social interaction in the Thai culture helps us to understand the Thai value concerning youth versus age as follows: (1) argument with parents or older persons are not encouraged and are sometimes prohibited; (2) a younger person should not teach religion to an older person; (3) a young man is able to teach religion to his or her own parents when his status changes from layman to Buddhist monk; (4) parents usually guide or make decisions on important matters for their children (For example, a young couple could not get married unless both sets of parents agree); and (5) on a bus, monks, women, children, and old people usually have the seats. Others who occupy seats when these are standing should get up.

Most new missionaries and new Christians are young. They should pay respect by *wais* to an older prospect first, to affirm this cultural value. Such a first impression would help open their hearts to the gospel. This would show that gospel presenters were meek from a Thai's viewpoint.

A young Christian should share with an older person politely but not with a teaching attitude (Komin 1991:159). They should establish and maintain rapport with the family of the inquirer early. New converts should be encouraged to continue identification with their community (LCWE 1980:13). They should always be humble, loving, and responsible to their family.

The Concept of Equality versus Hierarchy and Rank

Some cultures place value on hierarchy. In many of those cases, the vertical differences between people are justified on the basis of harmony and what is good for all in the culture (Dodd 1995:118).

Americans learn as schoolchildren that "All men are created equal." Taken from the Declaration of Independence, this value is burned in the American psyche as a "self-evident truth." If egalitarianism is the central theme in the American social structure, then hierarchical relations are at the heart of the Thai society.

The significance of the concept of hierarchically structured Thai society is concerned directly in intercultural communication. Thai society provides language, both verbalisms and non-verbalisms, for each level of its structure for people to communicate to each other. For example, a young Christian girl who comes from a lower rank in Thai society may encounter difficulties in her Christian witness to an older male government official because their daily lives rarely intersect unless she takes a role as helper in his household. By knowing verbal and non-verbal language, such as behaviors and pronouns used in each level of social structure, missionaries and Thai Christians can communicate and build relationships smoothly.

The Concept of Material versus Spirituality

Many cultures value material accumulation of goods and wealth. North Americans accumulate goods as a measure of wealth and success. The symbols of material well being and wealth obviously vary among cultures (Dodd 1995:122).

Dodd continued to mention that too often we prematurely judge a culture by its material features. A person who values technological features may overlook a rich cultural heritage in such areas as art, language, and interpersonal relationships. But Thai culture understands that spiritual growth is more important than amassing wealth. Material possession can sometimes be a sign of poor spiritual health and can be disruptive to society.

Unfortunately, some Western missionaries offend host cultures, both Christians and non-Christians, by their materialistic lifestyles which I believe are normal to them but disturb the host cultures greatly. A missionary who lives in a big house, drives a good car, dresses in good Western clothing, and eats good food in good restaurants can hinder his ministry with local Christian workers who work with him but live an opposite lifestyle. Non-Christians can misunderstand the Christian life. They may think that to be a Christian is only to be rich and blessed by God materially. A materialistic lifestyle can divert the Thai's intentions from spirituality to materialism. "Be simple in your own lifestyle" is a good policy. The lives of many Peace Corps volunteers touch the hearts of Thais because they live a simple lifestyle. Thais would like to see missionaries live in simple ways. Missionaries should consider living their lives in such a way that they will not be a stumbling block to the spiritual growth of the people with whom the work. Lifestyles often speak louder than words. Christians should be able to show their meekness in their lifestyles (LCWE 1980:18). Christians should not use material goods as means to manipulate relationships (LCWE 1980:12). They should not pursue any hidden agendas in developing relationships (LCWE 1980:12).

The Concept of Change versus Tradition

Cultures can be thought of as if on a continuum, from relying on tradition at one end to embracing innovation on the other end (Dodd 1995:122). Like Americans, Thais do believe in change, but they have never felt the same compulsion as Americans. In Buddhist values, change is the most certain thing of all; it is what existence is all about—constant cycles of *ubat* (birth, beginning) and *wibat* (death, ending, passing away). Since change is so all pervasive, it would be presumptuous, foolish, and certainly futile for humans to interject themselves in an active way into this process.

Missionaries should not require an instantaneous conversion from the Thai unless the Holy Spirit does his work in their hearts (LCWE 1980:11). A change should come naturally by the power of the Holy Spirit. The meaning of Christianity should be stressed more than the form. It is the duty of the church and the new believers to help communities and their families in the early stages of cross-cultural communication to understand this change.

Christians should approach Buddhists with humility and loving persuasion, backed by the testimony of a dynamic personal relationship with Jesus (LCWE 1980:10). A Christian's credibility is vital to the audience's acceptance of their message as credible (LCWE 1980:10). Christians should not present the gospel as a challenge but as offering benefits and help (LCWE 1980:10).

The Concept of Independence versus Dependence

At the heart of a North American's identity is self-reliance. A Chinese anthropologist, Francis Hsu, points out that the self-reliant American, however, strives to eliminate from his life both the fact and the sense of dependence upon other (1981:293).

In Thailand, the relationship is one of dependency. One such relationship is that of patron and client. The patron, like a parent, is totally responsible for the welfare of his clients. He not only provides them with basic food stuffs and a small income, but must also give them blankets when their old ones are in tatters, extra rice when a festival comes, and straw for their cattle when the supply runs out. Clients, in fact, can ask a patron for whatever they think they may grant, but this is not considered begging any more than when Christians ask God for help.

For this reason, the social network or web in Thailand is closely knit together. Missionaries should not be surprised when young Thais are asked to accept Christ and say that, "Let me go back home and ask permission from my parents." Individual conversion will separate a Christian from the social network and stop church growth. Missionaries should dare to win the whole family. Group decisions should be the target and goal of missionaries.

The Concept of Confrontation versus Indirection

The American preference for bringing problems out into the open and discussing them in a frank, candid manner so that "we can see exactly where we stand" contrasts sharply with the Thai tendency to avoid direct confrontation so as to preserve surface harmony (Fieg 1980:61).

Thais hate confrontation. Among Thais, serious and permanent damage is done to a relationship when a stage of open argument is reached. Face-to-face conflict is not viewed as a satisfactory solution to most problems. In Thailand it may not only be necessary but also desirable to beat around the bush in order to forestall an abrasive, open clash. Such an approach can appear evasive and insincere to Americans, whereas the American style can be seen as harsh and insensitive by Thai standards. Americans tend to see events as problems to be solved (Stewart and Bennett 1991:155). Americans naturally confront problems in a direct manner.

Christians should be aware that Thai people have big egos, a deep sense of independence, much pride and dignity. They cannot tolerate a violation of the ego self (Komin 1991:133). Christians should not make the Thai lose face in the process of confrontation; and in some instances, Christians should avoid criticism (Komin 1991:135). Missionaries should develop a *"kreng jai"* quality (consideration for others) (Holmes and Tangtongtavi 1995:46) and should not show their aggressive personality (Komin 1991:146). All confrontive strategies, especially direct confrontation of all kinds must be avoided (Fieg 1989:76; LCWE 1980:10). Christians should rely on the faithfulness of Christ and the power of the Holy Spirit and not pressure people (Bavinck 1960:247-272). They should seek to relate to others as neighbors and equals, regarding their beliefs as worthy of serious consideration.

Understanding the Differences between the Religious Concepts of the Thai and Americans

In this section, I will compare the religious concepts of Americans and the Thai as systems. Christians and non-Christians in Thailand have perceived Christianity as a religious system. Its coherent doctrines can be rejected or accepted as a whole system (Hughes 1989:41). This whole system will be viewed and discussed in this section as: (1) the differences in theological concepts, and (2) the differences in experiential concepts.

The Differences in Theological Concepts

In this section I will mention five points of differences between the theological concepts of the Thai and Americans. First, the difference between the theological concepts of Americans and the Thai rests upon their attitudes toward God (Hughes 1989:41). Theravada Buddhism holds atheistic ideas. God and gods are not necessary. American Christians hold a theistic idea. There is one God, omniscient, omnipotent, omnipresent, Creator, Redeemer, and Judge (Seamands 1981:173). This first contrast means that Christianity suggests people rely on a Power outside of themselves (Hughes 1989:43). The religious concept of the Thai does not provide help and aid with coping in their lives from outside sources.

When crises and difficulties occur in Buddhists' lives, Christians may use this concept to introduce Christ as the way out of problems.

Second, amidst the impermanence of the world and life that Buddhism stresses, there stand as E. Stanley Jones said, the unchangeable Christ and the unshakable Kingdom as the Bible affirms (Seamands 1981:174). Modernization and rapid change in the socio-economical system speed up the natural impermanence of Buddhistic ideas to a degree that may bring crisis to Buddhists' lives. Introducing Christ and his unchangeable words for Buddhists to hold onto in the times of crisis and suffering may affirm the usefulness of the differences of this value.

Third, Buddhism centers on humans—their needs and their efforts. Christianity centers on God—his purpose and his provision (Seamands 1981:173). When Buddhists encounter a dead-end street in their lives, they usually seek invisible means of support. Some Buddhists may accept that this is derived from their Karma but most of them seem to seek outside sources for their psychological coping. When this situation occurs and Christians introduce God's provision as new hope for their lives, this may affirm the usefulness in the Christian witness to the Thai. The research of Dr. Philip J. Hughes, a professor at Payap University, Thailand, affirmed this fact in his book, *Proclamation and Response* (1989).

Fourth, Buddhism claims there is nothing eternal or immortal inside the human body, no permanent ego. Christianity claims that human beings have eternal souls, that individual existence and selfhood are real (Seamands 1981:174). This concept can be used in dialoguing with Buddhists. Using the Buddhist position, Christians may ask them that if there is no permanent ego in the human body, what element is it in the human body that perceives *Nirvana*. There must be something since the human body is able to perceive it, or Buddhists would not know whether they have reached it or not.

Fifth, the basic teaching in Buddhism is that of suffering. The basic problem in Christian faith is sin. Salvation to the Buddhists is being released from suffering, receiving deliverance from the endless chain of birth-death-rebirth. Salvation according to Christian scriptures is deliverance from sin and reconciliation to God. In Buddhism, each one works by his own effort to achieve salvation through meditation, good deeds, and knowledge. The Christian faith declares that no one can save himself or herself. Salvation is the gift of God (Eph. 2:8) (Seamands 1981:175). The difference in this concept may be used in the Christian witness by introducing indigenous analogies as follows. Thai Christians may suggest to Buddhists that it may not always be true that human beings are able to deliver themselves out of their sins. In Thailand, on every December 5, King Rama IX releases thousands of prisoners from jail before their terms have been fulfilled. This is done by his own power and out of grace. Those prisoners who have been released come to know that their freedom, which they received from the King's kindness, was not derived by their good works.

The Differences in Experiential Concept

Philip Hughes (1989:45) cited a 1989 statistic that there are at least 30,000 Christians in northern Thailand. These people left Buddhism to become Christians. Hughes wondered what had attracted these people to Christianity and in his research, discovered that they had been in contact with Christian families. Christianity gave these people meaning. Christian values were planted into their hearts. They learned that they can depend on God in times of trouble (1989:45).

Hughes did his research by conducting a survey of Buddhists and Christians who live in the northern part of Thailand in 1981. He provided questionnaires to 386 Thai Buddhists, 71 Thai Christians who had not studied theology, and 42 missionaries associated with the Church of Christ in Thailand (1989:48). One question asked was what the reasons were that religion was so important to them. Ten reasons were suggested which the students rated in terms of their importance to them. It is interesting that for eight out of the ten reasons for the importance of religion, the responses of the Christians and Buddhists were very similar. Buddhism was important to Buddhist students for the same reason that Christianity was important to the Christian students (Hughes 1989:46). Both religions were said to give their adherents a sense of well-being and happiness, a sense of meaning in life, and provided opportunities to their members to help other people (Hughes 1989:46).

Those who converted from Buddhism to Christianity experienced the care and concern of Christians, particularly when facing some problem. Hughes suggested that the results of the questionnaires among students, and of interviews conducted in the churches, revealed that few people responded to the gospel because of its message of salvation and forgiveness of sin. For the Thai Christian students, forgiveness of sin was seventh out of ten reasons for the importance of religion. On the contrary, missionaries who responded to the same question mentioned that forgiveness of sin was the primary reason for the importance of religion.

This may be the reason why missionaries have kept on witnessing and preaching, passing the message of the gospel through the cognitive domain of the Thai. Missionaries must overcome their difficulty with differences in numerous religious words between the two religions. Words such as God, sin, love, and salvation produce different meanings in the minds of the Thai. Time for diffusion of the gospel may be required. This may be one reason why sharing the gospel with Buddhists in a short period of time and challenging them to accept Christ as their Lord and Savior brings frustration to missionaries as well as to Thai Christians.

If salvation and the message of the gospel are not perceived by Buddhists to be of primary importance at first, what is? Hughes' research provides a graph (see following page), which shows at least three areas of significance shared between missionaries and the Thai.

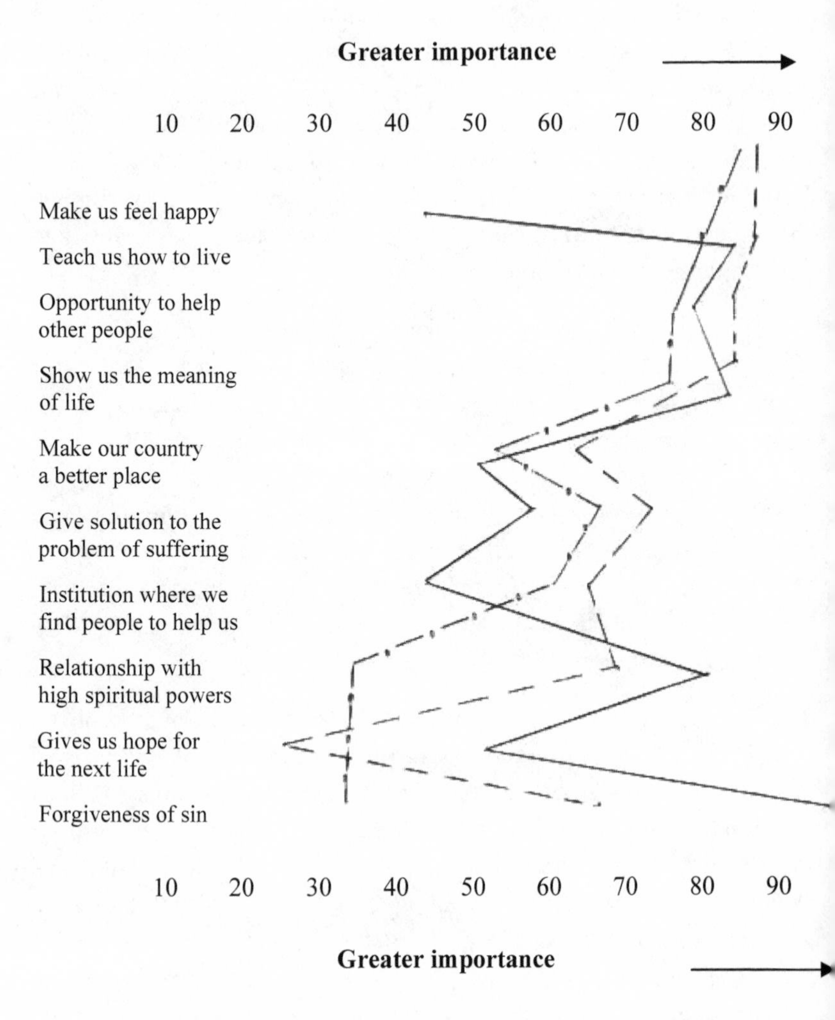

——— = a group of 42 missionaries associated with the Church of Christ in Thailand

- - - - - = a group of 71 Thai Christian students at Payap University not studying theology

—·—·— = 386 Thai Buddhist students at Payap University

Source: Philip J. Hughes, *Proclamation and Response* (Bangkok: Payap University Archives, 1989), 48.

Illustrating the relative rating of ten reasons for the importance of religion by groups of Thai Buddhist and Christian students and a group of missionaries working in Thailand, the graph proves the following:

First, Thai Buddhists and Christians agree that religion make them feel happy. A good religion must touch our affective domain, make us feel happy. Missionaries seemed not to agree with the Thai because religious values of missionaries are concerned with the doctrine of salvation from sin, but the Thai are interested in practical outcomes of religion. Thai Christians agree with Thai Buddhists in This matter, implying that Western Christianity could not change the religious values of Thai Christians to be like American missionaries. This implies that when the Christian witness provides the Thai with benefits and help, it may affirm this finding of differences in religious values.

Second, missionaries are concerned with the importance of the forgiveness of sin in witnessing to Buddhists while both Thai Christians and Buddhists are not.

The third difference is that Christianity offers its followers a relationship with a Spiritual Power. For many people this is the crucial difference between the two religions. It is when people feel that they no longer cope by themselves and they need help form outside that Christianity offers good news. Christianity attracts people in trouble for it tells them that they can turn to God and depend on God's help (Hughes 1989:47).

Reframing the Gospel from Biblical Sources

This section argues that if Christ were a missionary in Thailand, he would use the meek approach to witness to the Thai. It will help missionaries and Thai Christians to learn what the incarnation model looks like when performed by Christ in Thai culture. I will use Scripture passages to support my argument.

This section describes biblical meekness or Christ's meekness as required in the Christian witness in Thailand. Culturally speaking, it is effective because it approaches the affective domain of the Thai. I have studied the concept of meekness from the Old and the New Testaments. I have also observed the meanings from (1) *Webster's New International Dictionary* (1957); (2) examination of the Scripture passages where the biblical term is used; and (3) the *New International Dictionary of New Testament Theology Vol. 2* (Brown 1986:256-257), and *Dictionary of the Bible* (Davis 1954).

> Meekness is one of the marks of the humility of Christ. It is also grounded more fundamentally in the interrelationships of the Trinity. It is the sum of the earthly incidents and physical restrictions to which Christ was subjected, such as birth, education, passion, as distinguished from the incidents, such as resurrection, ascension, glorification which constitute the exaltation of Christ (Webster 1957:1213).

Meekness is a mark of true discipleship and does not imply a weak or vacillating nature (Tenney 1963:522). It means gentleness, humility, consideration, mild friendliness. It is a quality shown by friends, while stern harshness may be expected from an enemy (Brown 1986:256).

Meekness applies to those who would rather suffer wrong than do wrong and who therefore enjoy God's favor (Num. 12:3). Believers are commanded to be meek and to show a lowly spirit to one another (Eph. 4:2; Col. 3:12; Tit. 3:2) and to unbelievers, especially when making a defense to everyone who asks Christians to give an account for the hope that is in them (1 Pet. 3:15).

A teacher should be meek and gentle when correcting those who are in opposition, that God may grant them repentance leading to a knowledge of the truth (2 Tim. 2:25).

Meekness is part of the fruit of the Spirit (Gal. 5:23) and a characteristic of Jesus (Matt. 11:29; 2 Cor. 10:1). Jesus Himself was sent to minister to the meek (Ps. 45:5; Isa. 11:4; 29:19; Zeph. 2:3).

God assures help for those who are meek; they will receive ultimate victory (Pss. 22:26; 25:9; 37:11).

God also will beautify the meek with salvation (Ps. 149:4). This concept is opposed to unbridled anger, harshness, and brutality. It represents character traits of the noble-minded, the wise man who remains meek in the face of insult, the judge who is lenient in judgment, and the king who is kind in his rule (Brown 1986:256-257). Those who want to serve the Lord and those who want to come to the Lord must clothe themselves with all humility, with tears and with trials (Acts 20:19). They must have this mind among themselves (Phil. 2:5). Jesus Christ shows the meaning of self-humiliation by becoming obedient unto death, even the utmost shame of the cross. He had no other support than the incredible promise of the faithfulness of God (Pss. 22; 25:18; 31:17; 90:3; 119:50, 92, 150).

Paul's exhortation to humility is also rooted in the effective reality of Christ. Romans 12:16 warns against haughtiness and recommends that the readers give themselves "to humble tasks" or "associate with the lowly." Jesus Christ had to be meek in order to provide salvation to the world (Phil. 2). The foundation of this promise, admonition, and warning is found in Jesus' own way of life as he interpreted it in his invitation in Matthew 11:28ff. He is meek and lowly in heart. The two thoughts stand parallel and show that Jesus was submissive before God, completely dependent upon him, and at the same time humble before humanity, whose servant and helper he had become (Matt. 20:28; Mark 10:45; Luke 22:27).

Matthew 18:1-5 with its teaching on humility shows that Jesus' call to discipleship should not be confused with ethical attainment. The command to humble ourselves like the child placed among the disciples does not mean that we lessen our worth in God's sight. Rather, humility is to know how lowly we are before God. At the same time the use of the word "child" is a reminder of the Father in heaven.

Meekness: A New Approach to Christian Witness to the Thai People

This section contains a design for a meek approach with the suggestion that missionaries and Thai Christians consider this new approach. I will argue that my new approach is necessary as an alternative to Christian witness in Thailand, using explanation and reasons from the Scripture. I intend to convince missionaries as well as Thai Christians of a better way for their own ministries for Christian witness in Thailand.

In this section I want to show that it is possible for missionaries and Thai Christians to learn how to use the new approach to Christian witness to the Thai. With Christ, all things are possible. The Holy Spirit will open the eyes of missionaries and Thai Christians to see the way through this difficult task. Completely trusting in God's words will help missionaries and Thai Christians assure their source of power to work in human hearts.

A "meek" approach is not a "weak" approach. It is rather a biblical approach. I would like to ask missionaries and Thai Christians to withhold their judgment while they are reading this section. I also would like them, at least, to try to apply this new approach by conversing on religious matters with some Buddhists, even aggressive ones who may have had bad or negative experiences with some aggressive Christians in the past. They will begin to see a new and positive reaction from the Buddhists which may set a new hope for Christians.

The present approach used in Thailand is a mixture of Western cultures and a theological approach which may not fit Thai cultural and religious values. Jesus is meek, and meekness is part of the fruit of the Sprit (Galatians 5:22-23). A combination of Thai culture and biblical approach is more practical to the Thai than the current combination of western culture and theological approach.

A Meek Approach Requires Humble Attitudes toward Buddhism

A humble attitude toward Buddhism means that missionaries and Thai Christians should: respect Buddhism and Buddhist faith, mention positive things and good things in Buddhism and admire some of the teachings of Buddha, study Buddhism seriously and find its authenticity, know that God loved Buddha and God agreed with some of the teachings of Buddha, realize that the truth in Buddhism is God's truth, since all truth is God's truth, and realize that God loves all human beings because God created them all in God's image, and human religions reflect God's prevenient grace.

These attitudes create resilience in the minds of gospel communicators to have more capacity in absorbing negative attitudes and expressions of some Buddhists, to listen to their wrong ideas in their belief systems, to empathize with their stubbornness in their own faith, and to have patience, kindness, and understanding, in searching for more understanding from them.

These attitudes help those who have carefully studied Buddhism and confronted its error more selectively and powerfully than the ones who fulminate against everything traditional without studying any of it. These attitudes help missionaries and Thai Christians to develop a genuine, sincere, and long-term relationship with Buddhist friends and lead missionaries and Thai Christians to understand a number of cultural elements and behavior of Buddhists in their society.

This attitude, as I see it, helps missionaries and Christians escape from the "unworthiness" involve in a proselytizing witness and may challenge our motives (concern for our glory, instead of Christ's), our own methods (trust in psychological pressure or in material inducement, instead of the Holy Spirit), or our message (focused on the alleged falsehood and failures of others, instead of on the truth and perfection of Jesus Christ) (Stott 1995:54).

A Meek Approach Requires a New Attitude toward Thai Culture

Since Thai culture values "ego" and "face," missionaries and Christians should not apply techniques that include straightforward, negative performance feed back, strong criticism, and face-to-face confrontation with the Thai. A challenge should be avoided. Western cultures are good about face to face confrontation. Missionaries and Thai Christians should not look down on or violate the ego of the Thai and their dignity. Monarchy, Buddhism, and the nation should not be touched unless one has knowledge about them.

They should not develop a teaching attitude toward the elderly. A loud voice and argument should not apply in Christian witness. American people usually have a louder voice than the Thai. A religious discussion should be soft and smooth. Preaching of the gospel at the pulpit with a loud voice or shouting the word of God, especially when elderly people are in church is interpreted as rude. For Buddhists, *Dharma* should not be shouted by religious leaders.

Missionaries and Thai Christians who are flexible, situation-oriented, and those who love fun and *sanuke* can also relate to the Thai and lead them to Christ efficiently (Fieg 1989:58). Using Thai words correctly helps missionaries and Thai Christians are in the social system.

Missionaries and Thai Christians should be able to display their love, kindness, sincerity, commitment, humility, and mercy through their lifestyles. The Thai require certain qualities in the lives of gospel communicators in order to relate to them well. Developing listening ears and adapting to Thai culture are required for developing a bonding relationship with the Thai.

Missionaries and Thai Christians should witness smoothly and softly to the Thai. They should have a quality of *pranee-pranorm* (compromise with a smooth relationship), *ru-jai* (know the heart), and *mee nam jai* (have a gracious heart) to the Thai. These are key elements in Christian witness. Right manners applied by missionaries and Thai Christians at the right time and in the right place should be known and are required by missionaries and Thai Christians to reduce opposition and melt down a number of barriers erected by Buddhists. Missionaries and some Thai Christians are able to know these behaviors by developing a close relationship with the Thai.

A Meek Approach Requires a Long-Term, Genuine, Sincere Relationship with Buddhists without Strings Attached

This means that missionaries and Thai Christians should develop a bonding relationship along the webs of social networks by using appropriate roles and status in Thai society. This kind of relationship does not allow missionaries and Christians to simply use it as a means to fulfill the task of missionaries and Christians in their Christian witness. It is a relationship that has no hidden agenda. It is a relationship for the relationship's sake. This bridge of genuine relationship will not collapse, though receptors of the gospel may reject Christ at first. Missionaries and Thai Christians should continue to build these bridges to connect Buddhists and Christians together as individuals or as communities

Our examination of the category achievement task orientation revealed that a good relationship, not task, wins all. Missionaries and Thai Christians who are worked-oriented, aggressive in witnessing, and who consciously evaluate their success by the number of saved souls may be frustrated and discouraged constantly. Good relationship, not task, wins all.

Buddhists would like to see a manifestation of ethical elements from Christians' lives such as the fruit of the Spirit, sympathy, sacrificial living, humility, sincerity, unconditional love, mercy, peace of God, and politeness.

Relationship must be smooth, consistent, and natural. "*Jai Yen*" (cool heart), "*Ta Norm Nam Jai*" (hold the heart of others with care) concepts are required. At first, the gospel can be explained through the Thais' understandings of Buddhist faith. Biblical concepts should be built on the concepts that already exist. When these are perceived firmly by Buddhists, then more biblical elements can be added to shape and correct Buddhists' inadequate concepts.

A Meek Approach Requires a Presentation of the Gospel that Brings Benefits and Help, not Threat

A presentation of the gospel which brings benefits and help, not challenge and threat means that missionaries and Christians should not communicate the gospel that results in breaking of relationships. The gospel truth shared by missionaries and Christians should build up and strengthen relationships, and should not start with saying that Buddhists will go to hell if they do not believe in Christ today. They should not look down upon all idol worshipers as evil doers, make Buddhists lose face, or lead Buddhists to be interested in something that they do not have any background to understand.

Missionaries and Thai Christians should present the gospel to Buddhists at first in such a way that they see and understand concretely how the gospel is able to bring to a sense of well being, happiness, and a sense of meaning of life. There are a number of elements of gospel truth that Buddhists are able to perceive right away. Missionaries and Christians should demonstrate the power of the gospel in terms of care and concern for Buddhists as individuals or as communities, particularly when they are facing problems and crises. Christ should be presented to them as, "The Man for others," and the one who is able to release the suffering of Buddhists *(Pad Pao Khaum Took)*. After that we may present the theological side of the gospel and explain to them the cause of their suffering, and the cure of the suffering. Buddhists need the forgiveness of sin through Christ's death on the cross. They must come to the point where they repent from their sins. It should be noted that missionaries and Thai Christians should mention the cost of discipleship to them as well.

A Meek Approach Requires a Time for the Diffusion of the Gospel

This simply means that missionaries and Thai Christians should not seek magical formulas in condensing the contents of the gospel into a capsule or as brief as possible in order to share with them in less time. The "Four Spiritual Laws" can be used more effectively in the Western world than in the Eastern world. In the Western world or secular industrial world, efficiency may be measured by greater production in less time. In religion, however, this may not be the case. Time as appointed and designed by human beings from other cultures should not be a leading factor in Christian witness in Thailand. Missionaries and Thai Christians should not participate in what many missionaries called "hit and run" evangelism. But missionaries and Thai Christians should *Jai Yen* (cool heart) and allow longer term to build up their relationship with Buddhists because a genuine, long-term, and sincere relationship requires a longer time to build; allow themselves to become cultural insiders; demonstrate Christ-likeness; live among them so that they know Buddhists' needs; and spend time in dialoguing and laying down biblical foundations for them so that Buddhists can understand thoroughly what the gospel means.

A Meek Approach Requires Indigenous Strategies for Cross-Cultural Communication of the Gospel

Indigenous strategies for cross cultural communication of the gospel mean that missionaries and Thai Christians should know how Buddhists use meaningful indigenous media to convey their ideas, how missionaries and Thai Christians can improve their credibility as gospel communicators, how missionaries and Thai Christians can be family-focused in their Christian witness, how to demonstrate God's care and concern through social concern, and how to find suitable roles and status for missionaries and Thai Christians to develop genuine relationships with Buddhists in the Thai society.

From this point, I will discuss indigenous strategies for cross-cultural communication of the gospel as already mentioned in this chapter. They are concerned with these elements: use meaningful indigenous media; establish credibility of the communicator and the church and develop family focused evangelism; demonstrate social concern and find suitable role and status.

Use meaningful indigenous media: The library research suggested that in Thai culture, oral communication tends to predominate while printed media have low impact. Thai culture has its own primary communication systems, such as indigenous song, dance, drama, music, story telling, illustrations, and other arts. The best media for each culture should be used in evangelization. Use and adaptation of local media should be encouraged in all evangelism. Indigenous illustrations, key historical illustrations, parables, symbols, and analogies are encouraged for use in Christian witness (LCWE 1980:9). In urban areas and some rural ones too, Western forms of media such as film and songs have been used indigenously. Christian communicators should carefully study the principles and process of indigenization behind the acceptance of such media and not follow Western modes (LCWE 1980:9).

Establish credibility: Research suggests that a factor crucial to Christian witness is the credibility of Christians. Fieg suggested that in a hierarchical culture, higher status carries more credibility than lower status. In Thailand, the king has the highest credibility and workers, the lowest (Fieg 1989:16). In all relationships, there were distinct superior and subordinate roles. Authority and power are considered natural to the human condition, seen as being derived from moral and ethical excellence of those who lived by it (Fieg 1989:16).

The credibility of the communicator is vital to the audience's acceptance of his message as credible. Missionaries and Thai Christians should be able to develop their credibility among Buddhists. A sympathetic understanding of the Buddhists is needed. A Christian approach should always be with humility and living persuasion, backed by the testimony of dynamic personal relationship with Jesus Christ. A living demonstration of the gospel is required (LCWE 1980:10).

The credibility of the church as a whole is a crucial issue in the effective communication of the gospel. Through the eyes of the Buddhists in Thailand, the Christians church is an alien import and this becomes an obstacle to the gospel communicators. The Thai church should attempt to establish culturally relevant forms and expressions for the church. Thai churches should allow the local context to determine its own forms and expressions in the Christian witness and in the life of the church (LCWE 1980:10).

Evangelism of whole families rather than of individuals is vital. Individual conversion loses its impact in Thai society and encounters various opposition forces. The individual should be encouraged to prepare to win the whole family. Developing a relationship with members of the family and community should be done naturally in the early stage of the Christian witness.

Demonstrate social concern: Buddhists see Jesus Christ as a man who does good things. Jesus Christ is the man who lived for others in the eyes of Buddhists. He healed the sick, helped the poor, did good, and showed compassion to the oppressed. A careful study of the gospels reveals that evangelism and social action are two facets of the Christian faith (Seamands 1981:66). The Thai church should demonstrate social concern and welfare with evangelistic activity spontaneously, with no strings attached. The outreach must be carried out in a needy community naturally. Today great care must be taken not to spoil new inquirers or produce "rice Christians" with dependent attitudes.

Historical research demonstrates that successful and influential missionaries were those who put themselves in an appropriate Thai role and status. Interview results also indicate that Buddhists are not familiar with the role of missionary. Since missionaries do not have roles inside the Thai social structure, the Thai don't know how to relate to them. They are not sure how to use personal pronouns for missionaries and for Thai ministers. Thais wonder, "Are they medical doctors, or teachers, or priests, or Peace Corps volunteers?" In a hierarchical system, people should know roles and status of the other people in order to communicate with each other well. Jesus Caswell, Constantine Phaulkon, and George McFarland are good examples of powerful and successful missionaries in Thai history.

The present method used by missionaries and Thai Christians is to develop a relationship with Buddhists and find opportunities to share the gospel. Generally, Christians use one-way communication. The new approach suggests a two-way communication-dialogue approach. Christians should learn from Buddhists of their needs, ideals, and knowledge in Buddhism. Through a dialogue approach, both parties gain knowledge of the others. A dialogue approach produces no argument. The communication process flows smoothly without interruption. Aggression and barriers don't develop, and Christians are able to converse with Buddhists as the Holy Spirit guides. A designed encounter turns into a natural encounter. People are free to discuss subjects about which they know little. Both parties enjoy conversing. By this method, Christians come to know various aspects of Buddhists' lives and needs.

Buddhists have their own needs and religious ideals. These may be material needs, social needs, or religious ideals. Christians should show interest and concern for those needs. Acceptance and encouragement for Buddhists to fulfill their ideals and needs should be recognized. Theravada Buddhism basically teaches the ability of self to reach religious ideals—to be good and follow the five precepts or Buddha. Through a genuine relationship, if Christians are able to show repeatedly and in a concrete way to Buddhists that their ability to reach their ideals can be fulfilled through the Holy Spirit who lives in Christians, then through this approach Buddhists will begin to realize the power of the gospel on their own. Christian lifestyles which demonstrate the goodness of Christ to Buddhists are the most important element for the meek approach. If their desires and needs can be fulfilled by help in a biblical way and by the power of prayer of Christians, then Buddhists will come to their own conclusion that Christ is the Lord. When Buddhists encounter crises, Christians' prayer and genuine help done in the Sprit of Christ by the whole body of the Christian community can confirm to them that God's love and presence are in their midst.

Conclusion

I have attempted to design a meek approach for the Christian witness in Thailand using data derived from library research. The meek approach can be observed in various areas of cross-cultural communication and the Christian witness. The new approach aims to follow the biblical meekness. It suggests that missionaries and Thai Christians adjust their attitudes toward Buddhism and Thai culture. This can be done by serious study of Buddhism and Thai culture, which, in turn, may lead them to appreciate both. Factors related to the new approach are concerned with developing a genuine and sincere relationship, indigenous strategies and media in presenting the gospel, credibility of both the church and gospel communicators, social concern, and family-focused evangelism. The efficiency of the new approach depends on how one can utilize each factor to optimum efficiency. All factors should be applied at the same time, if possible, in Christian witness in Thailand.

I have based my findings in this chapter on the research of scholars. The new approach of Christian witness consists of: humble attitudes toward Buddhism; requiring a proper attitude toward Thai culture; developing a long-term, genuine, and sincere relationship with Buddhists with no strings attached; presenting the gospel bringing benefits and helps not challenges and threats; allowing time for diffusion of the gospel. Indigenous strategies for cross-cultural communication of the gospel must be concerned with: using meaning indigenous media; establishing the credibility of the communicator and the church; developing family-focused evangelism; demonstrating social concern; finding a suitable role and status of missionaries and Thai Christians.

6

Where Are Your Temples?

Do Christianity and Buddhism Share a Temple Ethos?

Steve Spaulding

Background to the Discussion

Sitting across the table in a dingy Indochinese hotel dining room from one of the prominent leaders of the church in the country…There's a look of concern that comes over his face. The churches are now being confronted by religious leaders over their viability—in the form of the question: "Where are your temples?" Where is the edifice that reflects your spiritual rootedness, place and authority within the society, membership, professional class, territory, financial strength, religious rites and public worship?

As the son of missionaries in Buddhist Asia, I grew up in the shadow of temples, observing elaborate village ceremonies, including death and cremation rituals. As the grandson of the founder of a major North American Bible school, I also spent every Sunday attending church, variously called the sanctuary, or "Tab" for tabernacle, and reverently singing refrains such as "The Lord is in his holy temple, the Lord is in his holy temple, let all the earth keep silence."

The background to this discussion then is both personal and missiological. But as we'll see, it arises from several quarters: the religious—in this case, Buddhist—world into which the Christian message first comes, the missionary community introducing an alternative society, inquirers and young believers coming into the new faith, and eventually, the leadership of the churches who represent any staying power for the minority religion.

The Question: Where are Your Temples?

From missionaries

I was first confronted with this question by a missionary, someone who had worked for years among Indochinese refugees in the Los Angeles area and who seemed well-versed in cross-cultural dynamics. His contention was that any lasting and culturally sensitive work among Indochinese would have to contend with the temple religion of Buddhism, and find ways to shape church to some degree along temple lines. This was not just a matter of indigenous architectural concerns. It involved a whole array of social and religious expectations on the part of peoples raised within a Buddhist *cultus* of temple, complete with rites, sacrifice, professional caretakers, cruciality of space, the housing of deities and holy artifacts, as well as distinctions in religious, gender, age and other roles.

From national church leaders

Years later I was conversing with the national church leader mentioned above. He had been distraught over the same question put to him by Buddhist leaders in his country. It was apparently a matter of religious pride, prestige and place which had the Buddhist hierarchy nonplussed. Why would a religion intent on mass conversion, church planting and a felt impact in the country not have large edifices to stake its claim, establishing visible centers of worship to be its own beacon on a hill? After all, was not Burma (Myanmar), for example, "The Land of a Million Pagodas"?

From religious leaders

The religious leaders themselves have put this question squarely to the indigenous church of nations in the Buddhist world. While the question may be loaded, it may also be the sincere inquiry into the nature of the Christian religion and reference to the apparent indispensability of a temple ethos within Buddhism and its host society.

From inquirers and converts

Lastly, honest inquirers both within and outside the church might be the most pertinent here. What is the viability of a religious alternative which does not have resources sufficient to erect its own alternative sanctuary? Is there a *dynamic equivalent* to the system in which they are existing, sometimes at great cost or already ample discontinuity?

Dimensions to the Discussion

Anthropology of religion

First, in approaching this topic of temple, we need to establish some functions and meaning to the temple part of Eastern/Buddhist religion. Comparisons can then be made with the functions and meanings attached to both the early Jewish and more contemporary Christian parallels.

In Buddhist societies, temples fulfill religious, social, psychological, anthropological/sociological, spiritual, and other functions. To what extent has the Christian missionary enterprise failed the Buddhist communities to which it has come by not adequately establishing a dynamic-equivalence structure?

Biblical theology

Given the direct correspondence between any talk of temple within New Testament Christianity and its roots in the Jewish temple system, some discussion ought to be given to the origins of temple in the OT and especially the relationship between tabernacle and temple. This will then be reflected in some of our dealings with the transitions and crisis associated with the establishment of the new Christian movement within the context of first century, second-temple Judaism.

Ecclesiology: How is church temple?

While it is clear that the many functions of temple in Buddhism do not correspond directly with the Christian institution of church, there is sufficient overlap between them in order to:

- Clarify or correct any validity of a one-to-one correspondence in the answer to the original question, from the receptor cultures;
- Address directly some of the institutional accretions of Christendom which may be a major hindrance to receptor cultures in understanding the true nature of the faith and of the church. This can be done through approaching especially what occurred in the transition from second-temple Judaism to the early Christian sect through the vocation and work of Christ and his immediate community, the apostles. Focus here is primarily on Jesus' ministry years and the climax of his career in relation to the Jewish temple, as well as Stephen's trial and martyrdom with the subsequent dispersion;
- Clarify an ecclesiology from the two perspectives of "How do we gather?"—more at the visible institution, often foremost in people's minds both inside and outside the church—versus "Of what do we consist?"—more at the underlying purpose and vital life-signs of the community of the King.

Missiology

Contextualization in the milieu of rapid advance: From a Christian mission standpoint, there is a global burgeoning of efforts at "rapid church planting movements" which have had attendant implications for ecclesiology. In fact, one popular recent definition of church planting movements begins with the qualifier "rapid" (Watt 2002). In other words, it's not a contemporary church planting movement unless it's yielding quick and relatively high numerical results. The advantage of some of these movements is its intentional avoidance of importing unnecessary foreign institutional trappings, which would normally allow for greater initial growth, a minimum of encumbrances and a requirement of much greater local engagement in exegeting the Scriptures for appropriate local renderings. This bias for fruit-bearing in mission, and specifically in the area of church-planting, is and will continue to have significant if indirect influence upon our missiology. In the case of associations between church in the populace's mind and church in a minimalist ecclesiological sense, there is bound to be some dissonance.

Indigenization and long-term stability: There is some concern within the broader evangelical mission community that such rapid reproduction of simple church without sufficient forethought on the inevitable elements of institutionalization might yield unnecessary aberrations, something which has substantial precedent in history. On the other hand, the progressives argue persuasively that it has been precisely the deadening weight of institutional ossification which has provided the larger church with both gross nominalism, ample error and/or dismal, if any, growth. Does a discussion of temple within the Christian faith provide a part of the solution here?

There is a related field of questions in the area of Buddhist-Christian conversion and the issues of social continuity or dislocation in the process. Is the question regarding the need for dynamic-equivalence temples more at a personal, psychological level? A communal/social level? Is it the community (as it considers the alternative belief and religious system, in search of an assuring set of symbols of religious stability, continuity and visibility)? Is the temple ethos one which actually draws the person or community into the realm of the divine, and in that sense acts as a means of grace on a spiritual level? Or is there, on the part of the missionary community, an over-concern for dynamic equivalence models and idealized noninterference?

Angst regarding church in an especially postmodern milieu: While this paper deals primarily with the distinctions between two religious realities in Asia, the ironic cotemporaneous popularization of Buddhist thought in pop-culture and the advent of postmodernity especially in the West points to crises happening in both the church and the culture of the West which will have significant influence on global Christianity. There may be connections here with the discussion of temple in both religions.

Foreignness of ecclesial forms: Finally, from a mission standpoint, there has been the persistence of embarrassingly Western forms of church planted throughout the non-west and specifically Buddhist spheres, which has reinforced the local assumption that Christianity is fundamentally a foreign and invasive religion, rather than something which can authentically find a home within the existing culture. Some groups have sought to reduce this dissonance by building visible church structures that appear identical to Buddhist temple architecture. On the face of it, this would seem like a reasonable and rather simple step of contextualization. The question needing addressing here is whether there is any sort of dynamic equivalence occurring in this process.

Loud Silence

The most fascinating feature of this question is the pregnant silence one finds on the subject, when in fact temple is one of the most conspicuous markers for most religions, certainly Buddhism and Judeo-Christianity included.

"Temple" in literature

Christian: Rarely indeed will one find mention of temple in Christian theological works, including works on ecclesiology. Within Christian theological literature, temple discussions are relegated largely to OT studies of specifically Israel's monarchial period and briefly to Pauline categories or metaphors of church in the NT. Of course, there is tacit agreement within almost all Christian communities that temple as a religious category mutated through the work of Christ from a physical structure centered in Jewish faith on Jerusalem to a spiritual and social reality embodied in the church which he founded—the people of God being the true temple—at least for the duration of the so-called "Church Age." But as we shall see, this can be somewhat of a smokescreen for other governing metaphors in the communities both within and outside the church.

Perhaps the theologian responsible for generating a whole new interest in temple within the Protestant/Evangelical community is N. T. Wright, the Anglican Canon of Westminster and Oxford New Testament scholar for almost three decades. His treatment of the temple is restricted almost exclusively to first century Jewish conceptions, expectations and how Jesus conceived of his own vocation as both consummatory and replacing of the temple and its *cultus* as Messiah.

But as a contemporary and practical Christian reality, temple as a visible expression of church does not appear much in theological or practical Christian literature. The irony here is that there is clearly a subterranean acquiescence to the idea that not only is the mystical Church the temple of the living God from a Pauline standpoint, but that the buildings which the church in Christendom has erected bear a resemblance to or hold some continuity with the OT temple. This is partly what we explore in this paper, since the question "Where are your temples?" is not merely a reflection of Buddhist (or non-Christian) ignorance but rather of the caricature put forward by seventeen centuries of Christendom's highly visible institutionalism.

We look in vain, though, for an extensive apologetic or theology of temple in relation to this almost overwhelming caricature within the visible Christian religion.

Buddhist: Rarely as well will one find even passing mention of temple in books introducing the inquirer to Buddhism. It is in the study of anthropology and sociology of religion—the etic perspective—that one discovers occasional coverage of the topic of temple. Is this because temple simply fits conceptually within the much larger category of institutionalization, of which all religions partake equally over time?

I contend that part of the silence on the structure within the literature, juxtaposed against the prominence of the edifice and function of the temple in both Christendom and Buddhism is due to a realization that the visible structure does not well represent the heart of the religion and has in most cases become a prime perpetuator of religious institutional power.

Edifice complex in the community of adherents

Within the Christian scene worldwide, there is still almost universal association of the word "church" with place and event. This is to say that while most theologically trained Christians will immediately denounce this universal association of church with buildings and services, the same majority revert to language which continues this very one-to-one correspondence. Church is first and foremost something we go to or drive by. Secondly, it is an event that occurs usually once or twice a week, something we attend. Thirdly, it may be a local fellowship or broader denomination in which one holds some sort of membership. Membership implies fees, and so we all support or tithe *to* our churches, which consume almost all of these gifts on their infrastructure, professional clergy and maintenance as facilities. Webster certainly bears out this order of understanding with its first choice in defining "church" (1) a building, especially for Christian public worship [Merriam Webster].

Buddhists hold a remotely similar view of their temples. We will explore various functions of temple in most religious societies (including Buddhist, Jewish, and Christian) and find that while cultures vary in their view or prioritization of these functions, there is considerable overlap among them all.

The silence here refers to the distance between the clergy's and the faithfuls' acceptance of and high dependence upon the visible edifice and the accompanying paucity of sanction for the same from within the creeds, doctrines, and religious apologetic.

Edifice complex in the wider populace

In an atmosphere amenable to church planting in pioneer Christian mission situations, it would seem especially incumbent on the Christian mission to discover what is in the mind of the audience already when something as central as church is introduced into their cultural framework. This intersects quickly with paradigms of religion which are held, promoted or reinforced by national or ethnic powers or governments. The popular image of Christianity—and hence its church[es] is often wittingly or otherwise associated in Asian cultures with foreign, relatively recent, aggressive, "Western," invasive *religion.* While this is a mostly negative association, and not altogether justified, it is one which unfortunately is reified by local and national authorities—political and religious—intent on maintaining the religious—and, by extension, economic or other—status quo. It translates into a type of edifice complex insomuch as local or national governments can use the visible structures as a means of monitoring, managing and ultimately limiting the growth of the church through its most evident and resource-intensive physical plant. Church-burning is a commonplace within areas of persecution. Church-vandalism is the equivalent in freer societies, all equally misleading but accepted terminology for the edifice-as-temple-as-church.

Temple Ethos and the Functions of Temple

Given the paucity of a proper apologetic for temple within most of the tradition in either religion, what then *is* a temple ethos? What are the legitimate functions of temple in these major faiths, given their prominence in the overall religious landscape?

By ethos we mean a temple world or the aggregate of functions which religious temples, their structures, symbols, artifacts, professionals and frequenters fulfill. In discussing the kind of religion that Buddhism is, anthropologist of religion David Gellner gives one list of the array of functions that religious practices in general might fulfill:

- the legitimation and expression of the household or family group
- the legitimation and expression of the locality (or village or tribal sections or caste, etc.)
- the legitimation and expression of the nation or ethnic group.
- the sanctification of the stages of the life-cycle.
- the socialization of the young and provision of a moral code.
- the provision of a path to salvation from all ills—i.e., a soteriology (Gellner 2001:323).
- While these are clearly the anthropological observations of religious function, they illustrate a wide array even within one discipline's perspective of what a society might attach to its temple functions—as a visible, centralizing force in the overall religion.

Based on my understanding of Gellner and similar summaries of functional religion, I have formulated here a number of probable functions for temple, beginning with the Jewish temple ethos of the Old Testament, and considering the social, societal, religious, spiritual, and political domains of other religious systems centered around temple:

- ***Pointing:*** Physical symbol/ a Godward sign
- ***Meeting:*** Place of centered communal worship
- ***Celebrating:*** Place of encounter with the divine
- ***Instructing:*** Center of teaching and continuation of the religious heritage
- ***Dwelling:*** Divine house or resting place (vs. derisive language God uses in Is. 66)
- ***Preserving:*** Symbol of rootedness, permanence, reassurance, presence/reminder
- ***Sanctifying:*** Creation of sacred place and establishing sacred people (sacrificial systems)
- ***Protecting:*** Providing power-protection from malevolent spiritual forces, people or deities
- ***Stratifying:*** Social and spiritual separation, and reinforcing hierarchical structure and binary relation
- ***Creating Art***: Architecture, gift, work
- ***Building Structure:*** Involving cost and time (vs. "In three days I'll rebuild it")
- ***Dominating:*** Power-center for the establishment (i.e. what Jesus countered)
- ***Conquering:*** Territoriality, a sign of mission conquest (medieval and modern)

There is overlap within this list, and it certainly may not be comprehensive. While a few of these functions derive from a negative notion that religion+time=institution=>domination, most of these features would connote positive and cohering elements in religious life of any society. Categories which seem contradictory to a NT treatment of the new temple ethos are italicized, and those categories which seem directly to overlap between any religious symbolism in a temple ethos and that of the NT church are bolded.

Primary Domains Affected by Temple in Most Religions

The Spiritual

a. In most temple contexts, "power-protection" is intimately associated with temple function, both in terms of establishing or maintaining sacred space, rites of protection against malevolent powers or vindictive deities, rituals of blessing and celebration of festivals of gratitude for such power-protection or other provision.[1]

b. The temple is also a pointer to the divine, oddly whether in a pantheistic, animistic, monistic or monotheistic context.[2]

c. Correspondingly, temple represents encounter with the divine or transcendent. God means to meet with his people—in a particular place and time. Temple usually expresses the nexus of this intention.

d. Temple is both symbolically and concretely the center of worship. This speaks directly to the inherent inclination towards idolatry within any temple ethos, for the closer one gets to the physical center of worship, the greater the temptation to worship the pointers to the divine rather than the true object to which the signs, symbols and structures point.

The Religious

a. Temple is the centerpiece of a religious society's rites and rituals, whether of birth, marriage, death and a host of other critical festivals, celebrations which tie the temporal to the eternal, the immanent to the transcendent and the menial to the meaningful.

b. Temple is the grand intermediary between the *laos* or masses and the holy both in terms of place and people. For all temple institutions have a temple mount or sanctified ground and a temple class or religious professionals who are set apart for holy practices to which the masses are not granted access. This is a *sine qua non* it seems of most established religion.

c. Temple is often the fountainhead of religious instruction, from which emanates the conserving elements of religious belief, the reinforcing of primary tenets.

d. Temple represents institutionalization of the religion. In this sense, by its grandeur and prominence it speaks to the permanence and stability of the religion. Its attendant professional class of priests, monks, clergy manifests its durability, the assurance of staying power over the generations.

e. Temple generally elicits a sacrificial system, whether propitiatory/soteriological or simply pragmatic and self-perpetuating, extracting resources from the populace to maintain its physical plant and operations.

f. Lastly, temple is a house for the god, and therefore a domestication of deity; put crudely, a manageable and convenient holy place to set perimeters about our creator, protector, provider, judge, savior, etc.[3]

The Socio-Cultural

a. Temple has as much a social meaning and function as a spiritual or religious one. It is a community center, often used for more than strictly religious functions, yet making sacred the secular by virtue of its primary associations with the transcendent.

b. As such, temple represents social continuity, permanence, stability. Destroy the temple and you have often cut the lifeline of the community's very identity and survival. Even the poorest rural communities in temple societies have scrounged up the resources to erect their own religious edifice, as much for their own social cohesion and identity as out of religious obligation to local or transcendent deities.

c. As Gellner points out, temple is also a center of learning, specifically moral instruction and this especially for the socialization of the society's younger generation.

d. Temples generally reflect local art, architecture, and hence culture. The most ready expression of local cultural art forms can be found in the temple architecture and artifacts within the compound.

The Anthropological

a. From a social-relations standpoint, the temple is itself a statement of position, place, prestige and hierarchy, and distinguishing of every member of the society by strata in relation to the holy, whether by age, gender, disability/deformity, ethnicity or vocation. The physical layout of the entire temple vicinity and internal structure distinguishes one group from another in general access to or restriction from the holy.

b. The power of place is intuitive in any temple structure.

The Political

a. The imposing presence of a highly visible religious structure says something about the political establishment of any society. State sanction must be present for temple to function openly and appropriately. Where a society has politically agreed to pluralistic expressions of religion, multiple temple systems can vie for or appeal to niche populations. But in most cases, the society's political establishment has tended to favor the prevailing and historic religious tradition, often in symbiotic fashion. Separation of church and state is not the historic pattern, and even where this has been established, there is rarely a long sustaining of such an ideal.

b. There is in the history of religion within nation-states a nexus between nationalism and national religion which has fueled both trenchant resistance to any religious competitors as well as some of the severest nationalistic conflicts.

c. As such, temple often embodies a negative extension of the domination system of the political establishment. This is also reflective of the unseen domination system of demonic powers which will use religious hierarchies to oppress people.

The Economic

a. The property and industry associated with elaborate temple structures has been wittingly or otherwise erected and supported by the poorest of peoples throughout history. Karl Marx was incensed with the manner in which religion, from his perspective, was rightly caricatured as the one institution which by default never gave back, a kind of economic black hole, and the temple at its center presented the greatest expenditures of energy and expense.
b. These structures are then maintained through equally elaborate systems of temple collections, ritual ceremony costs, and especially the support of its professional clergy/priesthood.

Attention is not given here to gross social and sexual abuses of temple systems,[4] which have indeed occurred within every temple milieu over time, and which might rightly be considered as part and parcel of the long-term implications of temple institutionalization within religiously corruptible systems. Within this consideration is also the presence of the demonic in a particularly religious garb—a religious spirit which is clearly part of the domination system which strips dignity and destroys humanity through the use of religious symbolism, strictures and open oppression.

To conclude, there is wide diversity in the function of temples across the religious spectrum, but these functions fall largely within the social, religious and anthropological or cultural spheres. The following sections will deal with whether Buddhism and

Christianity have a temple ethos and what the answers will mean for missiology.

While temples function at these various levels in most religious contexts, can common ground be found between Buddhist understandings, expectations and assumptions and the temple understanding of contemporary Christian church and mission?

Is There a Buddhist Temple Ethos?

In the typical encyclopedia of religions, the index entry for temple contains far more occurrences of illustrations/photographs than actual textual references. It seems the institution is appreciated for its aesthetics far more than defended for its religious function.

What was the Founder's position and conditioning in this regard? Much of the history and pilgrimage of the *Gautama* Buddha has mythical qualities and is anecdotal, but it is common knowledge that a significant part of *Siddartha's* maturation was in juxtaposition to the sixth century BCE Indian animisms and pantheon. The shrines, temples and millions of attendant gods of his Hindu homeland were in large part the cause of the Buddha's early launch into an atheistic philosophy of high ethics and contemplative detachment. He established the community—the *sangha*—of followers very late in life and seems to have given little thought or preparation to the inevitable institutionalization of a religion.

From the Theravada core and reflected in most other Buddhist traditions, temples provide the most consistent visible connection for the sangha—community of those entered upon the Middle Way of merit-making toward enlightenment—in their practice of contact with holy things (other holy things including *sutras*, *stupas*, Buddhist statues, ancestors, deities and spirits) (Earhart 1993:924). The scholarly portrayal of Buddhism in most streams/traditions is largely unapologetic for the encrustations of local animisms which normally accrue to the temple system. While technically Buddha is not a god, there is worship of the Buddha and often a wide array of local deities and spirits supported within most temple systems. For example, in references to both Chinese and Japanese systems, temples are by definition the residence of god(s) or Buddhist divinities, represented by statues and revered through scripture recitations, offerings and rituals (:1071, 1185).

Secondly, the temple in Buddhist religious life is connected with the almost omnipresent monastic orders. In this case, it is the representative, material setting apart of the holy from the unholy, the residence and retreat for those on the path toward enlightenment, and especially the locus of the teaching of the Buddhist way, for the monk is not only a meditative pilgrim but also connected to the laity through the function of teaching, and the temple is the primary location for this activity.

In Thailand it was maintained that almost one-half of all of the primary schools in the country are *wat* [temple or monastery] schools, taught by monks as well as laymen. While the actual number of students in these schools is a much lower percentage of the total school-age population, the impact on society would be enormous. Monks have consistently been involved in counseling on a wide range of personal and civic matters, reinforcing the centrality of the temple *cultus* in the village or even city life (Lester 1973:115).

The placement or location of the temple within the village has always been strategic, balancing the taboos of power and place with the central role the temple has in civic life, standing apart from the clustered houses, yet the hub of village life (Earhart 1993:927). Temples have for centuries been the favored place for religious functions as well as generic community gatherings.

Of course the ritual life of the Buddhist community is attended by the temple and most crucial celebrations and commemorations: annual festivals and entreaties, holy days and rites of passage like ordination, and preeminently those rites surrounding death, are all attached to temple proceedings and location.

At the popular level, one veteran missionary, based on decades of work in Southeast Asia, affirmed that for many Buddhists the two primary means of making merit are: (1) going to temple and (2) building temples, since this is so money intensive and therefore exacting such sacrifice, and then so impressive that the hope is some merit for the life to come has been achieved. This is reminiscent of popular-level Roman Catholic behavior before the Reformation and throughout many corners of the more conservative RCC world even today. Merit-making as centered on a temple ethos seems frighteningly close to the aberrations we point to within the Christendom model of church: facility-intensive and eliciting all the wrong motivations and activities for favor with God.

Another latent function of temples, not apparent in the standard presentation of the religion but introduced indirectly in the discussion of its missionary nature (and hence, the outer borders of the religion's demographic centers), is the visible, territorial placement of temples as representative of Buddhism's expansion. The Burmese have proudly maintained that Myanmar is "the Land of a Million Pagodas," clearly a statement of Buddhism's omnipresence in the culture and the value placed on physical reminders of this almost imperial territoriality. When dealing with Buddhism's expansion into the West and other traditionally non-Buddhist arenas, the numbers of temples are prominent as indicators of relative acceptance of or resistance to the new religion, similar to the notion of receptivity to Christianity by the presence and number of visible church buildings—i.e., South Korea. Max Weber in his study of religions distinguished between emissary, promissory and commissary missionary activities, based on the degree of pressure with which the obligation to convert others is felt within the religion. Buddhism would fit within the emissary category where Christianity would fit the promissory and Islam the commissary, in that as an emissary missionary religion, Buddhism highlights the establishing of a presence and minimizing differences between one's own religion and the religion one encounters while retaining commitment to the tradition (Sharma 1993:129). It could be debated whether in fact due to this more pliable nature, Buddhism "assumed a national form to a far greater extent than missionary religions of the promissory or commissary types." And the argument might work the other direction when East Asia's nationalized Buddhist traditions capitulated to the advance of communism in the twentieth century. But of these three world religions, it seems that history bears out that Buddhism is the most accommodating.

From a survey of the role of temples in different contexts such as Nepal, Thailand and Japan, different Buddhist societies and subcultures have developed differing models of use for temples, so that generalizations can be problematic. Yet as cited in the list of overall functions, there is a broad commonality among these very different contexts in: domestication of the religion, a centralizing and stabilizing social force or center, an association with the professional religious class and duties of the community to support the religious cults, a strong sense of power-protection and spiritual space or territory, the primary locus of communal rites and rituals, and a house or shrine for the local deity (or deities).

There is an almost universal temple/monastery presence within Buddhism, yet the religious literature does not give it pride of place or even a solid apologetic. It seems to have become a sociological necessity in bolstering the institutions and staying power of the religious system accruing to Buddhist tradition.

Is There a Christian Temple Ethos?

Merriam Webster defines "church" as (1) a building, especially for Christian public worship. What exactly are we saying if we seek an answer to the question *Is Christianity a temple religion*? Posing the question this way is, in a sense, unfair, since religion and even Christianity is being inserted as part of the equation. This is intentional, of course, as temple has emerged as a fundamentally institutionalizing force across religions. Most pietistic followers of Christ recoil from the notion that Christianity is a religion. Andrew Walls draws a word picture of the two competing tendencies within

Christianity—one toward domestication and rootedness and the other a more pilgrim or missionary impulse (1996). Others such as Ralph Winter and Art Glasser—both of whom taught at Fuller's School of World Mission—made the distinction between the modality versus sodality structures in Christendom.

In answer to the question of a Christian temple ethos, we proceed from three points: (i) Biblically, we can find evidence against a physical temple continuity in the NT (see table below). (ii) Theologically, there is both strong NT support for a temple reality in the essence of the church and scant support for the "temple" as it is attached to "churches" in the popular mind. (iii) Practically, in the general population there is wide acceptance of a temple ethos attached to the physical structure and activities of the institutional church.

Ironically or sensibly, both Buddhist and Christian religious histories hold up the founder as iconoclast, introducing into their heavily institutionalized and religiously corrupt environs radical new communities, recognizable not by an alternative institution but by a lifestyle and vital community (fellowship) of followership to the founder. Over time the community, gaining acceptability through a fiery trial of persecution, establishing moral credibility and numerical growth, ultimately became an institutionally sanctioned center of the originally antagonistic society, domesticating its radicalness in structures which increasingly drew separation between the holy from the unholy, until the faithful associated the religious experience with the physical symbol, revisiting the very institutional nominality from which the founders recoiled. In this sense Christianity and Buddhism do, negatively, share a certain temple ethos.

The simple chart below portrays the proximity in the histories of critical elements to the emergence and sustaining of a temple ethos in both religious traditions.

"Temple" Postures	**Buddhism**	**Christianity**
Theological underpinnings	Ambiguity or silence	Ambiguity or silence
Founder	Rejection/discontinuity	Replacement: continuity/discontinuity
New order	Creation of New Community: *sangha*	Creation of New Community; church
Popular culture and clergy	Necessity by Accommodation	Necessity w/ Tacit Theological Embrace

Other parallels and contrasts can be drawn between the common understandings and functions of temples in various Buddhist traditions and those within Christian "church" counterparts. Within each religion, there is vast disparity among different traditions/denominations on the "meaning of the temple." For the proper roots of Christian self-understanding of temple, we turn to a biblical—Old and New Testament—survey.

A Biblical Survey of Temple

> Therefore, brothers, since we have confidence to enter *the Most Holy Place by the blood* of Jesus, by a new and living way opened for us *through the curtain*, that is, his *body*, and since we have a *great priest* over *the house of God*, let us draw near to God with a sincere heart in full assurance of faith, having our hearts *sprinkled to cleanse us from a guilty conscience* and having our *bodies washed with pure water*.... Let us not give up *meeting together*.... (Heb. 10:19-25).

There is a sense in which the crux of this paper derives from two simultaneous hinge points of history in which we find ourselves: the one being the twilight of so-called modernity and the other being the dawn of what Philip Jenkins calls *The Next Christendom,* or the twilight of Christendom-as-we-know-it. These two transitions are contemporaneous, have clear interrelationship but are also distinctive.

But the primary point of departure here is to steer clear of contemporary landscape changes and to deal rather with the biblical record and equally momentous transitions between the old and new covenant eras and their direct bearing on our understanding of 'temple ethos' in the current maelstrom of Christian ecclesiology and mission among Buddhists.

To a panoramic perusal of the biblical material, then, we turn with an emphasis on the following: the establishment of temple in relation to its roots in the tabernacle system, Christ's treatment of the temple, Stephen's trial, the Apostle Paul's ecclesiology, other dominant NT motifs drawing upon temple language and symbolism, and overarching conclusions.

Old Testament Tabernacle and Temple Systems

When God claimed the people of Israel for himself and first established the nation as "my treasured possession…a kingdom of priests and a holy nation" (Ex. 19:4-6) he was making a statement as to his wider mission. For as Filbeck points out, as God's treasured possession, they were to be the vehicle of the message of God to the nations. The words "treasured possession" literally mean "moveable goods that are valuable." The emphasis here is on two things: (i) the portability of the message, and (ii) the high value God placed on his people (Filbeck 1994).

How did the temple *cultus* come into being for the Israelite people? There is no need for a scholarly answer here. The temple has its roots in the tabernacle system associated with the Exodus and the large worshiping community of Israel en route to the holy land. There is no question from the biblical record what the source of the tabernacle is. The entire episode on Mt. Sinai originates indubitably from the initiative, action and speech of a sovereign YHWH, intent on saving a people for himself that all the nations under heaven might come to know him.

Only after the tabernacle has been in use, traversing the wilderness with the pilgrim people and entering the Promised Land, do kings—themselves symbolic of a move against the original intent of their rightful King—sought a permanent resting place for their deity, incidentally coterminous with their own need for kingly palaces. 2 Samuel 7:4-13 is telling for its divine denunciation of David's innocent enough impulse to house the living God:

> That night the word of the LORD came to Nathan, saying: "Go and tell my servant David, 'This is what the LORD says: Are you the one to build me a house to dwell in? I have not dwelt in a house from the day I brought the Israelites up out of Egypt to this day. I have been moving from place to place with a tent as my dwelling. Wherever I have moved with all the Israelites, did I ever say to any of their rulers whom I commanded to shepherd my people Israel, "Why have you not built me a house of cedar?" Now then, tell my servant David, 'This is what the LORD Almighty says: I took you from the pasture and from following the flock to be ruler over my people Israel. I have been with you wherever you have gone, and I have cut off all your enemies from before you. Now I will make your name great, like the names of the greatest men of the earth. And I will provide a place for my people Israel and will plant them so that they can have a home of their own and no longer be disturbed.... [T]he LORD himself will establish a house for you....

In this passage there is ironic juxtaposing between God's resistance of domestication and his intent to bring his people to a place of peaceful rest and residence. In answer to David's intention to build a proper house for God, God's retort is that he has been in charge of Israel's history and even David's emergence as leader for the people.

God is not only clear in his response that there is and never has been a need to house him; he also turns the discussion back to the people and their king, whom he has moved, both out of Egypt in the great exodus as well as David from the pasture to the throne room. God seems to see their need to house him as a mere reflection of their own need for stability and rootedness. Even this, though, as reflected in the sermon of Stephen, is not a desire of God in the long run. While he calls his people into a Sabbath rest, there is little indication that God desires the people to settle permanently in one place. This after all would contradict God's grander purposes for the nations, and might render the people complacent or, in the end, superciliously religious.

The "tent" throughout the OT was almost always generally known as the "tent of meeting." The "temple" on the other hand was not referred to as a "temple of meeting" but rather as "The house of the Lord" or "Temple of the Lord."

Jeremiah 7 is a powerful indictment on the people's inclination to invoke the temple as a kind of talisman or good luck charm, just as Isaiah 58 speaks of the pseudo-fast of the people. In both cases it is justice and the destruction of idols that God is looking for. The warning is always that if justice is not done and if the idolatry is not done away with, the land will not tolerate the residents—will spew them out, banish them to far away places. Even this "house that bears my name" has been contaminated by idolatry and immorality and will not stand.

Bethel predates Shiloh, as Jacob's version of the house of God: and indeed this was strictly on the basis of the "meeting." Jacob had it right, inasmuch as nothing about Bethel—a stone for a pillow?—leant itself to the idea of a proper (noble, substantial, magisterial) dwelling place for a Sovereign Lord.

At the dedication of the temple there appears to be an odd understanding that this mighty and costly project is really a bit of a practice in futility—since at least twice in the middle of the prayer of dedication, Solomon prays:

> But who is able to build a temple for him, since the heavens, even the highest heavens, cannot contain him? Who then am I

> to build a temple for him, except as a place to burn sacrifices before him?...But will God really dwell on earth with men? The heavens, even the highest heavens, cannot contain you. How much less this temple I have built (2 Chron. 2:6, 18)!

Citing the Exodus, God makes a proper mockery of any attempt to domesticate him, that very time when by divine decree he gave Moses the elaborate heavenly pattern for the tabernacle. There seems at least in the mind of God a poignant distinction between tabernacle and temple.

There is also a presage here of a biblical motif often overlooked and in direct relation to the institutionalization of faith: the claim of God to be on the move. "I have been moving from place to place with a tent as my dwelling" may in fact be a paradigmatic statement on the very nature of God in salvation history, and his desire for the way in which worship is authentically to be done.

The OT ends with Malachi's prophetic words that: "*My name will be great among the nations, from the rising to the setting of the sun. In every place incense and pure offerings will be brought to my name, because my name will be great among the nations,*" says the LORD Almighty (Mal. 1:11). This contrasts dramatically with God's reserved right to uproot and "make a byword among the nations" the very temple which was to house his name at the dedication of Solomon, if the people rejected his kingship and squandered their vocation as a light to the nations (2 Chron. 7:20). But the censorship of Israel's missed calling is clear; the functions of the temple will in the end be uprooted and flung to the very ends of the earth—somewhere in Malachi's future—so that God's missionary impulse, his original sanction for the Jerusalem temple, will be satisfied.

Walter Brueggemann presents a compelling case for "Rethinking Church Models through Scripture" in an examination of the three structural models for the people of God in the OT: the Exodus, the Monarchic and the Exilic periods. He cites these three as the main arrangements for the gathering, worshiping and civil ordering of God's people under radically different circumstances. The intent of the study is actually to review where the contemporary [Western?] church stands in the wake of post-modern trends and realities. Brueggemann sees the current church situation as one of a dying modernity model which was reminiscent of the monarchial and highly institutional period of the OT. This period is the one to which the Biblical student naturally inclines when seeking an ideal and dominant center—literarily, historically and theologically—and yet it comprises only a relatively short 400-year interlude between the patriarchal and exodus motifs prior and the exilic model following. The period of the monarchy constitutes an established, culturally legitimated church. Brueggemann's footnote: "An analogue exists between the royal-temple establishment in ancient Israel and the Constantinian establishment of the church. Thus, the 'end of the Constantinian period' in the church is congenial to my argument."

Brueggemann is making the case for the legitimacy of models of church which do not have cultural dominance or a "temple-royal-prophetic" bearing, a pattern of stable religious institution, sympathetic civic leader, secularizing intelligentsia and passionate prophecy—all as a cultural package. He dares to suggest that this is the governing model of modern, established Christianity in the West (n.d.:131). But he then sets out to establish the legitimacy of pre- and post-monarchy models which do not have cultural sanction, and are characterized by: cultural/religious pluralism, little influence over public policy, temptations to cultural syncretism, strategies and mechanisms for survival—i.e., recovery of memory and rootage and connectedness, intense practice of hope and intense textual community. He characterizes the pre-monarchic model as an authentic "new church start," the monarchic model as "temple community" and the post-exilic model as a "textual community." Each of these is distinct, yet the third period has much more in common with the first and in fact 'jumped over the monarchic period to find resources in the early sources that could sustain it.' The late community went back to the early community (:136).

From the vantage point of pioneer mission in Buddhist contexts, it is obvious from Brueggemann's arrangement that the pre- and post-monarchial features would be most pertinent and applicable. Yet much of modern mission has been just that: 'modern' and, by extension, characterized by, or at least attempts at, more Christendom/monarchial/culturally dominant expressions of church. His closing statements are incisive:

> A move from temple to text requires a reconsideration of our social location, of the resources on which we can and must count, and of the work we have to do about the infrastructure that has largely collapsed. While we may find "wilderness-exile" models less congenial, there is no biblical evidence that the God of the Bible cringes at the prospect of this community being one of wilderness and exile. Indeed, this God resisted the temple in any case (cf. 2 Sam. 7:4-7). In the end, it is God and not the Babylonians who terminated the temple project. In the face of that possible eventuality in our own time and circumstance, the ways for the survival of an alternative imagination in an alternative community call for new strategies (:137-138).

Brueggemann's analysis of "post-Christendom West" seems to coincide with the elements of a pre-Christian Buddhist context, as well as pre- and post-monarchial Israel.

Christ's Treatment Of and Relationship To the Temple

The Synagogue, introduced into the life of the people of God by necessity between the two testaments during their exile from the holy land, needs brief mention here as an alternative with pros and cons in Jewish life.

- Synagogue is a kind of half-way house or an extension of some of the temple functions within an exilic era people of God. It carries a vestige of the 'holy place' (with holy men, literature, times, practices) for those who are separated from the original.

- It houses the Word of God vs. the Ark of the Covenant.
- Its primary function is social and instructional; the place of reading, revering and listening to exposition of Torah as the community of God in a non-temple construct.
- It could not be seen in the numinous or celebrative and redemptive functions of the tabernacle/temple system, especially in regard to the sacrificial system.
- It was the primary form of meeting place which Jesus, entering ministry during the Roman occupation and traversing the countryside (while coming up to the temple on specially holy days), exploited in his ministry years for teaching and confronting the religious practice, ethic and teaching of the Jews in his time.
- It was also the locus of Paul's missionary advance, as one obligated to "the Jew first," but also became at times the center of his general teaching/discipling ministry. Although it is also clear that Paul did not make any connection between the establishing of the church(-es) in his missionary journeys and the synagogue of the Jewish diaspora.
- It might be seen, explicitly or more often implicitly, as a sort of model of congregational church life-in-practice (structure and functions) whereas temple is viewed often as the archetypal model of church in its spiritual life.

How did the coming of Messiah bear on temple in the Judeo-Christian continuum? What was Christ's interaction with the Jewish temple of his time and what was his particular vocation when it comes to any subsequent dealings with temple?

The New Testament gospel writers had much more to say about Jesus' views, actions and relation to the temple than most evangelical minds would realize. The work of N. T. Wright has done more to remove this fog than anyone else in recent memory.

As an ecumenical evangelical, Wright is a first-class historian of Jewish first century expectations and the political and religious milieu into which Christ emerged announcing the reign of God. He convincingly portrays Christ's vocation as largely centered on the controversies of the torah and the temple and his intent to both fulfill and replace the entire temple system with…*himself.*[5]

The New Testament has the greatest number of occurrences of the word "worship" in two telling passages, one dealing with Jesus' appraisal of temple in light of his new dispensation of worship—in conversation with the Samaritan woman; and the other coming from Stephen's lips in the defense of his life before the Jewish Sanhedrin. In both cases, the issue at stake is the role of the temple as the central symbol for worship in the Jewish mind and history.

Jesus' encounter with the woman at the well is deep with symbolism pertaining to Jesus' mission and calling. His radical approach to women, Samaritans and the immoral is all captured here in this one brief conversation. Yet, the passage unveils in parallel fashion his regard for the temple as a cosmic expression of God's communion with humanity and how his vocation was to eclipse the entire institution. The woman's apparently diversionary side trail into discussion of places of worship allowed Jesus an excursus on his messiahship in the context of temple and worship. For her, the popular Jewish myth held that worship was a matter of place and event; for Jesus, it was soon to be (indeed already present) a matter strictly of spirit and truth.

> Jesus' clash with the Pharisees came about not because he was an antinomian or because he believed in justification by faith while they believed in justification by works but because his kingdom-agenda for Israel demanded that Israel leave off her frantic and paranoid self-defense, reinforced as it now was by the ancestral codes, and embrace instead the vocation to be the light of the world, the salt of the earth (Wright 1999:58).

Most contemporary writing about Jesus rightly focuses on the Temple, what Jesus did there and what happened as a result.

The Temple was of course, in this period, the heart and center of Judaism, the vital symbol around which everything else circled.[6] It was the center of Israel's national and political life: the chief priests who were in charge of it were also, in company with the shaky Herodian dynasty and under Roman supervision, in charge of the whole nation. Furthermore, the Temple carried all kinds of royal overtones… (Wright 1999:62-63).

> Though Jesus' action in the Temple must naturally be seen within this wider context of disaffection, it goes way beyond it into a different dimension. His attitude to the Temple was not "this institution needs reforming," nor "the wrong people are running this place," nor yet "piety can function elsewhere too." His deepest belief regarding the Temple was eschatological: the time had come for God to judge the entire institution. It had come to symbolize the injustice that characterized the society on the inside and the outside, the rejection of the vocation to be the light of the world, the city set on a hill that would draw to itself all the peoples of the world….During his Galilean ministry, Jesus acted and spoke as if he was in some sense called to do and be what the Temple was and did. His offer of forgiveness, with no prior condition of Temple-worship or sacrifice, was the equivalent of someone in our world offering as a private individual to issue someone else a passport or a driver's license....[The destroyed temple] would be followed by the establishment of the messianic community focused on Jesus himself that would replace the Temple once and for all….And all this judgment-with-finality was directly in line with the tradition of the prophets, especially Jeremiah. "When we allow these positive symbols to generate a larger picture of Jesus' intentions, we find once again that the focal point of it all is the Temple" (:64-66, 70).

More pertinent to the discussion however is the very cause of Jesus' death, and, by extension, that of Stephen's. The first-century Jewish context was volatile from the revolutionary standpoint. A long string of would-be messiahs had come and gone, a number of them in violent protest against both the Roman occupation and the Jewish acquiescence and religious corruption. The temple was the apex of Jewish identity as God's people and of religious rite and activity. Corruption had reached intolerable depths and protests had come from all corners within the conscientious and contentious Jewish majority.

The advent of Jesus as Messiah had to confront the temple system, which Jesus did with decisive and subversive aplomb. Jesus is both accused of and quoted as predicting the destruction of the temple and replacing it supernaturally with a Messianic substitute of his own making (Matt. 26:61; Mark 14:58; John 2:19). This was tantamount to blasphemy from a common first-century Jewish understanding, but was tantamount to suicide from the positions of power in the Jewish religious establishment. Wright demonstrates convincingly the two-pronged approach of the religious hierarchy to pit Jesus' kingship claims against the Roman political regime and his temple claims against the Jewish consciousness of an inviolate house of God—to conspire a foolproof sentence of death from all sides.[7]

Jesus' temple action—the casting out of the money-changers and their trade-in-religion, was much more than angry reaction to religious oppression or misuse of the house of prayer, though these were utterly pertinent. It was also highly symbolic of all Jesus had come to do by way of judgment and issuing in of God's new messianic order through his people. Jesus touched the very nerve of Jewish religious self-identity through his temple actions and citations, touching off a furor which culminated in his raucous trials and crucifixion. According to Walter Wink's summary of Jesus' temple action:

> We cannot enter the mind of Jesus to retrace his motives. Whatever he may have intended by his act, the church gradually discerned that his life and teaching had undermined the entire theology of holiness on which the Temple cult was based. Jesus' death, they also came to believe, had exposed

> and annulled the whole system of sacrificial victimage, and thus terminated Temple slaughter—in short, sacred violence.
>
> ...His action was understood symbolically. It was not a "cleansing" or reform of the Temple, to restore it to pure sacrifices or to eliminate business activity from the Temple precincts. The Temple could scarcely function at all without these sellers and money changers. Rather, the Gospels depict Jesus as enflamed by the separatism and exclusivity of the Temple ("my house shall be called a house of prayer for all the nations," Mk 11:17a). He is shown attempting to shut it down entirely by preventing payment of the Temple tax, the obtaining of sacrificial victims, and even its use as a shortcut....The Temple was the embodiment, institutionally, of holiness understood as separation—a holiness that prevented direct access to God by all but "undefiled" Jewish men. Jesus abolishes the pollution system maintained by the Temple through its inherent separation of the sacred and the secular. This separation worked greatly to the financial advantage of the priestly ruling elite ("but **you** have made it a den of robbers," Mk 11:17b)...the violence that countless animal sacrifices were supposed to quench was never satisfied...The church understood his [Jesus' crucifixion] act as a sacrifice to end all sacrifices that exposed the scapegoating mechanism for all the world to see (:125).

Consider then this connecting thread from the early days of his ministry to the early years of the NT church:

- Jesus' claim to lordship over the Sabbath and superiority over the temple in the context of God's desire for "mercy, not sacrifice" (Matt. 12:6)
- Jesus' denunciation of routine temple business, his violent temple clearing, recorded by John at the beginning and by the Synoptics near the end of his ministry years (Matt. 21; Mark 11; Luke 19; John 2)
- Jesus' minimizing the temple's glory and declaration of divine judgment (Mark 13:2; Luke 21:5)

- Jesus' bold claim to replace the judged temple system with a temple of his own making (John 2:19)
- Jesus' rebuke of the domestication and robbery of God over against the temple's original purpose of international blessing (Mark 11:17)
- The trial of Jesus in which various claims were made to his intention to destroy the temple (Matt. 26:61; Mark 14:58)
- The mockery at the scene of the crucifixion by various ones re Jesus' claim to destroy the temple and in three days restore it (Matt. 27:40)
- The tearing of the temple curtain at the moment of Jesus' death—the symbolic destruction or making redundant of the holy of holies through the once-for-all shed blood of the eternal covenant (Matt. 27:51)
- The trouble which Stephen and Paul got into with Jewish authorities over temple actions or statements of judgment (Acts 6:13,14; 21:28; 24:6)

Stephen's Defense and Martyrdom

Stephen's sermon, taken in context, is a simple defense before the Sanhedrin of his personal stance on the issue of the temple. He had been lumped together with Jesus as one who spoke against this holy place. The circuitous reiteration of Israel's history, with which his hearers were at least as familiar as anyone else in Israel, almost constitutes a death-wish on his part for its studied departure from the cherished temple myth of the Sanhedrin and popular Jewish religious imagination. Of course having a Greek name might not have helped his situation, but Stephen perfunctorily aligned himself with his new Messiah and rendered the Temple obsolete not on some personal bias but rather on the very history of this chosen people's God.

Among the recurring themes of Stephen's sermon are the following:

- Appearings and visitations and the inability of God's people to grasp their intent
- Lands, their leaving, repossessing, the holiness of particular but impermanent space; and the particular place of God's appearings and presence
- Chosen, improbable agents of God's liberation and leadership/rulership
- A thrusting out from the familiar or removing people from their comfort zone (exile)
- The things which hands (human vs. divine) have made and their relation to worship
- All these themes have a direct bearing on the answer Stephen was to give regarding his stance on the temple. So Visits and appearances or seeing just as Stephen sees Jesus at the Father's right hand in the end.
- Abortive revelations: God twice moves Abram toward Canaan (propensity to settle prematurely?); Joseph waits until his brothers' second visit to truly reveal himself to them; Moses' first visit to his brethren is a dismal failure; there are intervals and "second comings" through out the sermon if you will.

Exiles and being thrown out, foreigners are everywhere throughout the chapter; God meeting his people en route, emphasizing the pilgrim, this is a chapter of, among other things:

- nature of this call; Abram's Mesapotamia/Haran/Terah, Jacob's Canaan, Joseph's Egypt, Moses' Sinai/Midian. We have no sure home here, but God will meet us on the way. Or, negatively, the divine suspicion of both the *familiar* (leave your home... but God was with him) and the *fabricated* (What house will *you* build for me; have not *my hands* made all of these things?) Their severe discipline of exile was directly related to the worship of things their hands had made. It is almost as though God is moving or working always "out there" – beyond the borders of our current commitment, allegiance and familiarity…

Was this the problem with first century Judaism and the temple cultus? Note the disciples' fawning over the temple grandeur. While Jesus had cleansed the temple, he was simultaneously unraveling its ultimacy.

- Where does God dwell? David and Solomon answer this by the classic and innocent desire to domesticate the Maker of heaven and earth....whereas their patriarch Jacob had it right, by naming his pillow in the wilderness "none other than the house of God" – an awesome place, for therein was there an encounter with God Almighty, the God of promise, the God who converses with sinners (Gen. 28:16-17). This is the common and alien made holy by visitation.
- Much about "land" and "inheritance" and yet a somewhat frustrating suspension or constant delay of this inheritance, or disappointment at its final realization....Is this partly due to the fact that Abram's inheritance was so much more than the land of Canaan, but rather, in the words of Paul, the *world* (Rom. 4:13)?
- Very little about the beloved temple itself—which is the focal point of his defense. Stephen seems intentionally to be drawing attention to the nations *other than Israel*, the divine encounters *other than in the temple*, the lands beyond the promised land. Why? Because God is not the God of Israel only but of the nations; his sovereign designs lie anywhere people will truly and spiritually worship him. The temple (read election) was not the end but the means to a far grander end, God's glory and worship among all peoples.

Is it ironic, altogether natural or provident, that immediately after Stephen's high-profile martyrdom, over the redefinition of the place of the holy away from the inviolate temple *cultus* within Jerusalem, the community of Christians emptied out into the surrounding countryside under the weight of a fresh outburst of persecution and irreversibly altered the demographics of the faith into an international dispersion and mission?

In his excellent commentary, *The Message of Acts*, John Stott notes that "Stephen is seen by some as showing a bias towards the [tabernacle—versus the latter temple] because it was mobile. But he expresses neither a preference for the tabernacle nor a distaste for the temple. For both were constructed in accordance with God's will" (1990:138). Stephen's sermon allows, contra Stott, for a clear distinction between what God instituted in the impermanent or mobile tabernacle ethos, and the intent of finding a dwelling place or house for the divine in that of the temple.

Three observations need to be made in this regard. First, while Stephen does not seem to favor one form over the other, he clearly rehearses the divine dictates regarding the building of the original tabernacle as well as its mobile status—within the context of a message dominated by the superiority of a God who is ever-present among his people, especially regardless of their location in relation to the holy as a religious grounding.

Secondly, the claim that both the temple and the tabernacle were constructed in accordance with God's will is not, at least evenly, supported. The construction of the tabernacle is unequivocally, start to finish, a divinely initiated program (Ex. 20-27). The temple, conversely, is recorded as the brainchild of King David, who doubtless sincerely desired a better house for God than the by-then old and well-worn temporary structure resident at Shiloh. The erection of a "more substantial and permanent" (Stott) dwelling place for God can be tied directly to the monarchy which itself had been resisted by God as an acquiescence to pagan nationalisms and a subversion of his own Kingship (Deut.17:14ff; 1 Sam. 8:5ff). Yet the claim could also be made that the monarchy as well was constructed in accordance with God's will, insomuch as God took the final initiative and blessed the monarchy so long as it gave place to his divine supremacy and law, redeeming it for the ultimate purposes of Messiah's identity and lineage. The temple did indeed become a structure in which God was willing to continue to 'put his name' or even to dwell—in a manner of speaking—yet the caveat always remained, that this was a far cry from the uniqueness of a deity who is Creator of all and whose dwelling is always first and foremost within and among people.

Lastly, Stephen never actually mentions the temple. He has been asked to defend the accusation as to whether he, apparently like Christ, has spoken "against this place," but instead goes into lengthy excursus on the divine source of the tabernacle, only alluding to the later temple founding as a substandard ("…nevertheless, the Most High does not live in houses made by men") and decidedly human attempt to find a "dwelling place" for him "who does not dwell…," whose hands have made *all these things*.

Early Church Ecclesiology and Pastoral NT Temple Theology

In a discussion on the cessation of OT sacrifices, Walter Wink delivers another blow to the temple system through study of Stephen's sermon, (the entire sacrificial system being tied inextricably to the temple compound):

> Luke's reconstruction of Stephen's speech includes the charge that Israel's first sacrifice was not to God but to the golden calf, and that God's punishment was to give them over to offering sacrifices to the gods Moloch and Rephan and the host of heaven. But God, he reminds them, does not dwell in houses made by hands—a point Paul later makes to the Athenians. That constitutes a fundamental rejection of the validity of sacrifice from its inception.…Furthermore, Paul is, in very short order, speaking of the body of Christ as a new temple of which believers are individually members. But if our own personal or corporate bodies can be thought of as temples of the Holy Spirit (1 Cor. 6:19-20), or if we can present our bodies as living sacrifices to God (Rom. 12:1), what further use is the Temple? If Jesus has died, once for all, to free us from sin, then the Temple is superfluous, superceded. Jesus' death is the end of ritual sacrifice. When he dies, the curtain before the Holy of Holies is torn from top to bottom (Mk 15:38), a symbolic statement of the exhaustion of the Temple's holy powers. Spiritual sacrifice has taken the

> place of animal slaughter (1 Pet.2:5). God desires mercy, not sacrifice (Mt. 9:13; 12:7; Hos.6:6) (1992:124).

The Apostle Paul, it must be said, is the primary ecclesiologist for all of Christian church history. And Paul indeed tied his doctrine of the church to the historic temple of the people of God. But this he did very much in the vein of Christ's and Stephen's precedents.

There is a simple path one can take in the discovery of Paul's emergent ecclesiology, and that is his conversion. Paul made much of his conversion, both from Luke's record of his recounting of it to multiple missionary audiences as well as by extension through his pastoral writings. Jesus intercepts the persecutor of the church by a most unusual introduction: "Saul, Saul, why are you persecuting *me*?"

Jesus is appearing in a *heavenly* vision to Paul—from above, and claiming complete identity with those whom Paul persecutes, the young Christian movement, *from below*. "Who are you, Lord?" Paul, aware he is dealing with the Transcendent, an awesome heavenly voice, attributes Lordship to his divine Interlocutor. "I am Jesus, whom you are persecuting." Jesus identifies himself—a name Paul could associate with the people of the Way—but again identifying completely with the people of the young Christian movement so immediate and undivine to Paul's consciousness.

This first personal interchange between a heavenly Christ and the persecutor of the same, earthly, Christ is the most basic building block for an ecclesiology which speaks of the church as (1) the body of Christ. Paul physically persecuted and imprisoned real bodies, and was taught at his conversion that this was in fact the body of Christ; an incarnational ecclesiology, filled with metaphors of a flesh-and-blood, dynamic and immanent nature; and (2) the temple of God as a radical new spiritual entity (i.e., people); a whole new understanding of edifice which is again dynamic, living, mobile, universal and local; a building in process under the sovereign hand of God himself, not remotely of any human construction and built solely upon the foundation of Christ.

When we approach the great treatment of the Jewish faith in the context of the NT (Hebrews), we're faced with further discontinuity. There is no mention of the temple in the entire book, much of which is devoted directly to temple functions and their interpretation into the new covenant community. Interestingly, seven out of ten NT usages of the world "tabernacle" are to be found in Hebrews (mostly in Heb. 8-9). Five of the six NT usages of "sanctuary" are in Hebrews (6-9). Sixteen out of 30 instances of "covenant" and 27 of 71 NT instances of "priest" are also in the book.

The entire discussion of Jesus' high priestly role after the order of Melchizedek is a lengthy excursus on the circumventing of the temple establishment to show the extent of the blessings of the pre- and post-temple priesthood of Christ. Where Jews would have been inclined to associate priesthood with the localized temple system, the writer of Hebrews painstakingly separates these two, in order to grant a better covenant for a much larger constituency, those who could not celebrate the Jerusalem faith and fulfill its sacrificial requirements.

When the familiar temple practices are visited in Hebrews, they are cast further backward into the pre-temple, tabernacle *cultus*. And the purpose of the discussion seems to point to the sanctifying of those very things, places and people which have no access to the holy *place*. Sacrifices of the fixed temple are replaced by the sacrifice of praising lips and selfless sharing with others. The enduring city of Jerusalem and the stability of its temple court are unsure, replaced by the hope of an eternal city yet to come, and the scandal of Christ's scapegoat sacrifice is to be embraced by all those who go with him *outside* the gate—for true sanctification. Note especially Hebrews 13:10-16.

The Apocalypse and Temple-Tabernacle Revisitations

There is a fascinating capsule on the whole distinction between tabernacle and temple—in the final episode of John's revelation—in which God's new, or rather renewed, creative order is being introduced.

> And I heard a loud voice from the throne saying, "Now the dwelling [*tabernacle*] of God is with men, and he will live with them. They will be his people, and God himself will be with them and be their God (Rev. 21:3ff).

After a lengthy and glorious description of the New Jerusalem, coming down out of heaven from God, John makes the point that:

> I did not see a *temple* in the city, because the Lord God Almighty and the Lamb are its temple. The city does not need the sun or the moon to shine on it, for the glory of God gives it light, and the Lamb is its lamp (Rev. 21:22-23).

While the *skene* of God, his (mobile?) dwelling is come in among men—eternally, the *naos* of God—his shrine or temple—is not to be seen, since God Almighty and the Lamb are its permanent structure and establishment. Walter Wink elucidates:

> In the New Jerusalem, according to Revelation 21 and 22, there will be no temple, no altar, no sacrifice (21:22), even though the imagery of those chapters draws directly from Isaiah 60, where the wealth of the nations flows to Jerusalem specifically to beautify the sanctuary. The offering of sacrifice was a universal rite in the religions of the ancient world—so much so that the church's refusal to perform sacrifices brought down upon it the curious charge of "atheism" (ibid.:125).

Summary

- Judeo-Christianity could be purported to be a temple religious system. Judaism certainly lays the groundwork for this. The OT is precedent and sanction for solid temple moorings for our faith. Yet even here there is a shadow of doubt cast at the outset (2 Sam. 7). The prophets end with a mixed message of last days and the exaltation of a temple mount—among all the nations—and a castigation of the temple system as it is perceived by latter monarchial and exilic Israel (Jer. 7; Mic. 3:11-12; Zeph. 3:11).

- Jesus can be seen as—at the core of his vocation—both confronting and fulfilling the temple tradition. N. T. Wright has explicated this from a biblical theology study. All four gospels either allege (through trumped up charges) or portray explicitly (John) Jesus' intention to "destroy this place" in order to raise it—his body, the true temple—up in resurrection metamorphosis.
- Stephen's sermon is a defense against the charge that he's been speaking against this holy place and quoting Jesus' claim that he would destroy this holy place. His death can be seen as the self-accusatory playing-out of his defense.
- The early NT church's identity seems devoid of a physical temple continuity. The Church's early history, while begun in the temple courts, is one of unintentional flight from the temple. The persecution arising out of Stephen's death, symbolic as it was of a rejection of the visible temple system, precipitated a mass exodus from Jerusalem, and de facto cessation of temple use and pilgrimage in the lives of almost all new believers who received the Word beyond the borders of Jerusalem, Palestine and historic Judaism. Paul, the great apostle to Gentiles, also seems to fall within the purview of the conclusions of the church in Acts 15, in which the constraints are almost entirely lifted for Gentile believers (in terms of ritual, place, event—externals) and the faith is boiled down to universally accessible and transformational experience and values—meeting Jesus. N. T. Wright points out that consciousness of Messiah's judgment on the temple system was well entrenched in the early church's psyche before it was played out literally by the Romans in AD 70, so that the temple did in fact experience an early, intentional eclipsing.

- John's portrayal of Christ and Christology—as it ties to ecclesiology—is possibly the clearest at illustrating the impact of this transition. The new community of the King is to express itself in communitarian (trinitarian?), self-sacrificial love (vs. animal sacrificial propitiation). God is made fully available to every community through the incarnation of His Son in the life of this new social order. The shekinah of the Old Testament associated so closely with the tabernacle and later with temple (2 Chron. 7:1), is now resident in the community of the King, with no further mention of former function of the provincial, Jerusalem-based locus.
- The epistles, specifically 2 Corinthians and Hebrews, speaking at length of the former things and the Mosaic system compared to the new covenant understandings and provisions, must be seen as a frontal attack on the inviolate Jerusalem institutions.

Read this story now with early Christian eyes, and what do we find? That the temple, for all its huge importance and centrality within Judaism, was after all a signpost to the reality, and the reality was the resurrected son of David, who was the son of God. God, in other words, is not ultimately to dwell in a human-built temple, a timber-and-stone house. God will indeed dwell with his people, allowing his glory and mystery to tabernacle in their midst, but the only appropriate way for him to do this will not be through a building but through believing human beings, redeemed *imago dei.*

Jesus—and then, very quickly, Jesus' people—were now the true Temple, and the actual building in Jerusalem was thereby redundant, and, incidentally, destroyed. We must remind ourselves, crucially, that the Temple was, after all, the central incarnational symbol of Judaism. The temple was the place where heaven and earth actually interlocked, where the living God had promised to be present with his people.

Jesus, at the very center of his vocation, believed himself called to do and be in relation to Israel what, in Scripture and Jewish belief, the Temple was and did.…He rather than the Temple was the place where and the means by which the living God was present with Israel (Wright 1999:110-111).

So, Is Christianity a Temple Religion?

If we answer this question in the negative, what exactly are we saying? In fact, we can answer strongly in the affirmative: that there IS a temple remaining for the people of God upon which the entire negative assertion is predicated. 1 Corinthians 3:17 promises God's judgment on anyone—in this age—who destroys God's temple! Yet in this rendering the temple has moved from Jerusalem to Corinth, from edifice to populace, from ritual to *koinonia*—in Paul's message.

A Negative Answer

But in the negative, we cite the following by way of an overwhelming NT transition:

- The temple belongs to Jesus as God's Messiah: "My house shall be called a house of prayer for all nations;" "My father's business;" "My father's house."
- Jesus is "greater than the temple" from the outset (Matt. 12:6).
- Jesus is the temple; his *body* in particular is the new temple—as he so poignantly stated before his questioning disciples and critics (John 2:18ff). By way of extrapolation, when Paul maintains for the Colossians that in Him, all the fullness of the Godhead *dwells* in bodily form (Col. 1:19; 2:9), he's paralleling John's statements of incarnation (John 1:14—the Word, equal to God, becoming flesh and tabernacling among us; and John 10:30— Jesus: "I and the Father are one;" "if you've seen me, you've seen the Father."
- Jesus declared with some finality God's judgment on the physical temple (Mark 13:2), "Your house is left to you desolate" (Matt. 23:38).

- Jesus' victory over the forces of darkness at the moment of his death was accompanied by the great sign of the cessation of the temple barrier in terms of access to God, the rending of the temple curtain, the great separation of the people from the Most Holy Place and the great clergy-laity divide of high priest and the common faithful (Matt. 27:51; Mark 15:38; Luke 23:45).
- Jesus' body is his church. (i) He identifies fully (and twice) with his incarnation in earth post-Pentecost in Saul's radical and unforgettable conversion experience (Acts 9); (ii) Paul later with groups like the Corinthians—for all of their carnality and internal conflicts—was bold to declare them "now" the body of Christ; and almost in the same breath, remind them they are the temple of the Holy Spirit (1 Cor. 12).
- The church is the temple of God in this age. (1) In 1 Cor. 3:16-17, the Corinthians (plural) are warned of God's judgment on those who destroy the temple, which is now to be understood as the church ("you")—don't destroy God's temple, the church! (i) Paul's entire context here is the history of his own church-planting, apostolic ministry, as a 'master-builder' of the church of God in Corinth and Asia, building the church on the foundation stone, Christ. (ii) Remember that Corinth was a pagan temple paradise, much like Athens, with its myriad gods, shrines, etc. and much like modern Asia's tenacious temple cultures. (2) In 1 Cor. 6:17, the believers are reminded that their personal bodies are the "temple of the Holy Spirit, living in them." In 2 Cor. 6:16, Paul again stating emphatically "We are the temple of the living God." (3) In Eph. 2:21, Paul's treatise on the church in this seminal epistle again sees the church as dynamic, in process, and rising into a "holy temple in the Lord."
- Practically:

  (1) Our edifice complex cannot find NT sanction, but rather seems to demonstrate a reversion to a subset of OT, pre-messianic understandings.

(2) Our terminology has been misleading at best: (i) sanctuary: strictly derived from the tabernacle and temple system; ii) Altar: sometimes Lord's table, reflecting OT altar attachments; (iii) Lord's table: erecting a physical locus for what was to be a memorializing of Jesus' death at every meal shared by disciples; (iv) going to church, a come-to structure, a local place associated with meetings together and with God (through corporate worship); (v) "Bethel temple:" naming our buildings instead of ourselves as the locus of meeting with and priesting God; (vi) "cathedral" deriving in the Latin from "chair" or the bishop's official throne; (vii) going into a time of worship completely alien to NT (or even OT) parlance or commitments (Rom. 12:1-2; John 4).

(3) The use of this terminology is not merely cosmetic or semantic idiosyncrasy: it moves the general understanding of the meeting of God with his people and his re-presentation on earth away from human flesh and back into physical edifices which can *never* house the presence of God, and is a completely inadequate attempt at something God has made ample provision for—in the incarnation of his Son through the Body. So it empowers inanimate objects with divine function while stripping the Body of its proper and divine role in the earth. This has to be damaging to both Body-life and to witness, for the world has grown at least as accustomed as the church to thinking of church as primarily visible human institution and structures as opposed to an incendiary fellowship.

(4) Of course practically the costs to an edifice-dependent temple Christendom and therefore to mission have been obscene when taken together.

(5) Philosophically, though, this thesis does not throw down the gauntlet before all traditional church structures. That will at least have to wait for further insight and much more careful study of both scripture and church history. After all, we're never able to over-generalize on a religious system that has more than

survived two millennia. We are, rather, after the heart of a question which might take the church out of its captivity to a Euro-American Christendom and into a renewed opportunity to actually touch all of humanity, not simply a "little raft" of an elect enclosed within four walls.

- There is also the issue of worship and the consideration of cultural predispositions to worship in place. Encounter is a fundamental assumption of any true worship. Historically people look religiously to the numinous within specific time and specific space. This would surely be explanation for the propensity among Christians to rename their crude physical structures after the pattern provided by God to the OT people of God. And there is genuine room for that propensity within the framework we're dealing with here. The catch has been what sort of structure and limitations attend to the choices we have traditionally made in erecting local edifices to temple our experience.

  (1) The first question in a comparative religious study between the Christian and Buddhist contexts might be, given the fundamental tenets of Buddhism, what/whom exactly do Buddhists worship? The function of temple for Buddhists may be much more sociological than purely religious when filtered through the actual teachings and practices of the *sangha*.

  (2) A theological consideration here is the profane/sacred dualism from which we are all seeking to recover in a post-modern renaissance. A theology of the Kingdom, of common grace and of living all of life *coram deo*—before the face of God—tends us away from isolated or demarcated experiences of the holy—either in time or in space—and rather toward the routinization of the holy within the profane; the sanctifying of all of creation to the King to whom it all rightfully belongs through both creation and redemption. Salt and light speak to this interpenetration of the holy within/among, even overwhelming the common.

(3) Paul's treatment of the early church as the clear replacement of the Jerusalem temple (right around the time of its physical destruction in fulfillment of Jesus' words), seems to relate directly to this routinization or habituation of the holy. God has established this new society as his "holy nation," sanctified through the blood of Christ, to be for the praise of his glory *throughout the nations* (1 Pet. 2:9), indeed wherever they find themselves, and, in this vein, as the true, contemporary temple of God, radically decentralizing both the meeting place and the 'holy place' into a countless number literally filling the earth. It may be reminiscent of Joshua's conquering of the land of Canaan, since God had promised that anywhere he placed his feet would be his in God's name (Josh. 1:3).

(4) Jesus' treatment of the issue of the proper nature of worship with the woman at the well anticipates the same: A time is coming—and is now—when people will worship neither in this mountain nor in Jerusalem, but *in* spirit and in truth. This is a discussion of the matter of *location* of worship, and Jesus both universalizes and trivializes location by his response. God is after true worshipers for whom location is utterly irrelevant on the one hand and properly/potentially universal on the other. This would be good news to a despised Samaritan, and indeed to all those outside the prickly, rather formidable system of hurdles for acceptability within the Jerusalem establishment.

(5) When Jesus was in Jerusalem on his final Passover pilgrimage—to *become* the Passover—certain Greeks came to his disciples with an innocent enough request: "Sir, we would like to see Jesus." To which Jesus, as though suddenly galvanized, responds: "*Now* has come the *hour* for the Son of Man to be glorified." All the other hours were misplaced, but this is the hour. Why? Because with these Greeks coming into Jerusalem and seeking an audience with the true temple of God, we now have an embarking upon the great globalization of the faith. *All* must be drawn to the Son; he must be lifted up—n*ow*. The experience of God is simply too limiting if confined to

Jerusalem; there are only so many Greeks (read *goyim* or outsiders) who can be expected to make the pilgrimage (this is not a pilgrimage religion). We must make this quest for a sight of Jesus universally answerable. He is to be humanity's perennial (read time) and universal (read apostolic, catholic, place) Passover.

(6) If the church is the re-incarnation of Jesus, which we may robustly maintain in our ecclesiology, then if it is anything, it is accessible. When the Word became flesh, it did not temple among us but tabernacled among us. The difference is simple: the tabernacle was the mobile vehicle of the practiced presence of God…moving with the cloud and fire of God's designs beyond the horizons of the people's imagination and settledness. "We beheld" or as John says in his epistle, "we were witnesses" with all of our senses of this perfect self-disclosure of God. But now, as John so clearly reminds us, We are the primary remaining self-disclosure of God in the world—indeed, in the whole world (contra Christ's limitation to Palestine)—1 John 4:12. In fact, 1 John is the "as he is" book in Scripture. In this world, we are "as he is" (1 John 4:17). For all humanity to have an experience of the God we worship, the "temple" of his Body must be made available everywhere and at all times. This is the rationale for saturation church planting. Worship is the root and fruit of mission, occurring within the temple of God, Christ's Body, lived in and energized by his Spirit.

Questions of Religion and Institution

The more appropriate question here might be: "Is Christianity a religion?" Religious categories seem to require temple ethos, as part of the institutionalization of any movement or sect—which Christianity does share with all other religious movements. The early church was a sect by all religious-anthropological indicators—and by popular opinion.

Can we avoid the development of a temple ethos within religious movements as part of the inevitability of institutionalization? History would indicate that we cannot adequately resist institutionalization within maturing Christward movements. But this is where our theological understandings of "temple" need to impinge upon our understandings of movement and maturation. For there has been in recent years a widespread reaction to the degree of ossification and institutionalism within Christian denominations and movements. These tendencies might be summarized in two dominant dynamics common to much religious history: (1) The separation of the laity from professional religious class in the supposed interests of "leadership" and continuity—an often unwitting separation of unholy from holy people. (2) The mammoth investment in and maintenance of a physical edifice as the visible center for worship—hence, a separation of the unholy from holy space—and religious symbolism within the larger community. Both of these tendencies are most clearly manifest in "the temple compound" of any religion, a perennial reminder to the people of faith of, among other things, a fundamental separation, distinction and taboo of both place and people—to which only a few are granted full access.

If the Old and New Testaments can be distinguished by anything at all, it seems here would lie the boldest contrasts: (1) that in Christ, the *laos* or laity are all granted unmitigated access to holiness, to priesthood (1 Pet. 2:9), to God's throne room—or "the Most Holy Place" (Heb. 10:19-22), that no one individual is any longer to be elevated to "father" or "rabbi" (Matt. 23:9,10) and that leadership in the new order is granted under a title-less, character-defined criterion and universally-gifted community (1 Tim.3; 1 Cor. 12-14). To cite Snyder's vantage point: If we take the NT on its own terms, however, and analyze its own vocabulary of ministry, we find a "resounding negation" of the assumptions underlying the professional religionist view (1977:84); (2) that in Christ, the place of the holy is wherever the people gather [boldly!] in his name (Matt.18:20; Heb.10:19), and that the mission of this people is to move out into the profane and sanctify it; that forgiveness of sins and discipline of sinners (Matt. 6:14-15; 18:18), the sanctifying of one another (1 Cor. 7:14), a pleasing sacrificial system (Rom. 12:1; Heb 13:6; 1 Pet. 2:5), prayers and intercession, appropriate worship (Rom. 12:1), gifts and offerings (2 Cor. 8:19; Phil. 2:17), may, indeed *must*, be done in the context of the community of the King—not in some permanently specified or erected edifice or compound and not sanctioned by the office of professional clergy or an elevated priesthood.

Conclusions

Returning to the original question—rooted in the religious expectations of Buddhists, Christians and the general populace for whom the physical presence of a temple is equivalent to the center of the worshiping or religious community, we might propose the following conclusions:

- The question is sincere, real, and felt on both sides, Buddhist and Christian.
- From the perspective of religious sociology, it is also clear that a community of faith seeks and requires symbols and rituals which lend themselves to a temple ethos or "presence." From the vantage point of power, politics and religion, it is a fact of religious life that where the host society holds to one preeminent religious scheme, introductions of alternative missionary faiths meet with official and popular rejection or outright persecution. The host religion in most larger societies is somehow tied to state sanction or holds a symbiotic relationship with powerful societal implications. Some Christian leaders have desired a temple ethos as a kind of territorial or symbolic "taking the land" or establishment of a critical mass for both popular appeal (visible) and political clout (for the advance of religious freedom and ultimately a voice in national life).

- From the OT there is a mixed record on the Jewish temple, at least when it is compared with the introduction of the original tabernacle. The initiator, the induction, the physical make-up, the systems of maintenance and "location" were among some of the clear contrasts, but the greatest would have to be the corruption of the latter over time and God's mounting judgment upon it. From the NT there is ample evidence within Christ's teaching, prophecy, temple action and crucifixion, as well as Stephen's unmistakable treatise and Paul's (and Hebrews') elaborate ecclesiology of the complete replacement of the temple system and ethos in favor of first Christ himself and later the church as the new Israel and Jesus' body incarnate, achieving what the temple simply could not, in both universally accessible worshiping presence and universal priesthood.
- From the history of the church we have both a witness to the power of institutional faith and gross departures from the very costly NT replacement of the whole temple system with the body of Christ. (1) The wholesale association of church with edifice and all that this has cost the church in resource expenditure, misplaced identity, and especially the layered attachments of the holy as inaccessible and of religious with an underutilized physical structure. A house church movement in China, by contrast, has issued inflammatory language to demonstrate its aversion to the western church's love affair with church-as-building: "For every dollar spent on church buildings, a soul goes to hell." (2) The vocabulary built up around the church buildings has more often than not paralleled the OT temple model, taking captive critical functions of the NT church life back to inanimate and pre-Calvary symbolism.
- From the perspective of contextualization in mission, it seems on the face of it that church buildings and other edifices serving the Christian community would present a kind of dynamic equivalence or temple-centered worshiping communities for Buddhist-background believers. This illustrates the quandary or cul-de-sac which much contemporary mission has found itself

in seeking culturally sensitive expressions of NT faith in other religious contexts. John Davis deals with this quandary in the final chapter of *Poles Apart,* a book dedicated primarily to exploring contextual breakthroughs in Buddhist Thailand (where the church has historically and unhealthily mirrored much of western missionary and church traditions). The leadership of the church in many nonwestern contexts has often, in the supposed interests of church growth and dynamism, accommodated its style to the prevailing leadership of the culture, only to reveal its mirroring that sort of leadership which Christ castigated as monolithically Gentile and to be rejected by the new community of the King. As Snyder reminds, "The Church cannot uncritically take over structures from its own surrounding culture any more than it can uncritically import them from outside" (1977:142).

But can there be ritual without temple, sacrament without sanctuary, priesthood without priest-class?

- A censure of contemporary temple ethos from a biblical-theological angle would have to be qualified by a strong affirmation of local art and architecture in the emerging expression of the new community of faith, or at least proper disassociation of the theological realities of NT "church" from the cultural excellencies to be affirmed in most arenas of societal life. Apparently the Roman Catholic Church in Thailand chose to adopt local temple architecture in the erection of major church buildings, a mixed bag in the long run, while Protestant missionaries largely rejected the religious associations of the Buddhist context and chose rather Western architectural styles—a cultural mishap—or artless and strictly utilitarian edifice; in both cases, a rejection of local art/architecture and the creation of an oddity. The trick seems to be how to create an understanding of separation between the artifacts of culture—redeemed or reaffirmed through conversion of the community to Christ—and the true nature of the new community, the nature of its worship and indeed its God.

- The advent of a house-church ecclesiology and method has been motivated primarily by concerns for more rapid growth over against cumbersome facility-based institutions and programs as well as the ages-long separation of laity from the ministry. In the West it has accompanied the post-modern shifts away from the church's captivity to modernity. Yet from a missiological standpoint, house-church planting does provide at least a temporary sidestepping of the dilemma of temple both in terms of its physically imposing and religiously misrepresentative symbolism as well as its facility in re-centering the church around people as temple, the loving community of the King. A building, to use the now-familiar sociology categorization, is a bounded set, a clear delineation of the holy from the unholy, the insiders from the outsiders. A mobile and non-facility based tightly knit group of people/family/friends illustrates the centered set concept, without clear boundaries of sacred-profane, clergy-laity. Another strength of the house-church movement as it matures is the contrast of the image of God portrayed through either place-and-event ecclesiology of the more established institution from the people-in-loving-community ecclesiology of the less rooted, mobile and accessible younger networks. For it is humanity that in the end bears the *imago dei* and it is love which Jesus predicted would be the singular hallmark of his new community.
- Conversely in terms of structure, the persistence of especially urban mega- and meta-church superstructures with their attendant celebration or high worship imprint, has also had wide acceptance and set a model which many without the resources or leadership seek to emulate. A visit to rural Nepal will find youth groups scraping together their meager resources to put together an electronically wired praise band. And worship choruses composed in the West are often awkwardly translated/transliterated into local languages and have become a kind of *lingua franca* of the praise and worship movement globally. This propensity to praise is rooted in the Davidic,

monarchial model of the OT, a Christendom model of the church if you will. While the first months of the early church were attended by temple-court celebration, distinctly in the presence and under the watchful eye of the larger community ("before the nations")—a clear distinction from what is now done almost exclusively inside four walls—this practice diminished of necessity after the destruction of the physical temple and Jerusalem as the holy city. One theological weakness of this particular expression is its tendency to equate worship with collective, enclosed praise celebrations, whereas the NT presents a very different picture of worship as fundamentally a social reality of obedient discipleship and Christ-like lifestyle. This seems to be a leading rationale behind the simple church inclination of so many.

- As physical structures will almost inevitably go up (or be shared or taken over within the existing community) in the service of the growing movement, the following might be considered as parameters in sustaining a healthier ecclesiology and movement. (1) They are incorporated into the larger sphere of the artifacts of a redeemed, redemptive community in dynamic continuity and discontinuity with the culture's history. (2) They reflect the best in local art, an extension of the society's creative identity. (3) As facilities for use by the church, they are commissioned fundamentally for service within the larger community, multi-use; a servant structure. (4) As symbols, they are directed at and christened for the kingdom of God, designed for a church scattered as much as a church gathered or come-structure. They are never called churches or temples, and they don't necessarily constitute the primary meeting places for the growing number of disciples or the primary residence or edifice for leadership. (5) They could otherwise be erected or adopted for the purposes of: (i) a monastic way-station for apprentices/novices committing more fully for a time to the new faith; (ii) a service-center for administering aid to the poor, help for the sick, comfort for the bereaved; (iii) a community center, where such is needed, for generic community decision-making and celebrative/festival functions—including larger, more public worship gatherings.

Where are our temples? We maintain they are simply "the Body and building of Christ," wherever that is alive and intelligible; they are mobile like the tabernacle, dynamic like a building under constant construction, accessible like Jesus-in-the-flesh, holy, set apart but utterly tangible, the salt of the earth, the light of the world, mistaken for Jesus, signposts of the Kingdom—not of temporal wealth, beautiful as a bride, intimate as a family. Our temples are the only adequate this-worldly dwelling place of God, stable but anchored in eternity, visible but not perishable, former habitation of demons, the people of God wherever and whenever they gather in Jesus' name; in other words, everywhere. To erect temples in an effort at religious dynamic equivalence seems a recipe for failure: on the one hand a failure if we lack the resources to get it done competitively; and, on the other hand, a failure to communicate the God-on-the-move if we succeed.

Notes

[1] Nicalo Tannenbaum in an extensive anthropological study of the Shan of rural north Thailand goes to great lengths to demonstrate popular Buddhism's animistic fixation on power, power-protection and its relation to temple and other artifacts and practices permeating the religion.

[2] While we touch briefly on the irony of an atheistic founding of Buddhism and the gods which flourish within the overall popular Buddhist worldview—the persistent interdependence between the high-religious philosophical Buddhism and local animisms—it is not the general purview of this paper to discuss the reasons behind this complementarity and dissonance. Needless to say, Buddhism presents a rather unique

anomaly in the distinction between its founder's revulsion at the Hindu pantheon and the propensity to worship everything from monkeys to monks, relics to the Buddha himself. Doubtless similar wonder might be expressed, certainly by Muslims, over the Christian West's rather Jewish insistence upon the worship of one God, while apparently paying homage to a thousand other demigods of our making.

[3] Isaiah's treatment of idolatry has the tone of crude domestication in his artful description of the craftsman's god-manufacturing routines: Is. 44:9-20.

[4] Think of the well-known temple prostitution within Canaanite cultures, Israelite versions of the same, Hindu and Buddhist forms, and Christendom's stories of the abuse of spiritual power even up to the present. In this latter case, it would never have been sanctioned openly by the tenets or promoters of the faith, whereas the others seem to have been willing to institutionalize it.

[5] See especially Wright 1996, Chap. 9 "Symbol and Controversy" and Chap. 11 "Jesus and Israel: the Meaning of Messiahship," as well as his simpler essays in Borg and Wright 1999, and Wright 1999.

[6] For a lengthy treatment of the first century temple cultus, atmosphere, functions, compromise under Roman and Jewish corrupters and utter centrality/supremacy in Jewish faith and culture, see Roetzel, 2002: chaps. 1-3.

[7] Borg and Wright, "The Crux of Faith," *The Meaning of Jesus: Two Visions,* 100ff.

7

Islands in the Sky: Tibetan Buddhism and the Gospel

Marku Tsering

The Tibetans have had a special place in the minds of Christian mission thinkers for several centuries. Despite much prayer and effort, they remain virtually untouched by the Gospel. Many factors, ranging from faulty mission methods to demonic activity, have been suggested as reasons why this is so.[1] This paper uses a technique called root-cause worldview analysis to explain why ordinary Tibetans see the world in the way that they do, and to show how this affects their response to the Gospel.[2]

Origins of a Worldview

The word Tibet is used in this paper to mean the area of China in which most of the six million Tibetans live. It includes the whole of the present Tibet Autonomous Region, together with portions of the Chinese provinces of Gansu, Qinghai, Sichuan, and Yunnan. Most of this territory is a vast, tangled knot of mountains over two million square kilometers in extent, lying on average 4,000 meters above the level of the sea. The Tibetan borderlands are defined by the Himalayas to the south and west, the Taklamakan and Gobi deserts to the north, and a series of four great mountain ranges to the east. The latter are the scene of an extensive and violent geologic upheaval, which forms a very effective barrier to travel. These great mountain ranges and freezing deserts surround a high, dry plateau having cool summers and bitterly cold winters. Of special significance to Tibetan culture is the fact that this plateau has no direct access to the sea, the distance between Lhasa and the Bay of Bengal being greater than 800 kilometers across the Himalayas; nor does it have convenient access to inland China, as the great river trenches of the Salween, Mekong, and Yangtze rivers lie crosswise rather than parallel to the natural trade routes; nor is it easily approached from the north or west, because of the barrier formed by the Kunlun and Himalaya Mountains.

The ancestors of the Tibetan people occupied this harsh and isolated environment well before the end of the last ice age. We know this because they left their stone tools and pottery scattered widely across the Tibetan plateau.[3] Some of them occupied "lowland" (3,000 m. above sea level) river valleys, where they developed a farming culture based on the cultivation of wheat and barley. Others lived as herders on windswept high-altitude (4,000 m.) grasslands.[4] Still others settled around salt lakes, the source of an important commodity for trade within Tibet and (very importantly for the history of Buddhism) across the Himalayas. None of these environments was well-suited to produce food, so even at the best of times the population was quite thinly scattered over a very wide area. Mountain ranges, deserts, and rivers further separated the earliest Tibetans from each other. These geological facts had a series of important effects on the Tibetan people, and on their view of the world around them.

Linguistic Effects

People who live in thinly populated areas where travel is difficult tend to develop different ways of speaking. In the case of the Tibetans, several sets of related dialects, each with many local variants, emerged over the centuries. The dialect of one's home area, which might be spoken in a place the size of a single county, identified one as belonging to a particular tribe or group. It was also used as a shibboleth (cf. Jdg. 12:6) to exclude untrustworthy outsiders. Strong attitudes about various dialects (and those who speak them) have persisted to the present day, and on them turns an entire set of social, economic, and trust relationships, especially in mixed settings such as urban churches.

Cultural Effects

A series of petty kingdoms arose among the farming cultures of the river valleys. Living around these kingdoms was a nomadic society whose material culture was based on the use of animal products. Trade between farmers and nomads depended upon a set of mineral, plant, and animal-derived goods that anchored Tibetan culture to its high altitude environment, making it very "non-exportable." This limited its contacts with the outside world[5] and encouraged insularity in the culture at large.

Spiritual Effects

Tibet has a subarctic climate in a subtropical location. This combination of high altitude and low latitude makes for extreme weather conditions in which snow, rain, hail, and dust storms can occur in a single day. Unexpected storms could blight crops and cause slow starvation in a whole community, or catch a caravan on a pass and bring sudden death to a group of unwary travelers. Such a harsh, unpredictable environment placed a premium on control of natural forces by means of magic. And in fact, from before the dawn of recorded history, there was present in Central Asia a religious system which claimed to be able to do just that: shamanism.

A full description of shamanism is beyond the scope of this chapter, but most scholars agree that it arose in Asia as far back as the Neolithic period some 3,000 years before the present.[6] Its central figure is the shaman, a person of either sex who is involuntarily possessed by a spirit. This spirit enables the shaman to make spiritual journeys to the transcendent world, to know the past and future, heal diseases, control the weather, perform magic, avoid danger and find good hunting.[7] The shamanic worldview includes belief in personal energy (called *lungta* in Tibetan and *hiimor* in Mongolian), locality spirits called *lu*, artifacts such as stone piles (*do pung* in Tibetan or *oboo* in Mongolian) and practices such as walking clockwise around sacred places, burning incense for purification, setting aside animals for mystic purposes, and divination. Shamanism is not concerned with moral or philosophical questions, but sees itself as more of a practical tool for controlling natural and spiritual forces.

Shamanism remains the spiritual foundation for the worldview of most Tibetans (and Mongols) today. Such a worldview is 'occult' or hidden, in the sense that it believes in an unseen world of frightening or malignant spirits; and 'magical' in the sense that the powers of the shaman can be used to avoid harm by controlling or manipulating supernatural forces by means of magic. The eventual influence of these views on Tibetan Buddhism was profound and long-lasting. Even today, most of the religious practices that tourists see at temples and monasteries in Tibet or Mongolia are shamanist rather than Buddhist in origin.

A Different Buddhism

Though known as “Tibetan Buddhism,” the religious belief system of Tibet is a highly syncretized form of Mahayana Buddhism in which the voice of Siddartha Gautama is only a distant echo. Some 500 years after the Buddha died, monks in the Indian subcontinent began to formulate the teachings of what was later called Mahayana or "Great Vehicle" Buddhism. A full description of Mahayana Buddhism cannot be given here, but two of its central concepts had a lasting influence on the way that folk Buddhists in Tibet perceive the world around them.

The first of these was belief in a class of beings called *boddhisattvas*. The early Mahayanists taught that these beings had eliminated the causes of their own rebirth and delayed entry into nirvana so that they could be reborn and help others to escape from suffering. The Mahayanists multiplied these savior-Buddhas by the hundreds, so that by the end of the first century A.D., the historical Buddha was seen as just one of many Buddhas of the past, present, and future.

The second feature was a monistic view of truth. Like other philosophical monists, the Mahayanists taught that everything is ultimately part of the same whole. In such a system, seemingly opposite ideas like good and evil are meaningless at the deepest level. Conventional ideas of good and evil were relegated to the realm of 'relative truth' (*kun dzob den pa* in Tibetan) for those who were spiritually uneducated. Of course, belief in relative truth led to belief in relative morality, and the Tibetans became accustomed to behavior in their religious leaders which no other religion would tolerate.[8] By contrast, only the enlightened could attain the ineffable realm of "absolute truth," which cannot be put into words or doctrines.[9]

In the millennium after the rise of Mayahana Buddhism, it was deeply influenced by two other Indian religions: yoga, a system of psychological and physical training under a spiritual master, and tantra, a mystery religion that appeared in North India around the seventh century A.D. Tantra claimed to offer a 'short path' to enlightenment through ritual sexual intercourse, magical gestures (*mudras*), occult spells (*mantras*), mystical diagrams (*mandalas*), and individual occult relationships with specialized 'teaching gods' (*yidam*). Tantra had its greatest influence on doctrinal Tibetan Buddhism rather than at the folk level.

It was during the seventh and eighth centuries A.D. that a newly unified Tibetan state began to make contacts with Buddhist neighbors in China, India, and what is now Kashmir. A small class of Tibetan nobles served as royal patrons for the spread of Buddhism, and under their sponsorship a few early monasteries were built along the banks of the Yarlung, Kyichu (Lhasa), and Brahmaputra rivers. But as tantric Buddhism spread across the country in this period, so did conflict with Tibet's native shamanism.

The details of this contest are now encrusted in myth, but in the end, tantric Buddhism won at the political level because it had royal patronage, and because it brought with it writing, literature, art, and intellectual contact with the more advanced civilizations of China and India. But shamanism was by no means entirely defeated. It not only survived at the folk level, it profoundly changed tantric Buddhism by introducing to it many shamanic and occult practices (such as divination and uniquely Tibetan approaches to merit-making) which give folk Tibetan Buddhism its distinctive character today. At this folk level, both tantric Buddhism and shamanism strongly reinforced the occult-magical worldview espoused by the local shaman (by now a Buddhist monk) and his followers.

The struggle between shamanism and tantric Buddhism was repeated in every country to which Tibetan Buddhism eventually spread, and indeed it continues today in Mongolia, Buryatia, and parts of the Himalayas. In a sense, shamanism prepared the way for the spread of Tibetan Buddhism through the Himalayas (India, Nepal, Bhutan) and across Central Asia (China, Mongolia, Siberia). In modern times, Central Asian shamanism and Tibetan Buddhism are almost co-extensive along the Tibetan Buddhist cultural borderlands.

In the end, the lives and cultures of more than 60 people groups, from the Himalayas to Siberia, were shaped by this mix of shamanism and tantrism. Today this area is referred to as the

Tibetan Buddhist world, and it is linked by cultural, intellectual, and spiritual ties which were first forged at this early period of history, though only realized historically at a much later date.

Tibet in the 10th to mid-20th Centuries: Isolation and Identity

During the first half of the second millennium A.D., Buddhism expanded slowly as monasteries were built and the number of monks increased. By the 1600s, the monks of the Gelugpa order were powerful enough to seize control of the Tibetan government. Their claim to power was enhanced by the widespread belief that they could recognize a line of incarnate boddhisattvas, who governed the country as the Dalai Lamas.

The monastic government naturally did everything it could to promote tantric Buddhism. It filled government positions with monks and instituted a theocratic system which it called *chos srid gnyis 'brel* or "religion and politics together" (Goldstein 1989: 2). Aside from essential diplomatic contacts, the monks pursued an isolationist policy and showed little interest in the events of the outside world. Tibet became an island in the sky—physically, linguistically, intellectually, and politically isolated from the great cultures which surrounded it.

Isolation was perhaps a natural policy for the monks because it is a central theme in Tibetan Buddhism—a religion in which ultimate truth can only be realized by the individual in solitary meditation. Tibetan monks performed individual retreats lasting months or even years. A few even immured themselves for life.[10] Other monks went to remote hills and caves to meditate; their successors built monasteries at remote sites, often on a hilltop or rocky ridge away from settled areas. Tibetan Buddhism is, as the anthropologist Sherry Ortner observed, "a religion of anti-social individualism" (1978:157).

The monks also isolated themselves from contact with other (non-tantric) Buddhists, whose doctrines they mocked as "the Buddha's teachings for the less able." Under their rule, creativity withered and intellectual life shrank to the scale of conserving, classifying, memorizing, and commenting on the vast amount of scriptural material imported from India during the seventh and eighth centuries. As a result, the catalog and the memorized list became the paradigmatic tools of Tibetan intellectual life.[11] Artistic achievement was measured by conformity to norms established centuries before. Paintings had to conform to strict standards of proportion and color.[12] Writers were expected to use the established metaphors found in metaphor dictionaries. There was no popular literary culture, for only the monks could read, and they lived in intellectual, and to some degree, social isolation from their communities. Although the monks and the larger community were economically and socially dependent on one another, intellectually they were worlds apart.

This separation persisted for centuries and gave rise to a deeply-ingrained folk prejudice that religion is something to be delegated entirely to specialists. Under no circumstances was it a matter of personal choice or decision. The simple observance of ritual was enough to satisfy the religious impulses of most people.

The average Tibetan in this period was largely unaware of the world beyond his valley, or of the existence of any social or intellectual alternatives to his station in life. The life of the ordinary Tibetan was as wide as the valley in which he was born; or if a pilgrim, nomad or trader, the territory in which he roamed. Things outside this world had little relevance or interest. Tibetan Buddhism thrived in this atmosphere, nor was its influence ever challenged, since the Himalayas insulated Tibet from the competing pressures of Islam to the west, Hinduism to the south, and the Chinese world to the north and east.

Buddhism was not the only isolationist force in Tibetan society. As we have already seen, large distances, low population density, and difficult terrain promoted the emergence of dialects, not all of which were mutually intelligible. This gave rise to regional alliances that compromised Tibet's political unity and limited the development of a national consciousness. To this day, Tibetans identify most strongly with others from their home dialect area. When away from home, they usually seek social and economic relationships with others who speak Tibetan in the same way that they themselves do. It is not surprising that for the average Tibetan, the two powerfully isolationist forces of tantric Buddhism and one's local dialect of the language are the twin pillars of the Tibetan ethnic identity.

During the later part of the nineteenth and twentieth centuries, the monks' chief foreign policy goal was to maintain national isolation from the scientific and political changes going on all around them. It is surprising that they succeeded as long as they did. But the arrival at the capital city, Lhasa, of a British Indian army in 1904, and a Chinese army in 1910, were signs that the monks could not keep the world at bay forever.

The appearance in Tibet of modern Chinese culture during the 1950s resulted in the destruction of tantric Buddhism as an organized political force and its replacement by a government with a Leninist political culture. Buddhism was reviled as a feudal superstition, and Marxism-Leninism-Mao Tse Tung Thought became the new "pearl of great price." A vast corpus of Soviet and Chinese Communist literature was translated into Tibetan, and all sorts of modern technology arrived in the region as increasing numbers of ethnic Chinese came to Tibet. The new government made intense efforts to modernize Tibet in a social and economic sense, and to inculcate secular materialism as the dominant ideology. Widespread radio and television broadcasting and better infrastructure such as highways and airports led to some limited breakdown of intellectual isolation during the last third of the twentieth century.

With the easing of religious restrictions in the 1980s, tantric Buddhism enjoyed a limited revival. Monks were once again seen in the streets, and rituals revived in the monasteries, but the political power of the monks was gone. By the dawn of the twenty-first century, popular support for Tibetan Buddhism was still strong and broadly-based in the rural areas where most Tibetans live. While shamanism and tantric Buddhism continued as the foundational worldview of the average Tibetan, they now had to compete with modern secular materialism for the allegiance of educated and urban Tibetans.

In summary, Tibet's unique geographical position made it an ideal homeland for shamanism. Shamanism in turn became the foundation of Tibetan people's spiritual life. The arrival of tantric Buddhism during the seventh and eighth centuries further reinforced the occult-magical worldview fostered by shamanism. Tantric Buddhism, politically dominant, was able to exclude any new ideas which might promote change or challenge it. Centuries of political and intellectual isolation left the population inward-looking and disinterested in the broader world around them. In worldview terms, the arrival of Chinese culture in the 1950s did not greatly change this situation for most Tibetans. It did, however, open new possibilities for educated Tibetans in the cities, of whom we shall hear more later.

Tibetan Buddhism and Christian Missions

Perhaps the single most remarkable thing about the Catholic and Protestant efforts to evangelize the Tibetans was that so much effort met with so little success. The modern Catholic effort began with Father Antonio de Andrade's mission to western Tibet in 1624, and the Protestant effort began with William Carey's mission to Bhutan in 1797. Both Catholics and Protestants kept up a steady, and sometimes heroic, effort to share Christ with the Tibetan people through classical apologetics, evangelistic preaching, Bible translation, and distribution of Christian literature. Both groups ministered to physical needs through community development, agriculture, education, handicraft training, and medicine. One-to-one, group-to-many and community-based approaches were used.

Between the two groups, the Catholics seem to have somewhat greater numerical success as church planters, but neither group saw the level of response in Tibet that both had experienced in China (or even India) during the late nineteenth and early twentieth centuries.[13] This fact suggests that mission methods were not at fault; there was something unique about the dynamics of the Christian-Buddhist encounter in Tibet that hindered the progress of the Gospel. That "something" was almost certainly the worldview of the folk Tibetan Buddhist.

An Occult-Magical Worldview

At its simplest level, the Christian-Tibetan Buddhist encounter brought together two almost diametrically opposed worldviews. The relevant points of the Tibetans' occult-magical worldview can be summarized under the concepts of reality, truth, religion, scriptures, and culture.

Reality: Reality is unitary and there is no barrier between the physical and the psychological. Virtually anything that is possible in the mind is also possible in the physical world. Miracles, in the sense of remarkable occurrences that defy physical laws, are everyday occurrences and a part of the normal course of life.

Truth: Truth encompasses all possible opposites. Ultimate truth can't be reduced to propositions expressed in words. A thing is true if it is plausible. "Truth" as opposed to "falsehood" is an alien category of thought derived from non-monistic religions.

Religion: Religion is practice and ritual, not doctrine; method, not personal belief; its teachings are for others (monks and lamas), not self. Religion is not a matter of one's personal choice. All religions are good and their teachings are similar to those of

Buddhism. Any apparent contradictions between religious systems melt away in the ultimate unity of opposites.

Scriptures: Scriptures are materially holy and meant to be recited or used in magic and rituals. They are not to be read or understood by ordinary people.

Culture: Culture and Tibetan Buddhism are equivalent. Anything religious that is "not Tibetan" is not interesting and should be rejected. The only possible religion for a Tibetan is tantric Buddhism. To follow anything else is to cease to be a Tibetan.

The likely outcome of an encounter between this worldview and that of a messenger of the Gospel is self-evident: the Tibetan perceives the Christian's ethical concerns as identical to those of Buddhism, his good works as merit-making, his stories of Biblical miracles as nothing extraordinary, and the suffering Savior as one of many such figures in tantric Buddhism. The Resurrection is the tale of just another shaman who went on a journey to the land of the dead and returned three days later.[14] Prayers for someone's healing or exorcism in a "power encounter" are no more than the lamas do every day.[15] The conclusion that Christianity and Buddhism are "the same" seems entirely justified to most Tibetans.[16]

Many evangelistic encounters with Tibetans occurred at this point. Even if they don't, there are further barriers standing in the way of the would-be Tibetan Christian. For a Tibetan, the degree of worldview change involved in becoming a Christian is extreme. Immediate rejection by family and society, with its attendant economic, social, and (in China) political consequences, is another serious obstacle to faith. Implicit in the Tibetan worldview are barriers to comprehension of the Gospel message, and also barriers to its acceptance.

In summary, it is no wonder that the Gospel has had a difficult time among a people who see conservation of the past, rejection of cultural change, exclusion of foreign ideas, and preservation of national identity as vital themes in their intellectual and cultural life. When the history of Christian mission effort is reviewed against the background of the folk Tibetan worldview, it seems valid to conclude that Christian missions may have consistently underestimated the difficulty of bringing the Gospel to this people. It may be time for a rethinking of mission approaches.

Is Engagement Possible?

Perhaps the first step in such a rethinking is to recognize that there are no easy answers. The past 400 years of mission history has produced no example of an apologetic technique, a mission method, or a 'cultural bridge' which brought large numbers of Tibetan people into the Church. If the conclusions based on a root-cause worldview analysis are correct, it seems unlikely that new methods developed outside the Tibetan cultural area will be successful among the Tibetans either, though this may change if the influence of Buddhism declines in the future. A close examination of the record over time shows Tibetans coming to Christ in ones and twos, in scattered locations, over long periods,[17] independently of the techniques used to reach them.

Tantric Buddhism itself (as opposed to shamanism) seems to play a dominant role in such resistance to the Gospel. Among all the cultures of Buddhist Central Asia, those in which Tibetan Buddhism holds unchallenged dominance have been most resistant. Where Tibetan Buddhism has not yet established itself, or where it co-exists with a vital indigenous shamanism, the response to the Gospel has been greater (e.g. among the Tamangs of Nepal, or the Lepchas of Sikkim). Where institutional Tibetan Buddhism has been destroyed and replaced by a Soviet-style system for several decades, such as in Mongolia, church growth has been relatively rapid. So it seems that there is something in the Tibetan Buddhist worldview itself which promotes resistance to the Gospel.

That "something" is probably the Mahayanist view of the dual nature of truth, at least as formulated by Tibetan Buddhism. In his book *Truth in Religion*, the philosopher Mortimer Adler raised serious questions about whether truth-based engagement with

Buddhism was even theoretically possible. Adler noted Buddhism's denial of the principle of non-contradiction (which states that two propositions that are contrary to each other cannot both be true). He viewed this as a fatal logical flaw in the Buddhist system; a flaw which, at least from a philosophical perspective, subverts all efforts at truth-based dialogue (Adler 1990). While most folk Buddhist Tibetans are unaware of their religion's formal teaching about the dual nature of truth, this doctrine is now an integral part of their worldview, whether they can state it explicitly or not.

A Way Forward

It seems valid to conclude that substantive, truth-based engagement with the Tibetan Buddhist worldview may be humanly impossible. If this is true, then it certainly explains much of the history of missions among this people group. It also focuses attention on the point at which human resources fail and where dependence on God begins.

Trust God

Jesus tells us that "no one can come to me unless drawn by the Father who sent me" (Jn. 6:44). As Christians concerned for the Tibetan people, we need to renew our faith in the sovereign electing power of God, and trust Him fully to do the work of evangelism. There are many New Testament examples of God working directly in people's hearts even before they understood the Gospel: Nicodemus (Jn. 3), Cornelius (Acts 10), the Ethiopian eunuch (Acts 8), Lydia (Acts 16:14), the nameless centurion commended for his faith (Mt. 8), and many others. God still works in this way today, and we need to pray that we will meet the people whose hearts He has touched. When we do, we can be partners with the Holy Spirit in helping them reconstruct their Buddhist worldview[18] into a Christian one. A systematic study of the Bible is foundational to such an approach; the story of Creation is an excellent place to begin.

Be There and Be Ready

Many Christians are aiding China's development in the areas of education, health, agriculture, community development, and other fields. In the past two decades, the number and type of opportunities for foreign and ethnic Chinese Christians to enter the Tibetan cultural area have increased dramatically. It is likely that this trend will continue as the government emphasizes the economic development of the western regions of the country. Given these circumstances, Christian groups would do well to think about making plans for long-term service among the Tibetan people.[19]

Mission leaders bear a responsibility to make sure that those they send have adequate preparation. Expatriate (and Chinese) Christians need time for the hard work of becoming competent in Tibetan language and culture. This doesn't mean that each person must be a walking cultural encyclopedia, but it does mean that competence in language and cultural skills are not neglected in training and are available at least at the team level.

Tibetans are an overwhelmingly rural people, but some do live in the cities. Cities have been very strategic places from the earliest New Testament times (eight of the 27 New Testament books are named after the cities to which they were sent) because they offer anonymity, freedom from traditional sources of authority, and social spaces where change can occur. Tibet is no exception to this general rule, and so far, many if not most Tibetans who have become Christians live in cities. One reason for this may be that in recent decades a class of urban young people has emerged who know little or nothing of Buddhism; their focus is the pleasures of modern life as found in the nightclub and Internet cafe. If Church history is any guide, such people may be more open to Christ than others with established religious commitments.

More recently, opportunities for Christians to serve in rural areas have increased. Christians should not forget the many social, educational, health, and community development needs of the Tibetan people, most of whom live in rural areas. These are wonderful opportunities to fulfill both the Great Commandment and the Great Commission. Christians working in Tibetan cultural areas should incarnate the full range of biblical concern for man's physical, social, and spiritual well-being.

Build Up the Church

The two pillars of Tibetan ethnic identity are Tibetan language and tantric Buddhism. When a Tibetan becomes a Christian, one pillar of ethnic identity (Buddhism) is lost, and only one other remains (language). It is especially important that Tibetan Christians are able to read their own language.[20] This not only gives them access to the Bible, but allows them to express their Tibetan identity in a way that is highly valued by the culture. It demonstrates that a person can in fact be a Tibetan and a Christian.

Tibetan Christians in China also need access to Christian literature that is easy to read, and which addresses their needs and concerns. Much existing Christian literature has a strong Tibetan exile flavor and deals with themes that are not of vital interest to Tibetans living in China today. So there is much room for the work of Christian writers, artists, and musicians who can express themselves in ways that modern Tibetan people can understand and appreciate.[21]

Summary and Limitations

Tibet's unique physical environment proved ideal for the growth and persistence of shamanism. Shamanism in turn proved spiritually fertile ground for the growth and development of tantric Buddhism. The occult-magical view of reality fostered by both religions became the worldview of the average Tibetan more than a thousand years ago. This worldview is incompatible with the Gospel at a fundamental level. A review of the history of Christian missions to Tibet suggests that it is probably this fact which accounts for the Tibetans' disappointing response to Christian missions. The arrival of modern Chinese culture in Tibet has broken the power of institutional Buddhism, and secularized a small class of mainly urban Tibetans, among whom small but steady numbers of people are turning to Christ.[22] If present secularizing social and political trends continue, the outlook for church growth among the Tibetan people is considerably brighter than in the past.

This paper has attempted a root-cause worldview analysis for folk Tibetan Buddhists who live in the Tibet Autonomous Region of China. It would be somewhat different if applied to Tibetans from other parts of China under greater or more prolonged Chinese influence (e.g., Qinghai or Sichuan provinces), to non-folk Buddhists, or to Tibetan exiles. Root-cause worldview analysis is a technique that may prove helpful if applied to other peoples of the Buddhist world.

Notes

[1] For a thoughtful analysis of mission efforts among the Tibetans and other ethnic groups in China, see Covell 1993.

[2] Some readers may find such an approach rather mechanistic, but it is implicit in the way that the Apostle Paul, for example, approached the Athenian intellectuals in Acts 17:16-34. This passage amply repays careful study by anyone involved in ministry to Buddhists or Hindus.

[3] Artifacts from the Paleolithic and Neolithic periods can be seen in the Tibet Museum in Lhasa. They include stone and bone implements of various types, as well as examples of rock paintings found at Nagchu and Damshung. For photos, see Tibet Museum 2001.

[4] Life for these people was (and is) extremely hard. Snow may fall in any month of the year, and winter temperatures of minus 40°C. are not unknown.

[5] The Tibetans did leave their mountain homelands on military expeditions during the seventh to the ninth centuries, cutting the Silk Road and once

briefly capturing the Chinese capital at Xian. See Snellgrove and Richardson 1980.

[6] For a description of Mongolian shamanism written by a practicing shaman, see Sarangerel 2000.

[7] The so-called "witch" of Endor described in 1 Samuel 28:4-14 has many attributes of a shaman. Shamanic practices (as distinct from classic shamanism) are found in many cultures outside Asia.

[8] The sixth Dalai Lama was a noted profligate whose love poetry is still popular in Tibet today.

[9] Interested readers should see Newland 1992.

[10] For a description of Tibetan hermits in the last century, see Waddell 1988: 239ff.

[11] The Tibetans classified all their knowledge into ten subject areas: grammar, Buddhist logic, arts, medicine, Buddhist philosophy, rhetoric, composition, poetry, drama, and astrology.

[12] Artists are still expected to conform to these norms. For visual arts, see Rabgyal and Rinchen 2001.

[13] For a summary of these efforts, see Covell 1993.

[14] Even in modern Tibet, there are many persons who are believed to have died, made shamanic journeys to the world of the dead, and returned to life after periods of up to a week. Such persons are called *delog*. A typical delog's story is told in Drolma 1995.

[15] In a recent example in Tibet, a Christian was asked to pray for an ill member of a Buddhist family. During a subsequent illness the family invited both the monks and the Christian to come and make the patient better. When it was explained that for prayer to be effective, one had to follow Christ alone, no more invitations were given to the Christian. The reason given was that following Christ would mean rejection by family and society—it was just too costly.

[16] The view that Christianity and Buddhism are the same even appears in print from time to time, such as in the popular Tibetan magazine *sbrang char*.

[17] Fortunately, this is not true elsewhere in the Tibetan Buddhist World, where rapid church growth has occurred among the Mongols and among certain Tibetan-related ethnic groups in the Himalayas.

[18] A Tibetan friend of mine heard the Gospel many times, but took three years to become a Christian. Much of this time was spent in

reconstructing his former worldview into a Christian one. He is now a pastor.

[19] This statement is not intended to devalue short-term missions, merely to say that it may not be wise to build a long-term strategy around short-term methods!

[20] The written forms of Tibetan differ in important ways from the spoken forms of the language.

[21] For example, the catechism is a teaching method now out of favor in the West, but it has a long tradition and is much beloved in Tibet.

[22] This historical process also occurred in Mongolia, where it prepared the way for rapid church growth in the 1990s.

8

Structural and Ministry Philosophy Issues in Church Planting among Buddhist Peoples

Alan R. Johnson

Introduction

Missionaries involved in church planting among Buddhist populations wrestle with the problem of very slow church planting and church growth among existing congregations. One response to this has been to deal with issues of contextualization to see how the Gospel message and church life can be made to better fit the local context and thus become more relevant to the people. I personally believe that this is a very important piece of the explanatory "puzzle" as to why it is so difficult to plant churches among Buddhist peoples.

However, I have come to see this problem as being much more complex and multidimensional, with issues of contextualization being only one of a series of interrelated factors. I want to argue here that what may be the most significant reason for slow church planting and growth among Buddhist populations comes from the models of evangelism, ministry, church structure, and church life that are employed. I want to suggest that it is less a case of us not making sense to people from Buddhist backgrounds than it is one of perpetuating philosophies and models of ministry and ways of "doing church" that hinder our ability to plant and grow churches capable of multiplying rapidly and over long periods of time. Another way of putting it is to say that our problems lie more in what is normally considered under the topic of discipleship rather than evangelism.

Before discussing this proposition in more detail I want to illustrate how I came to this conclusion by sharing some of my own personal journey in church planting and development in Thailand.

"There has to be a better way!"

Prior to coming to Thailand in 1986 I worked in a large Assemblies of God church in the Seattle area for six years. My experience of ministry, which was quite typical for people coming out of standard church backgrounds, was one primarily defined by directing and running programs through lots of effort by a core of professional staff and a never-large-enough base of volunteer laborers. Although I have many pleasant memories from that time and it was a wonderful experience in terms of training for full-time ministry, some of my main remembrances are always being short of workers, and being very tired.

When I got to Thailand, after language school, our family moved to a medium sized province in the heart of central region. Our task was to work with a young Thai pastor and his wife to essentially replant a church that had fallen apart. I vividly remember my first Sunday, with our two families and small children and about six other Christians none of whom actually lived in the city but who all came in from surrounding villages. It did not seem to be a terribly promising core group to begin a new church plant with.

It was quite natural in this setting to use the only tools I had in my bag of ministry concepts-programs, event evangelism, and lots of hard work. Over the next two and a half years the pastor and I tried everything we could think of to reach people and incorporate them into the church. We passed out tracts, prayer walked, showed the Jesus film, did special events for Christmas, held open air crusades and revival meetings, taught English, visited people, tried small groups and bible studies, and had a booth at the annual fair. We were constantly busy, worn out and (in retrospect) rather stressed, and had stirred up a lot of dust and spent quite a few baht on these various activities. By the time we left for our one year deputation we had a group of about thirty-five people meeting that was still far from supporting their own pastor. I remember thinking that two couples worked full time for two and a half years with plenty of finance and we added just under thirty people to our Sunday morning church attendance. That is when I thought to myself, there has to be a better way to do this. By this time in my life I had been in vocational ministry for eleven years and quite frankly I was feeling tired and the glow and excitement was waning in the face of the constant weight of pushing the programs.

When faced with meager results, it is always a comfort to say that nobody else is really growing either or that the people are resistant. Yet deep inside I was not satisfied with blaming resistance as the sole reason for the slow growth.

Seeking Answers

My first attempts at looking for answers were focused on how to make the message more relevant. I have elsewhere chronicled the journey of how I became sensitized to the issues of message contextualization and the fruit of that research (Johnson 2002a). I discovered that while there has not been an overwhelming amount of material written specifically on Thailand, the issue of contextualizing the message as well as church life has received a great deal of attention in general.

During my year long deputation I began to examine other ways to reach and incorporate people into the Body of Christ. The two things that I ran into repeatedly in my early readings that were new to me and radically different than my first term work had to do with the concept of reaching personal networks, also referred to by its Greek term oikos, and that of non-professional leadership, more popularly known as "lay" leadership (Johnson 2002b). Our evangelism had been completely based on winning separate individuals, ignoring families and natural social connections. Consequently new believers were cut off from sharing back into their closest relationships. In addition to this the model of church life and evangelism was one that was driven by the trained professionals and was programmatic in nature. We had the sneaking suspicion that lay people were supposed to do "the work of the ministry", but did not have the slightest idea how to structure things so that they could. I was rather stunned to hear the Thai pastor I worked with actually say out loud that it takes five years for a person to be a believer before they can do anything.

So as I returned to Thailand for a second term I resolved to experiment with evangelism based totally in relationships and working through personal networks and that would be led by a bi-vocational leader without very limited financial assistance if any. Right as I was at the front end of this experiment, in God's providential timing, I was exposed to ideas and literature about cell churches and small-group driven ministry from a couple of pastor friends in the states who graciously sent me my first copies of these books.[1] The ideas I found there meshed completely with my new vision for empowering non-professionals to do ministry and doing evangelism through personal networks. Over the next seven years of ministry I found several opportunities to experiment with these principles first hand and also to teach them to others and observe the results.

The first experiment came in a ground up church plant attempt. We had a bible school trained couple who moved to a province and began working to support themselves. We worked at different forms of outreach and our first convert was a woman in her eighties whose hand was healed after prayer. We used this as our first entrance into an oikos. One by one people began to come to faith until we had a group of about fifteen believers who for the most part were connected in a couple of networks in one area of the city. This was quite a difference from my first term's work. In the space of a couple of years we had added fifteen people, with no outside finance, no programs, a bi-vocational worker, only a little bit of participation on my part, and meeting in homes. What is more is these Christians did everything on their own, if they wanted to do something they paid for it and gave their own offerings, whereas in my former place everyone expected that the church would provide for them.

Seeing a Pattern

In my third term I began work in a very different setting from my previous upcountry locations and circumstances. I connected with an existing Thai church plant that was three years old and had about fifty adherents. The pastor also shared a vision for small-group driven ministry led by lay people. One of my main jobs was to help in small group development and multiplication. The first group I worked with went from seven to twenty people in a few weeks as we worked on reaching personal networks and making the small group "outward" focused. But after a time it was apparent there was no leader ready to start a new cell so the pastor asked that I help another group. Eventually this cell group became a house church that now is connected to the mother church but meets separately.

The second group was led by a housewife with a few high school students attending. We started working the principles and very soon had our first convert from a house just a few doors down from our meeting place. After two years we counted just over twenty converts all who attended Sunday service and the cell, meeting in a total of five different groups and these groups were coached by this housewife.

In both these cases there was no finance, no programs, and no professional leaders other than me helping them with implanting basic principles. As I began to reflect on these experiences, I learned a number of lessons, two of which are relevant for our discussion. First, when we started doing evangelism based in people's relational networks rather than isolating individuals and giving them a "presentation" we found that people were more receptive. Second, when we structured around face-to-face meetings led by lay people and that were focused on reaching lost people, three things happened. First, people came to faith more rapidly, they became active believers rather than passive in worship and sharing their faith, and many of them went on to become leaders of other groups.

What really caught my attention as I observed these small Bangkok cells, was that I was watching Thai people share the Gospel in a zealous and passionate manner but in what I considered to be inelegant and certainly not-contextualized terms. Yet people were coming to Christ. This led me to develop what I called the "viral theory" of evangelism. Just as you cannot be "taught" to catch a cold, but must come into contact with the virus, in the same way we cannot "teach" people into becoming Christians. First you have to have someone with the virus of new life in Christ and just get them close enough to get into contact with the dynamic of that new life, and there will be people who come to faith. Getting lost people in close enough proximity with people who really have been changed by Christ made even the inelegant and inarticulate presentation of the Gospel make sense because they were seeing it lived out in front of them. It was not disembodied words, but a living incarnation of Jesus' power in a person's life that made the picture clear. The expression of new life in Christ provides the interpretational context of the message to begin to make sense and to begin to be seen as a life option for them. This is when I first began to understand that structure and context—both social and church—was even more important than message contextualization.

Further reflection help me to see that in my initial church planting experience our evangelistic model kept us from utilizing the natural social structure to share the Gospel through relationships, and our models of church made for a structure that effectively isolated those who have new life in Christ from those who do not. Hybels and Mittleberg (1994) have a nicer sounding formula than my viral theory that goes like this:

High Potency + Close Proximity + Clear Communication = Maximum Impact

This formula, like my viral analogy, addresses the issues of potency, that you must have Christians who have the real thing, a dynamic relationship with Christ; and the structural issue of proximity, where you have to be close to people to communicate the message.

This leads me back to my original thesis. I have watched Thai people come to faith not because of a contextualized message, as important as that is, but because what they did hear started to make sense in the context of a changed life. I propose that our problems in planting the church among Buddhist peoples have more to do with our assumptions and models of evangelism, church life, ministry and church structure that keep us from providing an interpretational context for our message and suppress the most natural carriers and conduits for the Gospel.[2]

Assumptions of the 1+1+1 Model and Associated Problems

As I started comparing the different ways of thinking about and doing ministry and evangelism I began to summarize the model that I grew up with and had been involved with in Thailand as 1+1+1. It consists of one building that is the "church" and the hub of activities, one full-time Bible school trained vocational minister whose job is to run the programs and care for the people, and one congregation or group of people who are to fit into the programs and receive spiritual nurture from the pastor. All of this equals "the way we do church."

By making a critique of this model I am not saying that it has not been used by God to produce much fruit, nor is it a structure that God is not using today. What I am suggesting is that in Buddhist contexts where there is a resistance to the message as being something outside and foreign, and where there is strong social solidarity in the society, this model has severe limitations. One reason why I think that church planters in Buddhist contexts have been slow to adopt new models of church is because the traditional model does work to a degree in places where there is receptivity to the Gospel and large numbers of Christians in the society. So there is the tendency to think that because this model worked in our homelands to a degree that it should also be fruitful in a new setting. However, for reasons that will be discussed below, I feel that among a resistant population the traditional model will not be effective and will generate a kind of Christian that is incapable of reaching their society and will not allow for church multiplication.

Assumption 1: The Building is the Center of Activity for the Believer

Even though we know theologically the church is not the building, in practice everything happens there. What this means is that very soon after conversion without ever even saying anything people begin to build a new social center around the activities in this building and soon are incapable of relating back to their own social structures to share Christ. In fact, the persecution they receive for their new affiliations drives them even closer to the "church" and away from their personal network.

Assumption 2: Ministry is Done by Trained Professionals

The pastor must have professional Bible school training and be full-time in vocational ministry. They care for the flock, run the programs, and direct everything that happens at the building.

Assumption 3: The Congregation are Consumers of Ministry.

Since the people do not have training they cannot do anything. This is unconsciously and unintentionally modeled to them by everything that happens in a Sunday service. They are taught to be passive consumers of the presentation. Thus churches are rated on "how good the product to be consumed is." Better worship, better preaching, means more people willing to come.

The Problem of Blindness created by Socialization Processes

I believe that the socialization forces of what we say through what we are doing in this model are so powerful that they virtually nullify all of the theological concepts that we talk about that are diametrically opposed to these three assumptions. Church leaders who have grown up in churches like this, gone to Bible school and interned in churches like this, and who have worked in planting or leading churches like this uniformly cannot "see" how all of this appears to the new believer, because it is so natural to them.

One of the exercises I use in teaching pastors or bible school students is to get them to role play making a "video" of their church service. I make them rearrange the chairs like in the church and we choose a song leader, speaker etc. While someone "videos" the others briefly act out their parts and I attend the service as a pre-Christian. When I ask them to run the video back and analyze it for what I learn as a first-time I can only get responses based on what I *heard* in the service and never based on what I have *seen* and *experienced*.

Finally after I prompt them with questions about thinking in terms of who has the power, who is in charge, who is up front, what are the different roles occupied, they start to see things in terms of the very passive nature of the attendee's church experience. People who come to this church model can sing, listen, and give, but there is not a whole lot after that. This is why even in the face of massive recruiting efforts and constant exhortation about "serving" and "using gifts" that there are very few takers. The structure and assumptions of this model completely undermine and subvert the verbal messages and teach something radically different.

When all the important stuff is done by trained professionals with the mystical bible school degree, there are very few connections with Christian service as it is conceived of as an up-front activity for people who are mechanics, housewives, salespeople, teachers, drivers, food vendors, or secretaries. In their minds they would have to leave their livelihoods to get professional training to do ministry.

In talking with one pastor about the cell groups in her church, she admitted that she has to lie to people in order to get them to do anything. She would call and say she was sick so they would lead the cell. If she attended, they would automatically make her do everything, refusing any involvement because their pastor was there.

Another downside is that since everything happens at the building, people have no time or ability to make relationships with non-believers. Even if there is not explicit teaching about forsaking worldly friends, there is a strong tendency for the church to become the new social center. Over time people become increasingly uncomfortable with the unbelieving friends and vice versa. Evangelism then is reduced to inviting people to come to the building so the professionals can share the message with them.

The Problem of Christians Barriered off from Those Without Christ

What you have in the end with this model is a pool of people who are philosophically and structurally barriered off from non-Christians and who do not see personal ministry to others as a part of their calling in Christ. Those who have the message of Christ are physically and mentally separated from the world of unbelievers and even when they do rub elbows with the lost world they are predisposed by the modeling given to think that only a trained ministry can share Christ with these people.

Where does this leave us with church planting among Buddhist peoples? In many places where there are already existing church movements that are small minorities in large seas of Buddhists it is this kind of church and ministry philosophy in one degree or another that is there already. I am not sure that people are rejecting Christ so much as they are rejecting a disembodied message connected to a social structure that places those who believe outside of their families and communities. Institutionalized Christianity or "Churchianity" makes very little sense, and they are quick to perceive, (as the evangelists are correspondingly slow to realize) the social implications for them if they were to become a Christian.

The Leadership Problem of Looking for "The Magic Answer"

What has been interesting to observe is how all of the literature and seminars sharing new models relating to meta-church, cell church, G-12 churches, training and multiplying leaders, house churches and church planting movements has been received by those using this traditional model. It takes very little reading at all to see that the fastest growing movements around the world have radically different ministry assumptions and models than what I have described above. The problem I find is that people coming from this background read the books and go to the seminars predisposed to look for "the magic answer" that will lead to growth and view it as a methodology, when in reality it is a complete new DNA code for making Christians and living the Christian life.

Part of the problem lies in the nature of seminars and teachings as well. I have realized that there are three types of "data" you can get in a seminar: a). low level concrete practices-"we did this," b). mid-level principles that usually wrapped in some kind of method-"you must release lay people by training them like this", and c). high-level abstract principles, values and assumptions. Oftentimes people who have been very successful as practitioners cannot fully explain the kinds of deep underlying assumptions and values that drive their methods. So pastors come looking for low-level concrete things to do when the real power is with the abstract principles. When they try to implement the concrete practices or principles at the mid-level they get frustrated because it did not work. But it did not work because those practices and principles were deeply embedded in a social context and value system both in the church and the society where it happened. When you strip that away the practice may not work at all. What traditional leaders have trouble doing is taking the very abstract and powerful general principles such as reaching networks and releasing non-professional ministry and developing their own values and assumptions and seeking how to apply it in their social context.

Church Planting Among Buddhists: Values for Building Dynamic Christian Communities

There is a mass of literature dealing with the nature of church and ministry.[3] Some of it is quite abstract and principled in nature while much of it is embedded in specific contexts and practices. In addition to this there is much debate among practitioners and scholars of church growth and missiology as to what are the best ways to plant and develop churches. Is it cell, meta, G-12, house church, do you use buildings, not use buildings, use paid pastors, not use paid pastors, etc.? I do not want to try and reproduce or rehash the literature nor do I want to enter into the debate. Two considerations underlie the approach that I will explain below. First, I do not believe there is a single right way or single best way or magic answer. Second, I believe in both/and thinking and believe that there is room for all of these pieces in the bigger picture. Principles need to be worked out in their specific local contexts.

What follows here are some concepts that I think can be helpful in developing forms that facilitate biblical functions. They focus on assumptions, values, structures, and ministry philosophy rather than on concrete activities. These are not "steps" that are to be done in some kind of order, but rather should be thought of as principles that inform action. These ideas and concepts do not "look" like anything, they can be enacted in many different forms and social settings and will look unique in terms of their forms in each one. Part of the big lesson that all of this is based on is that how you get to your goal is important as the goal itself because how you do it may introduce an ethos into the life of the church that hampers ever reaching the final goal.

For discussion purposes, I have separated the principles that follow into the major categories of church planting goals, training values, and ministry values. However, it is important to note that these are not stand-alone principles but are deeply interwoven together and in real-life settings they will impact all the activities in church life.

Church Planting Goals: Starting at the Beginning

It is one thing to plant a single indigenous church, but it is quite another to start a movement of rapidly multiplying indigenous churches. If we have this end goal in mind it will radically restructure the way we do things from the very beginning. Too often we have been encumbered by building-centered visions of what the church is like and with finding leaders capable of handling all that goes with it. A CPM is going to be facilitated by Christians who have dynamic new life in Christ, and who are mobilized to reach their networks and envisioned to take the Gospel to other localities who have never heard. Building and professionally oriented ministry does not do these things well.

People are hardwired by God; cream rises to the top:

A church planting movement requires that there be a continual flow of new leaders. Traditional thinking sees leaders going through a long process of training, and much of what is implicit in church growth thinking is that "better" leaders lead bigger groups. An unintended effect of this is that we gear our training to producing people who can lead and manage large groups, and this becomes a bottleneck in leadership development.

A pastor friend shared a fascinating idea about Exodus 18. I had always heard this passage used in terms of cell and leadership structure. But he suggested another angle, that people are hardwired by God to be able to lead different size groups. When I thought about this I realized that a corollary of this principle is that those with giftings to lead larger groups of people do not start leading large groups but work their way up as their skills and giftings emerge and are recognized. Perhaps rather than trying to train a few who can who can lead large groups, we should be training lots of people to lead groups of ten and then watch their giftings. The cream will rise to the top and these people can become key catalysts for further growth, leaders of networks of groups, and leaders of movements. The other corollary is that the kind of leader that God made the most of is leaders of groups of ten. Very few can lead thousands, but God has made lots of people who can love and care for a group of 10. It is a fascinating thought with huge implications for what the leadership structure and training methodology would look like in a church planting movement.

Refuse to settle for anything less:

I used to look at social contexts and think, how can people here ever fit into church life? That assumed that we were going to wrest converts out of their context and put them into our version of church life. Now I see social context and pray that the Holy Spirit will raise up His expression of a dynamic Christian community there that will fit their time frames and economic circumstances, and network of relationships. It may look radically different from 1+1+1 but it will be a true expression of the life and power of Christ to those people. Do not settle for extraction, set your heart on powerful Christians that will be used by the Spirit to transform their world.

Others will be content with less and be willing to splash money around in order to get quick results and some of your hard earned work may rush off looking for a better deal. Do not compromise the goals of an indigenous movement, this is where we have to trust and believe in the Lordship of Christ in the church.

Training Values: Everything We Do Teaches

I like to say that the national church starts with the first Christian. It is imperative to realize that absolutely everything that will be done, from evangelism to group meetings to leadership will become the standard for all believers who follow. Make sure they get the right message from the beginning. Look at what you are doing not in terms of what you are saying but what they are learning from what they see and experience.

Use nothing that takes away from core principles:

No structure will work without the right heart and passion. Many pastors try to bring in new concepts like small groups and relational evangelism and the believers hate non-believers and cannot stand to be around them. They have no heart, so the structure will never work. Jettison what hinders heart and compromises principles. If we believe in empowering others for ministry and something disempowers, then get rid of it. This is where brutal honesty and the ability to self-evaluate must be applied. We are often handed "toolkits" of things that do not work and feel obligated to use them because they were passed on to us. In planting churches among the least reached the advantage is you are starting from scratch. Use what facilitates your values.

Shoot for being reproducible:

Don't saddle the new church or movement with things that they cannot do. We do this all the time with our use of technologies and finance and then wonder why the local church is not doing anything. Again, if it is going to "send the wrong message" do not do it.

Train leaders on the job:

We talk about Ephesians 4:11-12 but then proceed to teach pastors who to do ministry but not train others to do ministry. It is a different skill set and philosophy of ministry all together. They need to know how to do direct ministry but they need to know that their primary task is equipping others.

Never stop at one:

To me one of the biggest downsides that has come with the emphasis on large mega-churches is the discouragement that people with different giftings have felt. The mistake that we have all bought into is that if you have the ability to lead a group of forty, we assume that forever we just lead the same group of forty. But if we apply the principles above about multiplication and empower leadership the leader of 40 can turn her work over to someone and then go out and reproduce another group of 40. Rather than letting people feel badly we should fill them with vision for starting new groups over and over again. Let the Holy Spirit raise up the leadership necessary to network these groups together.

Social Structure: A Bridge, Not a Barrier

When you have no believers you have to make your own oikos in the beginning. But as you reach people immediately work on their personal network and create understanding, acceptance and wherever possible bring other members to faith. Everything should be geared around building bridges into the personal networks that people have.

Loving and obeying God, the heart of the Christian life:

My last statement above leads me to this one. From before people come to faith they should be told that their life in Christ is not for them, it is to give it away to Christ and to bring others to know him. We cut the legs out of our multiplicative capacity by creating Christians who want to get something. From the first day let people know that as God heals, and moves in their lives that they are blessed to be a blessing. Keep everything focused on loving and obeying Christ and bringing Him glory by leading others to worship him starting in their personal network.

Make meetings participatory and Jesus focused:

First Corinthians 14:26 shows a very participatory meeting. When you get believers together from the beginning you must avoid creating the impression that you are "the teacher" and they are the "students." This will take serious work and creativity on the part of the church planter, but it is foundational for empowering ministry. You connect your meeting times with outreach into the oikos. This gives people a place to bring friends and relatives that is safe and non-threatening and gives them their first taste of Christian community. Teach them that when they gather that Jesus is in their midst, and believe that He will touch people and reveal Himself to them. To help keep the outward focus have prayer in every meeting for people in attendees personal networks.

Teach emerging groups to be responsible for themselves:

Let people know before they come to Christ what you expect a Christian community to look like, what they will do together. Refuse to do it for them. You are the facilitator and helper but they must do the work and be responsible.

Train responsible leaders who can take care of themselves:

It is always amazing to me to go somewhere and see that people even in the most dire of circumstances are surviving. Then suddenly the church comes to the community and now they can do nothing, it is all on the pastor. In the beginning it will be much better to start with responsible people and enable them to lead while still maintaining their livelihood.

Reach personal networks and lead a small group:

Focus on the skill sets that will bring growth and multiplication. Leaders need to demonstrate they can reach people in their network, disciple them, and that they can lead and multiply a small group.

These are the fundamental basics that are so often assumed and other forms of training at higher levels are brought in. There always needs to be ongoing and higher training for those so gifted, but make sure all leaders can do the basics.

Love pre-processed Christians and take them with you:

Christians and leaders already socialized into the old model will not feel comfortable at all with relational evangelism, face to face relationships, releasing people for ministry, and the lack of structure that these assumptions about ministry and evangelism will lead to. If in your work of church planting you are connected with such people, rule one is love them. God loves pre-processed Christians who are stuck in these models. Second, the best way by far to move towards change is not to teach or talk about what you are doing but to take them by the hand and ask them to join you. Many of these people really want to do something but do not know how and have nobody to help them learn.

Conclusion

There is nothing new here. If anything, I am suggesting that one of our biggest barriers to church planting in the Buddhist world is in our heads-in the assumptions, values and philosophies that shape our practices about evangelism, ministry and church. Even when we know better theologically the power of old practices still shapes our efforts. I hope that reading through the journey of how I reached certain conclusions and then considering these concepts in a more abstract fashion may be helpful working out new ways to apply them to produce powerful reproducing Christian communities among Buddhist peoples.

Notes

[1] Carl F. George, *Prepare Your Church for the Future* (Grand Rapids: Fleming H. Revell, 1991); Ralph W. Neighbour, Jr., *Where Do We Go from Here? A Guidebook for the Cell Group Church* (Houston: Touch Publications, 1990).

[2] John Davis has made a similar argument in his call for a theology of structure in the final chapter of *Poles Apart*. He believes that churches need to by dynamically equivalent to New Testament churches and culturally appropriate. He also notes that while the New Testament structures of servant leadership, plurality of leadership, releasing believers in ministry, facilitating the use of spiritual gifts, and an organic not institutional approach may not have been the cause of the growth of the early church, but such structures "enabled, facilitated and contributed toward such phenomenal growth" (Davis 1998: 253, 261).

[3] Anthony Ware, an Australian Assemblies of God missionary in Thailand, for a number of years has written a master's thesis entitled *Analysis and Development of a Church Structure to Facilitate Saturation Church Planting in Bangkok*. He has an extensive literature review that covers many of the major works on church planting and growth. I have used his work as the basis for the topical bibliography at the end of the paper. A pdf version of his thesis is available upon request by emailing Anthony at <a_ware@ozemail.com.au>.

9

People Movements in Thailand

Alex G. Smith

Introduction: The Christian Expansion Movement

Kenneth Scott Latourette, Sterling Professor of Missions and Oriental History, and Fellow of Berkeley College in Yale University, was possibly the greatest historian of the expanding flow and dynamic movement of Christianity from its inception. In his large one-volume *A History of Christianity*, Latourette suggested that the course and movement of the Church might be viewed as a series of "major epochs." In the Preface (1953:xxii) he noted three main criteria for discerning these "pulsations":

1. the expansion or recession of the territory in which Christians are to be found;
2. the new movements issuing from Christianity; and
3. the effect of Christianity as judged from the perspective of mankind as a whole.

Latourette's approach to viewing Church History as a series of movements of peoples entering the faith, and the consequent effect on societies, was refreshingly unique. Earlier in his series of *A History of The Expansion of Christianity*, released from the mid-1930s on, he developed these dynamic Eras of Expansions in describing the story of the Church.

People Movements with their normally attendant church multiplying movements were the most significant factor producing the expansion and growth of the Early Church, and of that in each succeeding generation and century. Donald Anderson McGavran wrote: "*Christendom arose out of People Movements*" (1981:39). Whether it was in the cultural basins of the Romans, the Barbarians, the Vikings or other peoples across Europe, Asia, Africa or the Americas, people movements have been the key mechanism that God has used to expand, strengthen and consolidate His Church.

People movements are not exclusive to Christianity. Among African, Asian and other animistic tribal societies worldwide, such movements have occurred, often with whole tribes and groups moving from their spiritistic religion into Buddhism, Islam or other belief systems. In such cases they have, at least subliminally, retained and syncretized some and often most of their animistic meanings. One special observation is notable: many of the current Asian Muslim peoples had converted en masse from Buddhism. Centuries prior to that many of these peoples had changed as whole groups from their animistic roots to Buddhism. Some outstanding examples are the Indonesians, Malays, Afghans, and the Uighers of Northwest China.

People Movements Defined

The term Mass Movement or Group Conversion was often employed throughout mission history. J. Waskom Pickett's epochal book, *Christian Mass Movements in India*, which was first released in 1933, used these terms but really explained and described many a people movement.

Donald Anderson McGavran traveled widely in India with Bishop Pickett and as a result was forever indelibly impacted. It was McGavran who first used the term *People Movement* in his classic book printed in 1955 titled *The Bridges of God: A Study in the Strategy of Missions*. In November 1954, Kenneth G. Grubb wrote in the Forward to this book: "Dr. McGavran's Thesis can be put in one sentence: it is a contrast between the "People Movement"- to use his own term—and the "Mission Station Approach" (1955:v). The latter focused on the method or strategy of gathering scattered, mostly isolated individuals into churches, usually "one by one against the tide" of their societies.

As he developed his term, McGavran identified "People" with varieties of people groups: a tribe, a caste, a clan or lineage, some extended families, a linguistic group, or a tightly knit segment of society. People Movements occur, wrote McGavran, when "relatively small, well-instructed groups—one this month and one several months later—become Christians." He later defined the process of People Movements as a series of *"multi-individual, mutually interdependent conversions"* (1980:340). In the 1970 first edition of *Understanding Church Growth*, McGavran gave his classic definition of people movements:

> A people movement results from the joint decision of a number of individuals—whether five or five hundred—all from the same people, which enables them to become Christians without social dislocation, while remaining in full contact with their non-Christian relatives, thus enabling other groups of that people, across the years, after suitable instruction, to come to similar decisions and form Christian churches made up exclusively of members of that people (1970:297).

Three Interrelated Church Growth Concepts

Three primary principles of Church Growth are interrelated and interdependent in seeing new movements of people groups coming into the Church.

First is identifying the Homogeneous Units of the populations, the different parts of the mosaic. This differentiates the specific people groups in a particular population.

When people movements occur, they are mostly focused quite heavily on one unit of population, a particular homogeneous unit. The coherence of the identity of a people group usually includes three fundamental issues that serve to congeal or bind the homogeneous people unit together. These three key ingredients include: (i) a feeling of societal affinity; (ii) a consciousness of affiliated kind; and (iii) a sense of common identity.

Together these three produce a strong social cohesion among the members of that specific people group and actually weld them together as distinct from other homogeneous units. Furthermore McGavran declared: "People like to become Christian without crossing racial, linguistic or class barriers" (1970:198). So focusing energies and resources on one people group that is responsive is likely to produce a stronger movement than mixing equal energies on several homogeneous units at the same time.

Second is the principle of Receptivity, which measures and evaluates the different levels of openness and responsiveness among the kaleidoscope of Homogeneous Units within the population. In Sumatra the Karo Bataks' resistance for a century and a half exhibits this, compared to their receptive cousins the Toba Bataks. Not all receptive populations develop into Christian People Movements. In the last fifty years in India some twelve million untouchable caste Dalits turned en masse from Hinduism to Buddhism.

Third is the actual process and progress of the people movement as it is diffused throughout the highly receptive homogeneous units. This process may take several years or even decades to run its course. It may be considerably large such as a majority of a tribe, or most of a village, or a significant proportion of a dominant people group. On the other hand the people movement may be small like one extended family or a whole network of interconnected families, which is termed a "web movement." Whatever size it turns out to be, the primary dynamics of the movement will include the three principles of Church Growth noted above. In this process people movements also facilitate and accelerate desired indigenous church development. Both the speed of the expansion and the size of the growth usually keep the sociological dimensions of the people group in tact and encourage the immediate functioning of local leaders.

Sketch of Some Small People Movements in Thailand

A number of people movements in Thailand have helped augment the increase of the Church during the last couple of hundred years. Several small people movements in recent decades in Udon Thani, Ubon Ratchathani, Ban Tham (Phayao), Uthai Thani, and Bangkok are only acknowledged here, as most have been reported on and described elsewhere. This chapter will focus on the following four people movements: the Catholic mixed families, the Chinese in Thailand, the Sgaw Karen of Siam and the Northern Thai (Khon Muang or Lao as they were identified in the late 1800s).

Roman Catholic "Mixed Families" Movement

Roman Catholic missions to Siam started around 1511. Before 1934 Thailand was known as Siam. During the period of about three centuries the Portuguese were the dominant European influence of commerce and politics in Siam. The response of the Siamese to the Gospel of Christ was extremely slow. Stiff resistance was the norm. In fact the only response of any consequence that the Roman Catholic Church experienced was from the populations of mixed marriages with the Portuguese. *The Catholic Directory of Thailand* stated that in 1785, after almost three hundred years of missionary effort, the total Catholic Community in Siam was only 1,372. This comprised three specific people groups: "413 Siamese of Portuguese origin, 379 Cambodians of Portuguese origin, and 580 Annamites" or Vietnamese (1967: 11). Thus the only possible church growth for hundreds of years came from "mixed families" and their offspring. In this situation small people movements arose from among the three specific homogeneous units of population. The combination of these three small people movements comprised the Catholic Church.

Later on the Catholics extended their missionary work particularly into east Thailand. New people groups were gathered in the Cambodian speaking Thai and Chinese in Chantaburi, the Lao Isaan in Ubon Ratchathani, the Lao and Vietnamese immigrants in Tharee-Nongsaen and Udon Thani, and the Chinese in Bangkok, Nakhon Sawan, Ratchaburi and Surat Thani. In the large Chiang Mai Diocese a major growth movement has occurred in the last quarter of a century, adding 30,000 to the Catholic Church in the North. Among these were many Chinese and tribal peoples as well as northern Thai.

The ingathering of people groups of mixed race or of particular language or ethnic groups has been a pattern of slow Catholic expansion in Thailand. In 1972 the combined community of Catholics was 167,194. This grew to 189,609 in 1978 and increased to 278,480 by 2002.

The Chinese in Thailand

During the 1800s many Chinese traders sailed their tiny junks down from south and southeast China to Bangkok to ply their wares. They returned home with rice and other exotic products. In many Buddhist Temples scattered throughout the Thai capital, images of Chinese gods are still found today. These large stone sculptures were used as ballast in the little sailing vessels to help stabilize them on their southern sea voyages. In May 1832 David Abeel noted that some fifty junks were "still lying at anchor in the river" (McFarland 1928:7). Until the early 1900s most Chinese in Bangkok were males. While they maintained Chinese wives and families back in China, they frequently took Siamese wives in

Bangkok. Thus Bangkok had become affected and influenced through this common Chinese semi-migration (Smith 1982:53-55).

During the early decades of the 1800s China remained tightly closed to foreign missions. She only opened her doors to Europeans after the iniquitous British Opium Wars with China 1839-1842. Therefore in the initial Protestant Missions going into Siam, Bangkok was seen as *a springboard or stepping-stone to China*. The early missionaries to Siam, starting from 1828 were marking time waiting for China to open her doors. When that time came, many missionaries left Siam and transferred to China (Smith 1982:21-26).

Significantly, it was the Chinese and their Siamo-Chinese offspring who were the most receptive people group in Siam during these early years of Protestant missions in the 19th century. The American Baptists took seventeen years before they gained their first Siamese convert, the American Presbyterians nineteen years (Smith 1982:49). At the same time the Chinese response was immediate.

Early Protestant Missions

The first two Protestants to enter Siam on August 23, 1828 were Carl Gutzlaff and Jacob Tomlin. They met with the Phra Klang or Foreigner Minister of King Rama III, and were given a kind welcome. The newcomers were allowed to reside in Bangkok and granted permission to work among the Chinese. The curious populace, particularly the Chinese, swarmed like bees around these strange *farangs*. Gutzlaff's stores of Chinese books, literature and medicines were soon exhausted. The interest was so high that some Chinese traveled for three or four days to visit the foreigners (Smith 1982:14-15). Gutzlaff reported that in one Chinese "temple dedicated to the spirits of the ancestors, they found many willing hearers. Even the priest desired to know something of the Christian religion" (:54). This high interest of the Chinese brought repercussions on the missionaries. The fearful Jesuits encouraged their expulsion. The Siamese charged them with being spies trying to incite the Chinese. Under pressure even the Phra Klang requested an English merchant to ship them out of the kingdom (Pierson 1898:201). After Gutzlaff appealed, the pioneer missionaries were granted permission to remain in Bangkok but warned to distribute their books sparingly.

The Chinese were among the first to be employed in mission service and in Christian institutions. They were key assistants to the missionaries and often vital as language informants. Boon Ti worked with Gutzlaff, the only one he baptized. Next came David Abeel in mid-1831. Regular public worship for the Chinese was started in the new missionary's house. Within six months Abeel left and with him Tomlin. Gutzlaff had already gone to China in June 1831. So for the next five months no Protestant missionaries were left in Siam.

However, George McFarland noted that "Sunday services for worship had kept up during his absence, and regularly there were from twelve to twenty Chinese present" (1928:7). The initiative and receptivity of the Chinese kept the church alive. Because of ill health Abeel soon left Siam. In Singapore he met John T. and Eliza Jones on their way to Siam. The Joneses had served in Burma under the American Baptists. Abeel asked Jones to take care of the fledging Chinese church. The Joneses did so, opening their home for the services, which Boon Ti led in Chinese on their verandah every week. Jones did not speak Chinese but he observed that "the Chinese part of the population (was) by far the most accessible and inquisitive" (Gammell 1849:189).

First Chinese Church

William Dean joined Jones in 1835 and learned the local Chinese dialect and was wholly committed to the Chinese. In August 1835 the congregation of Chinese numbered thirty-four. Within two months it had increased to fifty. On July 1, 1837 Dean organized "the first Protestant church in the East, the first Chinese church in all of Asia" (Pierson 1886:76). Today that historic church is the Maitri Chit Chinese Baptist Church. Five years later, two of the members went with Dean to Hong Kong. These two were among the founding members of the First Baptist Church in Hong Kong on May 28, 1843 (Smith 1887:178). Twenty-two years later Dean returned from China to serve for another twenty years in Siam from 1864-1884, before retiring in the US.

The numbers of Chinese in the North and in rural areas were quite small, though their growing influx and commercial impact increased in time. The first report of any Chinese converts in the North was in 1893 in Lampang (Swanson 1984:144).

Below is a compilation of American Baptists' baptisms and memberships of the Chinese. Other Missions' Chinese members are not included (Smith 1982:21-22, 42-44, 193-194).

Year	Baptisms	Members
1833	4	4 (up to 35 were meeting by early 1835)
1835	3	6 (50 were meeting for worship late this year)
1837	?	11 (church organized and founded)
1839	6	20
1840	?	17
1841	7	24 (2 members left for Hong Kong with Dean)
1848	?	23
1853	?	35
1863	7	13 (last missionary left; 19 months without help)
1865	?	48
1866	5	53
1867	40	53 (2 new churches at outstations organized)
1872	?	78 (in all of the three churches)

Year	Baptisms	Members
1873	30	108
1874	137	230 (Bangkok with 4 outstations)
1875	90	317
1877	61	418 (6 churches, 7 chapels, 5 outstations)
1883	?	500 (in 5 churches)
1884	?	100 (Chinese mob riots; Dean left to retire in USA)
1889	?	13 (revision of member rolls)
1900	?	40
1907	?	90
1934	?	200 (includes Presbyterians and Baptists)
1938	?	600 (includes Presbyterians and Baptists)

Notes:

1. The "?" above indicates no specific record of baptisms available.
2. S. R. House reported that by 1848 "sixty names had been added at different times." The above list records 20 only, so another 40 are not reflected here.
3. S. F. Smith records that "between 1837 and 1866 fifty-one Chinese were baptized in Siam" (1887:182f). So another 26 are left unaccounted for during these years.

In the half-century following 1833, the known baptisms of Chinese recorded above totals 390. Adding Dr. House's missing forty and Smith's unaccounted 26 makes a total of 456 Chinese baptized in the first 50 years. The receptivity of the Chinese compared to the Siamese, helped the Chinese Church grow into a small people movement. In fifty years it had multiplied from a few to five hundred members by 1883. By contrast over a similar period the Presbyterian Mission had a total of only 74 members including Chinese and Siamese by 1883 (Smith 1982:51). The level of openness among the Chinese in Siam was considerable, but only meager missionary resources and personnel were assigned to reap this receptive potential harvest. A small people movement was initiated, but was virtually aborted as it struggled to survive and multiply.

Weaknesses

Despite the few missionaries focused on Chinese work, and the orphaning of the churches on two major occasions for extended periods, the Chinese congregations grew faster than did those of the Thai in and around the capital. Early indigenous initiative is often a key to growing people movements. Factors that affected the fluctuations of membership in the Chinese church included:

- The mobility and migration of the Chinese traders back and forth to China
- The death of members by rampant diseases such as smallpox, cholera, and typhoid
- The temptation of the Chinese to succumb to the addiction of opium
- The neglect of the developing churches and their abandonment by missionaries
- The lack of follow up and nurturing of new believers and their families
- The loss of some by transfer to other missions including the Presbyterians
- The penchant of the Chinese to take any opportunity to advance themselves and their business by attaching themselves to influential persons, such as the missionaries, with good connections in government and with the Court

The drastic drop of membership between 1883 and 1884 from 500 to 100 needs study. Unfortunately we do not know definitively what truly caused the explosive growth from 1867 to 1883. Nor do we know all the specific reasons for the sudden drop to one fifth of the membership in 1884 and further demise afterward. Here are some suggested causes:

- G. Winfred Hervey wrote that between 1882 and 1884 the "Red Letter Society," a Chinese secret organization, caused considerable chaos among the Chinese laborers in Bangkok, robbing, rioting and causing general confusion and disruption. The political repercussions of these riots spawned persecution and oppression, especially of Chinese Protestants in Bangkok (1892:923).
- The effects "of the power of the mobocracy in Bangkok" caused many Chinese members to fear further reprisals and more persecution. Hervey claims the revision of church rolls was a key factor in reducing membership (1892:924).
- William Dean's departure in 1884, after serving fifty years in mission, probably contributed also. He was well liked, spoke Chinese like a native, had a powerful presence with officials, and was highly respected in the Church he had founded. For many years the Deans were the only Baptist missionaries with the Chinese. The Board pressed all to withdraw from Siam several times, as late as 1872. Did the Christians have little confidence in the Mission after losing their champion?
- The disruptive Red Letter Society riots raised suspicion of the Siamese towards the Chinese. The government became more cautious about them. In Buddhist Siam, since "to be Thai means to be Buddhist," a Christian is already seen as a traitor, a non-Thai, and an aberration in traditional society. So to be Chinese also added to the insult. The Christian Chinese started to withdraw from any high profile that gave potential for more trouble. They isolated themselves. Some even reverted to Buddhism. This caused a significant falling off in the visible Church.

On the positive side, William Bainbridge who visited Siam in 1882, gave an outside, shrewd but sympathetic evaluation of the work. He identified certain weaknesses, but also saw tremendous strengths in the Chinese church in Bangkok. His careful examination in Siam convinced him that the missionaries had taken due caution to face the weaknesses of the Chinese in view of "the few past years of large in-gathering." He was "more favorably impressed" with the Chinese Christians of Bangkok than those elsewhere. Some of them exhibited vibrant living faith. They had built a home for old men with their own money to shelter their aged poor (1882:153). His observation may have been on target. Significantly even today several of the Chinese churches in Bangkok are among the biggest congregations in Thailand.

A Big Question

But in view of the potential people movement of this receptive group we must also ask why was the movement prematurely delayed? Why, with ten and a half percent of the country's population still being Chinesein the year 2000 equal to almost six and a half million—is there not a much larger number of Chinese Christians now (Johnstone 2001:618)? A current estimate of Chinese church membership in Thailand would be around fifteen thousand at best (CCT 10,000 + CNEC 1,750 + others 3,300). This is only about 0.23%, little better than the average percentage of Thai Christians per capita in the early 21st century.

The following table depicts the growth of two Chinese Christian Districts of the Church of Christ in Thailand:

Year	Pahk 7 (Presbyterian)	Pahk 12 (Baptist)	Total in CCT
1954	1054	372	1426
1957	1191	476	1667
1963	?	745	?
1968	1675	969	2644
1970	1779	924	2703

Year	Pahk 7 (Presbyterian)	Pahk 12 (Baptist)	Total in CCT
1972	?	998	?
1974	1883	1318	3201
1978	2378	1516	3894
2003	4783	5361	10144

The return of American Baptist Mission in 1954 was welcomed. Over the years of their absence, the American Presbyterian Mission had organized Pahk 7 as a Chinese District of the Church of Christ in Thailand, combining the Chinese congregations of both persuasions. In 1954 the Maitri Chit Baptist Church withdrew from Pahk 7 over the mode of baptism. Did returning missionaries influence this move? Later the Maitri Chit Church rejoined the Church of Christ in Thailand, with other Chinese Baptist churches, as Pahk 12. This fostered unity and cooperation. The Maitri Chit Chinese Baptist Church set an excellent model of both home mission from the 1950s and of cross-cultural mission from the 1970s. These initiatives aided the expansion of new churches and facilitated increased growth. of the Baptist churches. Presbyterian Chinese churches were also stimulated, particularly through the use of Thai services for the growing younger Siamo-Chinese populations in Bangkok and Chiang Mai. In almost a half century, the Presbyterian Chinese membership has grown three and a half times, and the Baptists thirteen and a half times—a commendable movement of explosion and extension.

The Tribal Karen Movement

In Thailand several tribal groups such as Karen, Lawa, Lahu, Eekaw (Akha), Moosur (Lahu), Khamoo and Mien (Yao) have experienced some small people movements. Here we will only sketch the Karen. There are at least three major Karen people groups in Thailand—the Sgaw, the Pwo, and the Red Pudong (Long Necked) Karen. Our emphasis focuses largely on the Sgaw Karen, which has the biggest population in Thailand, though the Pwo are much more numerous in Myanmar (Burma).

Back in the 1800s a major people movement among the Sgaw occurred in Burma, until about ninety percent of the Sgaw became Christian. The Pwo were less responsive than the Sgaw, but considerable numbers of the Pwo also came into the Church. Some small family web-movements among them occurred later in Burma and in Thailand. They reinforced the need to observe the three inter-related principles of church growth noted.

Outreach from Burma

It was natural that the Christian Karen and the American Baptists, who worked with them in Burma, should therefore be first to reach the Karen across the borders in Siam. The movement in Burma was started through Ko Tha Bya, the first Karen convert, whom Broadman baptized at Tavoy in 1828. He had been quite a wild man with a criminal past. A Burmese Christian redeemed Ko Tha Bya from the slave market where he ended up because of debt. Eventually this unmanageable fellow was passed on to Adoniram Judson. Under Judson's patient example and love he believed the Gospel (Anderson 1956:385-386). When Broadman opened the new station at Tavoy, KoTha Bya went with him, along with the first Siamese convert won in Burma and four Karen youth (Brain 1910:365, Judson 1883:344, Smith 1982:13).

While in a prayer meeting in Tavoy on December 20, 1829, Kho Tha Bya had a "strong feeling that God was calling him to go beyond the mountains and preach the Gospel to the Karen in Siam" (Hovemyr 1997:2). Two days later he left for the border with some Karen, but was turned back. At least one in the party, Muang Sekkee, successfully made the initial foray into Siam by January 1830 and proclaimed the good news there.

Burmese Karen made or attempted sporadic visits in 1848-1849, 1850, 1863, 1872, and throughout the next half century (Smith 1982:46). Again there was a hesitant mission from Burma, by both

Karen Christians and American missionaries. The attempt to reach the Sgaw in Siam in 1863, says Van Benschoten, faced "difficulties and dangers," causing the team to return home, falling "short of their destination" (1954:1). Over sixty Sgaw and Pwo Karen villages were scattered along the western border areas in Central Siam from Tak (Raheng) down to Phetchaburi—with many more in the far north.

Sangkhlaburi and Central

In the mid-1950s a Buddhist Karen Sect, named the Telekon, was discovered in this western border area. They had a legend about "the Golden Book," which was to be returned to the Karen by the Ariya (Maitreya), or future Buddha. During the time of the seventh leader of the Telekhon, the anticipated Ariya was to appear. He would usher in this Karen Millennium and unite the Karen in independence. The headquarters of this sect of several thousands was in Umphang district center (Hovemyr 1997:10-13). My mentor, Dr. McGavran, whose own mission with the Baptists was approaching the Telekhon, told me about this potential people movement. Missions hopes rose with the Telekhon's concept of the Golden Book and a prophesy that the Ariya was to come in the "form of a white man." Various missionaries with expectations for a people movement made at least half a dozen mission trips over the next decade to talk to the leaders of the Telekhon, but each time their efforts proved fruitless. Even when the seventh leader of the Telekhon was taken off to Burma and killed, no movement came about. The Telekhon's Buddhist influences precluded their acceptance of the Bible or of Christ being the fulfillment as promised in their legend. The sect eventually dissipated.

Much dedicated service was rendered at the Christian Hospital in Sangklaburi amidst struggles for survival. Through many heartaches and much toil of missionaries with Karen and Thai workers in the most primitive conditions, seven churches emerged in time. They were scattered along the Thai-Burma border. In April

1989 these churches were organized into Pahk 16 of the Church of Christ in Thailand. By that time the seven churches had a combined baptized membership of 478 with another 99 associate members. A total of 63 had been baptized during that year. By 2003 the combined membership of Pahk 16 rose to 1,104. A small movement finally began.

Response in the North

The main concentration of Karen was in northern Thailand. Only after 1880 was any serious effort to reach them made. This was through Christian Karen traders and teak lumber dealers from Bassein, Burma, who visited Lakon (Lampang). Daniel McGilvary reports that the Christian Karen laymen won "the first considerable number of converts among the Karen in Siam" (Feb. 11, 1881 letter). So, right from the start, the Karen in the north was a receptive group with the potential for a dynamic people movement. The report of this ingathering stirred the Burma Baptist Convention to revive the Karen Mission to Siam. They sent three volunteer evangelists. The evangelists traveled on to Lampang and then to three other fairly large Karen villages named Ban Nawk, Ban Kah, and Ban Thet. Each of these villages represented about forty homes, located north of Lampang towards Chiang Rai. While the evangelists preached the Gospel in Ban Thet, a Karen man stood up and spoke. U Zan, a Karen historian, summarized what he said:

> "I am the youngest among five brothers in our family. Our father worshipped the 'Eternal God'. We did not really understand what he was praying about or to whom he was praying. However, when he died he told us this, 'Sons, you will one day be brought a book from God. When this book does come, accept it at once. After the arrival of this book, God will come and rule the world.' And then the man continued, 'Last night I had a dream. I dreamt that three teachers were bringing the word of God to us. I have been waiting the arrival of these three teachers the whole of today without seeing anyone. Yet, just before dark, you arrived. This

> coincides with my dream and with what our father had told us before he died. This is enough reason to believe that this is indeed the true word of God" (pp. 4 -5).

The significant result of this timely convergence was that five hundred Karen in the three villages totaling one hundred homes, believed. Whole villages became Christian in the beginnings of a small people movement. Probably these were Pwo villages, but in time they became "Sgawized," partly because both the Karen Bible and the Hymn Book were printed in the Sgaw dialect. Since the worship language was Sgaw, the Pwo adapted to it. Over time the Pwo contributed many leaders to both Pwo and Sgaw churches in Burma and in Thailand. The involvement of the Pwo in pastoral leadership was as high as seven out of ten. They ministered in Sgaw language even though they were Pwo.

The three volunteer Karen teachers went back to Burma that year, never to return again. A fourth Karen who accompanied them from Burma had become a believer on the way. He remained behind for some time to help establish the new Christians. The Burma Baptist Convention then requested Mr. Webster to go to Siam to survey work in the North. During his visit later in 1881, he baptized seventy Karen and organized three churches in these villages, located north of Lampang. In 1882 Webster with Bushell and some Burmese Karen pastors returned to visit the churches, but none of them stayed to work there. They baptized another 170 Karen at Ban Nawk. In another village around "fifty Karen were reported as wanting to receive baptism" (Zan n.d.:7).

A Second Front

About the same time a second people movement appears to have developed among the Sgaw in the North along the western border with Burma, around Musikee and Maesariang. Though little data on this movement was recorded, three sizable churches arose at Meh Thaw, Meh Kwak and Meh Mawk respectively. Sometime around 1883 to 1884 disaster struck this fledging people movement. The Meh Thaw church, the largest with approximately two hundred or more members, lost one hundred and sixty of them when two thirds of the members reverted to the old spirit ways of their ancestors. What sparked those reversions? We have no details of the process, dynamics or decisions that led to this reverse people movement. The spirit worshippers closed ranks and expelled all the remaining eighty-one Christians from the village. Unperturbed, the faithful formed a new church at Meh Kwak. Around 1883, the total Sgaw membership in that area was 181 (Smith 1982:48).

Following this major defection at Meh Kwak the churches at Ban Kah and Meh Mawk also experienced defections. Though records are sparse and obviously incomplete, what is reported gives us a fair picture. The statistical records note only two or three churches, but there were no less than six churches in the early 1880s in north Siam: Ban Nawk, Ban Kah, Ban Thet, Meh Thaw, Meh Mawk and Meh Kwak. The first three at least were in the Lampang area south of Chiang Rai. The last three were most likely in the west around Maesariang.

In March 1884 Webster and his wife came to Chiang Mai with a view to going to work with the Karen at Meh Kwak. They spent the next year in Chiang Mai. During this period they visited the former villages north of the Lampang region and wrote: "The people here live about five days' journey from the town and they have carried on their own work for about three years, with a total membership of about one hundred and sixty. There are two churches and two schools, and those with some education are traveling and preaching" (Van Benschoten 1954:2). Apparently no note was made of a third village and church. Possibly the defections in Ban Kah were so serious, that the church had disbanded.

However, the 1885 Annual Report of the American Baptist Missionary Union noted that three Karen churches in north Siam had one hundred and fifty one Sgaw members. This was probably the two above in Lampang plus the Meh Kwak church along the western border. No further statistics of the Siamese Karen churches were reported until 1954. In the interim the American Baptist Missionaries had withdrawn and left the orphaned Karen churches to their own resources.

Major Growth

Despite the absence of the American Baptists for the next sixty years, the Sgaw people movement struggled on and even expanded. By 1954 the ABMU Annual Report says the Karen in Siam had twenty churches with eight hundred members, mostly Sgaw, though "some few were Pwo Karen" (1954:8).

Here are some selected statistics of the net growth of Protestant baptized Karen members:

Year	Members	Year	Members	Year	Members
1881	70	1902	180	1955	1,392
1882	240	1912	320	1962	2,497
1883	181	1922	340	1972	4,075
1884	160	1932	560	1980	7,087
1885	151	1942	575	1992	?
1886	133	1953	800	2003	2,398

The following are some reasons indicating why this Karen people movement did not become considerably larger, especially in the first half-century:

- The lack of continuity in commitment of both missionary and Karen workers
- Inadequate nurture, grounding, follow up and consistent teaching of new believers

- Insufficient preparation of converts to deal with resilient old spirit ways
- Neglected and inadequate pastoral care of the new and later older churches
- Failure to train local indigenous Karen adequately to care for and lead churches
- Mobility of Karen through their swidden (slash and burn) cultivation
- Control and oversight from Burma rather than autonomous local direction
- Cultural influences and political pressures from the dominant society
- Weak strategy without efficient focus on web movements and family evangelism
- The orphaning of the struggling people movements by the missions

Summary

From the turning of five hundred in one area in the North in early 1881, and maybe another three hundred in the western area, the Karen people movements looked most promising. At least six churches arose but three had serious defections within a few years. Many ups and downs were faced. More ingathering was experienced and more falling away. Yet despite all odds, the movement gathered strength so that by 1954 twenty churches had eight hundred members. In the first century the Karen churches grew from seventy to seven thousand baptized members. In the last two decades 1981 to 2003 the church membership tripled to more than 23,000 today. This includes the CCT Pahks 10, 16, and 19, plus another 5,000 from other denominations. The estimated Karen Christian community was approximately 50,000 in 2003. Here is an exciting example of a people movement that is largely developed from native initiatives and vision both from Burma and locally in Thailand.

Later missionary personnel also helped strengthen the movement especially from the mid-1900s. Both national and foreign servants are "workers together with God."

The Strong People Movement Among the Khon Muang of North Thailand

A Conglomerate of Languages

Within its borders Thailand has a complex mosaic of people groups. Approximately fifty tribal peoples speak different languages and dialects. The Chinese, Lao and Muslim populations also have several dialects each, as do the Thai. Within the majority Thai, at least four specific distinct language groups exist: Siamese or Central Thai, southern Thai (Pak Tai), Isaan (a Lao dialect) in the northeast, and northern Thai (Yuan-Muang-Lao). For this reason the Thai in the North were called the Lao in the early decades of missions, since their languages were similar to that in the country of Laos, which was under Siam in the 1800s until the French partitioned modern Laos off in 1893. The language of the North was also akin to that of the Isaan northeast region. To note these linguistic differences was important to help identify the distinct people groups, and to discern the varying levels of receptivity among them. In time the Central Thai language was adopted as the trade and governmental language, used to bridge across all these Thai tongues, which still continued to be spoken locally.

Initiating Interest in the Lao

Dr. Samuel House of the American Presbyterians was attracted to the Lao of the North in the 1850s. He attempted to visit their territory, but only reached as far as Pitsanuloke. Some Lao were here, but House fell short of the main Lao populations further north of Raheng (Tak), in Lampang, Phrae, Nan, Lamphun, Chiang Mai, and Chiang Rai. To the east was another Lao suzerainty of Luang

Prabang, which was also then under Siamese control. House saw the potential among the Lao.

Daniel McGilvary, an American Presbyterian, arrived in Siam June 18, 1858. A year and a half later he married Dr. Dan Beach Bradley's daughter, Sophia, on December 6, 1860. Following 1858 McGilvary with other missionaries had visited Petchaburi several times. It was projected to be the first mission station outside of Bangkok, located about eighty-five miles to the southwest (1912:48-52). In June 1861the families of McGilvary and McFarland were sent there to open Petchaburi. They found "many Laos villages and some Karens within a day's journey" from their new city. They also observed that the Lao "unlike the Siamese, seem to be ready and willing to receive and embrace the Gospel" (McFarland June 14,1861 letter).

This large colony of Lao comprised descendants of political refugees and captives from the Lao tribes, mainly from the Khorat area in the Northeast. They had become serfs under the protection of the King of Siam, who had assigned them residences in villages around Petchaburi. These Lao helped construct a royal palace for the King in that city (Backus 1884:38, Bliss 1891: 335). Near the city of Nakhon Pathom, where relics of the bones of Buddha are still revered, were some large villages of Lao people also. These were Lao Song. They lived about forty miles further north of Petchaburi and to the west of Nakhon Pathom. In the twentieth century a small people movement among these Lao Song also occurred, but that will not be detailed here.

The Call of the North

Around five to six hundred miles north of Petchaburi were the much larger populations of Lao, in half a dozen local kingdoms, each with its own territorial Lao lord or prince, all of whom paid tribute to the King of Siam in Bangkok. The most powerful prince in the North was Chao Kawilorot - Lord of Chiang Mai.

Prior to his moving to Petchaburi, McGilvary had "a slight acquaintance with the Prince of Chiang Mai and his family" in Bangkok in late 1860. Chao Kawilorot had arrived near the Bradley's compound on an impressive flotilla of boats with a great retinue of attendants, just before the McGilvary wedding. Dr. Bradley had already developed an open relationship with Chao Kawilorot and had befriended the Lao in his entourage. McGilvary therefore visited the nearby Lao camp frequently. Chao Kawilorot with his two daughters visited the McGilvarys the day after their wedding (McGilvary 1912:57).

In November 1863 McGilvary with Jonathan Wilson made an exploratory trip to the far North up the main rivers with their treacherous rapids and currents, and then from Tak on they traveled by elephants. The arduous journey took six and a half weeks. Providentially they journeyed from the capital on a tributary parallel to that on which Chao Kawilorot was journeying south to pay tribute. So they missed meeting up with him. Probably had they met, the story of the Lao people movement may have been quite different, for the Lao lord later proved to be an opponent of the venture (McGilvary 1912:59-60).

On return to Bangkok, McGilvary requested that the Presbyterian Mission Board in New York permit him to open a Mission to the Lao. The Board agreed. McGilvary and Wilson were released from the Siam Mission for this challenge. Unfortunately Wilson and several other staff became quite ill and had to return to the USA for an extended period. This shortage of personnel delayed McGilvary from immediately implementing his vision. Three years later, on January 3, 1867 he started north with his wife and two daughters. This dangerous journey took seventy-nine days on the rivers plus another ten days rest about half way at Tak. They arrived at Chiang Mai on April 1, 1867.

The Pioneer Struggles in Chiang Mai

After overcoming the difficulties of getting accepted and established in Chiang Mai, McGilvary, in 1867, baptized the first Lao convert, Nan Inta, a former respected Buddhist abbot. Within seven months six more Lao men were baptized. Of these seven men only one, a blind man, was employed in the mission as a watchman. All seven were held in good repute among the local people. On April 18, 1868 McGilvary organized the first church in the North.

But dark ominous clouds soon appeared. Chao Kawilorot, though cordial at first, felt threatened and accused the missionaries of causing a rice famine. He requested the US Consul to have them withdrawn to Bangkok. When official word from the Capital did not concur, the Lao ruler was furious. On September 10, 1869 he secretly ordered the arrest, torture and brutal murder of two of the Lao Christians, Noi Sunya and Nan Chai. The remaining believers, except for the blind Ngiew (Shan) watchman and a Chinese boy, fled fearing for their lives (McGilvary 1912:111; Nov. 1, 1869 letter). The missionaries themselves were in extreme peril for the next couple of months. When in November the officials from Bangkok arrived to confront the Lao king, he "turned white with rage and unleashed his wrath". He threatened to kill every Lao in his kingdom, who "forsakes Buddhism for the religion of Jesus." He added: "If the missionaries teach their religion and continue to make Christians, I will banish them from the country" (Wilson Jan 24, 1870 letter). Some allowance must be made for the irate king's anger in his making these threats, but his determination to prevent the planting of churches in his territory was obvious. However, the king did calm himself and finally agreed to allow the missionaries to remain, and permitted them to distribute medicines but not to teach Christianity. This sudden turn of events shocked McGilvary and Wilson, but they believed "that Providence will interfere." In February the Lao king was summoned to Bangkok to attend the royal funeral of the late King Mongkut. Chao Kawilorot, then in his seventieth year, fell ill in Bangkok. Though he rushed back northward, he passed away on June 29, 1870 just outside the walls of his capital, Chiang Mai.

Herbert Swanson astutely analyzes the drastic results of this violent attack on the young emerging church amongst the Khon Muang or Northern Thai (1984:18-20):

- The martyrdoms brought about "a fundamental change in who was willing to become a Christian." The early converts were people of respect and standing in the community, usually from the middle or middle high class. Afterwards the converts tended to be more from the lower oppressed and distressed classes.
- The content of conversion became changed from primarily a spiritual base to a social reason, from more ulterior motives rather than from pure ones.
- Kawilorot effectively squashed the potential immediate and large-scale people movement, delaying it for at least a decade.
- He also effectively delayed the development of the native Christian community for a decade.
- He frustrated preparation for the potential indigenous church and a native leadership movement by setting the stage for the development of Mission control and direction of the churches.
- He successfully destroyed "the attractiveness of the new faith for those with a stake in society."
- The status of missionaries changed in relation to the Christian community, from a humble servant mode to that of power figures, from lowly living conditions to patrons of the converts and property owners, emphasizing the prestige of the Mission.

The Birth Pangs of Planting Churches

The raw shock of the brutal martyrdoms scattered the tiny church. Understandably, quite some time passed before others were open to commit to the Gospel. Tertullian, one of the early church fathers, famously said "The blood of the martyrs is the seed of the church," but in this Lao situation, some eight years of slow survival growth preceded any signs of a stable congregation. A further two years passed before the Church in the North was officially constituted.

The next baptism after the tragedy was that of a Lao farmer in April 1872, two and a half years after the martyrs had died. Three more Lao men "in the prime of life" followed in December that year. In early 1876 the first woman, the widow of one of the martyrs, was baptized. Four other women who were the daughters of the martyrs or of existing Christians followed in the latter months of 1876. A small trickle entered the Church, but during the same period at least three of the existing members died. By September 30, 1876 only nine members remained. Yet through small encouragements and the vision of the harvest to come, by faith McGilvary requested the Board to send plans for a church building that would "seat 300 to 500 persons" (May25, 30, 1876 letters).

The strategy under the circumstances of survival had, of necessity, changed temporarily to a Mission Station Approach. Most of the newly baptized had been living on the mission compound for about two years. Nearly all of them came from areas outside and surrounding the Chiang Mai capital. Birthing pioneer churches is tough and takes perseverance and patience. From September 1876 to August 1877 McGilvary baptized another fourteen adults and five children. The Church had doubled within a year. The first decade ended with an adult membership of only about twenty in one congregation, but the next three decades would produce a people movement with more than six thousand in twenty-six churches.

The Beginnings of a People Movement

During the next two years the Church doubled again to thirty-nine members. That year in December 1879, the Chiang Mai Church was officially organized. Seven months later, seventeen members of the first church, all of whom lived in a cluster of villages nine miles southeast of the city, were released from the mother church. With five other members they organized the Bethlehem Church. This began in July 1880 as a house church, initially meeting in a widow's home. During 1880 two other churches were founded in Lampang and Maa Dawk Dang.

By September 1882 the combined memberships of the churches reached one hundred and forty adults with seventy baptized children. In the preceding five years one hundred and nineteen adults had been baptized. But in this case it only arose after a decade of slow surviving growth. By 1883 the recovery of the church in north Siam was accomplished and the stage well set with the momentum to facilitate an accelerated people movement among the Lao. By this time other missionaries had joined the mission team.

The Dynamics and Patterns of Growth

In analyzing the development that gave impetus to this regenerating of the growth of the church several factors stand out:

- McGilvary focused his evangelism especially on the *men "in the prime of life*." This meant married men with grown families and often older grandfathers who had the respect of their communities.
- The Lao structure leaned to a patriarchal society and thus frequently the women and their offspring followed the men into the church over time. I estimated that around forty percent of the converts were related to Christian relatives. A third of women joining the church had male Christian family connections (1982:74).
- Though the initial converts were not mission employees, during the early recovery stages, maybe one third of those who came into the church after the martyrs, lived and worked on the mission compound or were employed in the institutions. The rest, about one fifth, were independent converts.
- *Family Web Movements* were common. Jonathan Wilson, McGilvary's associate, wrote: "A pattern of our work here is the

gathering of whole families into the church" (Aug.1, 1882 letter). He insightfully pointed out that in the new Bethlehem Church of 22 adults and fourteen baptized children, 12 adults and ten children came from one single family-connection. In this web were five full nuclear families, representing Christians across four generations. A second family web comprised seven other adults, relating to three full families over two generations. In another village where strong local opposition delayed the baptism of one younger family, Wilson, in May 1880, baptized ten adults and eight children all related in one extended family web. Nan Inta, the first Lao convert baptized in 1869 was installed as the first elder of the Bethlehem Church. Before his death in 1882, his wife, three daughters, one son-in-law and the youngest son had become church members. Three other married sons remained outside the church (Smith 1982:75).

- Confronting witchcraft accusations was a common approach. One case to the opening of Maa Dawk Dang Church. The missionaries were advocates of those charged falsely of black magic when some calamity arose in their village. A trial was usually held. The local officials normally expelled the accused often with their family, burned their house, and confiscated their property. In this case, the missionaries purchased the property from the defendant and sent someone to be their watchman. Despite the threats of officials, who tried to force the accused to return the money, he stood firm and the missionaries refused to accept any return of the cash. This strategy protected the property of the offender from forfeiture. The alleged culprit was expelled and forced to live in the jungle where he built a temporary shelter. His family, however, remained in the home with the watchman, who was withdrawn after a month. Later, the villagers declared the missionaries had cured the condemned of his malignant demon and so after a time let him to return to his village. When the accused was baptized in 1881, two of the village officials, who had expelled him, asked for baptism. The church met for worship in the home on the offender's property.

Within six months the church had increased to twenty-four adults and fifteen children. One third of these were represented in two family web movements (Smith 1982:76).

- New church plants initially always followed the "house church" model. This was true of each of the churches mentioned above.

The Lao People Movement Gains Momentum

Following the painful struggles of the first sixteen years, an exciting movement quickly burst forth. By 1884 the Lao churches in the North totaled only one hundred and fifty-two adult members. A virile movement began in October 1884. The 1889 Annual Report of the Presbyterian Board of Foreign Missions revealed the consistency of this phenomenal spurt of growth with "Adult accessions to the membership at monthly communion for the last twenty-two consecutive months, and in fifty-five out of the last sixty-one months since October 1884." Additions to the movement continued every month at least through 1891 (1889:137, 1892:221).

The Lao people movement in the North maintained rapid and remarkable growth, multiplying steadily through 1914, as is evident from the following chart:

Year	Members	Churches	Year	Members	Churches
1876	9	1	1885	241	8 w. 10 elders
1877	21		1892	1,376	8 w. 26 elders
1879	39	1	1894	1,841	11
1880	83	2	1902	2,929	16
1882	140	4 plus 7 baptized children	1913	6,299	24
1884	152	4	1914	6,934	26

By contrast the Siamese churches in the South grew much more slowly than those of the northern Lao and did not reach their first 1,000 members until 1915:

Year	Members	Year	Members
1877	108	1902	323
1884	190	1913	662 in 13 churches
1892	308	1914	821

In forty-four years, McGilvary saw this phenomenal growth in the Lao people movement from four members to over four thousand by his death in 1911. He longed to see a similar movement among the Siamese in the South.

The Arresting of the People Movement

The strong Lao movement continued to grow steadily through 1914, but that growth seemed to be abruptly interrupted after that. Membership leveled off. According to the statistics, slight fluctuations up or down occurred over the next quarter of a century with some gradual small increases. Between 1914 and 1940 the annual average growth rate of the Lao northern churches was below one percent, only 0.7% per annum. By 1940 the church membership was 9,399, showing a net gain of merely 1,700 over twenty-six years. Whereas the twenty years prior to 1914 the church memberships had almost quadrupled, the following quarter century saw only an increase of one third.

Out of Steam?

The first question is: Had the movement run its course? Research into the statistics of the Church of Christ in Thailand and those of their associated Board of Foreign Missions of the Presbyterian Church in the U.S.A. were revealing. During the period

1914 -1940, the actual additions to membership by baptism of adults alone, totaled a surprising 16,132. This did not include many thousands of child baptisms conducted in those families. The only reasonable conclusion possible, points to the reality that the people movement had not stopped but was alive and well during this period.

I calculated that the net loss of members over accessions by adult baptism was an astounding 13,349 (1982:158). Suppose the majority of the additions by adult baptism had remained faithful members of the church and that deaths of existing members were balanced by the confirmation of those joining the churches through biological growth. Then the church membership would have tripled in that quarter of the century. By 1940 it could have reached 23,000 members. While that may be too ideal an expectation, it could have even exceeded it had those sixteen thousand baptisms been conserved, for they would also have become a new increased evangelizing factor to their extended families and networks of friends. The hard fact is that by 1940 the northern churches were reduced to 9,399 members. The Church did not reach 23,000 for another three decades in 1973. Even if one third of all the new additions had died, reverted or moved out of north Thailand, the Church could well have reached over 17.700 members by 1940. That would have been barely a reasonable rate of growth of three and a half percent per annum. But the bottom line is that *in spite of the influx of 16,132 adult baptisms by conversion, the net gain was only 2,783.*

Reasons for Loss

The next question looms ominously. Why then, was there such a great loss of this great ingathering, while the people movement obviously continued on? The shocking discovery of the probable real cause for the loss was the lack of adequate shepherding of the movement during these years. The causes for such a failure to fold and care for the new converts of such large numbers are significant.

Remembering that the high quality of missionaries, national pastors and native leaders had not changed, we conclude there must have been some major changes in priorities and in programs for the Lao Mission to have neglected such a vital need.

By analyzing mission records, reports and other documents of that era I gleaned some key clues. The Presbyterian Mission changed its emphasis in the North from gathering in and folding the people movement into churches, to the building and multiplying of educational institutions. Their priorities followed suit. McGilvary had put top priority on evangelizing the people and then educating the Christians so they would make a significant change and contribution to the general populace. So schools were already an important part of his and other missionaries' strategy for the Lao. A competing policy was strongly introduced from the Siam Mission in the South and increasingly implemented in the North after his death. This called for priority to be given to educating the youth of the general populace, not just those of Christians. Schools were suggested as the best method of evangelism and thereby hopefully of seeing many students become Christians (Smith 1982:94-95).

Had mission and church leaders cleared away the promotional fog and clarified the data prior to 1914, they would have learned that the North's policy was working better than the South's in terms of bringing accessions into the churches. For example, in the combined two years of 1913-1914 the Lao church accessions from schools totaled 223, while those for the same period in the Siam Mission reached only fifteen. In 1914 this represented eight percent of the student body among the Lao, but less than two percent (1.6%) in the Siam Mission. Furthermore between 1913 and 1917 the percentage of students in the schools that joined the churches was only 2.6% in the South Mission but 6.5% in the North's. This was still only a small percentage in the North considering that the majority of students came from Christian families. In the South three quarters of the students were from Buddhist backgrounds, while in the North over ninety percent were from Christian homes. It could be concluded then that the schools were not a primary or productive way to evangelize but that they were a fair way to conserve the Christian community (1982:126-127).

Confirmation of Changes

In 1938 Presbyterian missionary educator John L. Eakin observed, with a fair amount of pride, the change of mission emphasis which took place:

> One of the most startling results of missionary labors in Siam is the growth of the educational work, especially since 1911. At that time there were 37 mission schools... Only 800 students attended these schools. By 1925, there were 53 schools...over 3,000 students, an increase of 2,200 in fourteen years. After another thirteen years (1938) we find there are today 65 grade schools....honored by the government for their contribution to education. Moreover, the receipts of these schools have grown in the last thirteen years from $54,000 to $81,688, and the pupils from 3,000 to 5,569 (1938:286-287).

With less pride but just as emphatically, John L. Eakin could have added; "One of the most devastating results of missionary labors in Siam has been the arresting of the growth of the Church, especially since 1914." In truth, he was aware of the haunting neglect to preserve the Lao people movement by withdrawing vital personnel from the church ministry to fill the growing demands of the expanding schools. Key missionary evangelists/ church planters, national pastors and native evangelists were among those transferred from church work to the school work which had become considered more important. He wrote: "At first the need for more educational missionaries for this growing work was met by the increase in foreign staff. But, during the last ten years, with an ever decreasing staff, many ordained evangelists were of necessity drawn into full-time or part-time school work. Naturally, the evangelistic work suffered thereby" (1938:287).

Eakin's carefully chosen words "of necessity" revealed the change of the Mission's priority during the decades 1911-1940. My personal interaction with an elderly Christian Thai teacher, Muak Chailangkarn, who taught during those decades, confirmed the Mission's practice of withdrawing pastors and church planters to provide sufficient teachers for the educational institutions (May 3,1977). Alan Bassett was an American Presbyterian missionary who served in Thailand between 1917 and World War II. He told me that he was withdrawn from a promising evangelistic work and reassigned to teach science in the mission schools (Feb. 7, 1976).

In 1939 Alexander McLeish visited Thailand and wrote an insightful report printed in the War-time Survey Series through World Dominion Press. In it he concluded, "that the school in Thailand has not proved as vitally evangelistic as was hoped..." (1942:16).

Eakin could have revealed the effects of this drastic change of policy and priority on the local churches growth and memberships in the North from the following comparison:

1908-1914	3382 increase of members over six years
1914-1925	469 increase in members over nine years
1925-1937	131 *loss* in members over twelve years

(Dennis 1911:88; Beach 1916:64; 1925:101; Parker 1938:53)

This shows that the change in church growth occurred after 1914 and confirms that the large baptisms of over sixteen thousand, which were still coming in from the Lao people movement following 1914, were sadly not conserved nor incorporated into the churches.

Some overall causes producing this people movement need noting, since significantly still today, the majority of the Church in Thailand is from the North.

Key Causes for the Lao Movement

Two significant elements that God used in producing this explosion of growth were His human agents and the practical strategies and methods they employed. The right combination of the power of the Holy Spirit operating through dedicated persons, who earnestly prayed and used prudent pragmatic approaches, produced amazing results.

First, God uses people. Those whom God used here included the native Christians, the indigenous evangelists and native leaders as well as the missionaries from overseas, all with various gifts and abilities. He also works through His preparation of the people group in the environmental and socio-cultural dynamics that produce their level of receptivity. The stronger the mobilization and utilization of indigenous lay people and leaders becomes the focus of the strategies employed, the quicker the potential for people movements can be realized. Missionary identification with the people is essential, along with a most humble attitude and a loving spirit. The role of the missionary is crucial, especially in the pioneer stages. He may be required to be the first to preach the Gospel in order to introduce it to an unreached people group. However, the secret of success will lay with the degree of his willingness to encourage and to involve the new Christians of that people in their own evangelization and church planting—right from the earliest possible opportunity. The missionary must also know when, where and how to change his role in order to assist the fastest facilitation of a people movement and the multiplication of church planting at each stage of development. He or she may be a key but must never be a kingpin!

High spiritual quality is also a crucial element for both missionary and local believer. True spirituality is paramount, along with the attendant credibility needed to make the message real. "Who we are speaks louder than what we say." Key dimensions of spirituality, of "being" as well as doing, include:

- A confident view of a sovereign God in and throughout history
- A living faith in His working out His eternal purposes

- A prayerful dependence always on Him alone
- An unshakeable conviction that only God's Spirit does any converting
- An absolute trust in the power of the Gospel of Christ to do so
- A willingness to sacrifice and suffer if needs be
- A deliberate determination to hang in there with God in the face of opposition

Second, the programs and strategies that God uses are as important as the servants who use them. Spiritual harvest is seldom haphazard. The methods and plans God employs to produce His Church in any given people group are often both relevant and unique. The strategies and tactics that produce people movements are frequently dynamic and often specifically honed to affect the ongoing ingathering. Because of the variegated contexts of peoples, church growth within a specific people group is usually a highly complex phenomenon. The more the new people movement is dependent on God, and the direction of His Spirit and His Word, rather than on the missionary or the Mission, the healthier it will expand. Strong development relies on maintaining evangelistic fervor and providing adequate nurture and training as the people movement gains momentum. Neither can be neglected without impunity. Never stop evangelism in order to consolidate, as it is generally quite difficult to reinstall evangelistic motivation.

Crucial Strategies

Some of the key strategies and approaches that McGilvary and other of his missionary and national associates repeatedly put into practice include:

- Extensive itineration throughout the whole people group and territory was usually done by lengthy evangelistic tours. They broadcast the Gospel seed widely.

- Taking particular note of different people groups and their needs was emphasized. Though focused on the Lao or Khon Muang as they called themselves, McGilvary also identified the different peoples he came across such as the Karen (by 1880), Lahu (1886), Akha (1891), Khamu (1897), and later Yao. He was interested in them and shared the good news with the various groups.
- The level of interest and receptivity of different people groups was also observed and evaluated. McGilvary recognized a potential people movement among the Khamu in 1897. They were located north of Luang Prabang, which in 1893 had been taken over by France (Smith 1982:98,150). He returned to spend several months with the Khamu the following year, 1898. "McGilvary expected a mass movement to begin at any moment. Ten villages showed a serious interest in Christianity" (Swanson 1984:50). The Lao Lord of Luang Prabang objected and the French ordered McGilvary to stop the work and leave. For a second time he was frustrated in reaping an immediate people movement. Nevertheless in 1899 elders were sent from north Thailand and the following year about forty Khamu were baptized. Though cut off from normal care, the church was established. Today there is still a Khamu church of one hundred members in Laos that claims its heritage back to the days of McGilvary.
- Follow up of the responsive villages and areas where new believers arose, was carried out, despite difficult seasonal barriers, travel and communications of that time. Repeated contact and concern for fostering nurture and spiritual growth, without smothering the believers, were high priorities in future itinerations. Quality was as important as quantity.
- The goal was to multiply local churches widely. Even where there were only a few families who responded, sometimes in isolated locations, McGilvary always aimed to plant local churches. He organized a church often before there was a

mission station. This was the reverse of the normal mission strategy of the day.

- The focus was mostly on winning whole families, extended families and even villages into the Church as web movements. Believers were called upon to share the faith with their relatives, friends, communities, and nearby villages. Quantity was also just as important as quality.
- Seeking out those in local leadership and showing respect to them as well as sharing the Gospel with them was a mark of this movement in its earliest days. He related to village headmen, Buddhist abbots and respected adults in the community. Later on taking a role of being the champion of the oppressed, especially concerning witchcraft accusations, became common. The former was a stronger approach as it tended to work with the respected power people and the solid citizens of the community rather than the fringe peoples and outcasts of society. After the martyrdoms the latter was often used more than the former, which was employed in the initial stages. Both approaches were important but the former was probably needed more, primarily to establish the credibility of the church for all strata of society first. Then the door for the acceptance of the oppressed could be opened within the church. Unfortunately pioneer churches are sometimes based on fringe peoples outside the mainstream of society and this often brands the Church with a negative connotation in the community's eyes.
- McGilvary had a deep passion to mentor and train leaders. He did this primarily through the apprentice type model. Even at eighty years of age he would take new missionaries along with him to introduce them to his pattern of itinerating as he evangelized and nurtured the churches. He did the same with prospective older native laymen, those who were already respected members of the community. He trained workers on the road and in the field in evangelism, theology and biblical

teaching. Only later, was the institutional model of the resident training school for younger people used.

- By committing the new churches to the Holy Spirit and by continually praying for them, McGilvary launched the churches on their way to maturity and independence as indigenous self-supporting and self-directing bodies. Being mobile and not attached to one particular church, he precluded the churches from becoming dependent on him. This was also a mark in the people movement in the Karen, largely by missionary default, but nonetheless a significant help.

Summary and Conclusion

These four main case studies of people movements in Thailand highlight the difficulties and the joys, the drama and the frustration, the excitement and the struggle of people movements. A bird's eye view sees the successive phases of the movement unfolding: the pains of the beginnings, accompanied by the usual slow process of development, followed by the strong flow of the movement, and ending with the vital need to conserve the results of the people movement. It's quite a challenge. Throughout these complex proceedings of growth, weaknesses and strengths are learned. Cooperation of missionaries and emerging believers strain tense muscles and drain flagging energies. At the same time, holding hands and moving forward together against all odds, energizes souls in unity for the faith given for all peoples, tongues, tribes and nations. The sparks of hope glow bright as converts flood in. But when adherents revert, the pains of loss plague the participant trainer. The slackening of the movement's momentum challenges the concerned researcher. The exuberance of indigenous involvement in starting, enhancing and leading the people movement excites the mind and the heart. The lowly persons of character that God uses, and the empowered programs and methods He utilizes to bring the movement into full force, humble observers. A new and enduring thing is produced in time, the Church - His

Church. God produces His Church with a mission—His mission to bridge across families, clans, neighborhoods, communities and people groups to share His Good News to the ends of the earth and to multiply His local churches till the end of time. That is the way He has worked since the beginning, since the beginning of His age of grace. And so it shall continue through His Spirit, by His grace, with His servants and for His glory.

In conclusion, let us delineate the five major stages of a people movement:

Motivation: This is crucial, for without a Holy Spirit driven burden, little will be envisioned or attempted to see a people movement birthed. Prayer and sensitivity to the Spirit moved Kho Tha Bya and McGilvary to have a vision of the potential ingathering of the Karen and the Khon Muang respectively. Both native believers and foreign missionaries, excited by this kind of motivation, expect and see a ripe harvest gathered in. By faith and hope they anticipate the harvest to come. Often both indigenous Christians and cross-cultural workers may be catalysts that God uses to start the process and move it towards a people movement. Prayerful attitudes, intense spirituality, determined sacrifice and clear vision are powerful motivators for a people movement mindset and orientation.

Mobilization: Once a significant level of receptivity is recognized in a people group, then the efforts of combined personnel and resources of Church and Mission should be concentrated on that people. Time, energy, and teams of both national and missionary servants need to be released and deployed to focus on that potential people movement. A special need and goal for the orientation of this mobilization is training workers to reach whole families, extended families and related communities as a whole. Furthermore mobilization of intercession for the anticipated movement is critical, since people movements towards Christ are primarily movements of the Holy Spirit.

Momentum: Essentially this involves the developmental stage of the people movement from its initiation to its full strength. In some cases this may be fast or rapid. In many situations it will proceed much slower before it gains strength and accelerates. Frustration, trials, opposition, persecution, setbacks and struggles can be expected before the movement gains a full head of steam, before its foundational preparation for explosion is solidly laid. The momentum phase could be compared to a Jumbo Jet lumbering at first down the runway while it builds up adequate velocity, until the appropriate airspeed is reached to produce the lift required for take off. Similarly the momentum of a people movement, generally demands enduring the stress, strains, and pains of lumbering along until the critical mass of local indigenous churches provides the launching pad for a people movement. The involvement of early native believers and indigenous leadership in evangelism and nurture are among the key ingredients for building this momentum.

Another dimension of the importance of building momentum relates to the sociological theory of Diffusion and Homer Barnett's Communication of Innovations. This theory states that for any significant movement or change to occur, sixteen percent or more of the population of that people group must first accept the innovative idea or change, before it can progress throughout the whole population. This is started often from outside advocates, picked up by some insider innovators or early adopters, then through the opinion makers within the group, propelled out to the majority of population by later adopters. Statistics are vital in evaluating the percentage of genuine Christians among a given people group. Good evaluation and analysis with accurate statistical collating and graphing help guide us in noting the burgeoning momentum of the movement.

The Main Movement: In the wisdom and timing of God's "fullness of time," the main people movement itself will commence to reproduce and multiply itself. Often the explosion of the movement goes far beyond the control of the missionaries or indigenous leaders. Therefore, the native believers and their leaders must be ready to go with its flow. Energies should not be expended in trying to control the movement, but channeled to enhance its outward multiplication, as the Holy Spirit directs. Rather than being side-tracked, leaders choose better roles to encourage and train as many believers as possible for multiplying new house churches and church groups, especially among family webs and existing networks. Also the nurturing of the new families being gathered in is crucial in order to get them involved in extending the movement as soon as possible. First they are to be enfolded, second trained and third released for further evangelistic extension across their networks of relationship and natural networks.

Maintenance: This is vital to the health of the movement and also to its conservation. While taking measures not to short circuit the movement itself, the Christians' and leaders' major task is to nurture it, mature it and ground those garnered into churches. However, evangelism must not be stopped in order to consolidate. Like two rails of a train track, both continuing active witness and constant deepening nurture should be done *simultaneously*, if the maximum potential of the harvest is to be reaped. The post-baptismal care in a people movement is essential to conserve it. Resources and personnel need to be mobilized and redeployed for this critical stage, even if it means temporarily disrupting other existing "good programs" of the Church. Only then can a people movement reach its full potential.

10

A People Movement among the Pwo Karen in Northern Thailand

Jim Morris

I would like to give personal testimony to what God has done in producing a small people movement to Christ among the Pwo Karen people in the provinces of Chiang Mai and Mae Hong Son of northern Thailand. These are reflections on my pilgrimage following the desires God had put into my heart as a teenager. The Lord gave me a passion to see Christ "exalted in my body, whether by life or by death" (Phil. 1:20-21) and to "preach the Gospel where Christ was not known" (Rom. 15:20). This ambition took me from high school to training for missionary service at Prairie Bible Institute, to mission work in British Columbia with the Canadian Sunday School Mission, and finally to Thailand in 1957 with Overseas Missionary Fellowship (OMF). I had been deeply inspired by reading the biographies of Hudson Taylor, founder of China Inland Mission (CIM later renamed OMF), James Fraser, pioneer missionary among the Lisu people of Yunnan, China, and the writings of Isobel Kuhn. Through the ministries of Fraser, Kuhn and others God had produced a large people movement to Christ among the Lisu of China.

Missionaries had to leave China in 1950 because of the communists' takeover. In the early 1950s, John and Isobel Kuhn and other CIMers moved to northern Thailand to continue working among unreached tribal peoples in Thailand who were similar to those they had been reaching in Yunnan, China. My fiancée, Louise Imbach, and I were drawn to work with OMF in northern Thailand among an unreached tribal people group. We arrived in Thailand in 1957 as an engaged couple. After two years of studying the Thai language we were married and were assigned with another couple to pioneer a church among the Pwo Karen of northern Thailand.

Discovering a People-Movement-to-Christ Mindset

My understanding of missions was influenced by my experiences in North America with an emphasis upon individual, personal conversion. I did not understand the dynamics of people movements and group conversions. It was very helpful to read and reread *Behind the Ranges* and to hear the stories of Lisu missionaries. I learned lessons about prayer and patience, language and culture, how tribal people make corporate decisions, and the importance of winning families to Christ. J. O. Fraser became my hero. *Behind the Ranges* was my manual on people movements to Christ. His principles can be summarized in this way:

A. Plant indigenous churches with local leadership who in turn would repeat the process over and over again until the whole people group was reached.

B. Live with the people, learn their language and culture well, and build deep relationships. Seek to understand their point of view and attempt to become real to them. Point them constantly to the Word of God.

C. Do not focus on individuals but focus on winning whole families to the Lord. The clan system was so strong that, unless the elders approved, the family altar and sacrifices would not effectively be done away. Taylor prayed with increasing longing for a turning to Christ of whole households, men, women, and children (Taylor 1998:112).

D. Help the believers make a clean break with their old animistic and idolatrous practices.

E. Pray personally and get other to join in prayer for the missionary and the Lisu. Fraser was personally led by God to pray the prayer of faith that hundreds of Lisu families would turn to Christ. Fraser wrote a long letter home about his thoughts on "the prayer of faith" (Crossman 1982:124-137). He contrasted general prayer (that which is limited by lack of knowledge, vague, knowing very little about the details of the object of the prayer) and definite prayer (which is a definite request made in definite faith for a definite answer).

F. Be patient and persevere. It takes time for a movement for God to develop among an unreached people group. In the summer of 1916, 129 Lisu families turned to the Lord, about 600 people. This was two years after Fraser prayed the prayer of faith and seven years since he had first learned of the Lisu. In the next few years a large people movement occurred among the Lisu.

G. After people turn to Christ and burn their demon things, it is important to teach them to obey all that is written in the Word of God. Fraser realized that it would take time, much teaching, and patience to develop Christian character in the lives of the Lisu believers and leaders. The Lisu language was reduced to writing, a catechism written, the New Testament translated, and Rainy Season Bible Schools held. The Lisu believers were well taught in the Word and in obedience to the Lord. They saw a good example in Fraser and other missionaries who came to help in the work.

H. Follow indigenous principles from the start. From the very first the Lisu believers shared their faith and won their relatives and friends to the Lord. They served the Lord gladly without pay. The local community of believers would look after the gardens and fields of those who went to study at the Rainy Season Bible School. Local leadership developed and the movement toward God spread across the area. Lisu won other Lisu to Christ. Lisu churches reached out to plant churches in other villages and the work spread rapidly.

Defining a People Movement to Christ

I learned more about people movements from the writings and teaching of Donald A. McGavran. He wrote that, "People like to become Christians without crossing racial, linguistic, or class barrier" (McGavran 1990:163). In contrast the earlier mission station approach, McGavran described the process of a people movement thus:

> A people movement results from the joint decision of a number of individuals all from the same people group, which enables then to become Christians without social dislocation, while remaining in full contact with their non-Christian relatives, thus enabling other segments of that people group, across the years, after suitable instruction, to come to similar decisions and form Christian churches made up exclusively of members of that people (:223).

McGavran warned against bringing people to Christ one by one against the tide into gathered churches. "To Christianize a whole people, the first thing not to do is snatch individuals out of it into a different society. People become Christians where a Christward movement occurs within that society" (1999:324). He also explained small response in this way:

> A factor in the small response, whose importance cannot be overestimated, is that, partly because of the individualistic bias of the missionaries and partly because of the resistance of the hearers, conversions were mainly *out* of the nation. Converts felt that they were joining not merely a new religion, but an entirely foreign way of living – proclaimed by foreigners, led by foreigners and ruled by foreigners. Converts came out alone. . . A vicious circle was established: the few becoming Christian one by one set such a pattern that it was difficult for a Christward movement to be started, and by the lack of a movement converts continued to come one by one and in very small numbers. . . The person not only became a Christian, but he was generally believed to have "joined another race." (1999:329).

McGavran gives five advantages of people movements: (i) People movements have provided the Christian movement with permanent churches rooted in the soil of hundreds of thousands of villages; (ii) They have the advantage of being naturally indigenous; (iii) With them the spontaneous expansion of the Church is natural; (iv) These movements have enormous possibility of growth; and (v) These movements provide a sound pattern of becoming Christian. Becoming a Christian is seen to mean not change in standard of living made possible by foreign funds, but change in inner character made possible by the power of God. (1999:336-338).

In *Saturation Evangelism*, George Peters has a section on Household Evangelism and Group Movements. He says, "If we neglect household evangelism and group movements we are neglecting what are potentially the most fruitful avenues of evangelism God has given us" (Peters 1970:145). He gives Ten Steps to Group Evangelism:

1. Assign a Christian worker to a tribe, people, or community with permanent responsibility for this people and/or community.

2. Learn the language of the people well.

3. Study the culture and the religion of the people well, including the mythology.

4. Study the social structure of the people and community well. Most societies are held together and are guided by an organizational (decision-making body) and functional (decision-influencing individuals) power structure.

5. Communicate along the culturally-accepted channels of the power structure; avoid all possible offense, and conscious or deliberate violations.

6. Study major interest areas, areas of tension, frustration and imbalance, as well as consciously felt needs, and expressed or hidden aspirations, desires and longings.

7. Work for the closest possible cultural adaptations, social identification and religious empathy without falling into the trap of nativism (i.e. contextualization not syncretism).

8. Study carefully the mentality of the people.

9. Make a genuine attempt of evangelism by group penetration and permeation before you attempt evangelism by direct confrontation.

10. Do not isolate converts from their cultural context and social interrelationships under the pretense of separation (1999:206-214).

Also helpful for me was George Patterson's article entitled "The Spontaneous Multiplication of Churches" (1999:595-605). Jacob A. Loewen has also helped me through a series of articles in *Practical Anthropology* that were later collected in *Culture and Human Values* (William Carey Library, 1975).

Alex Smith and I worked in Thailand with OMF. He worked among the Thai and Lao in central Thailand, and I worked with the Pwo Karen in north Thailand. Over the years we were able to share ideas and stimulate each other in the fundamentals of pioneer church planting and people movements to Christ. I followed much of the same principles that we wrote about in *Strategy to Multiply Rural Churches,* especially the model of the functioning church (1977:21-29), and the strategy for effective church planting (:187-239). The elements of the proposed strategy were:

1. Explore for the responsive widely
2. Evangelize the receptive intensely
3. Establish church immediately
4. Edify members constantly
5. Evolve local pastors speedily
6. Extend new churches persistently
7. Evaluate the program continually

Designing a People Movement among the Pwo Karen

The Pwo Karen of this study lived in Hot, Doi Taw, and Omkoi Amphoes in Chiang Mai Province and Maesariang Amphoe in Mae Hon Song Province. About 40,000 Pwo Karen lived in an area 100 miles wide and thirty miles deep in 200 plus villages. The area was divided into a smaller number of Pwo Karen who lived on the plains and a much larger number who lived in the mountains. Louise and I lived among the Pwo Karen 1959-1990. Since then we have made occasional visits to them from outside Thailand.

In this section the verbs are not in the same tense; some are past; others present, and I'm not sure which tense is appropriate.

Pwo of the Plains: Some Pwo Karen lived in the plains along the Ping River in Amphoes Hot and Doi Taw. Those who lived on the plains reside very close to the Northern Thai and are greatly influenced by Thai culture and Buddhism. The Pwo are rice farmers and day laborers. Few owned their own land. About 5,000 of them lived on the plains in this area of Thailand. There were also those who lived in the Yuam valley in Amphoe Mae Sariang.

Pwo of the Mountains: The majority of the Pwo Karen lived in villages located between the Hot-Mae Sariang road border on the north and Omkoi town on the south—in Amphoes Hot and Omkoi in Chiang Mai Province and Amphoe Mae Sariang in Mae Hon Song Province. They were rice farmers. Many owned their own land. This was really Pwo Karen land. It was a compact area of Pwo Karen with minimal Thai influence. Those who lived in the mountains were animistic with a veneer of Buddhism. Pwo Karen had contact with Thai Buddhist temples in Omkoi town and when they visited markets located on the plains. Until recently there were no Buddhist temples in Pwo Karen villages in the mountains. Beginning in the 1970s the government began building Thai schools in Pwo villages. The teachers taught Thai language and Buddhism. Beginning in the 1980s Buddhist temples have been built in Pwo villages. Since that time the influence of Buddhism has increased among the Pwo Karen in the mountains as they have more contacts with the Thai. The Pwo Karen who lived in this area belonged to the same Pwo Karen language group. Dialects varied slightly across the area, but they could talk to each other without much difficulty. They called themselves *phlong* ("people"). They can be called northern Pwo in contrast to other Pwo.

Other Regions: There were other Pwo Karen in Thailand and Burma. Pwo Karen also lived in other areas of Thailand. There was and still is little or no contact between them and the northern Pwo. They spoke a distinctly different dialect. Today the majority of Pwo Karen live in Burma and are quite different in language and culture. This study is only about the northern Pwo of Thailand.

Our Approach

OMF began working among the northern Pwo in 1954. I entered the work in 1958 and was joined by Louise in 1959. We lived with another OMF missionary couple in Wangloong, the main Thai market town at the end of the road and the beginning of Pwo Karen villages. At that time there were no Pwo Christians in the whole area. There were a few Buddhist temples and Thai schools on the plains in Thai towns. There were no Buddhist temples or Thai schools in Pwo villages. Many Pwo occasionally attended a Buddhist temple. Hardly any Pwo children attended Thai school. This dialect of Pwo was not written. The Pwo books written in Burma were for Pwo dialects not mutually intelligible to Pwo in this area.

We came at a time when traditional Pwo Karen culture was beginning to feel the impact of modernity, including the building of roads, which brought the outside world much closer to them. With the roads came outsiders who wanted to exploit the jungle. First came Thai traders, who set up small markets and who exported jungle products. Soon the government built Thai schools in Pwo villages, which were now accessible by road. Thai teachers came to live in Pwo villages. Then came Thai Buddhist temples and Thai priests moved in. Slowly the age-long traditional way of Pwo Karen life began to change. They went from being subsistent farmers of the isolated hills to being rural peasants connected to Thai towns and cities by roads. They became more and more dependent upon the outside world with an increasing need for money, work, education, and medical help.

Preparatory: Our plan was to live with the people, learn their language and culture, to identify with them, relate to them as friends and fellow human beings, and introduce them to Christ. We looked to God for a people movement to Christ. We were to translate the New Testament into their language, train leaders, and plant indigenous communities of believers from the beginning. Our goals were to encourage the multiplication of biblical, indigenous church plants and to work ourselves out of a job.

This took time, energy and effort. We were in a pioneer situation. Earlier workers had made a small beginning before they left. We joined the one remaining missionary couple and were able to build on their foundation. We spent a lot of time doing linguistic and anthropological investigation and analysis. I spent hours taping stories, listening to them, writing them down word by word with a helper, and analyzing Pwo Karen texts which contained a gold mine of language, culture and folklore.

Secondary: We sought to help them in areas of their felt needs. We did a lot of simple medical work. People came from miles around to get medical help. We also had opportunity to pray for their healing. Over a period of time we were able to win the confidence of many Pwo by the help we gave them through medicine and prayer. They experienced the powerful work of the Lord in healing in some very difficult cases where the worship of spirits failed.

We also helped them agriculturally. In time we hosted work parties of agricultural workers from overseas who came to teach new technology and to introduce new seeds, and other improvements. We also wrote literacy primers and simple books, and held literacy classes. We prepared a Pwo-English dictionary and wrote language lessons for expatriate workers. We began to translate the New Testament into the Northern Pwo language.

Primary: Our main job was to share the good news about Jesus Christ with them. We did this by living among them and sharing life with them. We studied their oral literature and learned much about their worldview from their stories. They know about a Creator God, but He had left earth. It was Satan who taught them spirit worship and how to survive life, sickness, pain, and death. The more we learned about them and their mindset, the more we could relate the

Good News to them. We told Bible stories, starting with creation and the fall, followed with the main stories of the Old Testament, and then the stories of the Gospels and Acts. We used a simplified version of Chronological Teaching before New Tribes Mission developed "Firm Foundations." We prayed for the sick and for God's blessing upon Pwo in their daily lives. God demonstrated His power over Satan and spirits and His love and care for the people. They were beginning to experience that Jesus was more powerful than the spirits. Not that they were willing to turn to Jesus, but they were willing to turn to us for help.

We visited many of the mountain villages in the dry season and sat around many fires sharing with the people the best we could with the level of language we had learned. In the rainy season we lived on the plains learning language and culture, visiting local Pwo villages, and preparing teaching materials for the next dry season thrust of widespread evangelism.

The traditional Pwo Karen society was cohesive and resistant to change. Theirs was the Karen way of life, taught by their ancestors for hundreds of years. Added to that was a strong veneer of Buddhism. We were looked upon as foreigners – non-people.

Their leaders were gatekeepers, who reinforced the traditional Karen way of life. Many people struggled to find enough food to live. Theirs was a hand-to-mouth existence and they had developed a handout mentality. Marginal Pwo would be willing to turn to Jesus in order to receive a handout, but such converts would not produce a people movement to Christ. We need to be patient and find a way to win families to Jesus, whom the Creator God had sent to earth to rescue. We resisted accepting individuals who wanted to believe apart from family and friends.

God's Promises to Us

God gave us the promise of Isaiah 49:24-25: "Can the prey be taken from the mighty man, or the captives of the tyrant be rescued? Surely, thus says the Lord, 'Even the captives of the mighty man will be taken away and the prey of the tyrant will be rescued. For I will contend with those who contend with you and I will save your children'" (NASB). This was our assurance from God that He had sent us to the Pwo Karen and that He would work through our lives to bring many to salvation in Christ.

Prayer: In 1960 God laid two specific prayer requests on our hearts: that we could live in a Pwo Karen village, and that the first Pwo Karen would believe in Christ. We had been denied taking up residency in the nearby Pwo Karen village because we could not comply with their requirement that we would participate in feasting the village spirit to ensure harmony in the village and fertility of crops. But about mid-year God answered our prayers and we were invited to live in the village because of their desire to have our medical help closer at hand. They gave us a house on the edge of the village and pulled in the boundary of the village so that our house was technically outside the village borders. In this way we were not required to share in the village spirit worship.

Getting the first Pwo Karen family to turn to Christ did not prove easy. One day I was invited by a Christian Thai from a village of leprosy patients about four hours walk away, which I did not know existed, to go preach the Christmas sermon in their small church. The regular teacher from Chiang Mai city was not free to go that year. In this small, isolated village of sixteen Thai households also lived a Pwo Karen couple, who were leprosy patients, with their adult niece. Christmas day 1960 these three adult Pwo Karen accepted Christ, as I was able to explain the gospel to them in their own language. So God answered our prayers in an amazing way. We were able to live in a Pwo village and the first Pwo had turned to Christ!

I thought the fact that local Pwo Karen had believed in the Lord would open doors in surrounding Pwo villages and that other Pwo would believe, but we did not find any such response. They said that when and if they got leprosy they may become Christians out of desperation. But for now they would remain normal Karen.

A Pwo Karen family, who lived next door to us believed in 1964 and another family believed in 1965. God miraculously healed the husband, who was very sick with tuberculosis. Five Pwo Karen were baptized in 1965, but the little church soon split up a couple years later over petty issues. One family continued to follow the Lord and have remained faithful to the present time. After ten years of work (1958-1968) there were very little lasting results. What were we to do next?

We were discouraged because so few had turned to the Lord. God reassured us with promises from Habakkuk 1:5, "For I am going to do something in your days that you will not believe, even if you were told. For the revelation awaits an appointed time. It speaks of the end and will not prove false. Though it linger, wait for it. It will certainly come and will not delay." We understood that He was encouraging us to continue on and to wait for the "fullness of His timing."

About this time we met George Peters, professor of missions at Dallas Seminary. He encouraged us not to be discouraged. He said that pioneer work like we were attempting takes an average of eighteen years before there is a breakthrough. "Pray on," he told us, "Work on. Trust God. He will work according to His own timing."

A New Beginning

In 1969 we moved into the mountain village of Striped Creek, located on a new mountain road that connected the Thai District town of Omkoi in the southern mountains and the Thai District town of Hod on the northern plains with the main road to the provincial town of Chiang Mai. We were now living in a predominately Pwo Karen area of about forty to fifty villages with a population of about 10,000 Pwo. One hundred miles of new roads allowed us to have easier access to many of these villages.

We visited many villages regularly in a wide area both on the plains and in the mountains. We sat around the fire for hours listening to Pwo stories and telling Bible stories. We taught from Sunday school poster rolls and OMF evangelistic poster rolls. We played Gospel Recording records over and over until they wore out. We sang hymns and choruses. The Pwo love to sing. We taught literacy. We helped many with simple medicines. We made friends in many villages. They liked us. They liked our medicines. They liked the power of Jesus to heal, but they were not yet ready to turn from Karen ways to the "Jesus way.

We kept looking for where God was at work in Pwo Karen land. Where would the response begin? Finally the breakthrough came in Prosperity Fields village, located along the road from Hot to Omkoi. Prosperity Fields became a center from which the gospel spread in the Omkoi area. Striped Creek village, where we lived, became a center in the neighboring Hot area.

The spark that began to produce a people movement to Christ among the Pwo Karen in the Hot-Omkoi mountains was Mrs. Dee. She lived in Prosperity Fields village, where our coworkers lived. We were living in Striped Creek village, twenty miles to the north. Mrs. Dee believed in 1969. Her family wanted her to become the demon priestess for their clan. She decided to opt out by becoming a Christian instead. Her husband, Mr. Dee Waters, the son of the area headman, was in jail in Chiang Mai at the time. We had hoped that Headman Waters would believe and be a positive influence for Christ. But no, he was friendly but not willing to leave his old ways. Instead God began His work among Pwo in the mountains in the life of a poor orphan lady with little influence. The Lord's power was demonstrated through her weakness.

Mrs. Dee was the only believer in the area but God met her needs and the needs of her four small children. She was helped and taught by missionaries for a couple years. Then our coworkers left the work in 1970 and we were away on another assignment from mid-1971 to 1974. Mrs. Dee was left without missionary help, nevertheless she refused to worship the demons. She listened to gospel recording, prayed to Jesus, and stood firm in the Lord. The villagers did not help her, but the Lord did. He blessed her children with good health. Her rice grew and she herself was strong in the Lord and in spirit and body. She and her children became living examples that Jesus is stronger than Satan and the spirits, and that He cares for Pwo Karen as well as for foreigners.

Special prayer and breakthrough: At the OMF North Thailand Field Conference of 1974, the Lord gave our field a strong burden to pray especially for breakthrough among the Pwo Karen. OMF leaders in Singapore also took up the challenge and initiated a worldwide prayer thrust for breakthrough among the Pwo Karen of northern Thailand.

When we returned to Karen land in April 1974, we sensed that God was working in a powerful way. Three families who had seen how God helped Mrs. Dee and her children during the time she was alone were ready to turn to Christ. One of the new converts had been the spirit head of her clan. Mr. Dee came home from jail. He was so impressed by how the Lord had helped his family that he also believed. He became my right hand man, whom I was informally training for leadership in the newly forming church in Prosperity Fields. Pwo from other nearby villages began coming to him and to us wanting the Jesus power and wanting us to go to their villages. A simple church building was built by the believers in Prosperity Fields villages and this became the center for a developing work in the nearby villages. New believers would meet in their own village on the porch of a house until the group was big enough to build their own simple meeting place—often a platform with a leaf roof and no walls. From time to time the believers in the area came to Prosperity Fields for a joint celebration and special meetings like for Christmas, Easter, Karen New Year, etc. For these occasions the meeting place was enlarged with tarps or temporary leaf roofing. Visitors slept on the porches of the believers.

Developing a People Movement among the Pwo Karen

Early in 1975 my language helper and his family in Striped Creek believed. A few years before, he had put the Lord to the test by having me go with him to his fields to pray instead of his doing the spirit worship ceremonies the Pwo normally do in the course of a year. That year the Lord gave the family a good harvest, but they were not yet ready to burn their spirit things and turn to Christ. Now they were ready. A group of believers began to form in Striped Creek village as well. So the gospel continued to slowly spread from family to family and from village to village. A movement to Christ had begun. There were groups of believing families in a half dozen or so villages—a total of about 245 believers.

Planting Communities of Believers

A significant breakthrough came mid 1975 in Sop Lahn village, thirty kilometers south of Omkoi town in a small, isolated village of twenty-five houses in a heavy malarial-infested teak forest in a good rice growing area with a plentiful supply of water. About a third of the villagers were Pwo Karen. The rest were Sgaw Karen. Most of the villagers were bilingual. The headman ordered that I come to his village. This prosperous and powerful headman owned elephants, water buffaloes, cattle, and lots of rice fields but he was hooked on opium and was afraid of losing all his wealth. He remembered hearing gospel recordings years before that said Jesus was stronger than the spirits. Mrs. Dee's sister lived in Sop Lahn and so he sent word to Dee Waters to bring me to Sop Lahn village because he wanted to turn from the spirits to Jesus.

Since I was about to leave for furlough, I spent only one night in the village. The headman and his family believed as most of the rest of the villagers watched. Then he went with me and watched me help two other families burn their spirit things. In a couple other households he and I worked together, as I trained him how to do it. Then I watched him do it for a couple families. Then all the new believers came to the headman's house and I taught them how to have a simple worship service, using a tape recorder to guide them and how to pray, etc. Without knowing it at that time, I followed the Church Planting Movement model: model, assist, watch and leave! Thus a church was planted in Sop Lahn. In time that church became the center of a work of God in surrounding villages.

Upon returning from furlough I visited the village several times to hold training courses. Then a Sgaw Karen intern from Phayao Bible College went to live in the village and two new OMF missionaries were assigned the task of developing this church and extending the church to the many unreached villages deeper in the jungle. Over the next twenty years churches were planted throughout in about forty Sgaw Karen villages. The work continues to grow even to this day.

Teaching the Believers to Obey the Word of God

Most Pwo turn to the Lord in times of deep trouble, when their traditional ways have not worked. They are not concerned with sin. They are concerned with sickness. They are looking for some power greater than the spirits rather than looking for forgiveness. God reaches out to them in grace, meeting them where they are and leading them on by his redeeming power to transform them into what he wants them to be. Our pattern has been to respect people the way they are; to reach them where they are; to see God redeem them from what they are; and to renew them to become what he is (2 Cor. 3:17-18, Rom. 12:1-2, Eph. 4:20-24).

We were working with a non-literate society with an oral tradition so we began there. We taught using pictures and telling Bible stories. We wrote doctrine into hymns and choruses. We used the record player and tape players. They listened to the message over and over and memorized the songs and stories. We introduced ceremonies and special days to replace their old ways. They learned to pray for everything and to trust God to help them get well, grow rice, take care of their livestock, gardens and children and to protect them from spirits and to keep their souls from wandering away from them and causing sickness. Over time they inculturated biblical truth, internalized biblical functions, and were transformed by God's power in their daily lives. Some things in their culture that were neutral were retained. Other things needed to be eliminated and were replaced with functional substitutes. Some things needed to be altered, like their wedding ceremony and new things needed to be added, like worship, reading, etc. There is always the danger of syncretism and restructuring but the Word of God and the Holy Spirit guides them. Over time the personal lives of the Pwo Karen and their society are being transformed by His grace.

The Proliferation Process: Train and Multiply

From the first we were working and praying for a people movement to Christ among the Pwo Karen. Families believed as units. We tried not to dislocate believers from society. We sought to encourage and train believers to share their faith with their relatives and friends from the day they believed. They were taught to pray personally, to listen to the Bible stories, to learn the songs on the tape recorder, and to gather together for worship, instruction and fellowship in their village each Sunday. From Sop Lahn the gospel spread to many Sgaw Karen villages in the surrounding area. Once a key person believed in a village others were quick to join. From Prosperity Fields the gospel spread to Pwo villages along the road. Sometimes those needing help came to seek us or Karen believers.

The gospel also spread by teams going out to share the gospel in surrounding villages.

We conducted simple leadership training programs, teaching them how to read, how to tell Bible stories, how to pray for the sick and other needs, and how to lead a service. They had tape recorders with testimonies, Bible stories and songs. They also used gospel poster rolls and had a series of Bible story books with pictures that told the main stories from Genesis to Christ to Paul.

The main road was improving. Dry season roads to many villages were carved out of the jungle. I visited villages and new churches with my Landrover. I always took along Pwo Christians, both to encourage new believers in isolated villages, to evangelize new places and to train the older believers in doing the work of the Lord. I tried to do things in such a way that Pwo themselves could reproduce. Today many Pwo Karen own motorcycles and trucks, so my use of a Landrover was not all that out of the realm of possibility for a Karen.

Some young people went to outside Bible schools – either Phayao Bible School or the Baptist school in Chiang Mai or later to the New Tribes Chronological Training School in Maesariang. They have now started a Bible Training Center in the Pwo Karen language in the village of Striped Creek.

Once roads improved other groups started coming into Karen land. Some took over some of the churches we planted. They sent young people to short-term schools in distant places and began to pay workers. This caused us some trouble, but praise God some very keen young Sgaw and Pwo were used of God to spread the gospel far and wide.

Today there are communities of believers in most villages in the area. Some are connected with Chinese or Korean missions, some with Thai Full Gospel churches, or with Baptist Karen Churches. OMF related churches are still active in the area. Every time I go back to visit I hear of new places being reached. The work is now bigger than any one mission or person. We may have planted and others watered, but God is giving the growth. Church multiplication is taking place. A people movement has taken place but there is still much to be done for the gospel to change the Karen worldview and truly transform the society. To Him be the glory.

Discerning What has Happened to Date

We lived ten years with the Pwo Karen on the Hod plains and visited about twelve Pwo Karen villages often (1959-1969). A few families believed. Most moved to live in a Christian Thai Leprosy Village. There has been no significant movement to Christ among the Pwo Karen on the plains. Over the years only a few marginal families became Christian. A few Pwo Karen school children became Christians while living in the Baptist Hostel in Chiang Mai. Today there is a small church in one village on the plains but its influence is limited. Bouy Jee, the first Pwo Karen of the area to be baptized (1965), and his family have remained true to the Lord, but they have not been able to influence their fellow villagers to turn to Christ. Instead, folk Buddhism has gained the allegiance of the Pwo Karen who live on the Hod-Doi Taw plains. Buddhist temples in Pwo Karen villages on the plains are common today.

The movement to Christ began in the villages along the new road from Hot to Omkoi to Yang Piang in the eastern mountains of northern Pwo Karen land. We moved to Striped Creek Village, the gateway village to Pwo Karen in the eastern mountains in 1969 and lived there until 1979. A small people movement began in 1974 in villages along the road from Striped Creek in the north past Prosperity Fields village to Omkoi town in south and east to Yang Piang town—about sixty miles of road with lots of Pwo Karen villages in the area. During most of the 1980s we were in and out of Pwo Karen land. Two pairs of single lady missionaries helped develop the work. From 1974 to 1990 the work grew from about

200 believers to 1,000 Pwo believers in a dozen or so major villages. There were ups and downs, reversions and conversions. As the gospel took root in their thinking and bore fruit in their lives, the good news spread from Pwo to Pwo, from family to family, and from village to village. The second generation grew up with better educational opportunities and a greater understanding of the Bible. They have become leaders in the churches and have helped spread the movement in depth and breadth.

Other groups beside OMF have joined the work. In the Omkoi area there have been Full Gospel workers with connections to Thai and Chinese, and there are Koreans also. Their work has spread into the mountain Pwo villages to the west of Omkoi in what could be called the southern mountains. They have built on foundations which we had laid. Praise God for the growth of His church among the Pwo Karen throughout this area.

In the past twenty years New Tribes Mission has seen a significant movement to Christ in a group of villages located to the west of where OMF is concentrating their work. Further to the west the Baptists have been planting Pwo churches in the town of Mae Sariang and in many villages south of Mae Sariang town and toward Myanmar. Sop Lahn soon developed into a dynamic center for the spread of the gospel in a band of Sgaw Karen villages located in the mountains between Omkoi town and Tak in the south. I understand that there are churches in forty Sgaw Karen villages in this area of Sop Lahn influence.

I have been away too long and much has happened since I left to be able to give an accurate account of the present day church growth among the northern Pwo Karen but an obvious movement of God has occurred here in the past thirty years. Thirty years ago there were no churches, no Bible Schools and only Mrs. Dee and her four small children who had recently believed in Jesus. Today there are scores of churches, hundreds of families and thousands of believers. The New Testament is in northern Pwo language. There are two

Pwo Karen Bible Schools and several Christian hostels for Pwo and Sgaw children to attend Thai schools. There are many capable leaders. With the joys comes the care of the churches. There are victories, and there are problems but God is working to build His church among the northern Pwo Karen.

God used outside messengers, models and mentors to begin His church growing among the Pwo Karen (cf. 1 Cor. 3:5-8). It took time for the understanding, diffusion and acceptance of new ideas (the gospel). It took time for the outside messengers to learn the language, understand the culture and win the confidence of the people. It also took time for the Pwo Karen to hear and understand the implications of the gospel as well as to get to know and trust the outside messengers.

It was an inside person who was the real innovator to spark the movement. The outside messenger was only an advocate for change. True change was the result of insider acceptance of the new ideas. The dynamic for growth was Karen reaching Karen for Christ.

The new ideas (the gospel) were validated by cultural stories, values and expectations. For example, the Pwo had stories of a Creator-God who would one day return, and about a lost Book from God. They had a messianic hope of someday having a better life.

God often used power encounters to show His power over Satan and the spirits in healing the sick, protecting from calamities and taboos, delivering rice fields from evil forces and curses. The defining question: Who is Lord? Satan? Spirits? Jesus? Their prior question was not about forgiveness, but about power. Jesus is Lord. He is greater than Satan. He is greater than spirits. He is able to protect, heal, deliver, and help people in their time of need.

We constantly laid foundations by telling Bible stories over and over again and relating the message to the daily lives of the Pwo. And we wrote songs packed with Christian teaching. Pwo love to tell stories and they love to sing. This was something they could pass on even before they could read.

We tried to limit our methods to what a Pwo could reproduce. We did not want them to become dependent upon foreign resources or missionary presence. Their dependence should be upon God.

We prayed, got others to pray for us and the work, and kept up-to-date information flowing to prayer partners. By example and by precept, we tried to teach Pwo Christians to pray regularly, too.

We involved Pwo believers in the work immediately: witnessing to family and friends, telling Bible stories, singing the gospel, and praying for others. The church in one village reached out to start a new church in a neighboring village. The aim was an indigenous, biblical church planting movement. God made things grow. All the greatness and glory is His.

Determining the Needs of the Future

There are churches in many Pwo Karen villages in the Hot-Omkoi mountains. There are Thai schools in major villages, and there are Buddhist temples in a few villages. In the future the pressure upon the church will come from the influence of Buddhism from the outside and the danger of worldliness and materialism on the inside. Nominal Pwo Karen Buddhists have proved responsive in turning from the spirits and Buddhism to the Lord Jesus Christ. But what about the more devote Pwo Karen Buddhists? How do we reach those who are still resistant to the gospel?

When we went to the northern Pwo, there were no Buddhist temples and no Thai schools in any Pwo Karen village. The Pwo Karen who lived on the Hot-Doi Taw plains lived close to the Northern Thai and close to Thai Buddhist temples and Thai schools. In the process of assimilation to the Thai culture and nationality, the ethnic Pwo Karen have taken on more and more Buddhist thought, language, and culture. The making of merit was right in line with animistic practices of seeking to control the unseen world of spirits and reality, which deeply affected the quality of their lives in terms of sickness, agriculture and prosperity. They saw the Thai as a superior race with power, possessions, and prosperity. They saw Buddhism as a means to these riches. Over the years, this group of Pwo Karen in Thailand have proved very resistant to the Gospel.

While the Buddhist Pwo Karen of this area understand the language of the Christian Pwo Karen, they have shifted more and more from traditional Pwo Karen culture, beliefs and practices toward a greater assimilation to Thai folk Buddhism therefore they have not accepted the Christian message. They identify more with Thai folk Buddhists. What needs to be done in evangelizing Buddhist Pwo Karen is the material for another paper.

Appendix 1: A Pioneer Church Planting Cycle

12. PROLIFERATION

11. Perfecting — 1. Purpose

10. Planting — 2. Prayer

9. PERSUASION — 3. PRESENCE

8. Permeation — 4. Preparation

7. Penetration — 5. Planning

6. PRESENTATION

The cycle begins with a person, church or a mission called our God to reach an unreached people group (Matt. 24:14).

1. **Purpose** = Fulfilling the great commission (Acts 1:8; Matt. 28:18-20; Acts 2:38-47). This includes making disciples, baptizing, teaching and church planting to the ends of the earth.

2. **Prayer** = Worship and praise, listening to God to determine His will, looking to God for personal help, interceding for the people to be reached, and resisting the evil one, etc.

3. **PRESENCE** = Actually being physically present among the people to be reached.

4. **Preparation** = Learning the language and culture and making relationships with the people. This could also include pre-evangelism, doing surveys, prayer walks, etc.

5. **Planning** = Setting out a strategy to reach the people for Christ.

6. **PRESENTATION** = Sharing the Gospel in a non-confrontational way. It is relational friendship evangelism,

rather than preaching at people. At this stage you are not calling for a decision. You are sharing your personal faith and life. You are seeking to relate to families, networks or villages for Christ.

7. **Penetration** = A key inside person understands and accepts the Gospel and becomes the key to reaching the rest of the group. (See Peters, *Saturation Evangelism*).

8. **Permeation** = The insider shares with friends and relatives and advocates for turning to Christ.

9. **PERSUASION** = A family or a group decide to follow Christ.

10. **Planting** = Immediately worshipping God as a community = planting an embryonic fellowship of believers (a church).

11. **Perfecting** = the "discipling ministry" or teaching them to obey the Word of the Lord (Matt. 28:20 and Col. 1:28; 2:6). Train local leaders. Help believers to apply the principles of God's Word to their daily lives. They should be growing daily in the grace and knowledge of Jesus.

12. **PROLIFERATION** = Multiply. This is the reproduction stage of evangelism, mission and church planting. It is believers winning unbelievers and churches planting churches. It is saturation evangelism and church planting among their own people. In time they should reach beyond their own people in mission to unreached people groups.

Repeat the cycle over and over, reaching the unreached until Jesus comes (Matt 24:14).

11

Incarnational Approaches to the Japanese People using House Church Strategies

Mituso Fukuda

Introduction

In order to help catalyze house church multiplication in Japan by providing resources for and networking house church planters, I founded the RAC Network. Though the acronym remained the same, the name of the network was changed in April 2002, from the Research Association for Contextualization to the Rethinking Authentic Christianity Network in order to reflect a new focus. Prior to 2002 our main activities were publishing missiological periodicals. Our vision was to see a contextualized Japanese Christianity.

The major reason why we changed directions stemmed from a strong desire to see New Testament Christianity actualized in Japan. It was discouraging and exhausting to see such little fruit come out of our publications, lectures and conferences. We realized that churches where direct access to God is encouraged and that have a flat and personal relationship structure, rather than hierarchical structures, reflect the lives of people most contextually.

I will try to describe how we changed our focus from just doing research to actually being in the field where we coach house church planters.

Contextualization and the Emergence of "Japanese Christianity"

When I was baptized about 25 years ago, I asked some long-time believers what percentage of the Japanese population was Christian. Their answer was that there was less than one percent. Today, I have to say that the real rate is far below one percent. Itami City, where I live, has a population of 190,000 with eight churches, including a Catholic church. Only 500 people participate in a Sunday worship service at least a couple of times a month—a rate of only 0.26 percent. Unfortunately this seems to be the average for all of Japan.

In the late 1980s, I came to realize that one of the major reasons for this stagnation was a lack of contextualization. The apostle Paul said, "Though I am free and belong to no man, I make myself a slave to everyone, to win as many as possible. To the Jews I became like a Jew, to win the Jews. To those under the law I became like one under the law (though I myself am not under the law), so as to win those under the law. To those not having the law I became like one not having the law (though I am not free from God's law but am under Christ's law), so as to win those not having the law." (1 Cor. 9:19-21) My evaluation is that Japanese churches have largely failed to become Japanese in order to win the Japanese.

Yasuo Furuya, a Japanese theologian, wrote that the "head" of the Japanese church is like a German-established church equipped by profound theologies without evangelism and contribution for the church fund; the "hands and legs" are that of American denominationalism whose system is highly democratic; but the "heart" is full of Japanese codependency (1995:38). The Japanese church is like a ghetto of intellectual elites who enjoy theological discussions and a clubby atmosphere but are not earnest in communicating God's love to their neighbors.

In the history of Japanese churches, church forms have continually been transported from Europe, the US and Canada and recently from Korea and other countries as well. They have at once been uncritically adopted and then abandoned when new success stories from other countries are introduced. For example, cell church strategies of a mega-church in Korea have been imitated by many churches in various denominations in Japan. Numerous copies of manuals on how to form regional small groups have been published. However, few churches have been successful, and no church has become like the church in Korea.

This "copy machine syndrome" has brought continual disaster to the Japanese churches. Six sure ways to destroy a church are: (1) Imitate the ways of a successful pastor. (2) Use his method of evangelism and pastoral ministry. (3) Teach the other pastor's experience as a principle or dogma. (4) Announce that this is the only way. (5) Communicate that other ways are sinful. (6) Oppose those who don't employ the "correct" way.

As Harvie Conn described, Christianity in Japan (as well as other Asian countries) has largely been a "potted plant" (1984:246). It was transported to Japan without really being transplanted. Therefore, my concern used to be the transplantation, or "critical contextualization" (Hiebert 1984:75-94) of employing Japanese cultural forms in Christian communication. I tried to find the essence of Christianity in the Western churches and then leave behind the Western cultural soils as much as possible and adopt only the essence and dress it with the Japanese cultural forms (Fukuda 1992).

However, recently I started to think about a fresh incarnation. If we could allow Christianity to emerge in Japanese soil without even considering the counterpart in foreign Christianity, it might be better. Both transportation and transplantation are based on the idea of the translation of a model whose starting point is, in the first place, a foreign idea, and which must then be interpreted and then introduced into the native soil. But a fresh incarnation emerges in the soil of a culture where the seed of God's words sprout.

The seed has already been planted in Japan. We have millions of translated Bibles and at least 200,000 committed witnesses as well as churches, mission schools, Christian hospitals, and church related publications. Our focus has to be on how to allow the Spirit of God to grow the seed. In my opinion, the house church is the ideal setting where God incarnates His heart in His church.

The House Church

As Banks stated, "Not until the third century do we have evidence of special buildings being constructed for Christian gatherings." (1994:41). Church historians estimate that the number of members of New Testament house churches rarely reached more than 15 or 20 people. This is why Simson suggests that there is a '20-person barrier" to overcome. He explains, "In many cultures 20 is a maximum number where people still feel 'family', organic and informal, without the need to get formal or organized" (2001:17).

The average size of the Sunday worship attendance in Japan is 34-35 people (Church Information Service, 1997). Many Japanese Christians think that their churches are too small and look to mega churches oversees as models. But our model as well as more important principles should be drawn from the New Testament. In reality, the problem of most churches in Japan is not that they are too small, but that they are already too big. As a result, Japanese churches have lost their attractiveness. They are not spontaneous or lively, but like a boring classroom, they are mostly irrelevant to the reality of peoples' lives (see Yamamori 1974).

If the church is small enough to maintain the dynamics of a family of God whose headship is Christ, the Holy Spirit will lead the members to apply the essence of Christian truth appropriately to the cultural environment of each house church. There should be no need to introduce structures in other places nor any need for a central administrative authority to make uniform the diversity of the churches (see Allen, 1992: 131).

Dean S. Gilliland believes that this contextual aspect is part of the reason Paul's churches survived under immense pressure, growing in each place and multiplying among the unevangelized. Gilliland stated, "Christianity was vibrant and alive because each local church found its own expression of the Christian life while at the same time it was joined in faith and truth to all other congregations that were also under Christ's lordship" (1983:209). It is easy to imagine that in these scattered small churches people would have shared their similar lives, related naturally with each other, and met the special needs emerging from the common socio-cultural context.

A house church seems to have several advantages in terms of contextualization. One advantage is that while the context of the traditional church exists in the relatively artificial environment of the so-called three "sacred Ps": sacred programs run by sacred people in a sacred place, the house church emerges and is centered in the context of daily life. The second advantage is that it is small enough to be flexible to adapt to its local culture. The third advantage is that it has a flat leadership structure, where the various cultural forms can be employed easily through open discussion. The expansion of the house church movement would likely reveal various contextualized church forms in Japan.

Examples of the Emergence of "Japanese Christianity"

We are finding that simple structures like participatory Bible studies where the Bible itself is the teacher, and everyone in the group is involved in the teaching/learning process as well as the application of what is being learned to daily life are effective ways to touch the hearts of Japanese people (2002:111-113).

For example, one day seven young people gathered in my house and joined a participatory Bible study. I was not there to teach, but just to observe. They chose a passage from Romans 6. I thought that it would be too difficult of a section for them as it included the concepts of baptism, dying and being resurrected with Christ. Several verses were read and a college student, who was functioning as a facilitator, asked what the "new man" and "old man" meant.

After some quiet time, one young man remembered a fight that he and two of his friends had had that afternoon. They were also there with him at the Bible study that night. After the quarrel, one had angrily said to the others, "Leave me alone. Stay away from me!" Some time later, both of them reconciled and were able to say each other, "Let's be good friends from now on."

The young man applied his experience to interpret the Bible verses and explained, "The 'old man' is like a person who says to Jesus, 'Stay away from me!' and the 'new man' is like a person who says to Jesus, 'Let's be good friends from now on.'" When the other young people heard his explanation, all of them understood the Bible verses and connected the meaning with their own spiritual journey. What an amazing interpretation! If I had explained those verses, I could have quoted profound theological statements about all of those subjects, but I wouldn't have impacted their lives in that way.

Let the Bible itself teach people! The young-man was used by God as an intermediator of God's truth using his own thoughts and terminology. Today in Japan, it is not the interpretation of a famous Bible scholar from the West that is needed, but a divine intervention of the Holy Spirit moving in the hearts and minds of people. "God chose the foolish things of the world to shame the wise" (1 Cor. 1:27).

The heroine of another story is an older lady. She had been coming to a house church meeting for a long time; however, my evaluation at that time was that she did not really want to have a life-changing experience. She grumbled continually at our meetings, "I could not do that even if Jesus told me to do that," or "I don't believe in the ideas of the Bible, because in my real miserable situation, I could not pursue such an ideal." Her negative statements sometimes seemed to have a serious impact on new comers.

Several months after we started using a participatory Bible study in the meeting, she made a comment on the Scripture verses, "Jesus said, "For judgment I have come into this world, so that the blind will see and those who see will become blind" (John 9: 39). She said, "This passage describes my situation. I was blind and I was a sinner. Now I understand that I could not see the truth anymore, even though I insisted that I could see. My sin was that I claimed I could see." When my wife and I heard her comment, we wept. It was not the fruit of a good sermon, but the work of the Holy Spirit in a small interactive setting that helped her to realize her sin.

The effectiveness of good preaching is often limited by the giftedness of a teacher. When a preacher is speaking and everyone is listening, even if the preaching itself is impressive, the listeners become a passive audience who want to be entertained more. Only a gifted preacher can continually satisfy an audience with new knowledge and breathtaking illustrations. Maybe he will establish a huge cathedral and a large following, but when he leaves, the people will most likely be scattered like sheep without a shepherd.

To ensure the contextuality of a church, it is necessary to allow people direct access to God through Jesus Christ. No one should be between God and His people except One mediator, the man Christ (1 Timothy 2:5). Ordinary people can hear God's voice and do the extraordinary work of God without the hierarchical administrative system of men. God will give contextualized answers to the questions that His people are asking from their real-life settings.

One more example of the emergence of "Japanese Christianity" is a new way of evangelism that we are seeing in Japan. One of the "hot" targets for evangelism in Japan is nurses. Three interesting characteristics of this group are: (1) They want to be healed. The work of a nurse is often like being a slave to the sick. People needing medical care surround them. Due to the stress of their hard work, they are tired and need to be healed. (2) They are involved in the New Age movement. They know the limitations of medical science. Some of them care for those who are dying and/or suffer from hopeless conditions. They tend to search in the spiritual world for answers to questions about man's finite existence. Although it is extremely expensive to participate in New Age exercises and various programs, their relatively high incomes allow them to afford it. (3) They give serious thought to the well-being of life. They are scientific people and are good at analyzing their psychological problems. But they have not been able to find the answers to the questions that are pressing in their lives. They are seriously seeking hope, purpose, happiness, and acceptance.

Recently, a nurse was led to accept Jesus into her life through a student of mine, who is herself a nurse. The process of her conversion was very different from what we see traditionally. This lady was a New Age practitioner who had even thought about studying abroad to become a New Age leader. My student led her to visualize her past experiences. Because she was familiar with visualization from New Age practice, she was very good at it. She saw herself and her ex-boyfriend in her imagination. Although he had once made her mad and had wounded her, strangely enough, she saw herself hugging him, and they were weeping together. She did not understand why she did such a thing. After awhile, she understood the whole picture. Jesus approached them and then hugged both of them with his warm hands.

When this lady saw Jesus in her imagination, He was bathed in tender light and she understood supernaturally that He would never leave her or abandon her. For her, conversion and healing came at the same time. The experience was so real that she cannot stop testifying about it to her friends. Just three days after her baptism, she shared her experience with a friend who had once been a partner in reading tarots. She led her friend to experience Jesus and the same thing happened in her friend's life. They began meeting weekly for prayer and accountability, and after three months they started a church in one of their homes where they used to read tarots. They have experienced God directly and are bold enough to share their experiences with other nurses, some of whom have already accepted Christ.

This new type of evangelism for nurses was not developed by clergies or missiologists. It did not happen in a big conference room or in a fancy cathedral with stained glass. It emerged in a family-like small group of Christians who had a passion for communicating Christ's love to their friends.

Conclusion

How can we release the biotic growing potential that God has given us? Some spiritualistic thinkers insist that we should throw away all institutional structures. However, for the healthy multiplication of churches, some simple and reproducible structures like participatory Bible studies and other house church strategies are needed. These structures should not be complicated and administrative, but simple, organic, family-like, relational and spontaneous, where ordinary people have direct access to God.

In these structures the most contextualized forms of Christianity can be developed. Although house church multiplication has not yet taken place in Japan, some cutting-edge experiments are being conducted, and hopefully, in the near future, a new breed of churches will emerge in the real-life settings of life in Japan.

References

1. Christian Opportunities in the Changing Demographic Context of Global Buddhism

Barrett, D. B., and T. M. Johnson. *World Christian Trends, AD 30–AD 2200*. Pasadena: William Carey Library, 2001.

________. "Annual Statistical Table on Global Mission: 2004." *International Bulletin of Missionary Research* 28, no.1 (January 2004): 24-25.

Barrett, D. B., G. T. Kurian, and T. M. Johnson. *World Christian Encyclopedia.* 2 vols. 2nd ed. New York: Oxford University Press, 2001.

Baumman, Martin. "Global Buddhism: Development Periods, Regional Histories, and a New Analytical Perspective." *Journal of Global Buddhism* 2 (2001): 1ff. www.globalbuddhism.org.

Lai, Whalen, and Michael von Bruck. *Christianity and Buddhism: A Multi-Cultural History of their Dialogue.* Maryknoll: Orbis, 2001.

Obeyesekere, Gananath. "Buddhism." *Global Religions.* Edited by Mark Juergensmeyer. New York: Oxford University Press, 2003, 63-77.

Walls, A. *The Missionary Movement in Christian History: Studies in the Transmission of Faith.* Maryknoll: Orbis, 1996.

W*orld Christian Database.* www.worldchristiandatabase.org. Accessed Nov. 2003.

2. Christian Mission in the Context of Buddhist Mission

Hiebert, Paul. "The Flaw of the Excluded Middle." *Missiology* 10, no.1 (January 1982): 35-47.

Lai, Whalen. "Limits and Failure of Ko-I (Concept Matching) Buddhism." *History of Religions* 18 (1979): 238.

Seamands, John T. *Tell it Well: Communicating the Gospel Across Cultures.* Kansas City, MO: Beacon Hill Press, 1981.

Turner, Victor. *The Ritual Process: Structure and Anti-Structure.* Chicago: Aldine, 1969.

Wilson, Bryan R. *A Time to Chant: The Soka Gakkai Buddhists in Britain.* Oxford: Oxford University Press, 1998.

Zahniser, A. H. Mathias. "Ritual Process and Christian Discipling: Contextualizing a Buddhist Rite of Passage." *Missiology* 19, no.1 (January 1991): 3-19.

_________. *Symbol and Ceremony: Making Disciples Across Cultures.* Monrovia: MARC, 1997.

3. Difficulties and Devices in Depicting the Deity of Christ to the Theravada Buddhist Mind

Abayasundara, Pranit Nisada. *Bauddha Samaja Palanaya Ha Aparadha Vidyava.* Kandy: As. Godage saha Sahodarayo, 1993.

Amunugama, Sarath. *Anagarika Dharmapala (1864-1933) and the Transformation of Sinhala Buddhist Organization in a Colonial Setting.* Kandy: Social Science Information 24/4, 1985.

Arasaratnam, Sinnappah. "The Dutch East India Company and Its Coromandel Trade 1700-1740." In *European Commercial Expansion in Early Modern Asia.* Edited by Om Prakash. New Delhi: Variorum, 1997.

Clough, B. "Missionary Letter. 27 September 1814." In *English Literature in Ceylon, 1815-1878.* Edited by Yasmine Gooneratne. Dehiwala, Sri Lanka: Tisara Prakasakavo, 1968.

de Silva, Chandra R. *Sri Lanka: A History.* New Delhi: Vikas Publishing House, 1987.

de Silva, Colvin R. *Ceylon Under the British Occupation, 1795-1833.* Vol. I. New Delhi: Colombo Apothecaries' Co., 1941.

de Silva, K. M. *A History of Sri Lanka.* New Delhi: Oxford University Press, 1981.

De Silva, Lynn A. *Emergent Theology in the Context of Buddhism.* Colombo: Ecumenical Institute for Study and Dialogue, 1979.

_____________. "Good News of Salvation to the Buddhists." *International Review of Mission* 57, no. 10 (1968): 448-458.

____________. *Why Can't I Save Myself? The Christian Answer in Relation to Buddhist Thought.* Colombo: Christian Study Centre, 1967.

Dharmasiri, Gunapala. *A Buddhist Critique of the Christian Concept of God.* Antioch, CA: Golden Leaves, 1988.

Dunn, J. D. G. *The Acts of the Apostles*. London: Epworth Commentaries, 1996.

Du Pre, Gerald. *Buddhism and Science*. Delhi: Motilal Banarsidass, 1984.

Geiger, William, and Mabel Richmers. *Culavamsa, Being the More Recent Part of Mahavamsa*. New Delhi: Asian Educational Services, 1998.

Gogerly, Daniel J. *The Evidences and Doctrines of the Christian Religion*, 1885.

____________. "Missionary Letter, 3 October 1831." London: SOAS Library Archives.

Gombrich, Richard. "The Consecration of a Buddhist Image." *Journal of Asian Studies* 26 (1966): 23-36.

Gombrich, Richard, and Gananath Obeyesekere. *Buddhism Transformed: Religious Change in Sri Lanka*. Princeton: Princeton University Press, 1988.

Gruber, E. R., and H. Kersten. *The Original Jesus: The Buddhist Sources of Christianity*. Dorset: Element Books, 1995.

Guruge, Ananda, ed. *Return to Righteousness: A Collection of Speeches, Essays and Letters of the Anagarika Dharmapala*. Colombo: Ministry of Educational and Cultural Affairs, 1965.

Hardy, Robert Spence. "The British Government and the Idolatry of Ceylon." *European Quarterly Journal* 12 (1841).

____________. *Commerce and Christianity: Memorials of Jonas Sugden of Oakworth House*. London: T. Constable, 1858.

____________. *Eastern Monachism*. London: Williams and Norgate, 1860.

____________. *Jubilee Memorials of the Wesleyan Mission*. Colombo: Wesleyan Mission, 1864.

___________. *The Legends and Theories of the Buddhists, Compared with History and Science*. New Delhi: AES, 1993.

Harvard, W. M. *A Narrative of the Establishment and Progress of the Mission to Ceylon and India*. London: 1823.

Ilangasinha, H. B. M. *Buddhism in Medieval Sri Lanka*. Delhi: Satguru, 1992.

Jayatilleke, K. N. *Buddhism and Science*. Kandy: Buddhist Publication Society, 1966.

Jayawardena, Kumari. *Nobodies to Somebodies*. New Delhi: LeftWord, 2001.

Karunaratna, Dabliv Saddhamangala. *Buddhism: Its Religion and Philosophy*. Kandy: Buddhist Research Society, 1988.

Kersten, H. *Jesus Lived in India*. Dorset: Element Books, 1994.

Kirthisinghe, B. P. *Buddhism and Science*. New Delhi: Motilal Banarsidass Publishers, 2004.

Knox, R. *An Historical Relation of Ceylon*. London: Royal Society, 1681.

Larkin, W. J. *Acts* (NTC). Downers Grove: IVP, 1995.

Lefebure, Leo D. *The Buddha & The Christ: Explorations in Buddhist and Christian Dialogue.* Maryknoll: Orbis Books, 1993.

Malalasekera, G. P. *The Pali Literature of Ceylon*. Kandy: Buddhist Publication Society, 1995.

Malalgoda, Kitsiri. *Buddhism in Sinhalese Society, 1750-1900: A Study of Religious Revival and Change*. Berkeley: University of California Press, 1976.

Marasinghe, M. M. J. *Gods in Early Buddhism*. Kelaniya: University of Sri Lanka, Vidyalankara Campus, 1974.

Mendis, G. C. *The Early History of Ceylon: And Its Relations with India and Other Foreign Countries*. New Delhi: Asian Educational Services, 1998.

Notovich, Nicolas. *The Unknown Life of Jesus: The Original Text of Nicolas Notovich's 1887 Discovery*. Sanger, CA: Quill Driver Books, 2004.

Paranavitana, S. "Pre-Buddhist Religious Beliefs in Ceylon." *Journal of the Royal Asiatic Society (Ceylon Branch),* XXXI, no. 82 (1929): 302-327.

Peiris, Lakshman. *Buddhism, Christianity and Sri Lanka.* <www.upali.lk/island/wed/mdwkrvw1.htm >.

Percival, R. *An Account of the Island of Ceylon*. Dehiwala, Sri Lanka: Tisara Prakasakayo, 1975.

Perera, H. R. *Buddhism in Sri Lanka: A Short History*. Kandy: Buddhist Publication Society, 1988.

Phadnis, Urmila. *Religion and Politics in Sri Lanka*. New Delhi: Manohar, 1976.

Rahula, Walpola. *The Heritage of the Bhikkhu: The Buddhist Tradition of Service*. New York: Grove Press, 1974.

Rahula, Walpola. *What the Buddha Taught*. New York: Grove Press, 1959.

Small, W. J. T., ed. *A History of the Methodist Church in Ceylon 1814-1964*. Colombo: Wesley Press, 1964.

Schumann, Hans Wolfgang. *Buddhism: An Outline of its Teachings and Schools*. Wheaton: The Theosophical Publishing House, 1973.

Spencer, Jonathan. *Sri Lanka: History and the Roots of Conflict*. Oxford: Routledge, 1990.

Tambiah, Stanley Jeyaraja. *Buddhism Betrayed? Religion, Politics, and Violence in Sri Lanka*. Chicago: University of Chicago Press, 1992.

Tennent, J. E. *Christianity in Ceylon*. New Delhi: Asian Educational Services, 1998.

Tract Society Annual Report. London: Baptist Missionary Society, 1833.

Weerasingha, Tissa. *The Cross and the Bo Tree: Communicating the Gospel to Buddhists*. Taichung, Taiwan: Asia Theological Association, 1989.

Wessels, Antonie. *Images of Jesus: How Jesus Is Perceived and Portrayed in Non-European Cultures*. Grand Rapids: Eerdmans, 1990.

Wijebandara, C. *Early Buddhism: Its Religious and Intellectual Milieu*. Kelaniya, Sri Lanka: Postgraduate Institute of Pali and Buddhist Studies, University of Kelaniya, 1993.

Williams, Harry. *Ceylon: Pearl of the East*. London: Robert Hale Ltd., 1951.

Wright, C. *The Uniqueness of Jesus*. London: Monarch Books, 1997.

Young, Richard Fox, and G. P. V. Somaratna. *Vain Debates. The Buddhist-Christian Controversies of Nineteenth-Century Ceylon*. Vienna: Publications of the De Nobili Research Library, 1996.

4. Gentle Strength and *Upāya*: Christian and Buddhist Ministry Models

Bowers, Russell H., Jr. *Someone or Nothing? Nishitani's* Religion and Nothingness *as a Foundation for Christian-Buddhist Dialogue*. New York: Peter Lang, 1995.

_______. "The Value of and Limits to Dialogue." *Sharing Jesus Holistically With the Buddhist World.* Edited by David Lim and Steve Spaulding. Pasadena: William Carey Library, 2005.

Carson, D. A. "Matthew." *The Expositor's Bible Commentary.* Edited by Frank E. Gæbelein. CD ROM ed. Grand Rapids: Zondervan, n.d.

_______. *The Gagging of God: Christianity Confronts Pluralism.* Grand Rapids: Zondervan, 1996.

Chin, Gail. "The Gender of Buddhist Truth: The Female Corpse in a Group of Japanese Paintings." *Japanese Journal of Religious Studies* 25 (1998).

"Death Rituals: Mistruth as a Positive Element of Upaya." https://www1.Columbia.edu/sec/bboard/003/reli2607-001/msg00189.html. Accessed 20 October 2003.

Fisher, Roger, William Ury, and Bruce Patton. *Getting to Yes: Negotiating Agreement Without Giving In*. 2nd ed. Boston: Houghton Mifflin, 1991.

Küng, Hanz. "A Christian Response." In *Christianity and the World Religions: Paths to Dialogue with Islam, Hinduism, and Buddhism.* Edited by Hans Küng, Josef van Ess, Heinrich von Stietencron, and Heinz Bechert. Garden City, NY: Doubleday, 1986.

Lai, Whalen, and Michael von Brück. *Christianity and Buddhism: A Multicultural History of Their Dialogue*. Phyllis Jestice, trans. Maryknoll: Orbis, 2001.

Lewis, C. S. *The Pilgrim's Regress: An Allegorical Apology for Christianity Reason and Romanticism.* Grand Rapids: Eerdmans, 1943.

Louw, Johannes P., and Eugene A. Nida, eds., *Greek-English Lexicon of the New Testament based on Semantic Domains. Bible Windows 6.0.* Cedar Hill, TX: Silver Mountain Software, 2001. S.v. makroqumi/a, aj *f* patience 25:167.

McGrath, Alister E. *Intellectuals Don't Need God & Other Modern Myths: Building Bridges to Faith through Apologetics.* Grand Rapids: Zondervan, 1993.

Matsunaga, Daigan and Alicia. "The Concept of Upāya in Mahāyāna Buddhist Philosophy." *Japanese Journal of Religious Studies* 1 (March 1974).

Rahula, W. "Bodhisattva Ideal in Buddhism." http://www.Saigon.com/~anson/ebud/ebdha126.htm. Accessed 1 November 2003.

Smart, Ninian. *Religion and the Western Mind.* Albany: State University of New York Press, 1987.

Stone, Jacqueline. "Medieval Tendai *Hongaku* Thought and the New Kamakura Buddhism: A Reconsideration." *Japanese Journal of Religious Studies* 22 (1995).

"The Lotus Sutra." Burton Watson, trans. (http://www.sgi-usa.org/Buddhism/library/Buddhism/LotusSutra/text/Chap02.htm. Accessed 16 October 2003.

Wilson, Liz. *Charming Cadavers: Horrific Figurations of the Feminine in Indian Hagiographic Literature.* Chicago: University of Chicago Press, 1996.

5. Meekness: A New Approach to Christian Witness to the Thai People

Ayal, Eliezer B. "Value Systems and Economic Development in Japan and Thailand." *Journal of Social Issues* 19 (1963): 35-51.

Barrett, David B., ed. *World Christian Encyclopedia*. New York: Oxford University Press, 1981.

Bavinck, J. H. *An Introduction to the Science of Missions*. Philadelphia: The Presbyterian and Reformed Publishing Co., 1960.

Brown, Collin, ed. *The New International Dictionary of New Testament Theology*, Grand Rapids: Regency Reference Library, 1986.

Davis, John D. *A Dictionary of the Bible*. Grand Rapids: Baker, 1954.

Dodd, C. H. *Dynamics of Intercultural Communications*. Madison, WI: Brown & Benchmark, 1995.

Fieg, John Paul. *A Common Core: Thais and Americans*. Yarmouth, ME: Intercultural Press, 1989.

Holmes, H. and S. Tangtongtavy. *Working With the Thais*. Bangkok: White Lotus, 1995.

Hsu, Francis L. K. *American and Chinese: Passage to Differences*. Honolulu: University of Hawaii Press, 1981.

Hughes, Philip H. *Proclamation and Response*. Bangkok: Payap University Archives, 1989.

Jeng, Timothy. "Strategizing Leadership Training." D. Miss. dissertation, Fuller Theological Seminary, Pasadena, 1981.

Kane, Herbert J. *A Concise History of the Christian World Mission.* Grand Rapids: Baker, 1978.

Kim, Samuel. "The Unfinished Mission in Thailand." Unpublished D. Miss. dissertation, Fuller Theological Seminary, Pasadena, 1974.

Komin, Suntaree. *The Psychology of the Thai People: Values and Behavioral Patterns*. Bangkok: National Institute of Development Administration, 1991.

Koyama, Kosuke. *The National Consultation on Theological Education.* Calcutta: Baptist Mission Press, 1968.

Latourette, Kenneth Scott. *A History of the Expansion of Christianity. Vol. 6.* New York: Harper, 1944.

Lausanne Committee for World Evangelization (LCWE). *Christian Witness to Buddhists.* London: Whitefield, 1978.

Neill, Stephen. *A History of Christian Missions*. 2nd ed. London: Penguin, 1989.

Nida, Eugene. *Message and Mission: The Communication of Christian Faith*. Pasadena: William Carey Library, 1990.

Seamands, J. T. *Tell It Well: Communicating the Gospel Across Cultures*. Kansas City, MO: Beacon Hill Press, 1981.

Stewart, Edward C., and Milton J. Bennett. *American Cultural Patterns: A Cross Cultural Perspective.* Yarmouth, ME: Intercultural Press, 1989, 1991.

Stott, John R. "Twenty Years After Lausanne: Some Personal Reflections." *International Bulletin of Missionary Research* 19, no. 4 (1995): 50-55.

Supap, Suprata. *Thai Society and Culture*. Bangkok: Thai Wattanapanich, 1994.

Tenney, Merrill C., ed. *Bible Dictionary*. Grand Rapids: Zondervan, 1963.

Webster, Merriam. *Webster's New International Dictionary of the English Language*. Springfield, MA: G & C. Merriam, 1957.

Wells, K. E. *History of Protestant Work in Thailand*. Bangkok: Church of Christ in Thailand, 1957.

Zahniser, A. H. Mathias. "Close Encounters of the Vulnerable Kind: Christian Dialogical Proclamation Among Muslims." *The Asbury Theological Journal* 49, no. 1 (1994).

6. Where are Your Temples? Do Christianity and Buddhism Share a Temple Ethos?

Borg, Marcus, and N. T. Wright. *The Meaning of Jesus: Two Visions.* San Francisco: HarperCollins, 1999.

Brueggemann, Walter. "Rethinking Church Models through Scripture." Paper at the Council of Conference Ministers of United Church of Christ, n.d.

Earhart, H. Byon, ed. *Religious Traditions of the World*. New York: HarperCollins, 1993.

Filbeck, David. *Yes, God of the Gentiles, Too*. Wheaton: Billy Graham Center, Wheaton College, 1994.

Gellner, David N. *The Anthropology of Buddhism & Hinduism: Weberian Themes*. New Delhi: Oxford University Press, 2001.

Lester, Robert. *Theravada Buddhism in Southeast Asia.* Ann Arbor: University of Michigan Press, 1973.

Roetzel, Calvin J. *The World that Shaped the New Testament.* Louisville, KY: Westminster/John Knox Press, 2002.

Sharma, Arvind, ed. *Our Religions*. New York: HarperCollins, 1993.

Snyder, Howard. *The Community of the King.* Downers Grove: IVP, 1977.

Stott, John. *The Message of Acts: the Spirit, the Church and the World.* Downers Grove: IVP, 1990.

Tannenbaum, Nicola. *Who Can Compete Against the World? Power-Protection and Buddhism in Shan Worldview.* Ann Arbor: The Association for Asian Studies, 1995.

Walls, Andrew. *The Missionary Movement in Christian History: Studies in Transmission of Faith.* Maryknoll: Orbis, 1996.

Watt, Eric. *Church Planting Movement.* No publisher data, 2002.

Wink, Walter. *Engaging the Powers: Discernment and Resistance in a World of Domination.* Minneapolis: Augsburg/Fortress, 1992.

Wright, N. T. *Jesus and the Victory of God.* Minneapolis: Fortress, 1996.

______. *The Challenge of Jesus: Rediscovering Who Jesus Was and Is.* Downers Grove: IVP, 1999.

7. Islands in the Sky: Tibetan Buddhism and the Gospel

Adler, Mortimer J. *Truth in Religion: The Plurality of Religions and the Unity of Truth.* New York: Macmillan, 1990.

Covell, Ralph. "Buddhism and the Gospel Among the Peoples of China." *International Journal of Frontier Missions* 10, no. 3 (July 1993).

Drolma, Dawa. *Delog: Journey to the Realms Beyond Death.* Junction City, CA: Padma Publishing, 1995.

Goldstein, Melvyn. *A History of Modern Tibet.* Los Angeles: University of California Press, 1989.

Newland, Guy. *The Two Truths.* Ithaca, NY: Snow Lion, 1992.

Ortner, Sherry. *Sherpas Through Their Rituals*. Cambridge: University Press, 1978.

Sarangerel. *Riding Windhorses: A Journey into the Heart of Mongolian Shamanism*. Rochester, VT: Destiny Books, 2000.

Snellgrove, David, and Hugh Richardson. *A Cultural History of Tibet.* Boulder, CO: Prajna Press, 1980.

Tibet Museum. *Tibet Museum*. Beijing: Encyclopedia of China Publishing House, 2001.

Waddell, L. Austine. *Lhasa and Its Mysteries.* New York: Dover 1988.

Wessels, C. *Early Jesuit Travelers in Central Asia.* Delhi: Book Faith India, 1998.

8: Structural and Ministry Philosophy Issues in Church Planting among Buddhist Peoples

Arn, Charles, Donald McGavran, and Win Arn. *Growth: A New Vision for the Sunday School*. Pasadena: Church Growth Press, 1980.

Berger, Peter L., and Thomas Luckmann. *The Social Construction of Reality: A Treatise in the Sociology of Knowledge*. New York: Anchor, 1966.

Davis, John R. *Poles Apart: Contextualizing the Gospel in Asia.* Rev. ed. Bangalore: Theological Book Trust, 1998.

George, Carl F. *Prepare Your Church for the Future*. Grand Rapids: Fleming H. Revell, 1991.

Hybels, Bill, and Mark Mittelberg. *Becoming a Contagious Christian*. Grand Rapids: Zondervan, 1994.

Johnson, Alan R. "The Power of the Oikos." *Enrichment* 7, no. 1 (2002): 86-89.

________. *Wrapping the Good News for the Thai*. Unpublished manuscript, 2002.

________. "A Contextualized Presentation of the Gospel in Thai Society." In *Sharing Jesus Holistically with the Buddhist World.* Edited by David Lim and Steve Spaulding. Pasadena: William Carey Library, 2005.

Kinsler, F. Ross, ed. *Ministry by the People: Theological Education by Extension*. Maryknoll: Orbis Books, 1983.

McGavran, Donald. *Understanding Church Growth*. Grand Rapids: Eerdmans, 1970.

McKinney, Lois. "Leadership: Key to the Growth of the Church." In *Discipling through Theological Education*. Edited by Vergil Gerber. Chicago: Moody Press, 1980.

Richards, Lawrence O., and Martin Gib. *A Theology of Personal Ministry: Spiritual Giftedness in the Local Church*. Grand Rapids: Zondervan, 1981.

Richards, Lawrence O., and Clyde Hoeldtke. *Church Leadership: Following the Example of Jesus Christ*. Grand Rapids: Zondervan, 1980.

Schaller, Lyle. *Activating the Passive Church: Diagnosis and Treatment.* Nashville: Abingdon, 1981.

Tillapaugh, Frank R. *The Church Unleashed.* Ventura: Regal Books, 1982.

Ware, Anthony. "Analysis and Development of a Church Structure to Facilitate Saturation Church Planting in Bangkok." M.A., Asia Pacific Theological Seminary, 2002.

9. People Movements in Thailand

American Baptist Missionary Union (ABFMS). *Along Kingdom Pathways* (1814-1940); *Along Kingdom Highways* (1941-1966). Annual Reports. Boston: American Baptist Missionary Union, 1814-1966.

Anderson, Courtney. *To the Golden Shore: The Life of Adoniram Judson.* Boston: Little, Brown & Co., 1956.

Backus, Mary, ed. *Siam and Laos as seen by our American Missionaries.* Philadelphia: Presbyterian Board of Publication, Wescott & Thomson, 1884.

Bainbridge, William F. *Along the Lines at the Front: A General Survey of Baptist Home and Foreign Mission.* Philadelphia: American Baptist Publication Society, 1882.

Bassett, Alan. Interview by author. Duarte, CA: Feb. 7, 1976.

Beach, Harlan P., and Burton St. John. *World Statistics of Christian Missions.* New York: The Committee of Reference and Counsel of the Foreign Missions Conference of North America, 1916.

Beach, Harlan P., and Charles H. Fahs, eds. *World Missionary Atlas.* New York: Institute of Social and Religious Research, 1925.

Board of Foreign Missions. "Annual Reports of the Board of Foreign Missions." In *Reports of the Missionary and Benevolent Boards and Committees to the General Assembly of the Presbyterian Church in the United Sates of America.* Philadelphia: Office of the General Assembly, 1870-1957.

Blanford, Carl E. *Chinese Churches in Thailand.* Bangkok: Suriyaban, 1975.

Bliss, Edwin Munsell, ed. *The Encyclopedia of Missions, Vol. II*. New York: Funk & Wagnalls, 1891.

Brain, Belle M. "Ko Thah Byu, The Karen Apostle." *Missionary Review of the World* (May 1910): 364-374.

Chailangkarn, Muak. Interview by author. Chiang Mai: May 3, 1977.

Dennis, James S., Harlan P. Beach, and Charles H. Fahs , eds. *World Atlas of Christian Missions*. New York: S.V.M. for Foreign Missions, 1911.

Eakin, John L. "Siam." In *Interpretive Statistical Survey of the World Missions of the Christian Church*. Edited by Joseph Parker. New York: International Missionary Council, 1938.

Gammell, William. *A History of American Baptist Missions in Asia, Africa, Europe and North America*. Boston: Gould, Kendall and Lincoln, 1849.

Gutzlaff, Charles. *Journal of Three Voyages Along the Coast of China in 1831,1832 and 1833 with Notices of Siam, Korea, and the Loo Choo Islands.* 3rd ed. London: Thomas Ward & Company, n.d.

Hervey, G. Winfred. *The Story of Baptist Missions in Foreign Lands from the Time of Carey to the Present Date*. St. Louis: C. R. Barns, 1892.

Hovemyr, Maria. *A Bruised Reed Shall He Not Break...A History of the 16th District of the Church of Christ in Thailand*. Chiang Mai: Office of History Church of Christ in Thailand, 1997.

Johnstone, Patrick, and Jason Mandryk. *Operation World, 21st Century Edition*. Pasadena: USCWM, International Research Office, WEC International, 2001.

Judson, Edward. *The Life of Adoniram Judson*. New York: Anson D. F. Randolph, 1883.

Latourette, Kenneth Scott. *A History of Christianity*. New York: Harper & Row, 1953.

McFarland, George Bradley, ed. *Historical Sketch of Protestant Missions in Siam, 1828-1928*. Bangkok: The Bangkok Times Press, 1928.

McGavran, Donald A. *The Bridges of God*. New York: World Dominion Press, 1955, 1981.

__________. *Understanding Church Growth*. Grand Rapids: Eerdmans, 1970, 1980.

McGilvary, Daniel. *A Half Century Among the Siamese and the Lao: an Autobiography*. New York: Fleming H. Revell, 1912.

McLeisch, Alexander. "Today in Thailand (Siam)." In *War-Time Survey Series No. 3*. London: World Dominion Press, 1942.

Merriam, Edmund F. *A History of American Baptist Missions*. Philadelphia: American Baptist Publication Society, 1913.

Parker, Joseph I., ed. *Interpretive Statistical Survey of the World Mission of the Christian Church*. New York: International Missionary Council, 1938.

Pickett, J. Waskom. *Christian Mass Movements in India*. Lucknow: Lucknow Publishing House, 1933.

Pierson, Arthur T. *The Crisis of Missions: Or the Voice Out of the Cloud.* New York: Baker and Taylor, 1886.

________. *The Divine Enterprise of Missions*. London: Hodder & Stoughton, 1898.

Smith, Alex G. "A History of Baptist Missions in Thailand." Unpublished Master of Divinity Thesis, Western Evangelical Seminary, Portland, 1980.

________. *Siamese Gold: A History of Church Growth in Thailand: An Interpretive Analysis 1816-1982*. Bangkok: Kanok Bannasan (OMF Publishers), 1982.

Smith, S. F. *Missionary Sketches: A Concise History of the Work of the American Baptist Missionary Union*. Boston: W. G. Corthell, 1887.

Swanson, Herbert R. *Khrischak Muang Nua: A Study in Northern Thai Church History*. Bangkok: Chuan Printing Press Ltd. Part., 1984.

Van Benschoten, A. Q., Jr. "A Thailand Missionary." Printed letter. Chiang Mai: January 1954.

Zan, U. "History of the Karen Church in Thailand." Trans. from Karen by Tongkham Songsaeng. Typescript, n.d.

10. A People Movement among the PWO Karen in Northern Thailand

Crossman, Eileen Fraser. *Mountain Rain: A Biography of James O. Frazer*. London: OMF, 1982.

Garrison, David. *Church Planting Movements*. Richmond, VA: International Mission Board of The Southern Baptist Convention, 1999.

Kuhn, Isobel. *Ascent to the Tribes: Pioneering in North Thailand.* Rev. Ed. London: OMF, 1968.

Loewen, Jacob A. *Culture and Human Values: Christian Intervention in Anthropological Perspective*. Pasadena: William Carey Library, 1975.

McGavran, Donald A. "The Bridges of God." In *Perspectives on the World Christian Movement.* 3rd ed. Edited by Ralph D. Winter and Steven C. Hawthorne. Pasadena: William Carey Library, 1999.

______________. *Understanding Church Growth.* 3rd ed. Grand Rapids: Eerdmans, 1990.

Patterson, George. "The Spontaneous Multiplication of Churches." In *Perspectives on the World Christian Movement.* 3rd ed. Edited by Ralph D. Winter and Steven C. Hawthorne. Pasadena: William Carey Library, 1999.

Peters, George W. *Saturation Evangelism.* Grand Rapids: Zondervan, 1970.

Smith, Alex G. *Strategy to Multiply Rural Churches: A Central Thailand Case Study*. Bangkok: OMF Publishers, 1977.

Taylor, Geraldine. *Behind the Ranges: The Life-Changing Story of J. O. Fraser*. Singapore: OMF International, 1944.

Winter, Ralph D., and Bruce A. Koch. "Finishing the Task." In *Perspectives on the World Christian Movement.* 3rd ed. Edited by Ralph D. Winter and Steven C. Hawthorne. Pasadena: William Carey Library, 1999.

11. Incarnational Approaches to the Japanese People using House Church Strategies

Allen, Roland. *Missionary Methods : St. Paul's or Ours?* Grand Rapids: Eerdmans, 1962.

Banks, Robert. *Paul's Idea of Community.* Peabody, MA: Hendrickson, 1994.

Church Information Service. *Japan Church Data At Glance*. Niiza: Saitama Japan, 1997.

Conn, Harvie M. *Eternal Word and Changing Word.* Grand Rapids: Zondervan, 1984.

Dale, Tony, and Felicity Dale. *Simply Church.* Austin: Karis, 2002.

Fukuda, Mitsuo. "Developing A Contextualized Church As A Bridge To Christianity in Japan." Doctoral Dissertation at Fuller Theological Seminary, 1992. (Published in Japanese in 1993).

Furuya, Yasuo. *Nippon Dendouron (Perspectives on Evangelism in Japan).* Tokyo: Kyobukan, 1995.

Gilliland, Dean S. *Pauline Theology & Mission Practice.* Jos, Nigeria: Albishir, 1983.

Hiebert, Paul G. "Critical Contextualization" In *Anthropological Reflections on Missiological Issues*. Grand Rapids: Baker, 1994.

Simson, Wolfgang. *Houses that Change the World: The Return of the House Church.* Waynesboro, GA: OM Publishing, 2001.

Yamamori, Tetsunao. *Church Growth in Japan*. Pasadena: William Carey Library, 1974.